SOCIOLOGY OF EDUCATION

An Introduction,
Second Edition

Sarane Spence Boocock

Rutgers University

UNIVERSITY
PRESS OF
AMERICA

LANHAM • NEW YORK • LONDON

Copyright © 1980 by

Houghton Mifflin Company

University Press of America,™ Inc.

4720 Boston Way
Lanham, MD 20706

3 Henrietta Street
London WC2E 8LU England

All rights reserved

Printed in the United States of America

Library of Congress Cataloging in Publication Data

Boocock, Sarane Spence.
  Sociology of education.

  Bibliography: p.
  Includes index.
  1. Educational sociology. I. Title.
  LC191.B628   1985   370.19   84-19607
  ISBN 0-8191-4333-2 (pbk. : alk. paper)

Reprinted by arrangement with
Houghton Mifflin Company, Boston

Figure 2-3: Reprinted from "Social class, parental encouragement and educational aspirations" in American Journal of Sociology by W.H. Sewell and V.P. Shah with permission of the University of Chicago Press. Copyright © 1968 by the University of Chicago.

Figures 3-2 and 3-3: From "Learning Patterns in the Disadvantaged" by Lesser & Stodolsky published by Harvard Educational Review. Copyright © 1967 by President and Fellows of Harvard College.

Sociology of Education

Contents

Preface ix

**PART ONE
INTRODUCTION**

Chapter 1 The Field 3
Learning in Schools
Changing Views of Childhood and Youth
   Models of Human Development / The Learning System
Notes

Chapter 2 The Design of Educational Research 17
Types of Sociological Theory
Methodological Decisions
   The Empirical Measurement of Learning/The Sample/The Setting
Conclusions
Notes

**PART TWO
THE STUDENT**

Chapter 3 Family Social Position 39
Socioeconomic Status
   SES and Linguistic Development
Race
Religion
Conclusions
Notes

Chapter 4 Family Structure and Interrelationships 65
Family Structure
   Research on Family Size and Birth Order
Parental Values and Aspirations
Interpersonal Relations and Interaction
   Parent-Child Interaction
What Is Good Parenting and Can It Be Taught?
Conclusions
Notes

Chapter 5 The Effects of Sex 84
Performance
Differences in Abilities and Personality Traits
   Motivational Comparisons
Socialization
   Differential Treatment in School
The Simultaneous Effect of Sex and Other Independent Variables
Conclusions
Notes

Chapter 6 Individual Abilities 102
Measurement of Intelligence
Origin of Intelligence
Cognitive Style
Creativity
The Consequences of Testing
Conclusions
Notes

PART THREE
THE SCHOOL

Chapter 7 The School as a Social System 127
The Sociologist's View of the School
   Schools as Institutions/Schools as Sets of Behavior/
   Schools as Bureaucracies
The Principal
The Teachers
Special Services Personnel
The Students
Conclusions
Notes

Chapter 8 Classroom Role Structure and Role Relationships 146
The Teacher Role
The Teacher-Student Relationship

Expectancy Effects/Evaluation of Classroom Performance
Student-Student Relationships
Conclusions
Notes

Chapter 9 The Class as a Social System 167
Size
Social Context
Classroom Technology
Communication
Classroom Reward Structure
Classroom Social Climate
   Climate Measures Based on Questionnaire Data
Conclusions
Notes

Chapter 10 Effectiveness of the School 191
Characteristics of Students
   School Size/Social Context/Social Climate/Equality of
   Educational Opportunity
Characteristics of Teachers
Nonhuman Resources
Some Methodological Issues
   Systems Analysis/Production Function Analysis
Conclusions
Notes

Chapter 11 The Adolescent Society Revisited 212
Coleman's Major Findings
Further Studies of Value Climate
The Components and Consequences of Peer Status
Processes of Peer Group Formation and Influence
The Relative Strength of Peer Influence
Youth and Society
Conclusions
Notes

PART FOUR
THE SCHOOL'S ENVIRONMENT

Chapter 12 Effects of the External Environment 245
Professional Administration
The School Board
The Public
   Attitudes of the Public/Parents

The Governmental Role in Education
Strategies for Change
   School Desegregation/Magnet Schools/Community-
   Controlled Schools/Education Vouchers
Conclusions
Notes

Chapter 13   Crosscultural Comparisons   277
Relations Between Societies and Schools
The Structure of National Educational Systems
   Models of System Structure/Alternative Models/Individual
   versus Group Orientation/Academic versus Productive
   Work/Ideological and Moral Instruction/Increasing
   Equality
Crosscultural Differences in Achievement
Conclusions
Notes

**PART FIVE
CONCLUSION**

Chapter 14   Where We Are and Where We Are Going   309
Changing the Schools
The Sociologist's Contribution
   A Research Agenda
Notes

Bibliography   325

Index   351

Preface

The first edition of this book was written because I could not find in the published literature a comprehensive discussion of the social factors affecting learning and education that I could use as background for my own research. Thus I attempted to provide such a discussion. I prided myself on having dealt with the major issues in at least a minimally respectable fashion in that book, and when the time came to begin revising it, I assumed that it would be a fairly routine task. It did not take me long to discover the error of my assumption.

For one thing, the intellectual climates that informed the two versions of the book are very different. The 1960s were years of unusually active educational debate and experimentation; the 1970s were epitomized by a retreat to the "basics." In the 1960s, there was a strong belief in R&D, a belief that just around the corner was a theory or a teaching device that would revolutionize the educational process—indeed the word *revolution* appears in the titles of many books and articles published during that decade. The publications of the 1970s have been more cautious, in many cases demonstrating the unreliable foundations of our earlier enthusiasms.

Some people claim that the research of recent years simply reiterates what we already know from earlier research, obscuring the rather ordinary findings by tortuous statistical manipulations. Although it is true that much recent work has a methodological elegance that distinguished only a few earlier studies, my own reading of the recent literature suggests that it goes far beyond what my colleagues refer to as "number crunching" or "dust bowl empiricism." If we have lost some of the naïve faith in innovation for innovation's sake that made the 1960s such an exciting time to be involved in the educational enterprise, this loss has been at least partly compensated for by the greater precision of recent work. And if we are still far from that elusive general theory of the learning system, recent work contributes a number of important links in the causal chain of relationships explaining learning differences.

The spirit of the past decade is illustrated by the continuing debate on many levels over the Coleman Report and, perhaps more important in the long run, by the large amount of careful reanalysis of the data from the *Equality of Educational Opportunity* survey. Probably no set of social science data has been more thoroughly probed by secondary analysis, and such nearly exhaustive exploration has served to distinguish those findings of the original report that hold up under careful scrutiny from those that could be interpreted differently or are true only under certain conditions.

Perhaps the best evidence of development in the field of sociology of education is that my revision of this book has resulted in a substantial rewriting of most chapters. About the only sections lifted verbatim from the first edition are descriptions of some of the classics of educational research—for example, Rosenthal and Jacobson's experimental manipulation of teachers' expectations, Flanders's discussion of classroom analysis, Jensen's paper on race and IQ, and Coleman's *Adolescent Society*. (In each case, however, our present perceptions of the work have been shaped by recent critical analysis and empirical replications.) Some chapters have been entirely rewritten (for example, Chapter 5), reflecting social movements that have increased the attention given to the educational problems of women and minorities, brought new scholars of varying social background and ideological orientation into the field, and shaken up prior assumptions that educational "disadvantage" can be explained by something in the biology and/or culture of the disadvantaged.

Some things have not changed in the interim between the completion of the first edition and the preparation of this one. My purpose is still "to describe and place in context some of the best research and the most important findings in the sociology of education." I still view the book as a progress and not final report—indeed, a final report in this field will probably never be written, certainly not by this author. I would hope though that a comparison of the two versions will show how much progress has been made. The amount and quality of sociological research on the social organization of schools and the schooling process have risen exponentially. If our areas of ignorance about schools and schooling are still frustratingly vast, we know much more than we did, and if the field of sociology of education is still far from maturity, it has moved from an uncertain infancy into a fairly hardy childhood.

In a book of this length many important and interesting topics must be omitted or treated more superficially than they deserve. I regret, for example, not being able to discuss more fully the research literature on learning in institutions of higher education, on the growing importance of preschool education and the implications of changing patterns of child care on subsequent scholastic achievement, and on learning in the context of sports or play activites as compared to the formal classroom setting. Some readers may disagree with my specific choice of topics to include and omit, but they can, I hope, sympathize with my desire to cover the topics I have chosen with some degree of comprehensiveness.

While the field continues to be dominated by the prodigious research of James Coleman, whose *Adolescent Society* and *Equality of Educational Opportunity* remain important focal points of this edition and who has in the interim produced important new studies on the position of youth and the consequences of our school desegregation policies, his accomplishments are no longer so singular. The literally hundreds of imaginative and well-designed studies coming out of research and development centers in this country illustrate the advantages of team efforts on thoughtfully delineated topics. The concentrated research activity on topics relating to achievement and educational equality in this country is mirrored by work in other societies (demonstrating among other things the commonality of our major educational dilemmas), and in this edition I have included more work by scholars outside the United States throughout the book, not just in the chapter on crosscultural comparisons. Yet another reason for optimism is that so many promising and well-trained younger scholars are now committing at least a major part of their research efforts to the problems outlined in this book; I have attempted to include a good sampling of their work.

I have always been fortunate in my colleagues. When I began my exploration of the sociology of education some fifteen years ago, the Department of Social Relations, and later the Center for Social Organization of Schools, at Johns Hopkins University, provided an ideal intellectual milieu—and, not incidentally, some initial financial support. During the past three years, my colleagues at Rutgers University have constituted an equally valuable social context. A grant from the National Institute of Education, for an intercollege faculty seminar on educational equality, has provided the time and resources for study of topics relating to several chapters of this book as well as the opportunity for regular interaction with colleagues, of whom Harry Bredemeier, Marilyn Johnson, Ann and Bob Parelius, Karen Predow, Randy Smith, and Ben Zablocki have been particularly helpful. A semester as a visiting professor at Hebrew University, Jerusalem, and several return trips to Israel under the aegis of the Ford Foundation, have, I hope, reduced my research ethnocentrism. I am especially grateful to three Israeli colleague-friends—Chaim Adler, Mike Inbar, and E. O. Schild—with whom I have discussed virtually every major topic addressed in this book.

Some reviews of the first edition pointed out, justifiably I believe, that the treatment of methodological issues was stronger than the treatment of theoretical issues. I have tried to redress that imbalance in this edition, and if I have had some measure of success it is in large part thanks to Walter L. Wallace, whose publications on social theory and whose personal suggestions have greatly influenced my own thinking.

I am indeed appreciative of the detailed and helpful critiques of my manuscript by several reviewers for Houghton Mifflin: David Adams, Ohio State University, Lima; James Fennessey, Johns Hopkins University; Harold S. Himmelfarb, Ohio

State University, Columbus; Eldon E. Snyder, Bowling Green State University; and Theodore C. Wagenaar, Miami University, Oxford, Ohio. Although I regret that I cannot thank them personally and that I could incorporate only some of the many references and other suggestions they offered, their comments influenced the final version considerably.

Friends, relatives, and coworkers have helped in countless ways to make an undertaking of this scope possible—even at times enjoyable. Special thanks are due to my son Paul Morris Boocock for his cheerful adaptation to my often absent-minded parenting during the past year. A nursery school student when the first edition was in progress, he is now a high school veteran who continues to be a major source of information and insight on what really goes on in schools.

Sarane Spence Boocock
Rutgers University

Sociology of Education

PART ONE

Introduction

The Field

Chapter 1

If there was ever a time and a country in which the sociological view was indicated, in a particularly urgent fashion, for pedagogues, it is certainly our country and our time. . . . It is not because sociology can give us ready-made procedures which we need only use. Are there, in any case, any of this sort? But it can do more and it can do better. It can give us what we need most urgently; I mean to say a body of guiding ideas that may be the core of our practice and that sustain it, that give a meaning to our action, and that attach us to it; which is the necessary condition for this action to be fruitful.   Emile Durkheim

The above statement was made just after the turn of the century by a Frenchman who was one of the founders of the modern discipline of sociology. Because sociology was such a new field, and a far from respectable one to many of Durkheim's contemporaries, he taught pedagogy at the same time that he was developing some of the basic concepts and research techniques of present-day sociology. As one of his biographers observes, the courses for primary- and secondary-school teachers that Durkheim taught throughout his life were "the cover under which sociology was first officially introduced into a French university" (Lukes, 1973: 109).

Although Durkheim was engrossed in the social problems of his own society, his message seems no less timely today. Every year in the United States, and in most other countries, more resources are devoted to formal education and more people spend more time in school. Yet educational systems continue to undergo wrenching crises, and satisfactory answers to fundamental questions about schools and education continue to elude us. What "should" students be learning in schools, and how do we know when they are learning "enough"? How is the amount or the quality of learning to be measured? Can schools produce a high level of cognitive learning without losing sight of other kinds of educational objectives, such as encouraging creativity, maximizing individual freedom, or providing greater equality of educational opportunity? What should be done about students who fail to learn? How can schools and their activities be more efficiently organized? Can schools be the instruments of more general social progress and reform, as John Dewey hoped, or is education at best a limited instrument of reform or at worst a substitute for more fundamental social change, as some contemporary critics have charged?

This book will attempt to develop a "body of guiding ideas" for addressing questions such as these. The subject of the sociology of education or learning is the learning environment, which includes the social characteristics of students, schools, and their surroundings that affect academic success. We want to explain what—and under what conditions—social factors have an impact upon school performance.

The sociology of learning is to be distinguished from the psychology of learning, which focuses upon the internal mechanisms by which the individual responds to and assimilates stimuli of various kinds. Although the ultimate advantages of interdisciplinary linkages are obvious—we shall, in fact, use findings from psychological research as the framework or givens in our discussion—so far, sociology lags far behind psychology in the learning field. This book's premise is that sociology has a contribution to make that is independent of the psychological learning theory dominant in the field.

Although the study of education and educational institutions began with modern sociology, the relationship between sociology and education has never been a comfortable one. Ever since Durkheim's day, sociologists and the sociological point of view have been accused of having an unhealthy influence on education and teachers. Until the mid-1950s, the research literature on the sociology of education[1] was small and tended to avoid the more controversial educational issues. For example, a number of studies described the structure and functioning of the school as a social system, in particular the degree to which schools share the characteristics of bureaucratic organizations generally. Many studies described the social background of teachers. But little sociological attention was directed toward the central function of schools, learning itself. Only during the past two decades, when research in educational sociology began to grow at a much faster rate, did sociologists attack directly the problems of how and under what conditions children learn or fail to learn.

Learning in Schools

Let us clarify further what we mean by the sociology of education or learning. Learning is, of course, a very broad concept. As one major sociological theorist, Talcott Parsons, has defined learning, it encompasses the entire set of processes by which individuals acquire "new cognitive orientations, new values, new objects, new expressive interests" (Parsons, 1951: 203). The particular kind of learning with which we shall be concerned—that is, the *dependent variable* that we shall be trying in this book to understand and explain—is that which is measured by a person's level of achievement or success in the formal educational system.

Learning, as it is conceived in this book, includes three crucial components. One is *change*. Learning involves a cognitive change leading to a measurable increase in some knowledge or skills. A student who can perform at time B some academic task that he or she could not perform, or perform as well, at time A is assumed to have learned something. Something happens to a person in a learning experience, so that he or she is in some sense not the same person afterwards.

A second component of learning is *substance*. Individuals do not just learn—they learn, or fail to learn, some *thing*. The commonly recognized things that are learned in school are knowledge (history, mathematics, and so on) and skills (reading, writing, computing, and so on). Sociologists have pointed out that schools teach other things as well. Indeed, one general criticism that is often leveled against educational research is that it is too narrowly focused upon cognitive or intellectual learning and pays too little attention to the host of other things that can be learned in school, from mechanical and physical skills to reasoning and decision-making skills, interpersonal and leadership skills, creativeness, citizenship, and work habits, including concentration, perseverance, and self-reliance. In a book titled *On What Is Learned in School,* Dreeben (1968) discusses four important social norms that are acquired during the process of schooling:

1. independence, or the capacity to act self-sufficiently and to accept personal responsibility for one's behavior
2. achievement, or the active mastery of assigned tasks
3. universalism, or acceptance of the notion that the same rules or standards apply to all persons in the same category or situation (for example, all first graders, regardless of sex or social origins, are expected to learn to read)
4. specificity, or the limitation of one person's interest in another to a relatively narrow range of characteristics and concerns (for example, teachers may know almost nothing about the interests, accomplishments, and problems of their students outside of school)

Dreeben feels that the learning of these norms serves to wean children away from the personal, affective relationships characteristic of the family world and to prepare them for the competitive, competence-based, and relatively impersonal relationships of the adult world. (For further discussion of alternative kinds of substantive school learning, see, for example, McPartland *et al.*, 1976; Coleman, 1972; Mayeske, 1975; Richer, 1975.)

A third component is some kind of *interaction between the learner and an instructor,* whether this be a teacher, another student, or some nonhuman teaching device. The learning that we are interested in occurs in a social setting, and academic success depends upon recognition by other people that one's performance is adequate or better. It may thus depend as much upon social skills as upon strictly academic or intellectual ones. As we shall see in later chapters, children from some social subgroups are more likely than children from other groups to possess the social skills that are correlated with school success.

Finally, it should be underscored that this book is about learning in schools.[2] Although, learning obviously occurs in other institutions, the skills and attitudes children acquire outside of school will be included in the discussion only when they help to explain differences in school performance. This limitation is imposed not only to provide a structure for the book, but because the discussion of formal educational functions increasingly is becoming synonymous with the discussion of schools. In small, simply organized societies, education can be carried out largely within the family, but in complex, industrially developed (or developing) societies, families rarely can communicate the specialized knowledge and skills required for many adult roles. In such societies there has been a trend toward "distilling from other institutions their normal educative functions and transferring them to the school" (Newman and Oliver, 1967: 75. See also Parelius and Parelius, 1978, and Hurn, 1978).

We shall, however, be concerned with both the formal and the informal aspects of school social structure. As Hurn notes, schools teach not only explicitly, through the formal curriculum, but also implicitly, through what he terms the "hidden curriculum" or what is "*implied* by the organization of the classroom and the rewards and punishments schools employ to regulate student behavior" (Hurn, 1978: 192). For example, how teachers and other school personnel communicate to students what is expected of them and whether they are measuring up to expectations may have as much effect upon their achievement as the curriculum materials used in a given school.

The kinds of things that can be learned at school are sometimes confused with the purposes or *functions* of schooling, about which there is as much debate and as little agreement as about whether children are learning "enough." One of Durkheim's fundamental assumptions, that education is "above all the means by which a society perpetually recreates the conditions of its very existence" (Durkheim, 1956: 123), has been called into question in the past decade by radical critics who argue that formal educational systems tend to perpetuate the inequalities of hierarchical class systems and that they should either be totally reconstructed or eliminated altogether (these two views have been most prominently argued in Bowles and Gintis, 1976, and Illich, 1971). Some observers feel that confusion over purpose is at the heart of our educational problems; that because our society is not sure of its own basic values, it "cannot be clear about the goals it wishes education to serve" (Keppel, 1966. See also Jencks *et al.*, 1972). Others feel that it is not that we lack clear goals but that we have so many of them. We expect our schools to do so much that our expectations are often unrealistic and conflicting. The literature on American education is filled with typologies and debates about the functions of education. The following list of the functions of school, formulated by Spady (1974), seems to incorporate the most important ones:

instructional function: Schools produce individuals equipped with the empirical knowledge and technological mastery needed for survival in the larger society.

socialization function: Schools produce individuals equipped with the attitudes, values, and interpersonal skills needed for the performance of adult roles.

custody and control function: In Western societies, children are legally obliged to attend school, and schools are responsible for their care during specified periods of time.

certification function: Schools provide course credits, diplomas, and other credentials that are accepted by other institutions as evidence that some set of requirements or level of competence has been reached.

selection function: Schools are a sorting mechanism that determines access to subsequent educational, occupational, and social positions and opportunities.

The various functions of schooling are not always congruent with each other, nor are they necessarily relevant to the needs of students in later stages of their lives. Spady himself points out that the custodial and certification functions may have negative repercussions on the instructional and socialization processes. Credentials may indicate anything from mastery of some specific skill to simply length of time spent in some kind of educational setting, and they may or may not be relevant to the roles or positions for which they are a prerequisite. Their sociological importance lies in the symbolic value attached to them by members of a society. As one analyst has put it: "What is important here is not that school-awarded credentials are relevant or irrelevant, but simply that *they are taken seriously* as screening devices for access to social roles and to subsequent education" (Green, 1969: 244-245).

As we shall see in later chapters, societies and societal subcultures differ in their perceptions of the appropriate functions of education, and even within a single society consensus is rare. Almost throughout the history of our society, there has been disagreement between those who feel that schools should focus upon a single function (for example, the back-to-basics proponents who would have the school concentrate solely upon the instructional function, dismissing the others as frills) and those who worry about excessive emphasis upon cognitive development. As one critic complains, "Marks in school subjects are virtually useless as predictors of creativity, inventiveness, leadership, good citizenship, personal and social maturity, family happiness, and honest workmanship" (Goodlad, 1966: 49). Finally, there are those, among whom Kenneth Boulding (1966) and Alvin Toffler (1970 and 1974) are the leading proponents, who say that the major function of schools today is to prepare students for the surprises of the future. Since the world of tomorrow will be one of ever-accelerating change, both technological and social, accompanied by an explosion of knowledge, formal education must develop in the young the habit of continual learning as well as the capacity for "social invention" to correct the discontinuities that result from rapid change.

Changing Views of Childhood and Youth

The goals a society sets for its educational system and what and how children are taught in school depend not only upon what is perceived as valuable and necessary for the smooth functioning of society but also upon society's view of what children are like. Although we tend to take for granted the way children are treated in our own society, it is important to remember that what we see is filtered through a cultural lens. As the following passage from Phillippe Aries's classic study, *Centuries of Childhood,* makes clear, our view of children has not always been the prevailing one, even in Western culture.

> Olivier Le Fevre d'Ormesson was born in 1525 of a father who was a clerk in the record office of the High Court, and a mother who was the daughter of an attorney in the Audit Office. He had two brothers and three sisters, who all died except for his brother Nicolas. He lost his father when he was five. At the age of eight, Olivier went to Navarre College. . . . However, the le Fevre family was not rich, and the widow could not afford to keep her two children at school. . . . Thus Olivier stayed at school only from the age of eight or nine to the age of eleven. At eleven "he was lodged with an attorney in the Audit Office to learn to write (that is to say to 'write to perfection,' to write deeds, the equivalent of typing today) and to earn his living." (Aries, 1962: 191–192)

In the sixteenth and seventeenth centuries, childhood could be very brief, with the young person early absorbed into the adult world to study or hold a job on the same basis as any adult. (Adolescence, to which behavioral scientists and educators now attach so much importance, was not even a recognized period in the life cycle until the late eighteenth century.) Formal schooling was available to only a small segment of the population and often was limited to three or four years, even for a person entering a profession. Moreover, because the function of the school was to communicate the knowledge and skills necessary to the operation of certain institutions—originally, the music and literature connected with the ceremonies of the church; later, the writing, arithmetic, and manual skills used in commercial activities—"for a long time the school remained indifferent to the separation and distinction of the ages, because it did not regard the education of children as its essential aim. . . . Thus it welcomed equally and indifferently children, youths, adults, the precocious and the backward, at the foot of the magisterial rostrum" (Aries, 1962: 330).

While these brief excerpts do not do justice to the richness of Aries's study, two conclusions are clear:

1. The very notion of childhood is a relatively recent conceptualization and one which is constantly adapting to the changing structure and needs of a particular society.
2. The image of the child held by a society affects the kinds of educational system it provides for him or her.

A review of various periods of American history reveals quite different views of the child. In the early days of our country, all able-bodied persons constituted a much-needed source of labor. In a society in which the majority of the population were children and in which idleness was a sin, most children worked by the age of six or seven, either sharing in the activities of their parents or working as apprentices and servants in the households of other people. A study of family life in the Plymouth Colony (Demos, 1970) shows that there was a surprising amount of "putting out" of children at all social class levels of the society, including quasi-legal arrangements in which the child would receive room and board and some form of instruction or training in return for assistance in the home or workshop. Until the mid-nineteenth century, it was also not uncommon for very young children to be playing full student roles. At the height of the infant education movement, around 1840, approximately 10 percent of all Massachusetts children *under the age of four* were enrolled as regular students, learning reading, calculating, and other basic academic skills (Kaestle and Vinovskis, 1978).

There seem to have been important changes in the position of children around the middle of the nineteenth century, when the ideas of Pestalozzi and other European pedagogical thinkers began to influence American thought. Pestalozzi argued that the young child's place was in the home, where he or she should be encouraged to play with toys rather than to "work" with books, writing materials, and tools. By 1860, children under six had all but been removed from the formal educational system, and child labor and the practice of sending one's children to be raised in other people's homes were much less widely accepted. The growth of industrialized cities in the post–Civil War period also brought increased recognition of the special needs of children, partly because Americans were faced for the first time with large numbers of children who did not belong anywhere in the society. Accounts of the period, such as Jacob Ries's *How the Other Half Lives* (1890) and the *Children of the Poor* (1892), include descriptions of swarms of unattended, often homeless children roaming the streets of New York and other cities. The visibility of homeless, mistreated, and delinquent children, further dramatized via analytical tools for defining social problems provided by the rise of social science in the United States, led to the enactment of child labor and compulsory school attendance laws and the creation of agencies and institutions devoted to the protection of children (Hawes, 1971).

The twentieth century has been characterized by the elaboration of childhood as a special period in the life cycle and by a parallel extension of formal education among older children, by now in separate and strictly age-graded schools (Kett, 1976). In a report of the Panel on Youth of the President's Science Advisory Committee (1974), it is pointed out that the United States educational system has been characterized by a continuing trend from "elite to mass," and that it is the first national system in which completion of secondary schooling is the norm and close to a majority of high school graduates plan some kind of postsecondary education or training. (These trends are also discussed in Karabel and Halsey, 1977: 105–118.) The increased popularity of adult education as well as the extension of higher education in general have led sociologists to posit a "lifelong education" model, a systematic restructuring of American education that would "promote education as a continuous process, to be experienced at all stages of the life cycle and to be integrated with work, family, and other major commitments." Lifelong education would "sever traditional ties between educational institutions and chronological age, eliminating the isolation of youth in age-segregated high schools and colleges, and encouraging people of all ages to move freely in and out of educational settings" (Parelius, 1975: 207).

The fastest-growing component of the American educational system is, however, at the opposite end of the life cycle, at the preschool level. Despite a reduction in the birth rate during recent years, so that the number of children aged three to five actually declined from 12.5 million in 1964 to 11.4 million in 1969 to 10.4 million in 1974, the number of children enrolled in preprimary programs increased from 3.2 million in 1964 to 3.9 million in 1969 to 4.7 million in 1974, an increase of 47 percent in a period in which the number of children in that age group decreased by 17 percent (Grant and Lind, 1975: 46–47; Levitan and Alderman, 1975: 32). There has been a trend in the last two decades toward more emphasis on intellectual development, and today few American nursery schools claim that their programs are entirely "play." Current preschool programs bear little if any resemblance to the New England infant schools of the early nineteenth century.

Models of Human Development

Thus a society's educational system reflects its view of children and youth, and the models of human development that are most influential at a particular time reflect the society's structure and needs at that time. Two models of human development have been particularly influential in the social science of recent years. One is the model of *developmental stages* formulated by the Swiss-born psychologist Jean Piaget. The second model emerges from assumptions concerning the universality of *competence* or *intrinsic motivation* among young children.

In Piaget's conceptualization,[3] the child passes through an ordered sequence of phases. Each phase has its own distinct view of the world, modes of thinking, and so on; at the same time, each has roots in and entails repetitions of the previous phases, although on a higher level of organization and differentiation. There is a continuity of development over the entire series, a continuous trend from simplicity to ever-greater complexity, from focus upon the physical world to the societal and finally to the ideational, from emphasis upon activity and doing to emphasis upon thought about what is being done and finally to abstract conceptualization.

Although there is within each individual the possibility of full development at each phase, in fact children achieve at different levels within each stage and many fail to realize their full potential. The implication for educators is that it is crucial both to understand a child's developmental stage and to provide learning tasks that will enable the child to reach his or her capacity. This does *not* mean pushing children to achieve academic tasks faster or younger—such efforts would, on the contrary, go directly against Piaget's theory—but rather structuring and enriching the learning environment to provide the fullest development congruent with each cognitive phase.

In this country, Piaget's ideas have had a broad influence on educators, particularly those involved in designing programs, such as Head Start, to raise the academic performance of poor children. His influence has been even more extensive in Europe. For example, the open classroom as developed by English educators incorporates many ideas from Piaget's developmental theories, in particular the degree to which young children can be encouraged to learn through self-directed activity and to shape a mental scheme of the world through direct, repeated experience using all of the senses.

One important consequence of defining childhood as a special period (or as a series of special stages) is that the child is not expected to make any real contribution to the productive life of the community. In a recent analysis of American child-rearing manuals, the authors note that

> the focus is on the individual child, his "self-realization" through "self-discovery" and "self-motivated behavior." While other people are to assist him in this process, they are not to get in his way. As for the question of the child's obligations to others—especially to those not his own age—the training manuals are strangely silent. (Robinson, Robinson, et al., 1974: 381)

The separation of children from the workaday life of the larger society is a condition that American children share with children in developed countries generally, but that distinguishes them from such contemporary societies as in Israel, where kibbutz children tend gardens and animals from a very early age and elementary school children in Jerusalem took on such community responsibilities as mail delivery and garbage collection during the Six Day War (de Shalit, 1970); or in mainland China, where elementary school workshops turn out machine components for buses and other heavy equipment, and school children spend a portion of each year in some form of productive labor (Committee of Concerned Asian Scholars, 1972; Munro, 1971. We shall say more about crosscultural differences in the allocation of responsibilities to children in Chapter 13).

Another emerging theme in recent research on human development is the universality of *competence motivation,* sometimes called *intrinsic motivation,* which is behavior motivated by an individual's need for dealing with his or her environment in an effective, self-determining way (Deci, 1975). The conceptualization of this motivation emerged from the observation that people seem to engage in many activities for their own sake, not because they lead to some extrinsic reward. The first systematically gathered evidence of such a motivation came from laboratory work with nonhuman animals in which it was discovered that rats, monkeys, and other laboratory animals often would continue to explore mazes and try to master other learning tasks even when such behavior would not be predicted on the basis of their bodily condition (hunger, thirst, need for rest, and so on) or the stimulus-reward structure of the environment. The traditional view of learning motivation—that learning occurs because a response produced by a stimulus is followed by reduction in a primary drive—would not explain the experimental finding that

> monkeys will learn to solve a three-device mechanical puzzle apparatus for no other reward than the activity itself. Other experiments with monkeys show an orderly increase in the number of correct responses in the learning of a six-device mechanical puzzle over a twelve-day period, though no reduction of hunger, thirst, pain or sexual gratification has followed manipulation of the puzzle . . . Butler has shown

that monkeys will learn which of two differently colored windows to press when they are put into an opaque box, and the only reward following their response is the chance to look out of the window for a 30-second period . . . Montgomery ran animals in a Y maze in which one arm of the letter Y led to a large maze that they could explore and the other arm was a blind alley. The animals learned to enter the arm leading to the opportunity to explore, which here functioned to reinforce their instrumental response at the choice point.

These recent studies of manipulation, exploration, and curiosity highlight the limitations of the drive-reduction theory of reinforcement. The activity of manipulating a puzzle and the activity of exposing the visual receptors to sufficiently complex and novel stimulation are, apparently, as capable of reinforcing antecedent actions as are the activities of eating when hungry and drinking when thirsty. (Atkinson, 1966: 185–186)

That children, like rats and monkeys, have a natural curiosity and desire for knowledge and skill is now widely held among educators and social scientists.[4] The implications of this view for educational practice are obvious, and it was incorporated into much of the criticism of American schools published during the 1960s. For example, the unifying theme of a collection of articles entitled *Revolution in the Schools* was that

children of all levels and kinds of ability and from all kinds of backgrounds can learn more, learn it earlier, and learn it better. . . . Furthermore, children can do this without any "pushing," propelled by their own curiosity and innate desire to discover and know and understand. (Gross and Murphy, 1964: 138)

A series of exposés of the American schools and the educational "establishment"—like Jonathan Kozol's *Death at an Early Age,* James Herndon's *The Way It's Spozed to Be,* and the multiple works of John Holt—argued that the most remarkable feature of the formal educational system is the efficiency with which it squelches the potentially powerful competence motivation of many children rather than using it to promote learning.

The Learning System

Perhaps the best way to gain an overview of the field of sociology of learning is to describe the territory that will be covered. Exhibit 1–1 is a map of the social components of the learning system, which can be used to organize the myriad of theoretical formulations and research findings discussed in the main body of this book.

Since the school system is set up for the purpose of effecting a particular kind of change (learning) in a particular class of individuals (students), we shall enter this complex system at the level of the individual student, in the left center of Exhibit 1–1. In understanding the student role, it is important to remember that the child does not enter school untouched by the past and the outside world. Each child brings to school a number of characteristics that differentiate that child from other children, that determine in part the nature of the school experience, and that

Exhibit 1-1
The Learning System

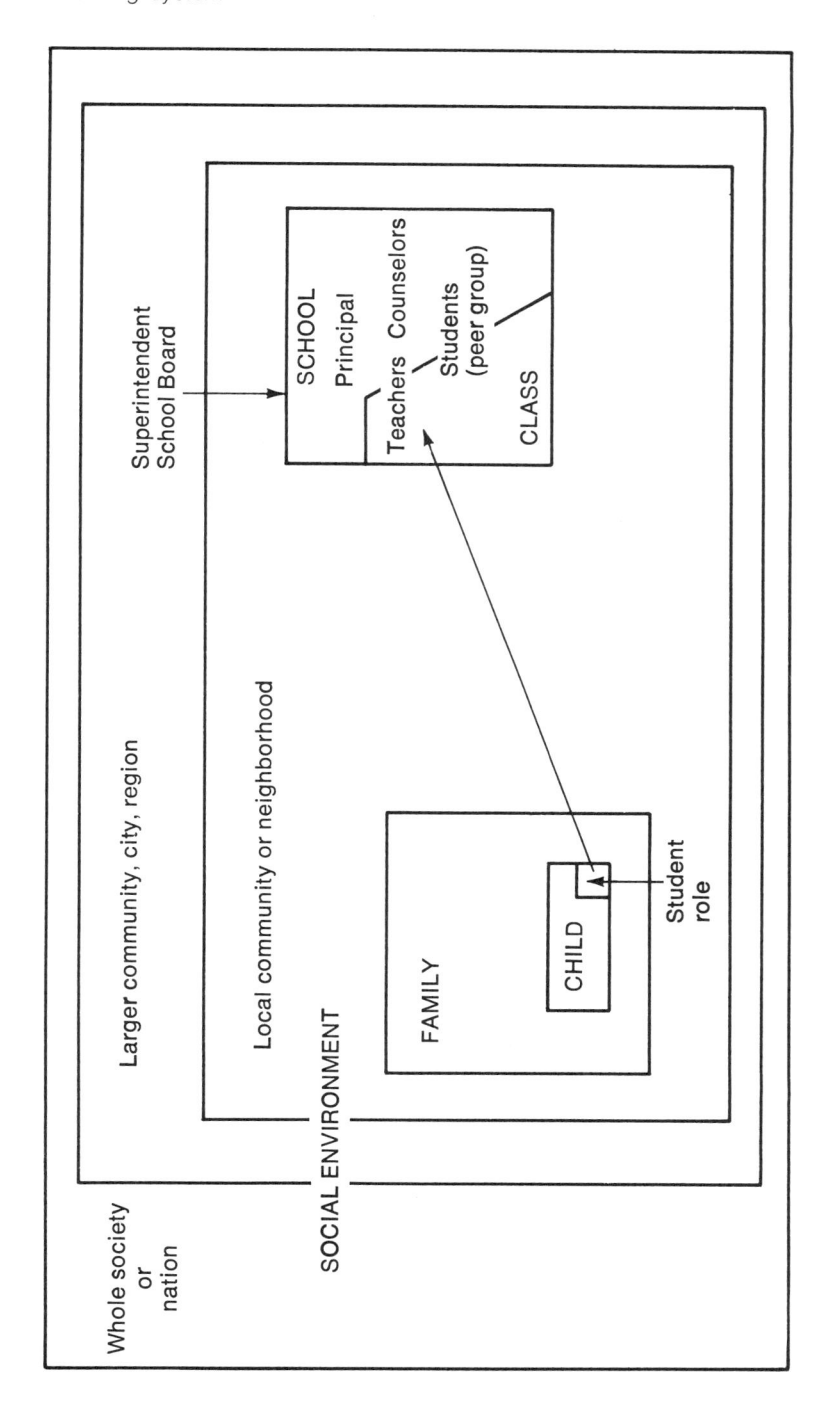

may have effects upon the school system itself. These characteristics include the individual's abilities and interests, values and attitudes toward school and learning, and the knowledge and skills he or she possesses already.

It is not really possible, moreover, to understand what is happening at the individual level without taking into account how the individual is affected by factors and processes occurring at other levels of the learning system. As Exhibit 1-1 indicates, personal characteristics of individual students are themselves affected by outside factors—by the structure, status, and values of the family, by the neighborhood, and by other layers of the environment. In sum, when they arrive at school, students have already been shaped by their backgrounds and environments, so that they possess a set of qualities, experiences, and expectations through which the influence of the school experience must filter. Part Two of this book will focus upon the student role, identifying the characteristics of the individual that are importantly related to success in this role and showing how they are interrelated with factors in both the in-school and out-of-school environment.

The individual level meshes with the group or system level of the learning system when the child enters the school, which is the subject of Part Three. Within the school, the child, in the role of student, interacts with teachers, counselors, principals and other adult or professional members of the school system, as well as with other students. The structure of the school as a social system, as viewed from a variety of sociological perspectives, is the subject of Chapter 7. Chapters 8 and 9 deal with the structure and dynamics of the classroom, including the type of teacher performance, teacher-student relationship, and classroom organization and technology that seem most productive of learning. Chapter 10 examines the sociological characteristics that distinguish schools from each other in ways that relate to their academic effectiveness.

The student peer group, the majority segment of the school population, is the subject of Chapter 11, where we shall examine the influence of the peer group upon individual and subgroup attitudes toward school and actual school performance.

Part Four deals with the school's environment as a part of the learning system. As Exhibit 1-1 indicates, the school system, like the individual student, is surrounded by a series of environmental levels, from the immediate neighborhood to the community, city or region, to the larger society or nation. At each level, the values and resources of the system affect the school's goals, resources, autonomy, and so on—and so the school is in a very real sense a sociocultural product. Chapter 12 in Part Four will analyze the role of the superintendent and his or her professional staff, the school board, and the other groups that together constitute the school's external social environment, with particular reference to the way in which the interaction of these groups may affect academic productivity. Chapter 13 will be devoted to some crosscultural comparisons of learning expectations and achievement. American sociologists have often been accused of research ethnocentrism, and certainly most educational research published in this country is based upon American schools and students. In an effort to correct this imbalance, efforts have been made throughout the book, to include studies and examples from societies other than the United States and Chapter 13 will include both crosscultural comparisons that show important similarities and differences between our educational system and systems in other countries, and data on selected societies that seem to offer important insights into some of our thorniest educational problems.

It is hoped that Exhibit 1–1 will serve as a frame of reference for Parts Two, Three, and Four. Although individual chapters must of necessity be treated as separate units, it is important to keep in mind that the components of the learning system are closely related. Also, although each chapter will pursue a different branch of the sociology of education, each is organized around the same set of general questions:

1. What do sociologists know about learning? What kinds of social factors are related most strongly to learning at a particular level of the learning system?
2. What are the implications of (1)? Given what we know, what components of the learning system can be manipulated to increase learning efficiency?
3. What *don't* sociologists know about learning at a particular level, or what additional knowledge would be most valuable?

In the final chapter, which constitutes Part Five, we shall attempt to pull together the answers to these three questions and to identify the directions in which our educational system and the sociology of learning seem to be moving.

Before plunging into the discussion of substantive findings, we shall take a detour that can be considered part of the introduction to the field. Chapter 2 will try to put into perspective the kinds of research strategies available to educational sociologists. We shall first consider the importance of the theoretical framework of research, and the types of sociological theories that may be used to explain differential academic achievement. Then, using a few landmark studies in the field to illustrate the range of possibilities, we shall consider the major methodological decisions and alternatives. The purpose of Chapter 2 is to help the reader who has not had extensive research experience to understand the structure and functioning of the learning system. That is, we shall not attempt to teach the reader how to *do* the educational research, but simply how to read and weigh the findings reported in the succeeding chapters of the book.

It is important to acknowledge at the outset, however, that neither Chapter 2 nor any other "aids" that we could provide to the reader will resolve all of the difficulties of reading and evaluating the subsequent chapters. This is not an easy book. The core problems addressed by the sociology of learning have challenged and baffled scholars, teachers, and policy makers for many years. Responsible research on such problems is by necessity complicated, and the results, even of studies on the same topic, often contradict each other. For the sociologist of learning, a tolerance for ambiguity is as useful as a tolerance for statistics! We can only hope that the persevering reader will be rewarded by coming to share some of the pleasures of discovery, the sense of accomplishment from helping to shape a still-young academic field, and the vision of better schools that have motivated the researchers whose work is presented in this book.

Notes

1. The terms *educational sociology* and *sociology of education* are sometimes used interchangeably. I have chosen to use the latter, because the best recent scholarship distinguishes between the two terms and also tends to view the latter as a more fully developed concept that has to some extent emerged out of the former. For a discussion of the distinctions between the two terms and the evolution from *educational sociology* to *sociology of education,* see Brookover and Erickson, 1975; Parelius and Parelius, 1978: Chapter 1.

2. It is also, in the main, about elementary- and secondary-school learning, although the preschool and postsecondary levels are the fastest growing levels of the United States educational system. Research on preschools and colleges or universities will be included where relevant in the following chapters, although their special characteristics and problems will not be treated extensively.

3. Piaget's scholarly output on the development in the child of causality, quantity, numbers and measurement, chance, morality, and other aspects of thinking is too voluminous to be fully documented here. A recent estimate was twenty-five books and over one hundred and sixty articles. Among the basic references are Piaget, 1948; 1951; and 1952.

4. Though there are scholars who disagree. For example, in a book arguing against compulsory education, Carl Bereiter (1974) claims that it is a myth (perpetuated by a small minority of teachers, researchers, and other education apologists) that all children start out life full of creativity and eager to learn. On the contrary, few people are by nature desirous of learning, formal schooling as presently practiced introduces as many social problems as it solves, and people should have a right *not* to receive formal education.

The Design of Educational Research   Chapter 2

One of the great unsolved problems of American education, or of education anywhere in the world is that of providing a continuous flow of dependable information on how well the schools are meeting the developmental needs of children and in what respects they are failing to do so.   H. S. Dyer

In an ideal world designed for the convenience of the social scientist, theories of the effects of schools on students could be tested in the following way: different kinds of schools would be created, students would be randomly assigned to these different experimental "treatments," and then the students could be followed over the years with numerous measurements made of their relative academic performance. Such a study, of course, is impossible.   Christopher Hurn

The only constant in educational research is the continuity of ambiguity.
      Ernest Boyer

One of the few common experiences that virtually all educational researchers (as well as all readers of this book) share is school attendance. To have been a student oneself and thus an insider to the very system one is studying is both an advantage and a hazard to the researcher. On the one hand, past experience may sensitize the researcher to certain things—upon entering a new school, he or she often notices things that are atypical or "feels" that the students are more or less friendly or interested; that the classes or certain classes are more or less stimulating, anxiety producing, or rigid; that the adult personnel are more or less competent; or that the general atmosphere is more or less attractive than in other schools. On the other hand, familiarity may cause the researcher to overlook or take for granted things that a stranger would find noteworthy. The behavior in classrooms, in school corridors, in the principal's office, on the school playground, which seems "normal" to most of us, would undoubtedly baffle someone entering a school for the first time. Indeed, it is difficult for anyone who has been a student to examine schools and schooling in a detached or objective way.

Sociology is, however, a discipline that attempts to understand social phenomena in an objective way, by using the scientific method. The sociology of education is based upon evidence about academic learning and the causal relations between learning and relevant social factors, and the main body of this book consists of presentation and evaluation of research studies on the social factors inside and outside of schools that are related to academic achievement.

In order to evaluate any piece of research as scientific sociological evidence, it is necessary to know something about how the research was conducted. While the studies that will be discussed in the following chapters vary in research design as well as topic, each has the following elements:

a research question or objective: what the researcher is trying to find out in this particular study

a theoretical framework: a general explanation of the type of phenomena being studied

a methodology: a scheme for gathering and analyzing data, specified by the theoretical framework, so as to answer the research question

a conclusion: an assessment of the answer to the research question and of its bearing on the theoretical framework

For the discussion in the following chapters, we have attempted to select studies that ask important questions about learning, like those raised at the beginning of Chapter 1, for example. We have also tried to select studies that are based upon a carefully formulated theoretical framework, although a number of critics have noted that the theoretical quality of much educational research is not very high (for example, Feldman and Newcomb, 1969), and we have included a number of studies that are better viewed as good data sources on a particular question than as models of sociological research.

Types of Sociological Theory

We cannot review here all of the theories or theoretical perspectives represented in this book, although in chapter summaries and in the final chapter we shall try to organize empirical findings in terms of their dominant theoretical themes. The major *types* of theories explaining learning or achievement are presented in Exhibit 2-1.[1] The major differences among sociological theories about learning, as indicated by the categories across the horizontal and down the vertical dimensions of Exhibit 2-1, are whether they postulate that

a. learning differences are better explained by causes that originate *outside* the school system (for example, effects of students' family background or of the society as a whole) or by causes that originate *inside* the school (for example, effects of teachers' behavior or of teaching materials)

Exhibit 2-1

Types of Sociological Explanations of Learning

Type of Cause	Origin of Cause Outside the School	Origin of Cause Inside the School
Learner's Mental Characteristics	1	5
Physical Characteristics	2	6
Learner's Environment Human Characteristics	3	7
Nonhuman Characteristics	4	8

Based upon Wallace, 1969: Chapter 1.

b. learning differences are better explained by characteristics of the *learner* him- or herself (for example, his or her attitudes toward school) or by characteristics of the *learner's environment* (for example, the organization of classrooms). Characteristics of the learner may be further divided into mental versus physical characteristics, and characteristics of the environment may be further divided into human and nonhuman characteristics. (These divisions will be clarified in the following paragraphs.)

The cells of Exhibit 2-1 (numbered from 1 to 8) represent the types of theories that result from combining these dimensions in various ways. Cells 1 through 4 pertain to theories that postulate that learning or achievement differences are primarily explained by things that happen to students outside of the formal educational system or before they go to school. Cell 1 theories explain learning in terms of individual students' mental characteristics. These kinds of theories will be referred to most often in Chapter 6, where differences in IQ and other individual abilities are discussed.

Cell 2 refers to theories that explain learning in terms of students' physical characteristics, including their height and weight, physical health, and physical appearance. There is evidence, for example, that children who are unusually small for their age do less well in school than their classmates. In Chapter 8, we shall review some studies indicating that children's physical appearance affects the way in which they are perceived and treated by teachers.

Cell 3 theories explain the learning of one person in terms of the number, density, turnover, and other characteristics of the persons around him or her. For example, children who live in crowded households or neighborhoods have different learning patterns and problems than children from sparsely settled areas, and the ethnic and socioeconomic characteristics of children's neighborhoods also affects their academic achievement. Theories of this sort are termed *demographic theories,* since they refer to the components of population variation and change.

Cell 4 theories correspond to ecological explanations of learning, and they postulate that learning is affected by such factors as geographical location, climate, and nonhuman environmental resources. For example, in some societies extreme climatic conditions affect both design of school systems and learners' school progress (including how long they stay in school). Students in modern industrialized societies are less susceptible to ecological conditions, although the difficulties of concentrating on school work on a very hot day, the difficulties of even getting to school during winter storms, and differences in the design of schools in Southern California compared to northern New England remind us that learning is not entirely free of ecological constraints.

Cells 5 through 8 pertain to theories that postulate that learning differences are explained by things whose causal origin is inside the school, whether they are experienced in school or are the results of schooling. Cell 5 theories pertain to the things schools do to students' minds. For example, Dreeben's analysis of normative learning, discussed in Chapter 1, argued that schools socialize students through the teaching of important social norms, which when adequately internalized enable them to perform the student role and later adult roles.

Cell 6, by contrast, refers to the things schools do to students' bodies. For example, in the traditional classroom students are required to sit quietly for long periods of time and are punished for boisterous physical activity. On the other hand, school breakfast and lunch programs and physical education classes are efforts by the school system to enhance students' physical development, and such programs are often justified on the grounds that good physical development will improve student academic motivation and achievement.

Cell 7 refers to theories about the social structure of schools, for example, about the ways in which the school role hierarchy, which shapes the pattern of interaction between students, teachers, and other school personnel, ultimately affects learning.

Finally, cell 8 theories refer to technological aspects of schools, including the design of classrooms and teaching equipment. Most educational reforms of recent decades involve a combination of social structural and technological changes. For example, the open classroom calls for a rich variety of learning materials and activities that students can control themselves (cell 8) *and* for changes in the nature of the student-teacher and student-student relationships (cell 7).

The research studies discussed in Part Three of this book, which deals with the school as a social system, are generally based upon theories from the right side of Exhibit 2–1 (cells 5 through 8). The different areas of Exhibit 2–1 also correspond to the various sides of one of the oldest, and major, debates in the sociology of education, which is over the source of different levels of school achievement. To put it another way, when children fail to learn, should we blame the students themselves (cells 1 and 2), their families or communities, the class structure, and other aspects of their environment (cells 3 and 4), or the schools (cells 5 through 8)?

Methodological Decisions

A research design is always a compromise. A full study of even a single classroom would require recording everything that went on during a given period of time (probably on film or video tape, since no single researcher could see and record everything and no two researchers would see the scene in exactly the same way), plus questioning the members of the group and examining available information on them to learn attitudes and past behavior that would not show up in observation alone.

To collect data in this depth would be an ambitious project in a single class, and to extend it to a whole school, or several schools, would be for all practical purposes impossible. Thus the researcher makes a choice out of all the things that could be studied and the methods of gathering and analyzing data. In order to gain some notion of the range of research alternatives, let us briefly consider from among the studies that will be discussed in the following chapters a few that represent very different approaches.

In a classroom study directed by Flanders, which is discussed in Chapter 9, the question raised was what teaching style produced the greatest increase in student learning in two academic subjects. Rather than trying to record everything that went on in the classes studied, the observers were trained in advance to use a rather elaborate coding scheme that categorized each unit of interaction. The coding scheme was based upon a well-developed theory of interaction patterns in small groups, and Flanders made some predictions about the results he would get before the data were analyzed.

Another classroom study, discussed in Chapter 8, is Rosenthal's analysis of the effects of teacher expectations upon pupil performance. Here the researcher manipulated the classroom situation by assigning some of the children to a special treatment that was not accorded to their classmates. Rosenthal's study illustrates the application of a particular kind of research design, the classical experiment, to the classroom situation. To the extent that a design meets the rigorous requirements of the experiment (including random assignment to the experimental treatment, a matched group of subjects for purposes of comparison, and measurement of all subjects before and after the experimental treatment), the researcher is justified in drawing certain kinds of conclusions that he or she could not draw in nonexperimental research.

A very different kind of study is the widely publicized and controversial *Equality of Educational Opportunity* survey, designed by James Coleman, Ernest Campbell, and a research team of sociologists, statisticians, and educational research specialists, under the auspices of the U.S. Office of Education and in fulfillment of one of the mandates of the Civil Rights Act of 1964. In this gigantic survey of approximately five percent of the schools in the United States, all students at five grade levels were given a battery of ability and achievement tests;

further information about them, their schools, and their communities was obtained from principals and teachers. The tests and questionnaires were produced and distributed by a national testing agency but usually were administered by the regular teaching staff in each school. The mountains of data returned were processed and analyzed by computer. At every stage of this ambitious undertaking, the research activity involved a variety of research specialists and the most meticulous attention to the technical details of administration and data handling. In keeping with the size and scope of this project, the empirical findings cover a wide range of topics, and they will be introduced in several different chapters in this book.

A final contrast is provided by the Strodtbeck study discussed in Chapter 3, which is based upon a small sample of high school boys purposely selected to contain equal numbers of boys designated as over- and underachievers. In this study, the researchers went into the homes of their subjects, taking recording equipment with them, and interviewed boys and parents at some length, both individually and as a family group.

These four studies illustrate only some of the design possibilities available. They also sensitize us to the need for caution in making comparisons between studies. Given that the way a study is designed and executed affects its outcomes and the confidence we can place in them, it is important to understand some of the basic dimensions of research design. Although the following discussion does not constitute a comprehensive presentation, it points to the alternatives that seem to have special relevance for sociological learning research. (For a more thorough treatment of the alternatives of research design, and suggestions on how to read and assess research reports, see Riley, 1963; Cole, 1972; or Selltiz, Wrightsman, and Cook, 1976.)

The Empirical Measurement of Learning

In Chapter 1, we discussed the concept of learning. In evaluating the research to be discussed in the following chapters, one should consider how good a fit there is between the researcher's conceptualization of learning and the empirical indicants chosen to measure it. While a first glimpse suggests endless variation in the measures used (which complicates the task of comparing the results of different studies), a closer examination shows that most studies use one or a combination of a few basic types of indicants.

Course grades are among the most common measures of learning. They supposedly reflect how well a student has learned the subject matter, but because they are given by the person who also taught the course they are especially susceptible to personal biases. (Recent studies of college grading suggest that the consistently improving grade averages over a four-year college career reflect the expectations of the faculty regarding achievement at the various levels rather than a truly objective measure of actual performance.) Another weakness of grades as a measure of learning is their lack of comparability. As college admissions directors know, a B or a C from different schools, or even from different programs or teachers in the same school, does not always mean the same thing. Whatever grades measure, they do affect students' subsequent educational careers and they are a good predictor of subsequent educational achievement. Within a given system, they can be used as a means of ranking individual students, providing one keeps in mind the possible subjectivity of the graders.

Tests are another commonly used indicant of learning. *Standard tests,* as the name implies, were developed to provide more objective and comparable indicants of academic abilities and achievement. Standard tests are of two general types: achievement tests, which measure the accomplishments and information the student has acquired from school and other learning experiences; and ability tests, which measure the student's aptitude for scholastic work. There has been much recent debate, however, about whether there is a clear boundary between the two kinds of tests and whether they are fair, in particular to children whose backgrounds have not afforded them the kinds of experiences and skills called for by the tests. The use of standardized tests as the major indicators of learning in the *Educational Opportunity* survey has been criticized for these reasons. This problem will be discussed further in Chapter 6.

The fact that researchers have reservations about standard tests and teachers' own tests and grades is indicated by the many *tests and questionnaires designed by researchers* for their own studies. For example, the achievement tests used in the Flanders study were designed by the research staff. Self-designed tests have the advantage of getting directly at what the researcher wants to measure, and they are necessary in areas where standard tests are not available, for instance, in measuring learning from a new kind of teaching device or method. Their weaknesses are their lack of comparability with results from other tests and the researcher's possible biases.

Another way to overcome the biases of grades and tests is to provide students with some *new learning task* distinct from their regular school work and observe how quickly and well they master it. This approach has been useful with children from disadvantaged or minority groups whose lack of familiarity with and confidence in formal classroom situations may have such a depressant effect upon their performance that it does not reflect their real capabilities.

While all of the above are methods of measuring *directly* students' information or skills, more indirect measures are also used. These include the highest education level reached and future educational plans or aspirations. The assumption of such indicants is that a person who has reached or who aspires to a high level of education has learned or is capable of learning more than a person whose attainments and aspirations are lower. The evidence indicates, though, that the correlation between education aspiration or attainment and more direct measures of learning is not terribly strong and that aspiration and attainment are affected by many factors besides intellectual ones.

Of course, none of these measures gets directly at many kinds of learning that occur in schools. As we noted in Chapter 1, the measurement of noncognitive or nonacademic skills and accomplishments is an underdeveloped area of sociological research, and little is known about the relationship between academic and other forms of school learning. It is indicative of the narrow focus of most research that at a recent conference on the effects of school and classroom structures on student outcomes, sponsored by the National Institute of Education, at which the assembled scholars were expressly instructed to consider how schools might nurture the broadest range of instructional and socialization outcomes, the discussions seldom moved away from the traditional indicators of achievement and aspirations.

The Sample

At the start, the researcher must decide whom or what to study—the research unit (individual students, schools, communities, or so forth) to use and the selection of cases to study out of the total population. The samples in the four studies described above range from 48 boys in Strodtbeck's study to some 900,000 children from schools all over the United States in the *Educational Opportunity* survey.

The latter study, one of the largest and most rigorously designed of those to be studied in this book, is based upon what is called a stratified, two-stage probability sample. Stratification involves choosing a similar or equal number of cases from each of a designated set of categories. Since the major objective of the *Educational Opportunity* survey was to compare the opportunities and performances of majority and minority group students, roughly half the respondents were white and the other half nonwhite. The total sample was also distributed so that there were over seventy-five thousand subjects in each of grades 1, 3, 6, 9, and 12. Since the geographical area and total population studied were so immense, the sampling was done in stages, the first to select the set of counties and metropolitan areas from which, in the second stage, the actual schools would be drawn. Within each of the strata designated, the individual cases were chosen randomly. A probability or random sample, in which every case in a population or population stratum has an equal likelihood of being included in the final sample, is the only kind that allows the researcher to make estimates about the total population and to compute the degree of confidence to be placed in his or her estimates.

As in all national surveys, there were difficulties in obtaining the truly representative sample specified in the original research design. For example, certain schools selected refused to participate in the study. Some of the data collected were unusable because of incompleteness, or coding and other kinds of processing errors. One important segment of the potential school population—school dropouts, for whom the issue of equality of educational opportunity is particularly relevant—was not included in the study. These and other problems are discussed in the report and estimates of the amount of bias introduced are calculated. It seems safe to conclude that the authors' findings and their interpretation of them represent an unusually accurate picture of American schools.[2]

The stratified, two-stage probability sample was appropriate for this particular study, but it is neither practical nor desirable for many kinds of research. Rosenthal, who wanted to study closely the effect of a particular aspect of teacher behavior and to manipulate the classroom situation, limited his sample to the children in the first six grades in a single school. He made no claims for the representativeness of his sample, but deliberately chose a school with a high turnover rate and a high proportion of students from a racial minority group, two variables related to low academic performance.

Yet another approach was that of Flanders. Here the population sampled was all *classes* in grade 7 social studies and grade 8 mathematics in one large metropolitan area. Class averages on questionnaire responses concerning the kinds of social patterns existing in the classes were calculated, and the eight highest and eight lowest classes were selected for the study. The important criterion in evaluating a study sample is the extent to which it fits the basic objectives of the study. While samples vary and can be judged in many ways, some of the more important variables are the *size* of the sample and whether or not it is *representative* of some designated larger population. (In the *Educational Opportunity* survey, the objective was "to provide estimates for a large number of school, pupil, and teacher characteristics for the Nation as a whole." Thus it was necessary to have a probability or random sample, and one large enough to assure sufficient cases in all the strata to be compared.) Another important variable is the sampling *unit,* which in educational research can be the classroom (in the Flanders study) or the school as a whole (as in the Coleman *et al.* survey) as well as the individual student.

The Setting

If one wishes to observe students in the process of learning, the natural or field setting in which to conduct research is the school. In three of our four sample studies, the work was conducted in the school. In the fourth, the Strodtbeck study, the researchers collected initial data in schools but did their interviewing in the homes of a selected group of subjects.

The major advantage of the field setting is that it allows the researcher to observe the social system operating more or less normally (keeping in mind that simply entering a social system for research purposes has some effects upon that system). Some researchers feel that the best way to "discover the meaningful aspects of the school's operation" is by "watching and listening to teachers and students alike, preferably with as few preconceptions as possible," over a fairly long period of time (Richer, 1975: 391). This viewpoint is succinctly expressed by Bronfenbrenner, who feels that educational research is too often the study of "the strange behavior of children in strange situations with strange adults for the briefest periods of time" (Bronfenbrenner, 1976: 158). The disadvantage of field research when the field is as complex and busy as most schools is that researchers cannot take in everything, and that they have little control over subjects and their activities. They can rarely ask a teacher to repeat a lesson or class, separate some students for special study, or make major changes in the content of a course or in the teaching methods used.

In order to focus upon particular aspects of the learning process or particular causal factors, the researcher may use the field setting but intervene in various ways. In the Rosenthal study, the researchers intervened to test the children and to identify some of them as academic "bloomers," although there was little interference in the regular classroom procedures between one test period and another.

When one wishes to study a specific portion or aspect of the learning system, with certain other aspects controlled, a more appropriate setting is a laboratory.

In educational research, this may be a specially constructed research facility with recording equipment, one-way glass for observation, and other technological devices, or it may be simply the researcher's office or an unused room in the school. The point is that the subjects are removed from their regular setting.

The first part of the Flanders study was a laboratory experiment "designed to study relationships between controlled teacher influence and its effect on dependent behavior among students. The laboratory approach was essential to the control of the students' goal perceptions and the assessment of dependence" (Flanders, 1960: 22). This part of the study was conducted in a spare room of the school, with students selected so that each of the thirteen groups had the same number of boys and girls and the same distribution of IQ scores. They were then assigned to one of four kinds of "treatment," based upon variation in the degree of teacher influence and the degree of clarity of presentation. By conducting his initial tests in this manner, Flanders was able to control certain characteristics of the student subjects, the presentation of the learning tasks, and the subsequent behavior of the "teacher" (a trained member of the research staff in this part of the study). He was thus able to study the way in which these variables were related to each other without having to take into account the possible effects of a host of other things that could be operating in a normal classroom.

As is the case with the other decisions researchers must make, their choice of setting determines the kinds of information they will obtain and how they can interpret them. Obviously, a full understanding of the learning process and the social factors that affect it requires studies from both field and laboratory settings. In this respect, the Flanders study is a very strong one, since the laboratory phase was followed by a field study with a larger sample.

Data-Gathering Techniques

Another major decision to make is what kind of data to gather from the sample one has chosen. The four studies we have used as examples illustrate considerable variety in data-gathering techniques. Again the reader is referred to a text on research methodology for a full discussion, and we shall simply outline the major alternatives.

1. *Observation.* This may range from simply putting a researcher into a class or other school situation to record all he or she can about what is going on, to the high structured form of observation developed by Flanders, in which pretrained observers classify selected aspects of teacher-student interaction according to an elaborate coding scheme.

2. *Interviewing or questioning.* The Strodtbeck study relied mainly on this technique, including individual interviews with boys and their parents and a special kind of group interviewing in which the family members were asked to resolve differences of opinion that had been revealed in the individual interviews. The group interviews were recorded, and by listening to the tapes the researchers were able to give each family member a "power" score based upon his or her amount of participation and the number of final decisions in accordance with his or her original opinion.

3. *Written tests and questionnaires.* With this technique, subjects produce their own data, which means that the researcher does not have to be present throughout the period of data gathering and that comparable data can be collected from a large number of subjects in a short time. The tests and questionnaires for the *Educational Opportunity* survey were mailed out to the thousands of schools in the sample and were administered in large assemblies or in a number of classrooms simultaneously. Coleman and his associates were thus able to collect a vast amount of information about the 900,000 students within a period of a few months.

This is the only practical method of gathering new data on a large sample. At the same time, it has certain limitations. Since it depends upon written communication, it is not an appropriate technique for use with young children or with older students who have severe learning problems, and when the researcher is not present during the administration, he or she cannot be sure that all respondents took the questionnaire under the same conditions and interpreted the questions in the same way. The researcher can overcome these weaknesses to some degree by careful pretesting of the data collection instruments.

4. *Available data.* In addition to generating new data by observing or interviewing members of the school system or by obtaining written information from them, researchers who can gain access to the great amount of data that schools and other educational organizations gather themselves can often save time and expense and get information they would be unable to obtain any other way. Most schools keep detailed records about individual students (grades, test scores, health, behavior and other problems, and family information) and about the school as a whole (class size, special classes and services, teacher and curriculum characteristics, and expenditures). The sample for the Strodtbeck study was based upon inspection of school records. Coleman and his colleagues used a variety of available data resources, including U.S. Census population surveys, the Office of Education National Inventory of School Facilities and Personnel, and school inventories from state departments of education. They also collected statistics on the physical facilities of schools and the academic and extracurricular programs from superintendents' and other administrative offices in each school district.

Many studies combine two or more of these basic data-gathering techniques. For example, Flanders and his staff also gave achievement tests to the students in the classrooms they observed. The Coleman and Strodtbeck studies illustrate the many studies that use available data as background for or in conjuction with the gathering of new data. The important thing in evaluating a study is whether or not the researchers have gathered data that have direct bearing upon the questions they are asking, and whether the technique used is the most efficient means of getting relevant information.

The Time Factor

According to the conceptualization developed in Chapter 1, learning is a dynamic phenomenon. That is, learning, by our definition, assumes change over time—the student who learns knows something he or she did not know at some previous time. Given this inherent characteristic of our dependent variable, the ideal research design would consider a set of students, classes, or schools continuously over some length of time. Over-time studies are termed *longitudinal* and are distinguished from *cross-sectional* studies, which examine a set of students, classes, or schools at one point in time. In real life, it is rarely practical to study any group of students, classes, or schools continuously for long periods of time, and a study generally is classified as longitudinal if measurements are taken of all subjects at fairly regular intervals over a fairly long period. None of our four sample studies can be said to be truly longitudinal, although the students in the Flanders sample were given attitude and achievement tests before, during, and at the end of the two-week teaching units, and Rosenthal's subjects were tested at the beginning and end of a school year.

One of the few large-scale, longitudinal studies in educational sociology is the Wisconsin Study of Social and Psychological Factors in Socioeconomic Achievement, designed by William Sewell and a group of researchers at the University of Wisconsin–Madison. The Wisconsin study began in 1957 with a statewide survey of more than ten thousand persons who were at that time high school seniors. A series of follow-up studies have been conducted, some of them with subsamples rather than the entire original sample of ten thousand. One of the most difficult problems in longitudinal research is retaining a high proportion of the sample members throughout the study, and the Wisconsin study is particularly impressive in this respect. For example, a tracing operation in 1974 succeeded in locating 97.4 percent of the original sample. A 1964 follow-up survey gathered information on respondents' educational and occupational attainments at that time. A 1975 follow-up was even more extensive, gathering information on current educational, occupational, and family status and social participation, and retrospective information, such as respondents' aspirations while in high school and the names of their best high school friends. The most recent follow-up, begun in 1976, added a subsample of siblings of the original sample members, and will provide rich information on family structure and influences that will permit

> extensive analysis of the influence of age, sex, birth order, sibship size, and child-spacing on educational attainment, while taking into account the complex logical interdependencies among these structural variables and their empirical relationships with socioeconomic status and ability. (Sewell and Hauser, 1976: 16)

In the *Educational Opportunity* survey, Coleman, Campbell, *et al.* attempt to draw conclusions about differential patterns of academic development among different racial-ethnic groups from cross-sectional data. During the 1965–1966 school year, the test batteries were administered to a sample of children at five different grade levels. The research staff began their analysis with the results of the twelfth graders, which they then compared with results from the other grade levels. From these comparisons the authors concluded that the gap that exists between white and minority group children when they enter school increases as they progress through the grade levels. What must be understood is that this conclusion was reached not by following a group of children through their school career but *by comparing different groups of children at different age and grade levels.*

Given the scope of the survey and the limited time available (a requirement of the Civil Rights Act of 1964 was that the report be submitted in the summer of 1966), a longitudinal study was clearly impossible. The study was thus designed to approximate the longitudinal model as closely as possible, by "matching" the older and younger respondents as follows:

> For each secondary school selected in the sample, the lower grade schools which feed their students into the secondary school were identified by the local school administrators, together with the percent of the feeder school students who would ordinarily attend the sampled high school. Each feeder school sending 90 percent or more of its students to a sampled secondary school was selected with certainty, and other feeder schools were selected with probability equal to the percent of students who go on to the sampled secondary school. (Coleman, Campbell, *et al.,* 1966: 554)

The researchers felt that, although they were not able to trace the educational growth of individual students over time, comparisons controlling for age and grade level could, "with appropriate caution, give some indication of relative growth rates among each of the ethnic and regional groups examined" (Coleman, Campbell, *et al.,* 1966: 219).

Analysis of Causal Relationships

A primary objective of the sociology of learning is to establish causal relationships between the dependent variables and various independent variables—that is, to determine the effects of relevant social factors or of changes in the learning environment upon students' achievement. Thus one advantage of longitudinal over cross-sectional studies is that they allow inferences about causal relationships. Changes in learning or achievement that are correlated with changes in an independent variable or variables suggest that the former may be at least partially caused by the latter.

1. *Experimental controls.* The most direct way to study causal effects is by controlled experiments. The classical experimental design is shown in Exhibit 2–2. The experimental group, which can consist of individuals or groups (classes), is subjected to a given situation or treatment with one or more control groups similar to it in all respects except the treatment factor. An important assumption of the ideal model is that subjects are assigned to the experimental or control group on a random basis. Thus, if d is different from d' (see Exhibit 2–2), this difference is assumed to be the result of the experimental variable—or of chance variation, the probability of which can be estimated.

Exhibit 2-2

Classical Experimental Design

	Before	Treatment	After	
Experimental Group	Test 1	Presence of sociological factor or new teaching method	Test 2	d = results of Test 2 minus results of Test 1
Control Group	Test 1	Absence of sociological factor or new teaching method	Test 2	d' = results of Test 2 minus results of Test 1

The experimental treatment normally is thought of as something new that the researcher introduces into the situation (for example, a new method of teaching or a particular way of grouping students). However, many research studies consist basically of a comparison between two or more groups that vary in one or more respects but where the variation was not controlled by the researcher—for example, comparison of the performance of a given type of student in different schools or programs of study or with different kinds or teachers.

The classical experiment has been the subject of countless articles and papers, many of which suggest additions to the basic design to allow researchers greater confidence in their results.[3] One variation is to test a pair of experimental and control groups only *after* the introduction of the experimental variable, to control for a possible effect of test 1. (When no "before" test is given, it is especially important that the requirement of random assignment to groups be met.)

A second extension of the classical design controls for the *novelty effect*—that is, separates the effects of the new program or equipment per se from the effects of simply doing something new or receiving special attention.[4] An example of a study designed to control for the novelty effect is Miller's (1967) experiment on Omar Moore's "talking typewriter," a technological innovation that consists of an electric typewriter with keys that cannot jam, a window or screen in which letters, words, or sentences can be displayed, and a microphone-speaker, all of which are connected to a computer. The child works at the typewriter—at first simply exploring its possibilities at will—and the responsive environment provides continuous audio-visual feedback, either repeating what the child has just typed or itself providing stimulus letters, words, and sentences (Pines, 1965).

Some early field studies with the equipment reported astonishing results. Very young children and children with severe learning handicaps worked voluntarily for long periods of time and gained reading and writing skills far ahead of their peers. Miller's study controlled for the special attention typically given to the young subjects trying out the talking typewriter by allowing only the regular teacher or staff member administering the program to be in the experimental classroom. All reporters, visiting educators, equipment designers, and so on were excluded. The result: the children averaged less than five minutes per ses-sion on the typewriter, and few learned even the alphabet—let alone how to read. The conclusion is that a good experimental design builds in some control for the powerful effects of attention or novelty, either by carefully approximating in the study the normal classroom conditions or by adding one or more control groups in which an alternative treatment or novel factor is introduced, preferably by the same persons who introduced the experimental treatment.

Another kind of effect to be guarded against is the *experimenter effect,* or the tendency of research results to turn out the way the researchers want them to. Rosenthal, the designer of the study on teacher effects described earlier in this chapter, also has written a full-length book on the experimenter effect (Rosenthal, 1966), which serves as background and companion piece to his own experimental work. In an example taken from psychology, experimenters who were told that they were working with genetically bright rats reported better performance in maze tasks than experimenters who believed they were working with dull or untrained animals—even though the animals actually had been assigned randomly to one or the other group. The experimenter effect, as Rosenthal conceptualizes it, combines the observer's tendency to "see" things consistently with his or her own expectations with a parallel tendency to influence the subjects so that they actually *behave* in the expected manner. The general strategy for avoiding this kind of bias is for experimenters to remove themselves as much as possible from the administrative process of the experiment, and to "blind" the data gatherers and analysts as to which are the experimental and control subjects.

There are, however, numerous difficulties in translating a model into an actual research design. Just to set up comparable experimental and control groups in an educational setting is more difficult in practice than in theory. In most schools assignment by classes rather than individuals to the experimental or control treatment is the only practical procedure, and researchers can consider themselves lucky if they can match the groups on some aggregate level measures (say, mean IQ or achievement scores), assure that the matched classes are taught by the same teachers, and assign the classes to treatments randomly. (Whether matching is done on the individual or group level, the requirement of random assignment to experimental or control treatment is an important one, since the possibility of bias is so large otherwise. It is difficult, for example, to evaluate much of the early work on progressive education, because children who attended progressive schools usually differed from the general population of children in background, motivation, and abilities. It is likewise difficult to evaluate the results of teaching innovations that are tested with students who have volunteered or been selected by teachers to try them.)

Another dilemma is whether researchers should, or can, control the behavior of the persons administering the experiment. "It is well known that almost any course works well in the classroom if it is taught by its inventors or by a few of their highly trained converts. . . . To get a valid test of feasibility, you must turn over the program to teachers who are a fair sample of the people who would be teaching if it were adopted on the scale for which it was intended'' (Moise, 1964: 175). But can teachers who have always run their classes along, say, authoritarian lines give a fair test to a teaching method involving much informal interaction among students and with no predetermined "correct" answers to problems—assuming such teachers are willing to participate in such an experiment? How can researchers be sure that two or more teachers supposedly using the same approach are in fact administering the experiment in the same way? In fact, how can researchers be sure the experimental treatment is being administered in the intended manner unless they do it themselves, or are at least present to observe? The dilemma is essentially the one described in connection with the field versus laboratory setting—are researchers more concerned with having the environment operate as "normally" as possible, or do they want to control factors that might complicate the particular process they want to understand? To add to the dilemma, the more researchers separate themselves from the experimental situation (in order to avoid novelty and experimenter effects), the less they know about what is really happening.

2. *Statistical controls.* To the extent that researchers can isolate and manipulate the system under study in accordance with the requirements of the classical experiment, they can make causal inferences with some degree of confidence. In most research situations, however, experimental control is not possible or practical, and in these situations *statistical* controls may provide some insights into the causal relationships among variables. Perhaps the biggest change in educational research since publication of the first edition of this book in 1972 has been the increased use of *multivariate analysis*—that is, analysis using multiple independent variables—and sophisticated statistical tests and measures to estimate the size of the relationships among variables and their relative and cumulative effects upon achievement. On the one hand, reporting of research results is now a more difficult task; on the other hand, discussion of causal relationships can be more concrete, less speculative than before. While we shall try to make our discussion of empirical studies clear to readers with limited background in statistics, it is important to realize that conducting research in the sociology of education now requires an understanding of the more important types of statistical techniques (including an understanding of how to use the packaged computer programs that have made extensive statistical analysis in the social sciences feasible).[5]

While a number of applications of statistical tests to empirical data will be described in the following chapters, we shall mention here, as examples, a few studies whose authors were among the first to use a particular statistical technique in a large-scale sociological study.

One kind of statistical analysis, which has been used to identify the ways in which learning environments vary generally and the ways in which effective learning environments vary from less effective ones, is factor analysis. *Factor analysis* is a technique that reduces a large number of items, or sets of items, to a smaller number of meaningful dimensions or *factors,* each of which, ideally, contains a cluster of items that are highly correlated with each other but have low correlations with all other factors. McDill, Meyers, and Rigsby, in a study discussed in Chapter 10, did a factor analysis of thirty-nine school characteristics, from which they obtained six dimensions of school climate, which they then related to various achievement measures. Factor analysis is an extremely complicated procedure that requires such extensive mathematical calculations that it was not widely used in the social sciences until the advent of packaged computer programs. McDill was later able to combine factor analysis with a second statistical technique, multiple regression analysis, in order to examine the relative and combined effects of climate dimensions and measures of students' family background, values, and abilities upon academic achievement.[6]

Multiple regression analysis is a technique that allows the researcher to look at the independent and combined contribution of a number of variables to the prediction of a criterion variable (usually postulated as the dependent variable). In the *Educational Opportunity* study, Coleman and his associates used multiple regression to identify the combination of family background, school, attitudinal, and other characteristics that would best predict the values of the dependent variable of verbal achievement—and the relative contribution of each of these independent variables.[7]

In situations where theory is well developed and the researcher can make fairly specific predictions in advance about the relationships among variables, the technique of *path analysis* may be appropriate. Like multiple regression analysis, which it resembles in some respects, path analysis enables one to assess the relative contribution of a given factor, although in this case one is interested in the contribution to the correlation between two other variables. The entire set of causal relations can be presented visually in the form of a path diagram, which places the variables relative to each other, with arrows indicating the direction of predicted causality and, where possible, correlation coefficients indicating the strength of the path. Exhibit 2–3 shows a somewhat simplified path diagram from one phase of the Wisconsin Study, described earlier in this chapter. The diagram shows that for girls, socioeconomic status (SES), family encouragement, and the student's own intelligence all had substantial and independent effects upon the dependent variable of college plans; that the independent variables were also related to each other; but that neither parental encouragement nor college plans are completely accounted for by the variables included in the study (that is, a sizable amount of the variation in each is accounted for by other, "residual" factors, the effects of which are also shown in our simplified diagram). Similar results were obtained for the male respondents in the sample, although the effect of SES on parental encouragement was greater for girls than boys, the effect of intelligence on encouragement greater for boys than girls.[8]

A well-documented report on the results of a statistical test will indicate whether the differences obtained (between two samples or subsamples, or between experimental and control groups) are significant. Significance tests help the researcher to decide how much confidence should be placed in the results. As we have seen, sociological research is generally conducted with samples representing some larger population in which the researcher is interested, and what is generally being tested is a hypothesis or hypotheses about the larger population.

Exhibit 2-3

Path Diagram Showing the Influence of Socioeconomic Status, Measured Intelligence, and Parental Encouragement on College Plans for Girls

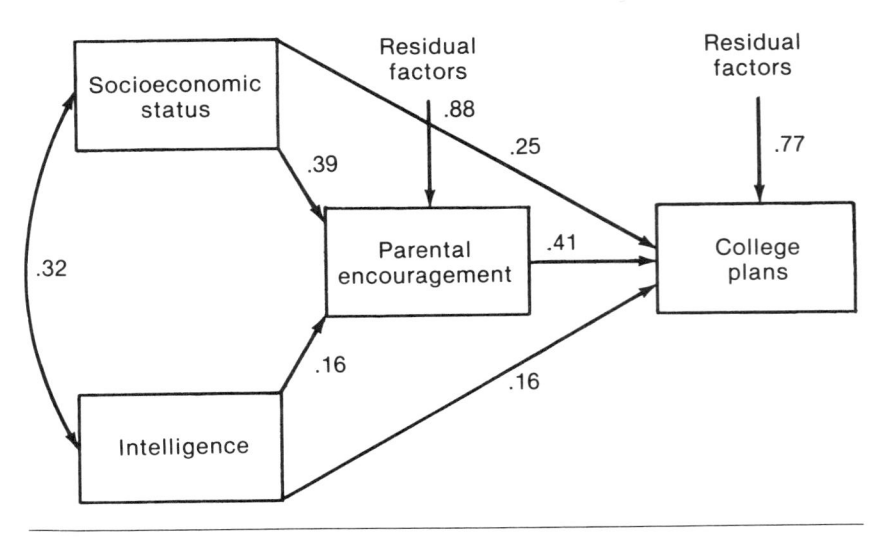

```
                          Residual              Residual
                          factors               factors
     Socioeconomic          |.88                   |.77
         status             ↓         .25          ↓
            \         .39                    ┌──────────┐
             \                                │  College │
        .32                Parental    .41   │   plans  │
             /            encouragement ────→└──────────┘
            /         .16              
       Intelligence                .16
```

Based upon Sewell and Shah, 1968: 567.

The standard procedure in testing for significance is to formulate a *null hypothesis,* which states that the obtained differences between groups or subsamples could have occurred as the result of chance alone. If the statistical test of significance leads to the conclusion that the observed differences could have arisen by chance only a small percentage of times in the absence of true differences between the two larger populations, the null hypothesis is rejected—that is, the researcher can conclude with some confidence that there is a genuine difference between the two populations. In the studies discussed in this book, the *level of significance* is usually set at .05 or .01, which means that an observed empirical difference will be deemed significant if the test shows that it would not occur by chance alone more than five times out of a hundred or more than one time out of a hundred, respectively.

There is a great deal of controversy, which is beyond the scope of this book, over the appropriateness of various statistical tests and tests of significance for sociological problems and data. Concerning tests of significance, two things are important to keep in mind: (1) that an empirical result that is statistically significant (or that passes a significance test at a given level of significance) is marked enough so that it is unlikely to have occurred sheerly by chance; and (2) the fact that a result is statistically significant does not necessarily mean that it is *substantively* significant or meaningful. For example, male and female students, black and Hispanic students, older and younger students might differ from each other in various ways that are statistically significant but that have no real importance in students' ultimate success in learning a given subject. In evaluating any piece of educational research, it is as—possibly more—important to be concerned with the theoretical and substantive importance of the findings as with their statistical significance.

Conclusions

The ultimate goal of this book is the construction of credible models that will organize the sociology of learning. To this end we shall describe and try to place in context some of the best of past and ongoing empirical research, to synthesize the most important findings from a large number of studies from the sociology of education and related fields. Our general strategy will be to look for consistent patterns in a number of studies that may themselves vary in type and quality.[9] We shall find a few landmark studies, studies that represent levels of theoretical and methodological sophistication not now characteristic of most research in the sociology of education. Some studies—among them, the Rosenthal study—will be given considerable attention because they test powerful ideas, even though on strictly methodological grounds they do not merit such attention.

In general, though, we shall find the balance between theoretical and methodological sophistication weighted heavily in favor of methodology. Indeed, a number of critics worry that educational research is becoming increasingly "methodology rich and theory poor," and at least some feel that our understanding of learning will be enhanced not by more finely controlled statistical analysis but by borrowing from sister disciplines, such as clinical psychology, analytic tools that will allow "greater qualitative analysis of learning behaviors, combined with the matching of this broader range of characteristics to the design of appropriate learning environments and experiences" (Gordon, 1976: 114).

There does seem to be a danger that the field will split into two research camps, divided by barriers of educational ideology as well as research design standards. One camp stresses comparability and generalizability, which requires large-scale studies with carefully constructed representative samples. The common criticism of such studies is that they too often use crude measures of learning. As one member of the other camp puts it, such research tends to measure what is easily measurable and amenable to powerful statistical techniques rather than what is theoretically or substantively interesting (Richer, 1975). The other camp stresses sensitivity to the details and nuances of life in schools. Such research is grounded in field observation, often of very small samples (for example, a single classroom). The criticism most often leveled against such studies is that while they are undeniably interesting and often insightful, their generality is extremely limited.

It seems obvious to us that the field needs sociological evidence from both camps. The studies that will be presented in the following chapters are drawn from both, and many do not fall clearly into either. It should also be obvious that not all of the studies chosen are perceived to be of equal weight. While we shall attempt to be candid and accurate in judging studies, our major concern is with what they add up to. By compiling a substantial body of empirical evidence, we hope not only to compensate to some degree for the deficiencies of individual studies, but also to move toward a dynamic and comprehensive model of the learning system.

Notes

1. Exhibit 2-1 is patterned upon a general scheme for classifying sociological theories developed by Walter Wallace, and the discussion borrows heavily from his book *Sociological Theory* (1969).

2. For the full sequence of steps by which this sample was chosen, see Coleman, Campbell, *et al.*, 1966: Appendix 9.2. A separate sample that included school dropouts was drawn by scholars at Florida State University.

3. Among the most thorough analyses of experimental design in educational research is a long paper by Campbell and Stanley (1963).

4. The *novelty effect* is often referred to in the research literature as the *Hawthorne effect*, after the industrial research project where it was discovered. See, for example, Riley, 1963: Chapter 11.

5. One of the first extensive discussions about making causal inferences on the basis of data from nonexperimental studies and that does not require an extensive background in mathematics and logic was Blalock, 1961.

6. See McDill *et al.*, 1967 for a full discussion of their factors and the methodology used to obtain them. For a more general discussion of factor analysis, see Fruchter, 1954; Harman, 1967; Henrysson, 1957.

7. The design of this analysis is described in a Technical Appendix (Coleman, Campbell *et al.*, 1966: 325-330). For a more general discussion of regression analysis, see Blalock, 1972.

8. For a full discussion of this study, see Sewell and Shah, 1968. For a more general summary of the method of path analysis, see Duncan, 1966.

9. For a discussion of this strategy of analysis and inference, see Campbell and Stanley, 1963: 36.

Part Two

The Student

Family Social Position   Chapter 3

The schools must sort all the human material that comes to them, but they do not subject all children to the same sorting process. Other things being equal, the schools tend to bring children at least up to an intellectual level which will enable them to function in the same economic and social structure as their parents.

Willard Waller

Our best general predictor of success in school is successful birth into a middle- or upper-class Caucasian family.   Edmund Gordon

    The second statement quoted above was made almost half a century after the first, and together they illustrate one of the most enduring findings in sociological research. In the years since publication of Waller's *The Sociology of Teaching* in 1932, an ever-growing body of empirical research has consistently shown that the family into which a child is born is one of the major determinants of her or his subsequent success in school. Scholars have not, however, reached agreement on certain aspects of this fact: the strength and permanence of the effects of family background compared to other influences in a student's life; the way in which different patterns of child rearing affect school performance; and the extent to which the formal educational system can offset the effects of family background and experiences. The general issue of family influence has been an especially sensitive one in recent years, as persons from low-income and ethnic minority groups have become increasingly, often militantly, resistant to suggestions that there is something defective about the way their families are organized and the way they raise their children.

    Because there are many different kinds of family influences that affect academic success both directly and indirectly through their interaction and through their effects on *other* variables related to achievement, two chapters will be devoted to this complex topic. In this chapter we shall consider the effects of *ascribed characteristics,* characteristics of the family that are attributed to the child simply by virtue of his or her family membership. These include social class or socioeconomic status and ethnic identity, the latter encompassing race, religion, and country of origin insofar as these differentiate the way in which individuals are perceived and treated by societies or societal subgroups. Race, which has been so strongly correlated with educational inequities in our country and many others, differs from other attributes in its visibility (usually, one's race can be identified on sight)[1] and its permanence (one cannot move out of one's race as one can move out of a social class or religion, for example). Religion will also be treated here as an ethnic characteristic, in that we shall be concerned mainly with the effects of being identified with a particular religion, regardless of whether one is an active practitioner of that religion.

In Chapter 4, we shall examine a second set of variables, those having to do with the way families are structured and the attitudes and behavior of family members with respect to one another. To put it somewhat crudely, the focus of Chapter 3 is upon what families are, the focus of Chapter 4 upon what families do.

Socioeconomic Status

The family characteristic that is the most powerful predictor of school performance is socioeconomic status (SES): the higher the SES of the student's family, the higher his or her academic achievement. This relationship has been documented in countless studies and seems to hold no matter what measure of status is used (for example, occupation of principal breadwinner, family income, parents' education, or some combination of these). It holds with a variety of achievement/aspiration variables, including grades, achievement test scores, retentions at grade level, course failures, truancy, suspension from school, dropout rates, college plans, and total amount of formal schooling. It also predicts academic honors and awards, elective school offices, extent of participation in extracurricular activities, and other indicators of "success" in the informal structure of the student society. It holds, moreover, even when the powerful variables of ability and past achievement are controlled. Finally, the relationship between family SES and academic achievement has been found in virtually every Western society for which empirical evidence is available.[2]

While everyone agrees that family status is important, the question of just *how* important has not been fully answered. Some social scientists argue that the modern family is losing its influence along with its functions, as the school and other institutions take over more of the socializing and educational tasks that used to be performed in the family. Others argue that despite extensive social change, a child's chances of success in school and in later life are still disproportionately—and some say unfairly—affected by the accidents of birth, and that the deck is stacked against children from poor families.

Measuring the effects of family background precisely is very difficult, because, as Christopher Jencks has pointed out, it is not a unitary concept with a consistent meaning in all contexts. Not only are there multiple indicators of status, but the indicator that most affects one kind of educational success (for example, scores on an ability or achievement test) may not be the one that most affects another (say, college attendance). From a reanalysis of several large surveys of educational and occupational achievement in America, using a variety of status indicators, Jencks estimated that family background explains close to half of the variation in educational attainment (Jencks et al., 1972: Chapter 5).

The most extensive and rigorous research on this topic is the Wisconsin Study of Social and Psychological Factors in Socioeconomic Achievement, which has been conducted for over twenty years by William Sewell and a group of associates. (The design of this longitudinal study of more than 10,000 persons was described in Chapter 2.) Sewell's important work has illuminated the complex process by which socioeconomic background (which Sewell has broken down into its component parts) and ability (also a multidimensional concept) jointly affect various measures of achievement, and how the effects of both background and ability are mediated by social psychological factors such as the encouragement and influence of parents, peers, and teachers. All of these variables have been put together in a mathematical model that, claims Sewell, explains 57 percent of the variance in post–high school educational attainment for the males in the sample, slightly less for the females. The Wisconsin model shows, for example, that "socioeconomic status has no effect on grades in high school independent of academic ability, but has strong direct and indirect effects on significant others' influence, and on educational and occupational aspirations, and through these on educational and occupational attainments" (Sewell and Hauser, 1976: 3).

There is also disagreement over the way in which family background and status ultimately affect educational achievement, although the effects seem to be both direct and indirect. Clearly, severe poverty can account for children's failure even to get to school, let alone learn anything there. The congressional investigations following the urban riots of the mid-1960s highlighted the correlations between poverty and such childhood health indicators as infant mortality rates, nutritional deficiencies, disease, and mental retardation—not to mention the probability of being bitten by rats. While the direct effects of malnutrition and other health deficiencies associated with poverty have not been precisely determined, the evidence does support the common-sense belief that they detract from children's classroom performance (McKay et al., 1978; Cravioto, 1968; Suchman, 1968).

Although Jencks estimates that money per se does not explain more than 15 percent of the overall difference in attainment between students from different class backgrounds (Jencks et al., 1972: 139), direct economic effects should not be overlooked. Lack of money to pay for basic school supplies (in some school districts, even required textbooks still have to be rented), inadequate clothing, or the need to help out at home with the housework or care of younger siblings may raise the absentee rates of many children or keep them out of school altogether. In virtually every study of school dropouts, a sizable portion gives the need to take a job or other financial problems as the major reason for leaving school or for not attending college (Miller, 1963; Astin, 1972).

In Chapter 4, we shall examine characteristics of family structure and interaction that affect school performance, but it is relevant here to note that these characteristics are themselves often related to family SES in ways which multiply the total influence of the family upon children's school success. One such characteristic is family size. Lower-SES children often start school with a verbal disadvantage simply because they are more likely to be born into large families where the opportunities for verbal communication with adults are limited, quite apart from the verbal facility or lack of it that parents may have (also class related).

Socioeconomic status is also related to a number of attitudinal variables that may serve as intervening or explanatory variables in the SES-school performance relationship. The basic thesis of a number of empirical studies is that middle-class parents communicate a set of values and a general outlook on life that incorporates educational and occupational success, which in turn produces higher actual achievement in school. For example, in a study of high school sophomore boys, Rosen (1956) found the middle-class groups higher on individual "need achievement" (measured by TAT-type tests), on cultural value orientations having to do with the implementation of achievement motivation (measured by questions on modes of coping with various physical and social environments—for example, "All I want out of life is a secure, not too difficult, job"), and on orientation toward the time dimension (the value of planning for the future). In fact, Rosen has characterized the typical middle-class family value system and child-rearing pattern as an "achievement syndrome," orienting the child toward success in school and later life.

During the past three decades, Melvin Kohn and his associates at the National Institute of Mental Health have been conducting studies on the relationships between social class, parents' values for their children, and parental behavior, particularly methods of discipline (Kohn, 1959a, 1959b, 1963, 1976). Kohn's studies are characterized by carefully designed samples. One consisted of two hundred middle-class and two hundred working-class white families with fifth grade children drawn by a two-step procedure. A selection of Washington, D.C., census tracts was made, based upon tract distributions of such status characteristics as occupation, income, and rent or value of home. Then families within these tracts were selected at random from lists of fifth graders compiled from public and parochial school records. In the early 1960s, Kohn compared this sample with a parallel one in Turin, Italy (Pearlin and Kohn, 1966), the findings of which will be discussed in the chapter on crosscultural differences in academic achievement. The other major sample used in Kohn's studies was of 3,100 men chosen to represent all American men in civilian occupations and interviewed by the National Opinion Research Center in 1964.

Respondents in this latter sample were asked to designate on a list of thirteen personal qualities: (1) which three they considered most important for their child; (2) which *one* of these three was the most important of all; (3) which three were the *least* important; and (4) which one of these three was least important of all. On each of the thirteen items, a mean rating was obtained for each of the five social class subgroups, based upon a combination of responses to all four of the questions. The items for which there is a statistically significant linear relationship between social class and mean rating—that is, the value of the correlation coefficient *r* is significant at the .05 level—and which the *lower*-SES parents perceive as more important than the higher-SES parents are:

good manners

neat and clean

obeys parents well

good student

Those for which the linear relationship is reversed—which are more highly valued by the *higher*-SES parents—are:

self-control

responsible

considerate of others

interested in how and why things happen

In other words, the middle-SES families, by comparison with their lower-SES counterparts, place greater emphasis upon *self*-direction. They want their children to be responsible and to control their own behavior, and this includes exploration of the world around them (finding out "how and why things happen" as opposed to simply being a "good student"). By contrast, the items that are relatively more important to the lower-SES parents are those that reflect conformity or obedience to external rules or authority (obeying parents and teachers) and having the *external* appearance or qualities that make a child acceptable to adults (good manners and cleanliness, in addition to obedience).

In the analysis of data from the Washington, D.C., sample, Kohn found that there are also differences between middle- and lower-SES parents in their behavior toward their children. These respondents were asked how they coped with a series of misdeeds ranging from fighting and playing wildly to disobedience and stealing. Most parents in both class subgroups said they tried to control their children's behavior first by such nonphysical means as ignoring them or asking them to stop. Only when misbehavior persisted despite parents' attempts to forestall it did they turn to physical punishment. At this point differences between lower- and middle-SES parents appear. Contrary to popular belief, the difference is not in the *extent* to which physical punishment is used—the middle-class mothers in the sample said they used it about as frequently as the working-class mothers—but rather in the conditions under which they choose it as opposed to alternative methods of control. Working-class mothers are most likely to punish severely when their children persist in physical aggression and severe fighting with siblings or other children, wild play that results in damage to the furniture, and other kinds of physical aggression by the child. Middle-class mothers, on the other hand, are most likely to punish what they call "loss of temper" when this reflects a loss of self-control. That is, they judge aggression not in terms of its extremeness of direction (even when it is directed against the mother herself) but rather in terms of the child's presumed intent. As Kohn puts it, "For the working-class parents, the 'important but problematic' centers around qualities that assure *respectability;* for middle-class parents, it centers around *internalized standards of conduct.* In the first instance, desirable behavior consists, essentially, of not violating proscriptions; in the second, of acting according to the dictates of one's own principles. Here the act becomes less important than the actor's intent" (Kohn, 1959b: 364–365).

The overall impression left by Kohn's studies is that the higher-SES parents want their children to understand the world around them and to come to grips with it through their own efforts, although control of their environment will require getting along with others; while the lower-SES parents are concerned mainly with avoiding trouble by means of meeting the demands of those in authority. It has been suggested that the lesser emphasis by middle-class parents upon conformity to external authority does not mean that they do not value, and indeed expect, good behavior of the sort that will lead to success in school, but rather that they do not see these things as problematic. In the relatively secure environment of the middle-class home, it is more likely that cleanliness and orderly behavior can be taken for granted than in a lower-SES neighborhood, where simply keeping one's children and home neat and clean and trying to control children's behavior so that they will not get into trouble takes a strong commitment and continuous effort.

SES and Linguistic Development

It is in the family that most children acquire language, which is, like values, both a product of social interaction and an important influence on all other forms of socialization and learning. Since language is a threshold skill for virtually all school work (and for the standard tests that are used to determine a child's place in the school system), children whose parents have facility in the kinds of language used by teachers and textbooks and who encourage their children to express themselves verbally are at a distinct advantage in most classrooms. Recent research by sociologists specializing in sociolinguistics suggests that this is most likely to occur in middle- and upper-class homes.

Some of the most influential, and controversial, research relating social class and verbal skills is by Basil Bernstein, an English sociologist who argues that the class structure gives rise to different family-role systems, which in turn encourage different modes of communication. In middle-class homes, children learn the kind of "elaborated" linguistic code (one that is based upon abstract general principles that apply to any situation) that is congruent with the conventional classroom situation, while working-class children acquire a more "restricted" code, which reflects their own limited life situation. Thus the poor academic performance of many working-class children "can be understood in terms of a confrontation between a) the school's universalistic orders of meaning and the social relationships which generate them, and b) the particularistic orders of meanings and the social relationships which generate them, which the child brings with him to the school" (Bernstein, 1970: 346. Other publications on this topic are Bernstein, 1961 and 1977).

Bernstein's work has been attacked by critics who accuse him of perpetuating an unjustified image of lower-class background as "defective" and in itself responsible for academic failure, though Bernstein himself argues that there is nothing intrinsic in working-class linguistic development as such that prevents a child from learning the more universalistic codes prevalent in the school. His conclusions have also been called into question by studies on children's linguistic development conducted by Doris Entwisle, which have shown that disadvantaged children actually may begin school with greater linguistic sophistication than their more advantaged peers. (Although, for the purposes of continuity of the basic arguments, we have grouped all sociolinguistic studies here in this section on family status, note that some of this research, including Entwisle's, involves racial rather than or in addition to SES comparisons.) Entwisle's studies concern the word associations of elementary school children. Most of the experiments involved administering a list of ninety-six stimulus words chosen to represent the different form classes (nouns, adjectives, and so forth) and frequencies of standard English. Each stimulus word on the list was said aloud by an adult interviewer and the child was asked to say "the first word you can think of." In order to make the young subjects comfortable, the test was administered in an informal, gamelike fashion, and both black and white interviewers were used.

While the experimental task obviously covers only a small part of the total range of verbal skills, word associations have a tendency to fall into fairly clear patterns according to the age of the child. Preschool children tend to respond to all words with a noun or with a *syntagmatic* response (a word that is related to the stimulus word in a meaningful sense and that usually directly precedes or follows it in a sentence; for instance, table-brown, or table-break). Between kindergarten and fifth grade there is a marked increase in *paradigmatic* responses (matching of words with their own form class, for instance, table-chair; responding to a verb with another verb, an adjective with an adjective, and so on). Because of these developmental patterns among children in general, individual subjects can be classified according to their level of verbal development. In addition, word associations have been found to be closely related to general linguistic competence and verbal comprehension. And they have the advantage of being easily obtained in large numbers from many children and of being easily analyzed by computers.

Comparison of a sample of black and white children of the same IQ range and from both high- and low-income areas of a large city showed:

> contrary to expectation, that slum children are apparently more advanced linguistically than suburban children at first grade. . . . While first grade slum children of average IQ give paradigmatic responses to about the same extent as gifted (IQ 130) suburban children, and although inner city black first graders of average IQ lag behind inner city white first graders, they give *more* paradigmatic responses than white suburban first graders of average IQ. Thus, at first grade the white child is slightly ahead of the black child when both are reared in the inner city, but the black slum child exceeds the white suburban child. The superiority is short-lived, however, for by third grade, suburban children, whether blue collar or upper middle class, have surpassed the inner city children, whether black or white. (Entwisle, 1970a: 14)

These findings were unexpected, so unexpected in fact that the researcher replicated the basic study in a number of settings and has reanalyzed her data in various ways in order to be sure that the findings were not the result of sampling biases or some artifacts in the statistical analysis. In addition to the differences in numbers of paradigmatic responses, Entwisle found differences between the semantic systems of black and white, middle- and lower-SES children. Analysis of the three most common responses for each stimulus word showed, for example, that black children were more likely than white children to give nonsense responses and less likely to give a "primary" or high frequency response (for example, "hot" in response to "cold"). For eight high-frequency adjectives, the percentage of primary responses ranged from 46 to 71 percent for white children, from 34 to 58 percent for black children. In sum, even by the early elementary grades, black and white children were, to a certain degree, not talking the same language.

While Entwisle's data do not provide any direct evidence about what accounts for the greater linguistic sophistication of disadvantaged children when they start school, it is interesting to speculate on the potential effects of certain already documented characteristics of their social environment. One is the virtually unrestricted exposure to television common to urban slum children. Although there is disagreement on the effects of television upon children's intellectual and social development, research evidence has indicated that while excessive television viewing has negative effects upon the academic performance of older children (both because it cuts into the time they might otherwise spend on homework and reading and because the intellectual level of most of the popular programs is below that of an intelligent adolescent), television serves a truly educational function for young children, introducing the kind of vocabulary and range of situations and experiences characteristic of the middle-class culture. (See, for example, the evaluation of the effects of Sesame Street in Cook *et al.*, 1975.)

Other clues may lie in the position of the slum child in the family and the nature of communication between children and adults. In the suburban home, children are taken care of for a longer time. Adults not only take time to talk with children (or at least feel guilty if they don't), but they also make genuine efforts to *understand* what the young child needs. When children cannot express their needs in readily understandable language, adults are likely to help them. Among the urban poor, children do many things for themselves at an earlier age—cross busy streets, use money, get their own meals, take care of young siblings. Adults do not have or do not take the time to interpret or translate requests formulated in childish syntax. If children are to survive in their environment, they have to be able to express their needs in the language of the adult world, whatever may be the language or dialect of the particular home or neighborhood.

These interpretations are congruent with the findings from another Entwisle experiment, which compared the word-association patterns of Baltimore city children with those of a matched sample of rural Maryland children and a group of Amish children who lived on very isolated farms without electricity (and thus without television and radio), with few books and magazines, and with limited interpersonal relations (contacts with non-Amish persons are discouraged by subcultural norms). The scores for the urban children were substantially higher. Entwisle concludes that

> rural residence impedes language development somewhat during the preschool period, so that first graders who live in the country are slightly retarded compared to first graders who live in the city. This is true irrespective of IQ level. Rural children of superior endowment quickly compensate, and by third-grade the difference is abolished. Rural children of lesser endowment still lag at third-grade, and it is not until fifth-grade that they are able to compensate fully. (Entwisle, 1966: 76)

The Amish children, moreover, lagged even further behind the other rural children at all levels. In summary, the more children's place of residence isolates them from exposure to the mass media and to other persons—both kinds of exposure are plentiful in the urban child's environment—the more likely they are to be retarded in verbal skills.

The implications of this research are ironic as well as important. For the linguistic advantage that disadvantaged children hold when they enter school is not recognized and is lost within a few years. While their social environment equips them rather well for learning in certain areas, either the failure of this same environment to train children for the role of student in the formal school setting or the way they are perceived and treated by the school itself manages to neutralize any initial advantage these children may possess.

Perhaps a more significant, if subtle, implication is that in our desire to explain we tend to categorize or label children as "successes" or "failures" on the basis of ascribed characteristics such as social class, race, or gender rather than upon actual aptitudes and performance. In the case of language,

> if [a person's] speech identifies him as a member of an out-group, when tagged as a member of that group he may be endowed with all the other modal qualities of that group—relatively low economic status, low educational status, values that emphasize immediate rather than delayed gratifications, relatively low power in the social hierarchy, or even having certain political leanings. (Entwisle, 1970a: 3)

That the stereotypes of the larger society can shape the self-image of minority-group children is indicated in a study of Jewish and black youth groups (Cahman, 1949). Questionnaire and interview data indicated that Jewish adolescents saw themselves as clannish, competitive, defensive, inhibited, and insecure; the black self-image stressed such weaknesses as drinking, fighting, carelessness, and lack of foresight. Although Cahman's sample was small and the findings may be somewhat dated by now, they do suggest that it may be the subtleties of interpersonal expectations and interactions among groups, rather than gross aggregate differences in potentialities, that constitute the real source of inequality of educational opportunity. The phenomenon of labeling will be discussed further in Chapter 7, where we examine classroom role relationships.

Verbal fluency may also be affected by the situation in which the student finds him- or herself. A study of the children of migrant labor families (Lein, 1973) compared the noncommunicative behavior of these children in school, where they were typically seen by teachers as all but ineducable, with their lively and highly verbal interaction with adults in their own homes and communities. Likewise, Labov's research on black children's language fluency demonstrates the pervasiveness of the effects of age, race, and familiarity of interviewers as well as the social structure of the interview (Labov 1970, Labov et al., 1968). A black boy interviewed alone in a schoolroom by a friendly, young, adult, white male, responded mainly in monosyllables with long periods of silence between his brief utterances. According to Labov, such defensive behavior is to be expected in a social situation "of an adult asking a lone child questions to which he obviously knows the answers, where anything the child says may well be held against him." Labov then goes on to describe the very different results obtained with the same children when the interview situation was restructured, concluding that

> when we change the social situation by altering the height and power relations, introducing a close friend of the subject, and talking about things we know he is interested in, we obtain a level of excited and rapid speech. (Labov et al., 1968: 340–341)

Labov also observed that lower-class black youth regularly engage in verbal "games," in which verbal facility is crucial to prestige and status.

Race

No other characteristic that the child acquires at birth has been the subject of more educational argument, analysis, and soul-searching than race. In recent years a considerable amount of sociological research has attempted to document and explain the differences in school success between black, Hispanic, and other racial minority children and their white counterparts. In Chapter 6, we shall examine the arguments and evidence on interracial differences in intelligence and other abilities. Examples of the different treatment received in the classroom by children from different racial groups will be included in Chapter 8. Differences in the schools attended by minority group children and the neighborhoods in which they are located will be examined in Chapters 10 and 12. What we shall examine here is the effect of being a member of a racial minority upon preparation for the student role and the ultimate likelihood of success in school.

Still the most comprehensive survey on this topic is the landmark *Equality of Educational Opportunity*—already mentioned in Chapter 2. The sample of about 625,000 (all the students at grades 1, 3, 6, 9, and 12 in about five percent of the public schools in the United States) included children from six racial and ethnic groups: blacks, American Indians, Oriental Americans, Puerto Ricans, Mexican Americans, and whites other than Mexican Americans and Puerto Ricans (referred to as "majority" or simply "white"). Coleman and his colleagues make clear in the introduction to the report that "these terms of identification are not used in the anthropological sense, but reflect social categories by which people in the United States identify themselves and are identified by others" (Coleman, Campbell, et al., 1966: iii).

Using as his major dependent variable the scores on a set of standard tests, Coleman found substantial differences among the various racial-ethnic groups.

> With some exceptions—notably Oriental Americans—the average minority pupil scores distinctly lower on these tests at every level than the average white pupil. The minority pupils' scores are as much as one standard deviation[3] below the majority pupils' scores in the first grade. At the 12th grade, results of tests in the same verbal and nonverbal skills show that, in every case, the minority scores are *farther below* the majority than are the 1st graders'. For some groups, the relative decline is negligible; for others it is large. . . . Thus, by this measure, the deficiency in achievement is progressively greater for the minority pupils at progressively higher grade levels.
>
> For most minority groups, then, and most particularly the Negro, schools provide no opportunity at all for them to overcome this initial deficiency; in fact, they fall farther behind the white majority in the development of several skills which are critical to making a living and participating fully in modern society. Whatever may be the combination of nonschool factors—poverty, community attitudes, low educational level of parents—which put minority children at a disadvantage in verbal and nonverbal skills when they enter the first grade, the fact is the schools have not overcome it. (Coleman, Campbell, *et al.*, 1966: 21)

Having established the substantial and consistent test score differences among the various racial-ethnic subgroups in their sample, Coleman and his colleagues turned to the task of trying to account for these differences. They first examined the orientations of students themselves, including their academic motivations, and their future educational and occupational aspirations as well as their feelings about themselves. Exhibit 3–1 compares the responses of whites and nonwhites in two areas of the United States with large black populations and where race relations and the differential opportunities related to race are exceptionally problematic. (Coleman's full analysis, which subdivided the sample into eight geographical regions as well as into the six racial-ethnic categories, is too extensive to reproduce here—the general pattern of results shown in Exhibit 3–1 is essentially the same in the regions not shown.) In addition to blacks, ethnic minority groups included in the analysis are Puerto Ricans, the group that is similar to blacks in educational disabilities, and Oriental Americans who have unusually *high* levels of academic achievement.

On attitudes toward school and academic work generally, black-white differences are negligible or even indicate a higher valuation of school and achievement by blacks. The black twelfth graders in these two areas of the country are as likely as their peers to want to stay in school now and to want to continue their education beyond high school and to spend relatively great amounts of time outside of school studying and reading books. They are even more likely to want to be the best students in their class and less likely to be truants from school. Where the black and white students do differ is in taking concrete steps to implement their educational aspirations. Not only do relatively fewer of the black respondents have definite plans to attend college *next year,* but also fewer have gone through the necessary preliminary phase of consulting college catalogues or officials. In sum, the black students approaching the end of their high school careers

Exhibit 3–1

Attitudes Toward School and Academic Work, by Race and Region

	White		Black			
% Respondents Who	Northeast Metropolitan	South Rural	Northeast Metropolitan	South Rural	Puerto Rican	Oriental American
Would "do almost anything" to stay in school	47	50	47	49	35	44
Want to be among the best students	36	46	48	69	36	46
Spend two or more hours on homework (daily)	51	47	57	54	41	64
Have not missed any school because of truancy	61	75	68	84	53	76
Read six or more books during previous summer	29	31	32	35	30	31
Want to get education beyond high school	86	83	86	85	66	93
Plan to go to college next year	46	35	31	30	26	53
Have read a college catalogue	73	58	59	49	45	70
Have talked to a college official	46	38	32	22	25	33
Plan to have a professional occupation	46	31	31	25	21	43
% Respondents Who Agree						
"Good luck is more important than hard work for success"	4	4	9	15	19	8
"Every time I try to get ahead, something or somebody stops me"	13	16	21	22	30	18
"People like me don't have much of a chance to be successful in life"	5	6	12	11	19	9

Data assembled from Coleman, Campbell, *et al.*, 1966: Chapter 3.

have essentially the same (generally high) valuation of academic achievement and higher education, but they are less likely to *do* the things that will translate their aspirations into reality.

By contrast to the blacks' pattern of responses, the Puerto-Rican students have the lowest percentage of positive responses on almost every item on Exhibit 3–1. They display lower aspirations, do less reading and studying, and are even less likely than blacks to be taking steps to continue their schooling beyond high school. The Oriental Americans, on the other hand, show a pattern of aspiration and activity that almost mirrors that of the white, majority group students.

Another set of attitudinal items that showed interesting racial-ethnic differences was the respondents' sense of control of their environment. The figures in the bottom three rows of Exhibit 3–1 show that both blacks and Puerto Ricans are more likely than whites to agree that "Good luck is more important than hard work for success," that "Every time I try to get ahead, something or somebody stops me," or that "People like me don't have much of a chance to be successful in life," items that reflect a lack of confidence in the individual's ability to control events in his or her life. These differences are more impressive when considered in conjunction with the related finding that sense of control of environment is also among the most powerful predictors of test scores. In a multiple regression analysis designed to determine the relative contribution of students' family backgrounds, their attitudes, the characteristics of their teachers and of their schools to variations in test scores, the researchers found that for black children sense of control of environment accounted for more test score variation than any other variable. Black children who did exhibit relatively strong sense of control had considerably higher achievement than those with low sense of control. The control dimension was less strongly related to achievement for whites, whose *self-concept*—their confidence in their own ability to learn—was a more powerful predictor of test scores. The authors conclude that there is a

> different set of predispositional factors operating to create low or high achievement for children from disadvantaged groups than for children from advantaged groups. For children from advantaged groups, achievement or lack of it appears closely related to their self-concept; what they believe about themselves. For children from disadvantaged groups, achievement or lack of achievement appears closely related to what they believe about their environment: whether they believe the environment will respond to reasonable efforts, or whether they believe it is, instead, merely random or immovable. In different words, it appears that children from advantaged groups assume that the environment will respond if they are able to affect it; children from disadvantaged groups do not make this assumption, but in many cases assume that nothing they will do can affect the environment—it will give benefits or withhold them but not as a consequence of their own action. (Coleman, Campbell, *et al.*, 1966: 320–321)

The relationsnips between the variables of race, academic achievement, and sense of control of environment may be summarized as follows:

Minority group children (in particular blacks and Puerto Ricans) are less likely than white majority group children to be good students (even if they value education and achievement).

Minority group children are less likely to have a sense of control of their own environment.

Children with low sense of control of environment are less likely to be good students.

Since the publication of *Equality of Educational Opportunity,* there has been some tendency toward narrowing the gap between majority and minority children. Comparing the relative educational attainments of blacks and whites, for example, the Pareliuses found that by 1975

> the median level of education attained by blacks who had been born between 1946 and 1950 was 12.5 years; for whites born in the same period, it was 12.8. Between 1950 and 1972, the proportion of blacks completing high school and the proportion with a college degree almost tripled. During the same period, the proportion of whites completing high school and college also increased, but at a slower rate . . . By 1975, the rates of college enrollment among younger blacks and whites who had graduated from high school were almost identical: 41 and 43 percent respectively for 18–21-year olds. However, even then, blacks were somewhat more likely than whites to drop out of both high school and college before graduation. Overall, then, black, as well as most other minority educational attainment, remains below that of whites, although the black-white gap has narrowed substantially. (Parelius and Parelius, 1978: 287)

Throughout the Coleman study, one ethnic minority group did not fit the pattern of lower scholastic achievement. On virtually every variable of intellectual value, aspiration, or achievement, the Oriental-American children were equal to or even outperformed their white, majority group peers. On the sense of control variables, they stood between the white students and the blacks and Puerto Ricans, perhaps reflecting a realistic awareness of lingering racial prejudice (or, as we shall see in the study to be considered next, the restrictions of an authoritarian family system), but on any measures of academic achievement or steps toward higher education they excelled. Is there anything in the background of Oriental-American children that explains their subsequent academic and occupational success?

One interpretation is offered by Caudill and De Vos, who studied Japanese Americans who migrated to Chicago from relocation camps at the end of World War II. Longitudinal comparisons of a group of first- and second-generation Japanese Americans (Issei and Nisei, respectively) with a sample of middle- and lower-SES non-Orientals on a variety of educational and occupational achievement measures showed that the Japanese Americans "achieved more in the space of four years in Chicago than other groups who had long been in the city, and who appear far less handicapped by racial and cultural differences" (Caudill and De Vos, 1966: 218).

The heart of the Caudill–De Vos study was an intensive clinical analysis of test, interview, and psychotherapeutic data from a subgroup of the total study sample. These clinical data suggest that the source of the Japanese-American phenomenon lies in "a significant compatibility (but no means identity) between the value system found in the culture of Japan and the value system found in

American middle class culture." Both groups valued politeness, respect for authority and parental wishes, diligence, and personal achievement of long-range goals. These shared values, plus a common "adaptive mechanism of being highly sensitive to cues coming from the external world as to how they should act," even to the extent of suppressing many of their true feelings, assured that the Japanese Americans, while acting in terms of the values and adaptive mechanisms of their own ethnic heritage, would at the same time project an image that would be favorably evaluated by Americans. "What has happened here is that the peers, teachers, employers, and fellow workers of the Nisei have projected their own values onto the neat, well-dressed, and efficient Nisei in whom they saw mirrored many of their own ideals" (Caudill and De Vos, 1966: 214–215; 226). Thus was built up a set of role expectations that both reinforce and produce achievement behavior. Teachers and others in important role relationships with Japanese Americans came to expect high levels of performance from them and they in turn fulfilled these expectations by actually obtaining relatively high-level jobs, which in turn reinforced the expectations of those around them, and so on. (Similar interpretations can be found in Okimoto, 1970, and Kitano, 1972.)

The authors also point out that communication of achievement-oriented values and skills was facilitated by the family structure of Oriental Americans, who "formed tight, self-contained communities controlled by parental authority and strong social sanctions." Ironically, the very family structure that was so conducive to success in American society was also a source of strain for the second-generation Japanese Americans, making it difficult for them to break free from their families. In other words, what may be very functional for success in certain social institutions, such as the school or office, may be less functional at the individual level, where it may hinder personal satisfaction and development.

Whatever the consequences of particular family forms for academic and occupational success, there is some evidence from recent research that both the dynamics of Oriental-American families and communities and the academic achievement patterns of Oriental-American students are changing. In a study of several samples of third-generation, Japanese-American high school students, Connor (1975) found that their grade-point averages tended to be somewhat lower or only slightly higher that their Caucasian classmates. Connor also found considerable evidence of assimilation into the high school culture, which was not characteristic of earlier generations of Oriental-American students. In one sample, 83 percent of the males were involved in athletics and other extracurricular activities and 85 percent of the females were active in student government or school clubs. Sixty-nine percent of the males and 79 percent of the females said that their friends were mostly Caucasian. Connor's interpretation is that in the past Japanese-American students concentrated upon their studies and earned higher grades than whites because other avenues of achievement were closed to them, a pattern that has changed during the past decade.

Although race has a clear impact upon school success or failure, and at least part of the effect is due to the systematic discrimination practiced against certain racial minorities, the exact extent of the purely racial effect is difficult to specify because race is itself related to other family characteristics. Probably the strongest relationship is between race and SES. Indeed, the thesis of a recent analysis of the achievement of American blacks, by a black sociologist, is that because of fundamental and interrelated changes in the structure of the economy and of race relations in the United States, the life chances of individual blacks are now affected more by their economic class position than by their race. Comparing the situation of blacks at various points in our national history, Wilson concludes that at present middle-class blacks, riding on the wave of political and social change, have benefited from expansion of opportunities in many sectors of society, while the black "underclass" falls further and further behind. Wilson claims, furthermore, that his hypotheses apply to all disadvantaged ethnic minorities. While blacks are disproportionately represented in the underclass population,

> the situation of marginality and redundancy created by the modern industrial society deleteriously affects all the poor, regardless of race. Underclass whites, Hispano-Americans and native Americans are all victims, to a greater or lesser degree, of class subordination under advanced capitalism. And since 1970 both poor whites and nonwhites have evidenced very little progress in their elevation from the ranks of the underclass. (Wilson, 1977: 18–19)

One of the few empirical studies to compare the performance of several different ethnic minorities controlling for SES is by Stodolsky and Lesser (1967). Working on the premise that "social-class and ethnic influences differ not only in degree but in kind, with the consequence that different kinds of intellectual skills are fostered or hindered in different environments," Stodolsky and Lesser (1967) tested a specially selected sample of 320 first graders, evenly distributed by sex and social class, in four different ability areas: verbal, reasoning, number, and space conceptualization. Since the researchers wanted tasks that did not require transfer from previous learning, they constructed tests that included only objects and experiences common to all social and ethnic groups in an urban area. Thus, they used pictures of buses, fire hydrants, police cars, and other objects to which all urban children are exposed, rather than the conventional giraffes, xylophones, and other objects that middle-class children are more likely to encounter in picture books, family excursions, and so on. Stodolsky and Lesser also controlled for "examiner bias" by having each child tested by a person of his or her own ethnic group and by extensive videotape training of the examiners.

Exhibit 3–2 shows the average test scores in the four intellectual areas for the four ethnic subsamples. Children in these four groups differed both in the absolute level of each mental ability and in the pattern among these abilities. For example, on verbal ability the Jewish children rank way above the others, and this was also their area of most outstanding performance. Although the overall pattern of Jewish children was relatively high, their average scores were considerably lower in the other three ability areas, and they were outranked in reasoning and space conceptualization by the Chinese children (who were weak in the verbal area). Black children, who were in the bottom or next to the bottom

Exhibit 3-2
Pattern of Normalized Mental-Ability Scores for Each Ethnic Group

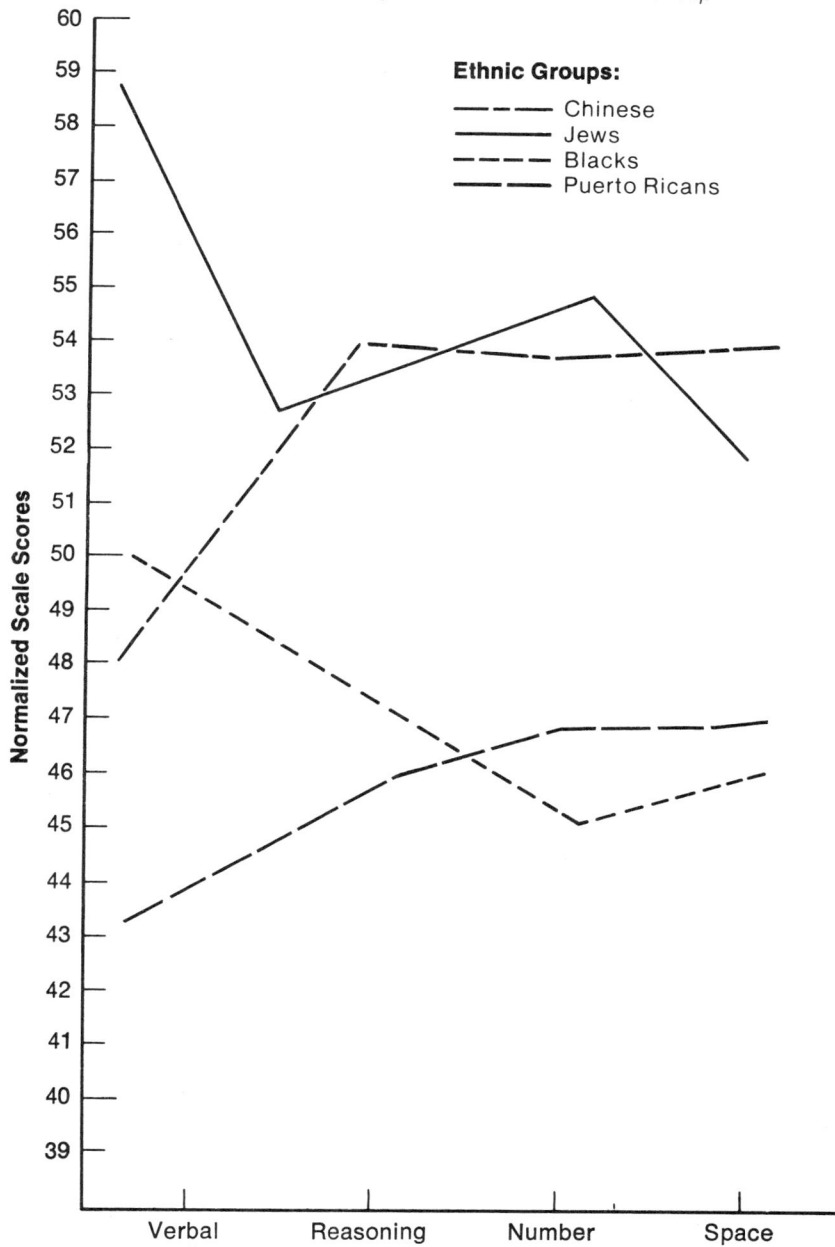

Stodolsky-Lesser, 1967.

rank in three out of four areas, performed relatively well in the verbal area. What is even more striking is that the ethnic patterns shown in Exhibit 3-2 are not changed by introducing the social status factor.

Once the pattern specific to the ethnic group emerges, social-class variations within the ethnic group do not alter this basic organization. For example . . . [Exhibit 3-3] shows the mentality pattern peculiar to the Chinese children—with the pattern displayed by the middle-class Chinese children duplicated at a lower level of performance by the lower-class Chinese children. . . . Parallel statements can be made for each ethnic group.

The failure of social-class conditions to transcend patterns of mental ability associated with ethnic influences was unexpected. Social-class influences have been described as superceding ethnic group effects for such diverse phenomena as child-rearing practices, educational and occupational aspirations, achievement motivation, and anomie. The greater salience of social class over ethnic membership is reversed in the present findings in patterns of mental ability. Ethnicity has the primary effect upon the organization of mental abilities, and the organization is not modified further by social-class influences. (Stodolsky and Lesser, 1967: 567, 570)

A replication of the study by the same authors (a rare phenomenon in social research, as we saw in Chapter 2), with a similar sample of children but in a different city, duplicated almost exactly the pattern of test performance reported above. Thus, the authors conclude that while both social class and ethnic-racial group membership affect the level of intellectual performance, it is ethnicity that fosters the development of unique ability patterns, with children from higher social classes simply reflecting the same ability pattern at higher levels of performance than their lower-SES racial-ethnic peers. Thus an important implication of this study is that certain cultural subgroups in our society may nurture special attributes and skills, and that pursuit of the goal of equal educational opportunity should not lead us to impose uniform modes of learning upon all children.

Recent analysis of historical data shows changes in the relative performance levels of various racial-ethnic-religious groups over time that seem to be better explained by changes in their social position in society than by changes in their basic aptitudes for academic work. In a study of the results of IQ tests administered in the 1920s and 1930s, Sowell (1977) found that many immigrant groups showed performance patterns similar to those of poor and minority group children today. Thus the average scores of Italian, Polish, Spanish, and Portuguese students were all in the seventies and eighties, indicating below-average intelligence. One set of data on Massachusetts students showed a higher percentage of black students with high test scores than Portuguese, Italian, Polish, or French-Canadian students. In some early tests, Chinese Americans did most poorly on tests of abstract reasoning ability, the mental ability on which Chinese-American children in Stodolsky and Lesser's 1967 study excelled (see Exhibit 3-2). At the time of these earlier testings, genetic explanations, arguing the particular disadvantages of various "racial stocks," were widely accepted. It now seems more likely, as Christopher Hurn has argued, that the differences between southern and eastern European immigrants versus the majority population

Exhibit 3-3
Patterns of Normalized Mental-Ability Scores for Middle- and Lower-Income Chinese Children

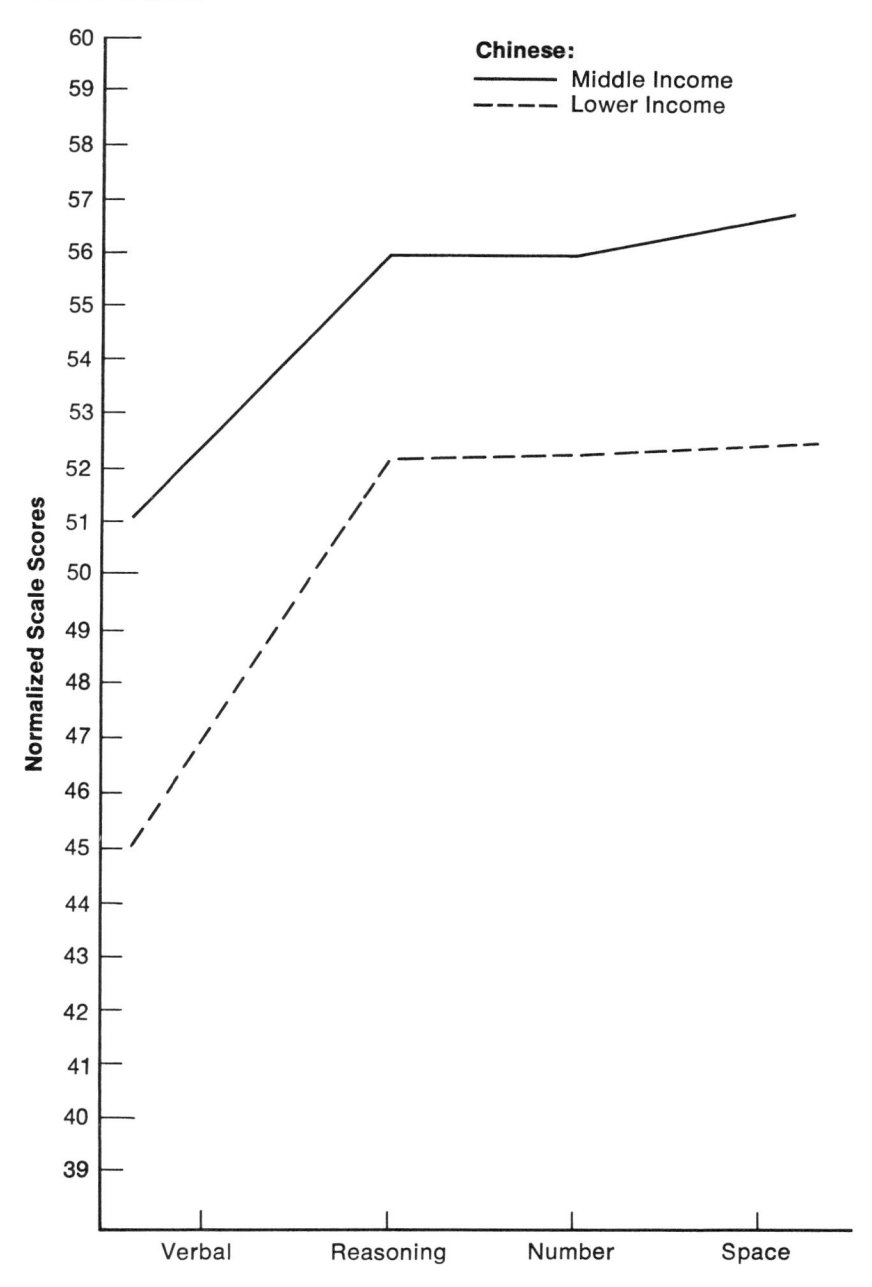

in the 1920s and 1930s and between whites and blacks today reflect "caste-like social differences" between different racial-ethnic groups than genetic differences (Hurn, 1978: 132. The relationships between ethnicity and abilities will be discussed further in Chapter 6).

Religion

The Stodolsky-Lesser study reminds us that the various components of ethnic identity are not always clearly distinct from each other. While Jewish children were in that study compared with children of different racial-ethnic groups, in this section we shall consider some studies in which Jewish children are compared with children from different religious affiliations. What is consistent about both kinds of studies is the general phenomenon of high achievement among Jewish subjects. As early as the 1940s, Terman's longitudinal studies of gifted children (Terman and Oden, 1947) showed that their Jewish subjects, while not differing significantly in mean IQ scores from the group as a whole, went on to receive higher grades in college, higher incomes, and to concentrate more heavily in professional occupations. The Stodolsky-Lesser data showed overall high performance by the Jewish children in the sample, with extremely high test scores in the verbal area. While the consistently high achievement points to the likelihood of factors specific to the Jewish culture that encourage and facilitate achievement, the first study in which systematic efforts to specify and measure these factors were made is the comparison of a sample of Jewish with Italian-Catholic families carried out by Strodtbeck in the early 1950s. These two groups were chosen because they had similar periods of residence in this country and it was possible to locate adequate numbers of second-generation families with early adolescent sons in the particular school system studied (New Haven), but their socioeconomic attainments and their rates of mobility *as groups* in American society differed markedly.

A sample of 1,151 boys between the ages of fourteen and seventeen in the New Haven public and parochial schools completed a questionnaire asking about their values, educational and occupational aspirations, parental expectations and control, and the balance of power within their families. The researchers also gathered information on the boys' school performance and the SES of their families. From this sample, Strodtbeck selected the following stratified group of Italian Catholic and Jewish boys for intensive study:

Family SES	Catholic Boys School Achievement "Over"	Catholic Boys School Achievement "Under"	Jewish Boys School Achievement "Over"	Jewish Boys School Achievement "Under"
High	4	4	4	4
Medium	4	4	4	4
Low	4	4	4	4

Total = 48

Achievement was determined by the extent to which the boys' school grades were higher or lower than would be predicted on the basis of performance on intelligence tests. Note that the sample makes no pretensions at being representative. In the context of New Haven as a whole, Strodtbeck "oversampled" for Italians of high SES. Note also that Strodtbeck's group contains a religious-ethnic combination. That is, his Catholic boys are Catholics of one specific ethnic background. Since there is considerable evidence that family structure, styles of life, residence, and even achievement vary among American Catholics of different national backgrounds (see Greeley and Rossi, 1966), one cannot specify in Strodtbeck's study which differences are due to the religious and which are due to the ethnic factor. (Recognizing the biases of his sample, Strodtbeck felt that "the stratification served our theoretical curiosity about effects of combinations of classificatory factors rather than the straightforward description objective of efficiently estimating parameters of incidence for particular populations" Strodtbeck, 1958: 160–161.)

The data were collected by Strodtbeck and an assistant in the respondents' homes, using a technique called "revealed differences." This technique involved interviewing the boy and both his parents, and then having the family as a group resolve disagreements in opinion that had been expressed in the individual interviews. Recordings of the interviews were scored both in terms of the content of the attitudes expressed and the structure of the interaction (the number of acts by each family member and the proportion of decisions "won" by each).

From an analysis of both questionnaire and interview data, Strodtbeck found that the Jewish families were more likely to hold three values postulated as important for achievement in the United States:

Belief that the world is orderly and amenable to rational mastery, and that the individual can and should make systematic plans for controlling his or her destiny (this is a close parallel to the sense of control of destiny items that Coleman *et al.* found to be strongly related both to race and to scholastic performance)

Willingness to leave home to make one's way in life

Preference for individual rather than collective credit for work accomplished

Examination of the data on resolution of family disagreements indicated more equalitarian relations in the Jewish than in the Italian-Catholic families. In comparison with the boys of Italian background, the Jewish boys were encouraged to express their opinions and to be independent. This autonomy, coupled with the Jewish parents' willingness for their sons to leave home to make their own way in life, meant that these boys could move out of the formal family setting and establish ties with other systems without having to rupture family ties altogether, as was the case in the traditional, authoritarian Italian families.

Notice that the picture of the Jewish family constructed by Strodtbeck is very different from that of the Japanese-American families studied by Caudill and De Vos. While the Japanese Americans' impressive performance in school and in the occupational world paralleled the Jewish pattern, their authoritarian family structure was closer to the Italian-Catholic model. The two studies are not really comparable because of differences in conceptual formulation and data-gathering methods, as well as geographical and other differences, but they do indicate that no single dimension can predict the achievement propensity of all religious or ethnic groups. Valuation of achievement is not a satisfactory predictor, because it appears to be a necessary but not sufficient condition for academic achievement. That is, if one took a cross section of racial-ethnic-religious groups in our society, one would find some groups that had both relatively lower achievement orientation and lower academic achievement as a group (for example, the Puerto Ricans in the Coleman *et al.* sample, the Italian Catholics in the Strodtbeck sample). However, there would also be groups that had reached the stage of recognizing the value of education and desiring it for themselves or their children but that had not yet learned the strategies for successful performance in formal educational settings (for example, the blacks in the Coleman *et al.* sample).

Further insights could be obtained by examining the *same* racial-ethnic-religious groups *over time*. The research by Sowell discussed in the previous section showed that the actual performance patterns of students from some groups changed, along with changes in public perceptions about their abilities. In contrast to the consistent superiority of Jewish students on tests of verbal ability in recent times, Sowell discusses a 1921 study that reported that Jews exceeded all other immigrant groups in the number of certificates for mental deficiency issued at Ellis Island.

Ever since Max Weber's classic work on the influence of religious beliefs upon social activity, *The Protestant Ethic and the Spirit of Capitalism,* there has been general acceptance of the notion that the set of concepts, values, and structures constituting a religious dogma has impact upon the believer's view of the world and his or her activity in it, in particular the extent to which he or she is concerned about and actually achieves worldly success. Weber's thesis was that Protestantism, especially the Calvinist sects, emphasized the value of hard work, coupled with an asceticism that denied any kind of sensual pleasure in the fruits of one's labor but hinted that success in worldly affairs might be an indication of God's grace. In contrast with Catholic dogma, with its emphasis upon the imperfectibility of human beings and their constant exposure to sin and moral conflict, Calvinist dogma was congruent with the development of both competitive capitalism and modern science. Analysis of historical materials by Weber and later researchers did in fact show a disproportionate number of scientists and successful businesspeople among Protestant individuals and countries.

More recent studies, including Strodtbeck's, have found Catholics less oriented toward educational and occupational mobility generally, less likely to attend college, and less likely to go into scientific careers if they do attend college. McClelland, whose *n* Achievement scale will be discussed in the next chapter, has found that Protestant parents tend to set earlier standards of independence for their children and has inferred that this would produce higher achievement motivation (McClelland, Rindlishbacker, and de Charms, 1955). In a study of the educational expectations of a national sample of white teenagers, Rhodes and

Nam (1970) found that the proportion planning to attend college was related to the religious identification of the respondent's mother, with the following rank ordering:

	% Planning College
Jewish	86
Large Protestant denominations (except Baptist)	58
Roman Catholic	55
Baptist and smaller Protestant denominations and sects	42

However, the relationship between religious background and academic success is not as simple as the theoretical arguments and some of the empirical findings suggest. In the same study, Rhodes and Nam found that the religious context of the school, as well as the religious identity of the individual student, made a difference. Catholics attending Catholic schools were more likely than Catholics attending public schools to plan college, though whether this is because parochial schools have an option of selectivity of students, which public schools do not have, or because students in parochial schools are pressured not just to attend college but to attend a Catholic college (the motive being to produce more good Catholics as well as more good students) cannot be explained with the study data.

Findings from a national sample survey that, unlike Rhodes and Nam's, controlled for several socioeconomic factors indicate that the achievement orientation of some subgroups of Catholics is as great or greater than that of comparable Protestants (Veroff *et al.*, 1962). As part of a larger study of mental health, 1,620 men and women were given a thematic apperceptive test of achievement motivation, similar to McClelland's *n* Achievement scale, in which imaginative stories told in response to a set of pictures were scored for references to indicants of achievement motivation. The proportions of men in each of the three religion categories who had scores above the median for the entire male population were as follows: Protestant, 48 percent; Catholic, 57 percent; Jewish, 68 percent. The finding that relatively more Jewish men had high achievement scores than either of the other religious groups was anticipated. What was unexpected was that the Catholic men's scores were higher than the Protestants'.

Further analyses designed to interpret this unexpected result showed that the motivation of Catholic men is more directly related to economic factors. Thus for the Catholics, the lower the income and the greater the number of children in the family, the higher the achievement motivation; for Protestants, the scores showed a slight positive association with income and none with family size. The effect of religious identity was also dependent upon place of residence, including geographical region and the extent to which one's religion was a minority religion in a given area. For example, Veroff and his associates found that the Protestants living in the relatively higher income areas of the industrial Northeast had higher motivation scores than Protestants in other regions of the country, and they point out that most researchers who have reported higher achievement among Protestants have also been studying this one area. While they concede that religious doctrine undoubtedly influences the way a child is socialized, including his or her orientation to academic and other kinds of success, they conclude that the effect of religion, like that of race, also depends upon other attributes of the individual and upon the social environment in which he or she is located. Thus:

> the situational effects that the social milieu has on these dispositions—region, socioeconomic status, education, income, size of family—may be so large as to cancel out any real differences between the personality dispositions of Catholics and Protestants which may be there. . . . Our impression is that the Protestant Ethic hypothesis when used to contrast achievement motivated Protestants and Catholics has many new facets to be considered within certain social conditions. The hypothesis does seem to work simply only at the upper status positions of a well integrated, fairly prosperous, economic structure, in the established Northeastern parts of the United States. Perhaps this region is more typical of the European structure Weber originally observed. Change in the tempo of capitalism in America, change in the Calvinistic ideology in Protestant groups, changes in direction to Catholic living in a highly mobile society, may all contribute to making the Protestant Ethic less generally discernible and outstanding as a way of life geared to achievement in modern America. (Veroff *et al.*, 1962: 217)

Conclusions

This chapter and the next one examine explanations for children's differential learning that are based upon characteristics of their families—that is, explanations that would be classified primarily in cell 3 of Exhibit 2–1.

The weight of evidence clearly indicates that a child's chances of success in school are greatly affected by the social position of her or his family. However school or academic success is measured, children whose parents have low socioeconomic status or who are members of an ethnic minority group that has a relatively low position in society are less likely than other children to achieve it.

One of the bitterest controversies in the sociology of education is over the *explanation* for the clearly documented relationship between family social position and school success. A number of theories have been proposed. The biological-genetic explanation, which proposes that there may be innate differences in intelligence between children of different races, and which is understandably offensive to minority groups who are designated as having inferior intelligence, will be discussed in Chapter 6. Battle lines have also been drawn between those who think that differences in achievement can be explained by cultural differences between persons of different social classes and ethnic groups and those who think that achievement differences are explained by differences in the quality of the schools attended by children of different status and ethnic groups. The first theory, formulated by Martin Deutsch (1963) and Frank Riessman (1962), holds that poor and minority families have a unique set of beliefs and customs—a "culture of poverty"—that limits the capacity to profit from formal education. (Basil Bernstein, the British sociologist whose work was discussed in this chapter, has also been accused of holding this view, although he denies it.) Characteristic of the culture of poverty are fatalism, feelings of frustration and alienation from the larger society, a present- rather than future-time orientation, resulting in an inability to plan for the future, and preference for physical over mental activities and gratifications. Thus "the lower-class child enters the school situation so poorly prepared to produce what the school demands that initial failures are almost inevitable and the school experience becomes negatively rather than positively reinforced" (Deutsch, 1963: 163). Because "culturally deprived" children are prone to so many learning difficulties, they need special or compensatory education that will change their self-image, motivation, and general world view.

The culture of poverty or cultural deficit theory is hotly contested by Kenneth Clark (1965, 1972) and others, who argue that the poor performance of poor and minority children is explained not by deficiencies in their upbringing but by the inferior quality of the schools they attend and the systematic institutional bias of schools and other middle-class institutions against such children. The culture of poverty theory encourages social stereotyping rather than educational reform and, by allowing us to believe that minority children are "different" from other children, it provides us with an unjustified alibi for their school failures. The solution does not require teaching white middle-class values to lower-class or minority children. Rather the whole public school system, especially in large urban areas, needs to be redesigned so that *all* children are taught the basic skills required for survival in complex modern societies. Clark and his associates have proposed a reform of the Washington, D.C. public schools based on such a model (Clark, 1972).

The arguments among opposing theories cannot be resolved with the research evidence currently available. And assuming that different subgroups in a society are differentially able to communicate to their children the attitudes and skills necessary to playing the student role successfully, *how* they do so has been only hinted at. In the next chapter we shall examine what goes on within the family that may produce differential success in school.

Notes

1. Of course, socioeconomic status and religion can have visible manifestations, such as clothing style or quality. The very poor may have poverty-connected health problems that affect their physical appearance. But these are mainly things that could be changed. With the proper "costume" an individual can pass for almost any social class, and in industrialized Western countries mass production has given the majority of citizens access to clothing styles formerly available only to the upper strata. One cannot do something about one's race in this respect. With the exception of a handful of individuals whose physical features are ambiguous enough to allow them to pass from one group to another, one's race at birth is a lifetime attribute.

2. The International Project for the Evaluation of Educational Achievement (IEA), which will be discussed in detail in Chapter 13, shows a consistent relationship between

family status and test scores in each of the twenty participating countries, varying in level of development as well as political structure and ideology.

3. A statistic that measures the extent of dispersion of scores around some central value or score. In this case the measure of central tendency was the *median* or midpoint score, above which fell half of the scores and below which fell the other half, for each test at each grade level in the sample. In most samples about two-thirds of the cases fall within one standard deviation on either side of the central value and almost all cases fall within two standard deviations. For a fuller discussion of measures of central tendency and dispersion, see Riley, 1963: Volume II, Section 3.

Family Structure and Interrelationships   Chapter 4

In our studies we were not only impressed by what some children could achieve during the first years, but also by the fact that the child's family seemed so obviously central to the outcome . . . The informal education that families provide for their children makes more of an impact on a child's educational development than the formal educational system. If the family does its job well, the professional can provide effective training. If not, there may be little the professional can do to save the child from mediocrity.   Burton L. White

The relationship between the family and the school is a complex and sensitive one in modern societies. In relatively simple societies education can be, and often is, carried out within the family or kin group (indeed, in such societies the school as a separate institution may not even exist), but in modern industrialized societies the educative function becomes more and more removed and is to some degree opposed to the interests and rights of the family. The difference between the social structures of family and school settings in modern societies has been analyzed by Dreeben, who pointed out that

> schooling demands the formation of social relationships more transient, more time-bounded than those characteristic of the family. The small size of the family, the great frequency of contact among its members and particularly between mothers and children, the intensity of emotional bonds, and the mutuality of support make it a setting well suited for establishing a relationship of dependency. The school provides a much larger pool of individuals within which a pupil establishes relationships. Annual promotion, moreover, limits the duration of these relationships to about one year, and ensures, at least with those formed with adults, that they will be broken. The school, then, constitutes a setting more conducive than the family to the formation of looser, more fluid social bonds inconsistent both with strong ties of dependency, and with authority based on enduring personal obligations to elders. (Dreeben, 1968: 21)

Chapter 3 focused upon the ascribed characteristics of families that are strongly related to the performance of children in school. Background variables, while they do explain a sizable amount of the variance in achievement, do not tell us much about *how* homes are effective or ineffective in socializing children to the student role, nor do they give a detailed picture of the range of home environments that occurs within given status categories. In this chapter we turn to the internal life of the family, and we shall consider the ways in which family structure, parental values and expectations, modes of communication, distribution of power, and child-rearing practices are related to academic achievement.

This is a more difficult task than the one we faced in Chapter 3. First, for obvious ethical reasons most of the available data on child rearing in America is based upon parents' or children's reports of their home life rather than upon actual observation within homes.[1] Second, most of the social-psychological research on family socialization does not link the family and school system. As we shall see, the particular combination of social motives most conducive to high achievement and the particular patterns of socialization most likely to produce them have not been clearly established. Third, the topic of family effects upon school performance is one in which the dangers of experimenter effects, as described in Chapter 2, are great. Since family experiences are such an important and emotion-laden part of everyone's life (indeed, it is difficult to separate our feelings from our theories), the probabilities are high that the researcher will "find" his or her personal view of the best kind of family life to be related to desirable learning outcomes. Thus, in reading research reports one must be sensitive to the possible effects of the researcher's personal ideology upon his or her research design and interpretation of results—not to mention the extent to which our own feelings color our reading of the work of others.

Finally, it is important to keep in mind that these internal or process variables are themselves often related to the ascribed characteristics that were discussed in Chapter 3. Some of these interactive relationships will be discussed later in this chapter.

Family Structure

The social structural framework within which family interaction takes place sets certain limits on the quantity and quality of socialization that occurs. In recent years, social historians have been reconstructing the size and structure of households in the past, and their findings contradict some of our romantic notions about the way families used to be. Large three-generational or extended families have always been rare. It is true, however, that households in the past were more likely to contain apprentices, servants, boarders, and other persons not related by blood. They were also more likely to contain children of a greater range of ages and the male head of the household, since his work was often in or near the home. While there is no evidence that homes in the past were consciously organized for the care of children, the economic and other functions of the home necessitated an organization which, at the same time, assured that a number of persons were available to help look after children.

While the two-parent nuclear family is considered the norm in twentieth-century America, there is, in fact, a great deal of variation in family structure in this country reflecting some important recent social trends. These include:

Large increases in the proportion of working mothers. For example, the labor force participation of married women with children aged six to seventeen rose from 26 percent in 1948 to 51 percent in 1974.

Substantial increases in the proportion of single-parent families. Over 15 percent of the children in the United States now live in one-parent households, and this percentage is much higher in cities and among certain ethnic subgroups.

Decreases in the number of adults populating family units. For example, the percentage of extended families with children under age six declined by half in the past twenty-five years. During the 1960s and 1970s, there was considerable experimentation with communes and other pseudofamilial households with several adults, but these never constituted more than a small minority of the households in this country.

A sharp increase in the proportion of illegitimate children. The percentage of illegitimate births more than tripled from 1948 to 1974, during an era when planned births among married couples declined considerably.

An increase in the number of children being cared for in day care centers and other arrangements outside of the child's home.

Studies of contemporary American families reveal that many are experiencing considerable stress in trying to coordinate their work and child-rearing responsibilities and that many are anxious about the kind of job they are doing as parents (see, for example, Kenniston and the Carnegie Council on Children, 1977. Some interesting case studies of "middle-American" families with two working parents and young children are contained in Lein, 1974).

Scholars differ in their interpretation of the implications of these trends. Some see in them the breakdown of the family, and some go so far as to blame the recent widely publicized declines in achievement test scores on changes in the American family. Others (for example, Bane, 1976) note that more children than in the past live with at least one of their biological parents and argue that the structure of American families has remained remarkably consistent over time. To date, however, the only systematic empirical research relating specific aspects of family structure to specific kinds of intellectual outcomes is on family size and the spacing of children.

Research on Family Size and Birth Order

The effect of family size is fairly clear; in general, the fewer the children in a family, the greater the achievement of each. The effects of birth order or sibling position are less clear. A study of a large representative sample of U.S. males by

Blau and Duncan (1967) found that the educational attainment and subsequent occupational career of first-born and last-born sons were higher than those of sons in intermediate positions, but that the relationship was also affected by family size. There was little difference in the achievement of oldest and youngest children in small families, but in large ones the youngest sons tended to be more successful that their older brothers, perhaps because in large families, older sons take on responsibilities and make sacrifices for younger ones to the benefit of the latter.

Another study, based upon a smaller and more selective sample but that contained both males and females, concluded that family size and birth order influenced a child's subsequent attainments by governing the "inputs" (time, money, and other resources) invested by parents in their children. For example, in large families or one-parent families the amount of time a parent can spend with each child is limited (Lindert, 1974).

The most comprehensive analysis published to date is by Zajonc, who proposes a "confluence" model of the effects of family size, birth order, and child spacing on measured intelligence.[2] As Zajonc formulates it:

> The basic idea of the confluence model is that within the family the intellectual growth of every member is dependent on that of all the other members, and that the rate of this growth depends on the family configuration. Different family configurations constitute different intellectual environments. (Zajonc, 1976: 227)

Zajonc tested his model against data from several large empirical studies—from Dutch, French, and Scottish, as well as American populations—and found that (1) Scores on intelligence tests increased with decreasing family size. (2) Test scores were higher among earlier- than later-born children when the intervals between births are not large, but that longer intersibling spacing appeared to cancel out the negative effects of later birth order and in some cases to reverse them. (3) In general, the greater the spacing between births, the higher the test scores. (Twins and other multiple-birth children had markedly lower average IQ scores.) In the case of only children, the benefits of small family seemed to be counteracted by the lack of opportunities to serve as teachers to younger children. The tutoring role assumed by many first-born children with younger siblings seemed to explain some of their greater intelligence. Last-born children suffer the same handicap of only children. (5) Children from single-parent families or children whose parents were frequently absent (such as children of servicemen on active duty) generally had lower test scores. The importance of parental presence is emphasized by the finding that remarriage of a single parent, especially when the child is young, resulted in improved intellectual performance.

Zajonc also argues that changes in family patterns, such as increases or decreases in the birth rate or changes in child-spacing patterns, are reflected in parallel temporal changes in intellectual performance. He feels, for example, that the recent declines in SAT and other achievement test scores can be partly, though not entirely, explained by changes in family configurations, including increases in the number of children living in single-parent families. At the same time, the birth rate and fertility declines of recent years mean that a greater proportion of American children will be first-born. While the small nuclear family does present many difficulties for the socialization of children, it may also have certain advantages for intellectual development.

It should be noted that not all scholars concur with the model and interpretations discussed above (see, for example, Schooler, 1972, for an argument against the existence of birth-order effects). Others question whether the same model is appropriate for all societies. For example, some crosscultural analyses indicate that a linear model like Zajonc's, in which additional children lower the intellectual environment of the family in a linear fashion, holds true only for Western societies. In Middle Eastern societies studied by Davis, Kahan, and Bashi (1976), older children often contributed to the intellectual environment of the family more than did their parents, especially in communities undergoing rapid cultural change, and in such situations being later born was an asset rather than a liability.

It has been suggested by some researchers that the sheer physical presence of both parents in the home may be less important to the child's development than the degree to which the parents are meeting the expectations attached to their roles. In a reanalysis of part of the data from the *Equality of Educational Opportunity* survey, Chad Gordon[3] constructed a measure of family structure based upon (1) the presence or absence of both parents and (2) their employment status. Some of the results of crosstabulating this family structure measure with a variety of dependent variables are shown in Exhibit 4–1.

The most positive attitudes and highest performances are found in families with both parents present and the father working (columns 1 and 2 of Exhibit 4–1). Whether the mother was working did not seem to make much difference (columns 1 and 2 alternate between first and second rank for almost all of the positive attitude and performance measures), as long as the father is employed. The most damaging family situations were those where the father was present but not working (columns 3 and 4), again regardless of whether or not the mother worked, and where the father is absent and the mother unemployed (column 6). Families with only one parent but where that parent is employed are in the middle (columns 5 and 7).

These results suggest that it is the relative economic security attached to alternative family structures that explains variations in children's self-image and success in school, and that the children who are least successful in the student role are from families where the major breadwinner is not meeting the expectations attached to that role (this includes families where the father is present but unemployed, even if the mother is bringing in some income). The data also indicate that the employment of women is not detrimental to their children's self-confidence or achievement. Students do well when the father is present and employed, regardless of the mother's employment status; and if he is present and unemployed, her employment does not noticeably help or hinder the situation (with the exception of especially low self-acceptance among children with working mothers and unemployed fathers). If the mother is raising the children alone, it is apparently to their advantage if she works (compare columns 5 and 6).

Exhibit 4-1
The Effects of Family Structure Upon Student Performance and Attitudes

	Both Parents Present				Mother Only		Father Only
Father employed? Mother employed?	(1) yes yes	(2) yes no	(3) no yes	(4) no no	(5) — yes	(6) — no	(7) yes —
% Respondents Who							
Say their parents have high aspirations for them	41.4	42.2	24.7	21.9	28.1	21.8	36.0
Say they are among the brightest in their grade	17.1	14.6	15.4	12.8	12.2	9.6	12.5
Say they are below average in their grade	2.1	3.0	9.2	6.4	6.5	8.5	4.2
Have a high grade average (A or B)	26.2	29.4	9.1	12.8	27.7	17.6	17.4
Have high overall competence	13.6	11.0	11.1	7.7	10.7	8.1	13.0
Have high self-acceptance	53.7	55.6	31.7	43.6	54.1	48.8	50.0
Have high self-esteem	26.2	30.4	13.4	12.3	26.2	13.8	26.1
Have high self-determinism	24.2	29.1	19.7	16.7	20.2	16.3	30.4
Have high verbal ability	60.7	63.0	16.9	19.8	37.8	29.1	60.0

Parental Values and Aspirations

It is clear that high-achieving children tend to come from families who have high expectations for them, and who consequently are likely to "set standards" and to make greater demands at an earlier age. We saw in the previous chapter that success is generally held in high esteem in our society and that most people recognize the hard work and sacrifice involved in attaining it, but that students and their parents differ in their estimates of the relative importance of personal initiative as against fate or luck as the source of success. They also differ in the degree to which they set high attainment as a specific goal for themselves and their children.

A study that illustrates the power of parental aspirations, but that at the same time shows that they are not synonymous with socioeconomic status, is Kahl's often-cited analysis of a sample of Boston high school boys (1953). Kahl's objective was to explain the educational commitment of students subject to educational "cross pressures"—who had some characteristics that would lead one to expect high academic commitment and performance and some that would lead to the opposite prediction. The two variables he chose to control were individual academic ability (IQ scores) and family SES.

Past analyses have shown that it is quite safe to predict that boys with high IQ's and fathers in white-collar or higher-SES occupations will go to college (cell *a* in Exhibit 4–2) and that boys with low IQ's and fathers in low-SES occupations will not (cell *d*). Kahl focused upon cell *b,* one of the two cells where prediction is problematic. He selected a sample of twenty-four boys from a larger survey known as the "Boston-Harvard Mobility Study." All of the boys tested in the top three IQ deciles in their schools. All of their fathers held low-level white-color or skilled to semi-skilled labor jobs. Half of the boys were taking a college prep course and planning to go on to college; the other half were not. Kahl conducted intensive interviews with all twenty-four boys to find out what influenced the decisions of students whose abilities and environments could lead them in two different directions. His conclusion: their parents. Unlike boys without college aspirations, those who planned to continue their education had parents who were not satisfied with their own status and who had applied steady pressure on their sons to do better. In other words, it was not class per se that explained differential behavior, but the degree to which families retained the values and outlook of their own class or instead looked to a higher class as a reference group.

Exhibit 4–2

Property-Space for Predicting College Attendance

		Socioeconomic Status	
		High	Low
IQ Score	High	a	b
	Low	c	d

Kahl's objective was to show that different kinds of socialization to the student role could occur within a single social class, and he did not compare the boys in his sample with boys from any of the other cells in Exhibit 4–2. His findings also suggest, however, that the mechanisms for inducing educational commitment may be different in different classes. He found, for example, that *none* of the boys in his sample, college oriented or not, valued learning itself. All viewed education purely as a means of achieving socioeconomic mobility; what distinguished the high and low aspirers was that only the former had internalized the success-achievement ethic as a goal for themselves. Learning for its own sake is a luxury that these working-class boys could not afford.

While Kahl's data are now almost thirty years old, the study is still timely because the basic findings have been replicated in many settings, including crosscultural ones. For example, in British research on children from families with borderline status between the middle and working classes, the most academically successful children were found to be those whose parents' social aspirations exceeded their present or expected status or who identified themselves with the middle class (Morrison and McIntyre, 1971: 47). Evidence of the power of parental aspirations can also be found in the reanalysis of *Equality of Educational Opportunity* data by Gordon introduced earlier in this chapter. Gordon constructed an index of perceived parental aspiration from four items, asking respondents: how good, as students, their mothers wanted them to be; how good their fathers wanted them to be; their mothers' educational desires for them; and their fathers' educational desires for them. Exhibit 4–3 shows the relationships between scores on this index and ninth graders' own aspirations and academic performance, both totals, and controlling for SES and race.

The totals show a strong positive relationship for each of the four items. For example, the first set of totals shows that only 15.3 percent of the respondents with low perceived parental aspirations wanted to be among the best students in their school, while 46.8 percent of the middle group and 74.5 percent of those with high parental aspirations wanted to be top students. The figures above the totals show the effects on that item of parental aspiration controlling simultaneously for race and SES. Reading from left to right across the various rows shows a fairly consistent and substantial pattern of increases. Almost without exception the higher the parental aspiration, the higher the proportion of students within a given race-SES subgroup with high performance or aspirations.

Analyses of historical data suggest that the value placed upon formal education has changed over time and that it is probably related to people's life circumstances. In an analysis of the role of education in the "escape from poverty," Herbert Gans notes that among immigrants to this country in the nineteenth and early twentieth century, parents not only offered little encouragement to their children to perform well in school, but on the contrary,

> many of them made strenuous efforts to keep their children out of school in America, partly because these schools treated them with hostility and believed that they

Exhibit 4-3

The Effects of Parental Aspirations Upon Student Performance and Aspiration Controlling for SES and Race

%Respondents Who	Race	SES	Parental Aspiration Low	Medium	High
Want to be among the best students	black	low	30.2	71.9	71.0
		working-class	17.6	59.0	77.4
		middle	20.8	58.3	79.7
	white	low	14.3	56.4	57.9
		working-class	12.0	41.3	66.2
		middle	11.3	35.1	79.2
		TOTALS	**15.3**	**46.8**	**74.5**
Have overall grade averages of A or B	black	low	26.8	44.8	40.0
		working-class	38.9	48.2	62.1
		middle	17.9	63.2	53.9
	white	low	33.3	50.0	60.0
		working-class	42.9	64.7	73.0
		middle	48.0	65.2	73.4
		TOTALS	**38.6**	**59.4**	**71.2**
Are in college preparatory courses	black	low	8.5	18.4	25.7
		working-class	12.5	15.7	28.7
		middle	7.1	44.7	41.5
	white	low	9.7	12.5	50.0
		working-class	16.9	37.3	57.2
		middle	18.0	54.2	66.4
		TOTALS	**13.9**	**36.1**	**52.8**
Want a BA or more education	black	low	22.5	34.2	62.9
		working-class	19.4	38.6	81.6
		middle	25.0	57.9	90.8
	white	low	12.5	32.5	60.0
		working-class	8.7	54.2	80.9
		middle	16.0	74.2	92.7
		TOTALS	**14.6**	**54.5**	**84.8**

were unteachable, but also because parents wanted the children to work and contribute to the family income, and the jobs which were available to them did not require education. (Gans, 1976: 64)

Only in recent years have these attitudes changed. As blue-collar wages began to go up, parents no longer needed their children's paychecks. Also, as parents realized that automation and the decline in manufacturing would eventually lead to a reduction in decent blue-collar jobs and that white-collar jobs could not be obtained without the proper credentials, they began to insist that their children graduate from high school, and that boys, at least, consider going to college. Such changes in attitude have escalated in the last decade.

These observations suggest a hypothesis about the role of education in upward mobility that is just the reverse of the conventional wisdom. Education, at least for the poor, is not a causal agent in the achievement of mobility but one of its effects, and education is not thought to be relevant to mobility until *after* parents have achieved a threshold of economic security in the primary labor market (Gans, 1976: 66).

Interpersonal Relations and Interaction

Child-rearing practices are the means by which parental values and aspirations are implemented within given family structures. In this section we shall consider the kinds of parental behavior and parent-child interaction that are related to academic performance.

In the process of socialization, parents communicate to their children expectations for the children's behavior, or behavior standards. These behavior standards consist of a set of motives with their associated activities and habits. Among the social motives most often studied by educational sociologists are achievement motivation, independence (versus dependence), and aggression (or activity).

Achievement motivation refers to the individual's response to situations where some standard of excellence can be applied to her or his behavior. It seems almost a truism that high achievement motivation will lead directly to high achievement itself. Indeed, educational innovations or curricular changes are often justified with claims that they will raise student motivation—and teachers and teaching methods generally are believed to be incapable of producing learning unless they also produce high student motivation or morale. The evidence so far, however, has not produced strong empirical support for this assumption.

Still the most widely used measure of achievement motivation, although it was developed in the 1950s, is McClelland's n Achievement scale, based upon the number and type of references to achievement elicited by a series of stimulus pictures (McClelland *et al.*, 1953). The number of studies using the n Achievement scale or some variation of it runs into the thousands. In a review of this literature, however, Entwisle (1970b) concludes that, despite its popularity, the scale has neither high test reliability nor strong correlations with grades or any other measure of school performance. Her own analysis suggested that the few statistically significant positive relationships between n Achievement and performance scores could be explained by the verbal productivity or the general intelligence of the subjects—that is, their high n Achievement score seemed to be a consequence of their having produced more intelligent verbalization in response to the picture, and this linguistic facility rather than the test as a whole was related to academic performance.

In sum, little of the variance in educational performance seems to be explained by current modes of measuring the motivation to achieve, although this lack of relationship may be due to weaknesses in the measures used, including lack of internal consistency and failure to separate out the unique motivational component from the other components that are related to academic performance.

Independence versus dependence refers to the extent to which the child participates and/or is given freedom to make his or her own decisions and the extent to which rules and discipline are justified on some kind of rational grounds. Independence is generally believed to be a characteristic of high-achieving children, and observers in ghetto classrooms have commented upon the excessive dependence of the students upon the teacher. Severely disadvantaged children are, in fact, often so "hyper-alert" to the teacher's whereabouts and actions that they fail to respond to the learning materials and activities provided for them (see, for example, Miller, 1967: 58ff; and Moore, 1967). More systematic empirical research indicates, however, that the components and consequences of independence motivation are complex. In several studies of young children (Crandall *et al.*, 1960; Crandall, 1964), it was found that high achievers are at the same time less dependent than other children upon parents and teachers for emotional support and instrumental help in carrying out intellectual tasks *and* more sensitive to adult expectations.

> It would appear, then, that achieving children, in contrast to peers who perform less well, do not need to depend upon adults but are somewhat compliant and conforming to their demands and accept and incorporate adults' high evaluations of the importance of achievement. They are also able to work without being immediately rewarded for their efforts, show initiative, self-reliance, and emotional control. (Crandall, 1964: 81)

In the language of social psychology, the high-achieving child has internalized adult values and expectations. The process of identification is a subtle one, the trick being not only to provide appropriate role models but also to create the right degree of dependency in the child by providing attention and affection that are linked to the child's performance, with the underlying threat of withdrawal of the attention and affection if the behavior is unsatisfactory. The properly socialized child looks to the parent for values and guides to behavior but is capable of operating without constant parental supervision. As Rosen puts it, the ideal is for the child "to act appropriately not because his parents tell him to but because he wants to." The word "appropriate" is a clue to a subtle but important point about the value of independence. What success-oriented parents want for their children is not true independence of judgment—which would, of course, leave the children free to choose goals other than achievement and success—but rather internalization of the success goals of the parents by the children so that they appear to strive for these goals under their own volition.

Aggression refers to a loose cluster of actions and motives around the theme of intent by one individual to hurt or control another. The antecedents of aggressive behavior in children and the relationship between aggression and learning are not very clear. It seems that extremes of parental behavior are most likely to produce this behavioral motive.

> Both permissiveness and punishment have been shown to contribute to the development of aggressiveness in young children. Since these two qualities of parental behavior can vary somewhat independently, there is possibility of variation in the amount of aggression produced in children simply by virtue of combining different degrees of these antecedents. (Sears, 1965: 134)

Effects of aggression motivation or behavior on learning are probably indirect or interactive with other individual or societal attributes. For example, the discouragement of aggressive—even active—behavior in any part of the school except the gym may explain why boys (for whom aggressive behavior is more likely to be tolerated, indeed encouraged) or children from inner-city ghetto neighborhoods where interpersonal aggression is an everyday occurrence have a hard time adapting to the aspects of classroom life that call for sitting quietly, following instructions, and so on. On the other hand, since academic success is at least partly based upon actual performance, girls who have been taught to equate femininity with passivity are also unlikely to have high achievement. The sex relationship will be developed further in the next chapter.

Parent-Child Interaction

Achievement behavior is believed to originate in the desire of young children to get a response from those around them. "Only later, and for some children, does approval from others for good performance become unnecessary and feelings of pride or self-approval constitute sufficient reinforcement to maintain or increase their achievement behaviors" (Crandall, 1964: 78). Findings from a variety of empirical research studies show that the quantity of adult-child interaction is related to children's intellectual development and academic success. There is a large body of evidence on the prevalence of mental and social retardation among children raised in orphanages or hospitals where the ratio of adults to children is low and there is little adult-child interaction. The importance of interaction with adults is underscored by the dramatic gains often made by institutionalized children when they received nurturance from substitute mothers, even if the substitutes were severely retarded themselves.

An often-stated platitude is that middle-class children learn faster than lower-class children because their homes and neighborhoods are more "stimulating." Anyone who has spent much time in an urban slum can testify to the barrage of stimuli that is a constant feature of such environments. The point is that only certain kinds of stimuli are linked directly to the developmental needs of children and to the demands of the school system. In the crowded households of the urban poor, the child is surrounded by stimuli, but they are seldom directed at the child in a meaningful way and they are often stressful. As one analyst put it, "the situation is ideal for the child to learn inattention" (Deutsch, 1963: 171). The middle-class family is usually better able to provide the books, play materials, trips to zoos and farms, and other stimuli that prepare them for the student role, and they may even provide coaching in school-related skills and tasks. A dissertation project by Dave (1963) reported that a third of the students in one algebra class in a middle-class high school received tutorial help at home equal in time to the time they spent in class. Moreover, the students who received help from their families had generally higher grades in the course than those who received no instruction outside of class. Another difference was that the relationship between math aptitude scores at the beginning of the course and test scores and grades at the end of the course was very high (+ .90) for the untutored students but was almost zero for those who received home tutoring. Although this was a small study, it merits replication, since it indicates that parents can, and do, provide concrete assistance with academic work as well as help in mastering the external characteristics of the good-student role.

While the communication of high expectations and clear definitions of appropriate behavior are a necessary antecedent to high academic achievement, researchers disagree about the degree of intrafamily closeness and warmth that constitutes the most effective socialization climate. One view is that the families of high achievers are characterized by relatively greater warmth, closer primary relationships, a greater amount and depth of intracommunication, and many shared activities. Applying the findings of research on group dynamics showing that high-cohesiveness groups adopt group standards more readily than low-cohesiveness groups to the family situation, Seginer (1978) hypothesizes that children from families that are highly cohesive and where the child also receives parental support will be most likely to accept family expectations concerning school achievement. An opposing view is that striving for achievement is most frequent among children whose relationship with their parents is more reserved, even unsatisfying (for instance, the review of studies conducted by Strodtbeck, 1958).

Both views oversimplify a complicated and controversial subject. Insofar as the first position suggests that warmth and acceptance are unconditionally functional for achievement, it is misleading. Unconditional love from parents provides no motivation for the child to achieve (since the child will receive love whether or not he or she achieves). Only when the power of the parent to withdraw or withhold love and approval is felt by the child does parental closeness itself promote achievement. Moreover, the assumption that the child feels a need for parental approval is not always justified. Studies such as Arnold Green's classic comparison of middle-class American families with Polish immigrant families (1946) have demonstrated that the need varies from one cultural subgroup to another.

On the other hand, for the more reserved parent-child relationship to promote high achievement, there must be clear definitions clearly communicated, as mentioned above. A child may perform very well for parents who maintain their emotional distance, but only if they effectively communicate high expectations to him or her.

The relationship between parental warmth and children's achievement is also conditional upon the sex of child and parent. A review of sex differences in intellectual development (Maccoby, 1966) found that a high level of nurturance or supportive behavior on the part of the mother during the preschool years was negatively related to subsequent academic performance among girls but positively related for boys (although the latter effect tended to disappear after a few years of school). What girls benefited from was *freedom* from maternal restrictions, plus supportive behavior from their *fathers*. A parallel for boys is Strodtbeck's finding that the fathers of boys with the strongest academic orientation were not only reserved with their sons but were also relatively nonassertive about achievement values or about their own position within the family.

> Oddly enough, the more the father subscribes to achievement values, the less the son's power appears to be—perhaps because the father is himself so energetic that the son assumes a reciprocal, passive role . . . the less the mother and son are dominated by the father in the power area, the greater the disposition of both to believe that the world can be rationally mastered and that a son should risk separation from his family. Apparently for a boy lack of potency in the family might well lead him to infer that he could never control his destiny anywhere. (Stodtbeck, 1958: 182–183)

The pattern suggested is that high academic performance is a product of a relatively close relationship with the parent of the opposite sex, but reserve or autonomy with respect to the same-sex parent.

While the parent-child relationship is inherently hierarchical, the greater power and authority of parents can be shared to some extent and children can be allowed to participate in family decision making. Although empirical research on the academic effects of differential family power structures and decision-making patterns is sparse, there is some evidence of positive effects of relatively equalitarian family structure on both attitudes toward school and actual achievement. The Strodtbeck study comparing the school achievement of Jewish and Italian-Catholic boys indicated that parental authoritarianism was related both to religious-ethnic background and (negatively) to achievement orientation. A crosscultural study relating family structure with educational attainment in five different countries showed that parental dominance was negatively associated with the probability of reaching secondary school, both between and within countries (Elder, 1965). In an analysis of the effects on students' development of "open" versus "traditional" family and school environments using survey data from 4,079 Maryland students ranging from grade six to grade twelve, Epstein and McPartland (1977) found that at all grade levels greater participation in family decision making was associated with more positive personality development (self-reliance, self-esteem, and feelings of control of environment) and school coping skills (satisfaction with school, classwork, and student-teacher relations, adjustment to the work-related demands of school, and involvement in class actions requiring the teacher to admonish or punish them). The authors summarize the effects of home environment as follows:

> Certain types of environments appear to be, on the average, especially beneficial. Family environments that emphasize trust, freedom of expression, and shared power or authority among parents and children encourage more positive student self-reliance, control of environment, and school coping skills. In addition, at least a moderate level of regulation or control at home appears advantageous for school coping skills, personal adjustment and advancement. (Epstein and McPartland, 1977: 34–35)

What Is Good Parenting and Can It Be Taught?

While the findings discussed in this chapter do underscore the importance of the parent role and do point to some aspects of family structure and process that contribute to (or detract from) children's intellectual development, we are far from having a full and clear picture of what constitutes a "good" family environment. To put it another way, a parent or prospective parent searching this chapter would find little specific advice on how to raise an academically competent child and would probably find the inconsistencies as well as the gaps in information disconcerting. Can social science offer any concrete advice to parents? Since the early 1970s a group of social scientists at Harvard University, under the direction of Burton White, has been trying to answer that question.

The design and administration of White's project are extraordinarily complex (and expensive), but its basic objective is rather simple. The researchers hoped by observing some families who were doing an outstanding job of raising their children (labeled by White as *A*) and some families who were doing a very poor job (labeled *C*) to identify those aspects of parenting that seem crucial to producing competent children. From an initial screening of over fifteen thousand families, in which the intellectual and social development of young children and their elder siblings was evaluated, thirty-three children under the age of six were chosen, about evenly divided between predicted *A*'s and *C*'s. The sample was by necessity very small because each child was visited in the home every three weeks for six months out of a year, and the observers took voluminous notes on the child's daily life as well as administering a battery of specially designed tests for various aspects of intellectual development (including IQ, language development, and reasoning ability).

White found that families did not differ greatly in their treatment of their children during the first year or so of life, but that when the child began to move about, to comprehend language, and to develop a clear, and often demanding, personality, the differences between *A* and *C* homes became apparent. *A* mothers seemed less worried about the possible clutter, interference, and accidents created by mobile youngsters, and they allowed their children considerably more physical freedom than *C* mothers, who seemed more concerned with keeping the home orderly and were more likely to keep the child in a playpen for long periods of time. *A* mothers were more attentive to their children's efforts at verbal communication and went out of their way to listen and talk to them. *C* mothers made more use of the TV as a companion for their children and more frequently expressed exasperation over the demands made on them by their children. Although *A* mothers were not constantly hovering over their children, and concentrated periods of formal teaching were rare, these women tended to respond to their children's interests and initiatives. As White put it, they got in a remarkable amount of teaching "on the fly" by picking up on a child's overtures (White and Watts, 1973. A brief journalistic description of the project can be found in *Carnegie Quarterly,* Summer 1973: 6–8).

The project has a number of weaknesses and limitations besides the obvious one of its limited sample. The focus upon "mothering" (the team studied only stay-at-home mothers; father-child or sibling-child interaction and the responsibilities and influence of anyone except the mother receive little attention) is irritating to anyone with feminist inclinations, and it also limits the applicability of the findings (since recent increases in labor-force participation have been most marked among women with young children). Class biases are also visible. The home visitors often seem overimpressed by affluent suburban homes with spreading lawns and children's rooms stuffed with toys and equipment; and temper tantrums and other misbehavior that in a working-class home are attributed to incompetent parenting are often excused or said to be "atypical" in a middle-class home. Finally, the requirements of *A* parenting call for more intelligence, understanding, patience, time, and energy than most people have, and the authors do not suggest any social rearrangements that would enable most adults to raise the quality of their parenting. However, the project is the most ambitious effort to date to identify the components of effective parenting and to provide actual behavior models that a parent can aspire to, if not attain.

Other attempts to synthesize what is known about the kinds of home environment that maximize intellectual development and school success are under way in a number of countries. For example, Marjoribanks, a social scientist at Oxford University, England, has constructed measures of a set of eight environmental forces within the home that produce "the most insistent and subtle influence on the mental ability development of the child" (Marjoribanks, 1972: 103). The forces were labeled: (1) press for achievement; (2) press for activeness; (3) press for intellectuality; (4) press for independence; (5) press for English; (6) press for "ethlanguage" (any language spoken in the home other than English); (7) mother dominance; and (8) father dominance. In an empirical study of ninety middle-class boys and their parents and ninety-five lower-class boys and their parents, Marjoribanks found statistically significant relationships between the environmental force measures and various ability test scores. Moreover, when the environmental forces were combined into a set of predictors they accounted for a large proportion of the variance in several of the test scores.

Recent research also suggests that the kind of home environment most conducive to academic success may differ for different subgroups and that, particularly in the case of ethnic minorities, family strengths may have been overlooked or misinterpreted. Until now, most research on minority children has been conducted by white, middle-class academicians, who have tended to take for granted an assimilationist model—that the best way for immigrant or minority groups to achieve mobility in the larger society is to copy the values and lifestyles of the majority population, discarding any features of their own culture (including language) that make them "different" from the majority population. A study of Mexican-American students by a researcher who is himself Mexican-American questions the benefits of cultural assimilation for that group (Garcia, 1975). Garcia found, on the contrary, that Mexican-American students who were *least* assimilated into Anglo society (who were active in the Chicano movement, and who came from homes where Spanish was regularly spoken and where pride in the Spanish heritage was emphasized) were more likely to go on to college and had on the average higher grade-point averages when they got to college.

A study that compared family socialization practices among Anglo-American and Mexican-American families with junior high school children found that the Mexican-American students experienced much less independence training and were granted relatively little autonomy in decision making (Anderson and Evans, 1976). A path analysis[4] linking family socialization practices (achievement training and independence training), self-concept, sex, and father's education with measures of school achievement found that direct attempts by parents to encourage and reward greater academic effort appeared to have the opposite effect in both ethnic groups, while active independence training resulted in significant gains in achievement. The Mexican-American students not only received significantly less independence training from their parents than did their Anglo-American peers, but the direct effect of independence training was relatively more important even than their perception of their own ability. The authors concluded that such family training may be critical if Mexican-American children are to perform well in classrooms structured to require student initiative.

In sum, understanding the kind of family environment that is most conducive to academic achievement requires: (1) examining simultaneously multiple components of family structure and process; (2) examining the (possibly) different effects of family environment variables upon children from different social backgrounds and ethnic groups; and (3) taking into account the social background and ethnic identity of the persons who conduct a given piece of research study.

Conclusions

The theme of Part Two is that being a student is in large part a role-playing activity. The child's initial view of the world and first experiences in role playing are furnished by his or her family. The last two chapters have reinforced the common-sense belief that the position of the family within the larger society and the way in which children are socialized within the family have a powerful effect upon the way children play the student role. Although our understanding of the interrelationships among various families as related to academic success is still incomplete, the findings we have assembled fit the general model diagrammed in Exhibit 4–4.

The empirical evidence has indicated that there is relatively little difference among families in their valuation of achievement. Most children and their parents value success and recognize formal education as an important ingredient. What differs is the degree to which a general yearning is translated into a workable set of life goals and strategies for reaching them. Parents of school achievers not only expect more and communicate this to their children, but they also teach them the *behavior* needed to fulfill their expectations. In sum, *what children who fail in school lack is role-playing skill not the desire to succeed, and because they do not know how to play the role of student, they are less likely to do the things that will lead to success.*

To date, the social position variables that are the subject of Chapter 3 have been better predictors of academic achievement than the family environment variables discussed in this chapter. This may be partly because they are easier to measure and the comparability from one study to another is greater. For example,

Exhibit 4-4
Model of the Relationship of Family Variables and School Performance

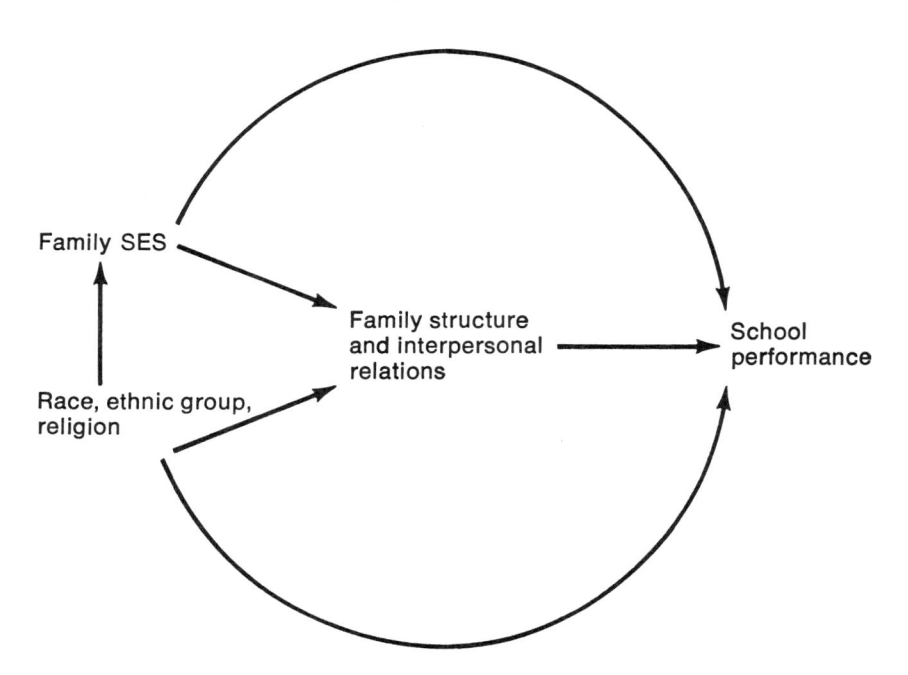

family income or race present fewer measurement and comparability problems than variables like family cohesiveness or the degree of academic guidance given to children by their parents. The range of home environment is wide and varied, and it is also likely that family environment affects the intellectual development and academic achievement of children from different social backgrounds differently. Research in this area is still far behind research on the effects of family background in theoretical and methodological sophistication, though large and sophisticated studies like the Wisconsin study, which previously focused upon family background variables, are now adding family structure variables (Hauser and Sewell, 1976).

It is now generally recognized that family environment may be as important as family status and, moreover, that it is more susceptible to manipulation. Thus, the last decade has seen the development and testing of a number of "home-based" or "home-intervention" programs to teach parenting skills and enhance intrafamily interaction. Some of these programs will be discussed further in the final chapter of this book, but it is relevant to note here that the theory underlying home-intervention programs represents another challenge to the culture-of-poverty theory, since it assumes that regardless of their social position parents can change specific aspects of their home environment.

Notes

1. It is interesting that most of the inside studies of American families were done by anthropologists, and they were usually done to provide comparative data with families in more primitive societies (Whiting, 1963). Close observation of family life is a standard operating procedure in anthropology—and we do not seem to worry so much about invading the privacy of the home in other people's cultures!

2. The most recent phase of the Wisconsin Study includes a subsample of siblings of the original sample members and will permit extensive analysis of family structural effects on educational attainment, but these analyses had not been completed when this chapter was being written (Hauser and Sewell, 1976).

3. The discussion of Gordon's findings here and elsewhere in this book is taken from an unpublished manuscript (Gordon, 1969) plus additional statistical data furnished by him.

4. See page 33.

The Effects of Sex Chapter 5

In light of the social expectations about women, it is not surprising that women end up where society expects them to; the surprise is that little girls don't get the message that they are supposed to be stupid until they get into high school. It is no use to talk about women being different-but-equal; all the sex-difference tests I can think of have a "good" outcome and a "bad" outcome. Women usually end up with the bad outcome.   Naomi Weisstein

A basic problem with research on sex differences is that it is almost always impossible to be blind to the sex of the subjects. Stereotypes about what kind of behavior is to be expected from the two sexes run very deep, and even when sex differences are incidental to the main focus of a study, the observers must almost invitably be biased to some extent.   Eleanor Maccoby and Carol Jacklin

Probably no area of the sociology of education has developed more rapidly during the past decade than the analysis of sex-role socialization and its effects on academic achievement. Increases in the number of female scholars (many of them with feminist orientations) getting Ph.D.'s in sociology, teaching in colleges and universities, and conducting research on the sociology of sex roles are already reflected in changing interpretations of male and female achievement as well as in the sheer quantity of new publications on this topic.

Sex,[1] like race, is an attribute acquired by a child at birth, and, like race, it is both visible and (with a few exceptions) permanent. At the same time, gender constitutes an important role in all known societies. It must be learned like any other role, and there is an extensive and growing literature, using a variety of research approaches, on what is expected of females and males in different cultures and how they are socialized to sex roles. In this chapter we shall be concerned with similarities and differences in the school-achievement patterns of females and males and the ways in which socialization to sex role affects performance of the student role.

A considerable amount of the debate of the past decade has been over the origins of sex differences—that is, whether the differential status and achievements of females and males are explained by innate (biological or genetic) differences between the sexes or whether they are explained by differences in the way boys and girls are perceived and treated. While this chapter is about the sociology of sex differences, it will be necessary to pay some attention to biological and psychological factors where they are relevant to understanding differences in achievement patterns. (Also as we shall see, research indicates that even abilities and skills that appear to be biologically based may be developed to a greater or less extent in both sexes depending upon the cultural conditions affecting their socialization.)

We shall begin with a comparison of the academic performance of males and females at various age levels and in different subjects. In a sense this is beginning at the end, since achievement is the dependent variable of our analysis, but it seems helpful to clarify at the beginning what we are attempting to explain. Then we shall consider two sets of independent variables. One set is primarily psychological, including the individual abilities and personality characteristics that are related both to sex and to academic performance. The second set is primarily sociological, with a major focus upon the modes of socialization of girls and boys with respect to achievement in general and school behavior in particular. We shall also examine some research in which the effects of sex will be analyzed simultaneously or interactively with other sociological variables.

Performance

In this country, each sex tends to outperform the other at some phase of the school career, and there also seem to be substantive areas of sexual "specialty" from the beginning school years. (The patterns to be described here are generally applicable to other contemporary Western societies, although the United States patterns are unique in certain respects.) Girls tend to have an initial academic advantage. At the elementary level, girls tend to outproduce boys in nearly all academic areas, and boys are six times as likely to have reading problems. In fact, the apparent learning disadvantage of boys in the early elementary years has led to serious proposals that the sexes be separated for the first few grades and that systematic attempts be made to recruit more male teachers at this level. At least through the high school years, girls achieve on the average better grades and are more likely to gain academic honors, such as making the honor roll, being admitted to school scholastic societies, or qualifying to take the National Merit Scholarship exams (though boys get more of the scholarships actually awarded).

If one breaks down performance into different subject areas, however, there are some male advantages right from the beginning. While girls perform better than boys in reading, writing, literature, and music, boys have higher interest and achievement in mathematics and science from the beginning of school, and the sex differences increase with age (National Center for Education Statistics, 1976: 42–49). These differences have been found in other countries as well. For example, the sex differences in mathematics achievement show up with special clarity in an international comparison among adolescents at two age levels in twelve countries, including the United States (Husen, 1967). Almost without exception, male students in these countries showed a greater predilection for math—the ratio of males to females specializing in or taking advanced math courses varies from 2/1 to 7/1—and higher achievement scores, even when the level of instruction was held constant and regardless of the type of problem.

By at least late adolescence, boys overtake girls in educational attainment, although the point at which this occurs is later in the United States than in most other countries. Sex differences in educational attainment are shown in Exhibits 5–1 and 5–2. Exhibit 5–1 shows the proportions of young people graduating from high school, entering college, and graduating from college during the past twenty-five years. The two left-hand columns of figures show that throughout this period the high school graduation rate has been consistently higher for females than for males, although the differences are not very great. Thus in 1954, 62 percent of the females aged seventeen or eighteen and 57 percent of the males graduated from high school; in 1966, 77 percent of the females and 73 percent of the males in that age group graduated; and in 1976, 76 percent of the females and 73 percent of the males graduated from high school. Also after 1966, the graduation rates of both sexes (which had risen dramatically throughout the twentieth century, from less than 10 percent in 1910) leveled off and have remained at a little more than three-quarters of the females and a little less than three-quarters of the males. The next two columns of the table compare the percentages of persons of college age who are enrolled in college. Here we see that up to 1972 more

Exhibit 5–1

Educational Attainment by Sex for Selected Years, 1954–1976

Year	Percentage of Persons Aged 17 to 18 Graduating from High School — Females	Males	Percentage of Persons Aged 18 to 24 Enrolled in College — Females	Males	Percentage of Persons Aged 21 Graduating from College — Females	Males
1954	62	57	*	*	*	*
1958	66	60	*	*	*	*
1962	72	67	*	*	14	21
1966	77	73	*	*	*	*
1968	*	*	36	44	18	26
1970	78	74	37	41	21	30
1972	77	73	38	38	*	*
1974	76	72	38	35	24	28
1976	76	73	43	35	*	*

*Data not given.
Source: National Center for Education Statistics: *The Condition of Education* Washington, D.C.: U.S. Government Printing Office, 1974, 1975, and 1976 editions.

males than females attended college, but that after that date there was a reversal in attendance rates by sex, so that by 1976, 43 percent of the females but only 35 percent of the males were enrolled. Note that college enrollment rates have actually declined among males since 1968, while they were increasing for females during this period. While the college enrollment rates are now higher for females than for males, the college graduation rate continues to be higher for males, as indicated in the last two columns of Exhibit 5–1. In 1962, only 14 percent of females aged twenty-one graduated from college, compared with 21 percent of the comparable males, and by 1970 the figures had gone up to 21 percent of females and 30 percent for males. Since that year, however, the graduation rate for males has gone down slightly while continuing to rise for females, so this sex difference may disappear or be reversed in the near future.

Exhibit 5–2 contains information on sex differences in the attainment of advanced degrees, showing both the total number of various degrees earned in 1965, 1970, and 1975, and estimates of the number to be awarded in 1980 (the figures in parentheses in Exhibit 5–2), and the proportion of these degrees that were, or are estimated to be, earned by females. For example, in 1965, 501,248 bachelor's degrees were awarded, 42 percent of them to females. First, comparing the figures in parentheses in each of the columns of the table shows that the total number of all kinds of advanced degrees has increased greatly, in most cases more than doubling in the decade between 1965 and 1975. Males still receive most of the higher degrees, and generally the higher the degree, the lower the percentage of females earning the degree. Thus in 1975 females earned 45 percent of the B.A.'s awarded but only 16 percent of the Ph.D.'s awarded. Third, the proportion of the degrees awarded to females increased over time. For example, the total number of master's degrees awarded increased from 117,152 to

Exhibit 5–2

Earned Degrees, by Level and Sex of Student for 1965 to 1980

Year	Bachelor's Degrees	Master's Degrees	Doctor's and First-Professional Degrees
1965	42	34	6
	(501,248)	(117,152)	(45,222)
1970	43	40	9
	(791,510)	(208,291)	(65,590)
1975	45	45	16
	(922,933)	(292,450)	(89,999)
1980 (projected)	46	49	25
	(1,010,000)	(360,100)	(106,000)

*Figures in parentheses are the total number of degrees awarded to males and females combined.
Source: National Center for Education Statistics: *The Condition of Education*. Washington, D.C.: U.S. Government Printing Office, 1975 and 1976 editions.

292,450. During this period, the number of degrees awarded to both males and females increased, but the proportion of the total awarded to females increased from 34 to 45 percent—that is, the rate of increase was greater for females than for males.

To summarize, in the United States graduation rates have been increasing at all levels of formal education during the past quarter century, although the high school graduation rate, which rose most dramatically between 1910 and 1963, has now leveled off. Throughout this period, the high school graduation rates have been consistently if slightly higher for females than for males, but the pattern of formal completion of education by sex reverses after high school graduation. While the proportion of females of college age actually enrolled in college has been higher for females than for males since 1972, females still receive less than half of all college degrees awarded, and the higher the degree, the smaller the proportion earned by females. This achievement gap at the higher education levels is narrowing, however, and if present trends continue, the proportions of males and females earning bachelor's and master's degrees will be approximately equal by 1980. These trends reflect major changes in the life cycle patterns of Americans, especially American women, and while it is not yet possible to link specific changes in educational achievement with specific changes in the culture of our society, it seems likely that the feminist movement of the past decade has influenced both.

Differences in Abilities and Personality Traits

One explanation for differential academic performance by females and males is that intellectual abilities and the qualities of personality that affect achievement are differentially distributed between the sexes. Until recently, most social science research reached conclusions generally consistent with popular stereotypes—for example, that males are superior to females on mathematical and mechanical aptitudes, while females excel at verbal fluency and tasks involving memory; that the personality traits of anxiety and dependency are more common to females, while males are more aggressive, active, and impulsive.

In the past decade, all of these conclusions have been called into question. Some of the debate has been largely ideological, stemming from accusations that gender stereotyping has prevented females (and sometimes males) from developing the full range of their capacities. At the same time, new research as well as re-examination of existing empirical evidence has led to new perspectives on the antecedents and consequences of sex differences. The most comprehensive review to date is by Eleanor Maccoby and Carol Jacklin, whose book on the psychology of sex differences (1974) includes summaries of all of the published literature the authors could find on how the sexes differ (or do not differ) on intellectual abilities, motivation, self-concept, and social behavior, plus an annotated bibliography of over one thousand studies published since the mid-1960s. Of the multitude of traits examined, Maccoby and Jacklin conclude that for only four is there convincing evidence of "real" psychological differences (that is, differences that are not simply or primarily due to education or culture)[2].

First, girls appear to have greater verbal ability than boys. Their verbal facility matures more rapidly than boys in early childhood, and their superiority at all kinds of tasks requiring verbal fluency increases steadily from age ten or eleven. However, the magnitude of sex difference varies considerably from one task or population to another, and a number of recent studies have shown no significant sex differences in verbal ability.

Second, boys' visual-spatial ability exceeds girls'. This is one of the very few ability differences that seems to be genetically based; biological research indicates that spatial ability is highly heritable, transmitted via chromosome combinations that are more common to males than females.

Third, boys' mathematical ability exceeds girls', although like verbal ability, the magnitude of sex difference varies from one study to another, and boys' and girls' acquisition of quantitative concepts and mastery of basic skills is similar during the grade-school years. Variations in the magnitude of sex difference may be partly explained by variations in the extent to which a particular task calls for visual-spatial and/or verbal skills, which we have seen are sex related.

Fourth, males are more aggressive than females, both physically and verbally. This difference has been observed in many different cultures and is found as early as any form of social play begins (usually by age two and a half). That aggression has a biological foundation is indicated by experimental research findings, with humans as well as nonhuman primates, that show that aggression levels are related to levels of sex hormones and can be changed by experimental administration of these hormones.

Despite these four differences in specific areas of intellectual or personality development, test scores also indicate that on all measures there is considerable overlap between the distribution of scores for the two sexes; and that on tests of total or composite abilities, the sexes do not differ consistently, and superior or highly developed ability is more or less equally distributed among boys and girls. Moreover, compared to the number of traits that do *not* appear to differ significantly by sex, the four characteristics discussed above make a very short list. Maccoby and Jacklin's review leads them to conclude that there is not empirical evidence for the following beliefs:

Females are more "social" than males. Research shows that males and females are equally responsive to social stimuli, are equally dependent upon their caretakers, are equally motivated to gain social rewards, have the same capacity for interpersonal empathy, and spend the same amount of time interacting with playmates.

Females are more "suggestible" than males. Research indicates no male-female differences in imitative behavior and that boys and girls are equally susceptible to persuasive communications and to face-to-face influence situations.

Females have lower self-esteem than males. Boys and girls are similar in overall self-satisfaction and self-confidence, although girls rate themselves higher in social competence, and boys rate themselves higher in strength and dominance. The only significant difference found in research is a tendency, found only among college-age students, for males to report greater confidence in their school performance and greater sense of fate control.

Females are better than males at rote learning and simple repetitive tasks. Research findings suggest that this unfounded belief is based upon differences in the kinds of tasks most societies assign to males and females, not upon any real psychological differences between the sexes.

On a host of other personality characteristics, including anxiety, competitiveness, dominance, compliance, and nurturant or "maternal" behavior, there is either not sufficient evidence to draw firm conclusions or the findings that are available are ambiguous or conflicting. Two conclusions do seem to be justified. One is that the relationship of a personality trait to sex depends upon the instrument used to measure it. For example, most research that finds higher anxiety among girls than boys is based upon self-reports. When anxiety is measured by observation of children's behavior in anxiety-producing situations, few sex differences are found. Thus, we do not know that girls *are* more anxious than boys but only that they are more willing to say that they are (which may reflect differences in socialization rather than differences in personality). Second, the relationship of personality characteristics to intellectual performance may be different for boys and girls. Some research suggests that timidity, caution, and other components of anxiety are positively related to IQ and intellectual interests for boys but not for girls.

As a whole, the research of the past decade has indicated that the number of differences in personality traits and intellectual functioning that can be attributed primarily to sex is much smaller than previously assumed, and, moreover, that the magnitude of a particular skill difference may be greater or lesser depending upon the extent to which individuals are encouraged to develop that skill. For example, although a large-scale international study of academic achievement found that in every country studied, boys scored higher than girls on math achievement, the sex differences were markedly reduced in those countries in which the learning conditions for boys and girls were most similar, and the least able girls in countries with well-developed math curricula outscored boys in countries with poorer educational systems or where girls' educational opportunities were more limited (Husen, 1967). Even an ability as apparently physiologically based as visual-spatial ability can be improved by training, and at least some crosscultural research indicates that in cultures or subcultures where children of both sexes are allowed considerable independence, sex differences in spatial-ability tests are slight or nonexistent (Berry, 1966; McArthur, 1967; Maccoby and Jacklin, 1974: 130).

While many earlier beliefs about sex differences have not stood up well under the impact of recent evidence and analysis, it does seem to be true that certain personality constellations are associated with high intellectual performance and that the most functional combinations may differ for males and females. Maccoby and Jacklin conclude that

> studies on personality correlates of intellectual performance have continued to suggest that intellectual development in girls is fostered by their being assertive and

active, and having a sense that they can control, by their own actions, the events that affect their lives. These factors appear to be less important in the intellectual development of boys—perhaps because they are already sufficiently assertive and have a sufficient sense of personal control over events, so that other issues (e.g., how well they can control aggressive impulses) become more important in how successfully they can exploit their intellectual potential. (Maccoby and Jacklin, 1974: 133)

Motivational Comparisons

A theory that has been frequently offered to explain the greater achievement of males over the long run is that the sexes differ in their *motivation* to achieve. Like much psychological theory, achievement-motivation theory was originally developed to explain the behavior of males, and most of the early research with McClelland's *n* Achievement scale (discussed in Chapter 4) was done with male subjects. Many studies have involved manipulation of the subjects' environment by means of introducing the task in a manner varying from "relaxed" to "aroused."[3] These conditional variations or cues had a distinct effect upon the performance of male subjects, independently of their individual differences in *n* Achievement, but early experiments showed that girls' scores did not increase significantly from relaxed to aroused conditions. For this and other reasons, there were few studies with female subjects until the 1950s when research by Field (1951) showed that while girls' need to achieve was not whetted by such arousal stimuli as talk about intelligence and leadership, increase in female scores could be produced by substituting such terms as *popularity* and *social acceptance*.

More recent reassessments of the evidence (in particular, Stein and Baily, 1973; and Maccoby and Jacklin, 1974: Chapter 4) conclude that when achievement motivation is measured using pictures or stories about males, female subjects respond with a high level of achievement imagery whether or not an arousal treatment is given, but males score lower in the absence of arousal. This result is interpreted by Maccoby and Macklin as indicating that boys require greater efforts to motivate them—which may explain their generally lower grades in school. Both male and female subjects typically score lower when responding to stories or pictures about females, which may reflect, accurately, the lower expectations for females in the society at large rather than the lower motivation of individual female subjects. Another explanation offered by Entwisle (personal communication) is that most of the females portraying achievement-oriented activities in the stimulus pictures for *n* Achievement tests are physically unappealing (they have glasses, heavy shoes, unattractive hair styles, and so on), and, moreover, they are seldom portrayed in positions of real status (for example, women office workers usually are engaged in clerical rather than managerial activities). Stimulus pictures showing attractive women in a variety of updated occupational settings might produce different responses from both girls and boys.

Recent work also discredits the claim that sex differences in achievement orientation are explained by the greater "task-orientation" of males and greater "person-orientation" of females—that is, that boys tend to achieve when they are intrinsically interested in the task itself, whereas girls achieve in order to gain praise and approval from others. Several studies have shown that the presence or absence of adults during an experiment did not affect either boy or girl subjects. However, males did perform better on a task when observed by peers, though there was no apparent "peer effect" for females (Meddock *et al.*, 1971; Horner, 1970). Thus if either sex is more person oriented, it appears to be males, though they seem to be differentially influenced only by the presence of a peer.

Some of the most interesting and controversial recent research on achievement motivation is Horner's work on "fear of success" or motive to avoid success. Horner argues that the traditional measures, focusing upon either hope of success or fear of failure, do not take into account the conflicts that often accompany achievement, in particular the desire to do well at school but not to outperform males that affects many females. To identify this potential conflict, male and female students were asked to write a story in response to a cue sentence like the following: "After first-term finals, John (or Alice) finds himself (or herself) at the top of his (her) medical school class." The stories were scored for the number of negative elements, either unpleasant events or unfavorable personal characteristics of the successful person. Horner found that 65 percent of the college women subjects described unpleasant events and attributes in discussing successful women, while only 10 percent of college men gave such descriptions of successful men (Horner, 1972).

Replications of the Horner studies have produced inconsistent results. One study using a more complete design, with subjects of both sexes writing stories about successful persons of both sexes, found that both girls and boys gave many more negative responses in stories about females than in stories about males, and that male subjects were even more negative about female success than were female subjects (Monahan *et al.*, 1974). However, a replication using a sample of several hundred college students writing stories to randomly assigned cues reported that the majority of stories contained some "fear of success" imagery and that there were no significant differences between male and female respondents in the instances of such imagery (Levine and Crumrine, 1975). A study controlling for race and social class found that significantly fewer black women at each of two colleges (varying in the social class distribution of the student body) gave motive-to-avoid-success reponses in their stories, and that there were no significant class differences in responses (Weston and Mednick, 1970).

In sum, the research evidence does not point to less achievement motivation in girls than in boys. In fact, under "neutral" conditions, girls tend to score higher than boys on *n* Achievement measures, while boys' achievement motivation appears to be positively stimulated by competition or the presence of peers. While their basic motivation may be as high as boys', girls do appear to be caught in a kind of double bind that may affect their ultimate achievement. They want to do well in school, but they also fear that very high achievement will bring social rejection or a lack of femininity.

The dilemmas faced by females motivated to high achievement are not, of course, new. A book published in 1953, Mirra Komarovsky's *Women in the Modern World,* contains reports by college girls describing advice received from parents, brothers, and friends, all urging the girls not to set their sights too high and not to reveal their intellectual abilities or achievement-oriented goals (say, to go to medical school) to potential boy friends, at least until they knew them well enough to judge whether such an admission would be offensive. The general process that is set in motion is a circular one by which certain activities (getting outstanding grades, going on for graduate or professional training) and certain subjects (math) are identified as masculine, which means that girls who might otherwise have the interest and the potential for such activities and subjects never cultivate them, which in turn reinforces the unfeminine image of such activities and subjects. This phenomenon has been popularized in recent years as the "feminine mystique" or the "woman-as-nigger" syndrome—the premise of which is that women in our society get talked out of and/or talk themselves out of high educational and occupational achievement.

The discussion in this section raises the possibility that some important differences in male and female achievement patterns may be explained better by differences in the way they are socialized than by innate physiological or psychological differences, and we shall now turn to the research evidence concerning socialization to sex roles.

Socialization

One formulation of psychosexual development (Simon and Gagnon, 1969) refers to sexual behavior as "scripted" behavior, underscoring its sociocultural, learned components as opposed to its biological ones. This view is based upon the observation that in all known societies the sex role is one of the first and most important in the child's repertory, and that in most societies boys and girls are socialized differently. What we are interested in are the socialization differences that lead to differences in the way boys and girls perceive and play the student role.

Sociological analysts of the family often refer to a basic sex-role division along what they term the *instrumental-expressive dimension,* a division that they see as universal. Instrumental functions include "direct responsibility for the solution of group tasks, for the skills and information prerequisite to the role in its adaptive aspects, and for the authority required to make binding managerial decisions." Within the family, when both parents are present, instrumental leadership is typically assumed by the husband-father, who is thus boss-manager of the family as well as of any economic or political units encompassed within it. As such, he is the "final court of appeals, final judge and executor of punishment, discipline, and control over the children of the family." Complementary to the instrumental role is the expressive role, which includes "responsibility for the maintenance of solidarity and management of tension" and care and emotional support of children. The expressive leader, normally the wife-mother, is the family mediator or conciliator. She is "affectionate, solicitous, warm, emotional to the children of the family," and by contrast with the instrumental leader is indulgent and unpunishing (Parsons and Bales, 1955: 317–318).

A study by Brim (1960) explored the behaviors encouraged in young boys and girls within the general framework of the instrumental-expressive dimension. The following list compares the personality traits that were classified by Brim as instrumental or expressive and that were also differentially encouraged in five- and six-year-olds:

instrumental-masculine
  tenacity
  aggressiveness
  curiosity
  ambition
  planfulness
  responsibility
  originality
  competitiveness

expressive-feminine
  kindness
  cheerfulness
  friendliness
  obedience
  affection

Brim's list suggests clues both to girls' greater success in school in the early years *and* to boys' greater success over the long haul. Such "feminine" traits as obedience and friendliness are apparently functional at the elementary level, or at least they are better understood by the typical female teacher than the active but as-yet-unfocused curiosity, originality, and aggressiveness displayed by young boys. Indeed, it has been reported in another study (Kagan, 1964) that young children view school as a feminine place; given a variety of stimuli to classify, they consistently labeled books, blackboards, desks, and other school paraphernalia as feminine. However, the characteristics that foster true intellectual growth are in the left-hand list. As school becomes less dominated by the female element, and as boys approach adulthood and the assuming of the instrumental leader role, the student role becomes more congruent with a boy's other roles.

In a study of socialization to sex roles by a Norwegian social scientist (Brun-Gulbrandsen, 1971), it was found that while most parents claimed to adhere to the general idea of equality and similarity in child rearing (more than 95 percent of the mothers interviewed answered yes to the question: "Do you think that boys and girls should be brought up in as similar a manner as possible?"), their responses to more concrete questions revealed rather differential treatment of daughters and sons. Only 77 percent of the mothers thought that boys and girls ought to assist equally with work in the house; almost all agreed that parents ought to place great emphasis on teaching girls housework because this will be useful to them if they become housewives. Concerning gender-related school subjects, about 80 percent of the mothers felt that boys should have less instruction in this area than girls; only 8 percent thought that girls should receive as much carpentry instruction as boys. Almost 60 percent thought that the then prevailing practice of offering fewer hours of theoretical subjects to girls than to boys was all right.

> Finally, we posed the question, "Who do you think ought to receive a better education, boys or girls?" Approximately half of the mothers thought that both should receive the same education, while the rest thought that boys should be favored—

were it necessary to make a choice. Not one expressed the view that girls should be so favoured. (Brun-Gulbrandsen, 1971: 64)

One of the questions raised by the most recent research on sex-role socialization is whether the treatment of the two sexes is really all that different. Maccoby and Jacklin conclude that at least during the first five years of life, boys and girls appear to be treated with equal affection, independence appears to be equally encouraged, and aggressive behavior equally tolerated in the two sexes. They do find some differences though. Boys are handled and played with more roughly and socialization pressures are somewhat more intense—boys seem to receive more praise, more criticism, and more physical punishment. The greatest differentiation, though, is in the area of specifically sex-typed behavior.

> Parents show considerably more concern over a boy's being a "sissy" than over a girl's being a tomboy. This is especially true of fathers, who seem to take the lead in actively discouraging any interest a son might have in feminine toys, activities, or attire. (Maccoby and Jacklin, 1974: 362)

The above discussion indicates that the father and mother play somewhat different roles in the socialization of children. There has been considerable research on which parent is more responsible for the child's psychosexual and sociosexual development and what type of parent-child relationships are most conducive to "satisfactory" development (though few studies have related specific parental attitudes or behavior to the subsequent intellectual achievements of their children). The findings are mixed. Robert Sears, who believes that masculinity and femininity are not simply opposite ends of a single dimension but rather "clusters of loosely organized qualities that can vary in strength among themselves" and that are not necessarily in conflict with each other (Sears, 1965: 134), concludes from his own observations of young children and their parents at the Stanford Laboratory of Human Development that children of both sexes are most likely to develop "feminine" characteristics under the following circumstances: (1) when their fathers have a high level of sex anxiety; (2) when their mothers are relatively nonpermissive and punitive toward aggressive behavior by the child; (3) when socialization of the child involves a great deal of ridicule and physical punishment; and (4) when great demands are made on the child about such things as table manners and toilet training. On the other hand, girls (but not boys) tend to develop "masculine" qualities when their fathers (but not mothers) are either very involved and affectionate with them or, at the other extreme, when the father is absent altogether. More "feminine" girls are found in homes where the father is more distant and strict, that is, where he is present but does not assume a close, caretaking role (Sears, 1965: 159–161).

Another study that examined parental behavior as a function of both sex of parent and sex of child concluded that both men and women take a tougher stance toward children of their own sex; fathers generally showed a greater permissiveness toward daughters than sons, and mothers showed the reverse (Rothbart and Maccoby, 1966). As we saw in Chapter 4, what little research there is linking parental behavior with children's academic achievement suggests that boys tend to benefit from nurturant, supportive behavior on the part of their mothers, while girls benefit from a lower level of maternal warmth and nurturance, with more attentiveness from their fathers. Sears's findings indicate that this pattern of child rearing is likely to produce "masculine" behavior in girls. To put it another way, for girls, child-rearing practices that lead to extreme "femininity" are the practices *least* likely to result in high achievement. The research on this topic is, however, far from consistent or conclusive.

Parents are not the only socializers of young children, and some recent studies of children's books, television programs, and other media influences argue that females are underrepresented in all of the media beamed at children and that both female and male characterizations reinforce traditional sex-role stereotypes. For example, a study of a sample of prize-winning children's picture books revealed a male-female character ratio of 11/1, and almost all of the active roles were filled by boys or adult men (Weitzman *et al.*, 1972). A similar analysis of a sample of popular children's television programs produced similar findings (Sternglanz and Serbin, 1974. For a parallel analysis of sex roles in the mass media and books in Sweden, see Liljeström, 1966).

Differential Treatment in School

The socialization processes begun in the home are continued in the peer group and in school. Children's play groups, even among the very young, tend to be sex segregated and to be sex differentiated by type of activity. Crosscultural anthropological studies, such as the Six Culture Study directed by Beatrice and John Whiting and their associates (Whiting, 1963; Whiting and Edwards, 1973), indicate that boys' free play involves more aggressive forms of activity, girls' play more seeking and offering of suggestions, assistance, and physical contact. In an observation study of several groups of Canadian kindergarten children, using video tape equipment as well as teams of observers, Richer (1977) found: (1) that most children played mostly with other children of the same sex, and the vast majority of choices in games were same-sex choices; (2) that boys typically played with toy trucks, cars, and building blocks, while girls played in the dolls' house, dressed up in women's clothing, and played at "Mommy going shopping," "Mommy taking care of the baby," and so on (girls were also the only children observed role-playing their teachers, who were all female); and (3) during activities in which the children sat together as a group, the girls always clustered closer to the teacher than the boys and were more likely to create "affective bonds" with her, by holding her hand, or stroking or hugging her.

In a study of the playtime activities of fifth-grade children, using diaries of their outside-of-school activities kept by the children themselves as well as her own observations and interviews in classrooms and playgrounds, Lever (1978) hypothesized that play and games serve as learning contexts for developing skills useful in later-life roles, and that in this society they contribute to the preservation of traditional sex-role divisions. Lever's data revealed six differences in the play patterns of boys and girls: (1) boys play outdoors far more than girls; (2) boys more often play in larger groups; (3) boys' play occurs in more age-heterogeneous groups; (4) boys' play occurs in less sex-segregated groups (that is, girls were more often found playing predominantly male games than boys playing girls' games); (5) boys' games last longer than girls' games and (6) boys play competitive games more often than girls. As she puts it, *girls played more* while *boys gamed more,* and she concluded that by comparison to girls' usual leisure activities

> boys' games provide a valuable learning environment. It is reasonable to expect that the following social skills will be cultivated on the playground: the ability to deal with diversity in memberships where each person is performing a special task; the ability to coordinate actions and maintain cohesiveness among group members; the ability to cope with a set of impersonal rules; and the ability to work for collective as well as personal goals. (Lever, 1978: 480)

There have been other recent studies that also demonstrate sexual differences in physical activities. (See Kidd and Woodman, 1975; Loy, Birrell, and Rose, 1976; and Maloney and Petrie, 1974.)

While the sex-role identity of most children is firmly established by the time they enter school, it also appears that schools themselves constitute an important setting for continued sex-role socialization. Richer found, for example, that teacher-student as well as student-student interaction tended to underline sex differences (Richer, 1977). Teachers tended to punish female acts of aggression more promptly and explicitly than similar acts committed by boys. Lining up to move from one activity to another was usually done by sex, or the teacher assigned a "boys' leader" and "girls' leader." Teachers made frequent reference to "my boys" or "my girls" (for example, "All my girls are here today"), and used sex to motivate participation or completion of tasks (for example, "Who can clean up the fastest, the boys or the girls?").

At the elementary school level, it appears that textbook revisions have so far paid more attention to strengthening the image of racial minorities than to changing gender stereotypes. For example, in *Our Country,* a first-grade text in the much touted series prepared by the Social Science Staff of the Educational Research Council of America, a four-page spread showing three men (black, yellow, and white) leaving their homes and arriving at their place of work is accompanied by the text: "Fathers go to work. Father may work in a factory. . . . in an office. . . . or in a barber shop." The next two pages tell the reader: "Mothers go to the store. Mothers buy food for the family." The pictures here show a multi-skin–colored trio of women entering and inside a supermarket. A little further on, in a discussion of the necessity of rules, the text reads: "Fathers follow rules at work," and there are pictures of the three men at work on an assembly line, at a desk, and in a barbershop. On the next page, as a kind of afterthought, is a single picture of the three women, who have by this time progressed to the check-out counter of the supermarket, with the comment: "Mothers follow rules too" (Boocock, 1971).

As we shall see in Part Three of this book, schools differ in their social structure and educational ideology, and it has been hypothesized that schools with more modern structure and ideology (schools based on the open-classroom model, for example) will produce children with less rigid or stereotyped sex-role attitudes. In a comparison of fourth graders in four schools classified as "modern" and "traditional," Minuchin (1965) found more sex-typed play behavior in the traditional school and greater sex differences in the performance of problem solving and coding tasks, although girls in general were more flexible than boys in their commitment to their own sex role. However, a comparative analysis of students in ten middle schools and six high schools in Maryland varying in authority structure (including the openness of the school program and students' participation in classroom decisions) showed sex differences in grades, course preferences, college plans, and involvement in disciplinary incidents; no sex differences in feelings of control of environment, standardized achievement, anxiety in school, prosocial behavior, and feelings about the quality of school life; and no significant differences between males and females in the effects of the school situational differences studied (Epstein and McPartland, 1977). Both the Minuchin and the Epstein and McPartland studies included measures of family as well as school structure and processes, and both found the modern or open families had effects on student attitudes and behavior similar to the effects of modern or open schools, but that the influence of family orientation was more pronounced. Thus, school experiences may reinforce or refine the child's developing concept of sex roles, but there is still no strong evidence that school reforms, at least of the sort attempted so far in this society, can in the absence of changes in family-socialization patterns bring about substantial changes in children's sex-role orientations.

The Simultaneous Effect of Sex and Other Independent Variables

We have already gotten some hints that sex-role socialization in the home may be affected by the parents' social status. Kohn's research on social-class differences in child-rearing practices (discussed in Chapter 3) also contains some data on differences related to the child's sex. The middle-class parents in Kohn's sample made little distinction between boys and girls with regard to what was regarded as desirable and what was punished—"the issue for both sexes being whether or not the child acts in accord with internalized principles." Working-class parents, however, were more likely to punish daughters than sons for fighting, stealing, and especially for refusing to do as they were told; boys often were allowed to get away with defiance to parents. Kohn interprets these differences as follows:

> The answer seems to lie in different conceptions of what is right and proper for boys and for girls. What may be taken as acceptable behavior (perhaps even as an assertion of manliness) in a preadolescent boy may be thought thoroughly unladylike in a young girl. Working-class parents differentiate quite clearly between the qualities they regard as desirable for their daughters (happiness, manners, neatness, and cleanliness) and those they hold out for their sons (dependability, being a good student, and ambition). . . . This being the case, the criteria of disobedience are necessarily different for boys and for girls. (Kohn, 1959b: 365)

A similar pattern has been shown with respect to the probability of entering college, although at this older age level, SES effects seem to reflect mainly differences in economic resources. In a comparison of 76,015 boys and 51,110 girls, controlling for father's occupation and student's high-school grade average, Werts (1966) found that the college-entrance rates of boys and girls whose fathers had high-status jobs were similar, but that among low-SES students boys were much more likely than girls to go to college. A similar pattern was found with respect to previous academic achievement; high ability boys and girls were equally likely to enter college, but among students with low high-school grade averages, boys were more likely to go than girls. The independent variables were, moreover, interactively related.

> There were more girls than boys in the A−, A, A+ grade category for all four groups of fathers' occupations (ratio 1.0), and the ratios were not much different in the four groups. . . . Since previously cited studies show that among able, upper SES students girls attend college as often as boys, the similarity of the ratios across the father's occupation groups at this highest grade level suggests that very bright, lower SES girls are as likely to attend college as their brothers. Low-SES boys with low grades outnumber low-SES low-grade girls to a greater extent than high-SES low-grade girls. This suggests that low grades are a greater deterrent to college attendance for low-SES girls than for high-SES girls. (Werts, 1966: 5,7)

What Werts's data indicate is that when the resources needed for high education—whether they be the student's own academic capacity or the parents' ability to pay—are freely available, sex does not make much difference in determining college attendance, but when such resources are in short supply boys get first choice at higher education.

A more recent study by Gail Thomas examines the joint effects of sex, race, and SES on college attendance for a representative national sample of United States students (Thomas, 1977). The data used were from a subsample of about fourteen thousand students participating in the National Longitudinal Study of the High School Senior Class of 1972. Thomas's multivariate analysis indicated that sex effects are not as pronounced as race effects and that the impact of sex is stronger among whites than blacks. However, much of the direct effects of race and sex on college attendance were found to be mediated by educational expectations, school-process variables (such as class rank and curriculum placement), and to a lesser extent on the influences of significant others (for example, parents and friends). When either or both family status and achievement test scores are low, a higher percentage of blacks than whites attend college, but when both these variables are high, racial differences in college attendance are not as great. The effects of family SES, independent of the influence of expectations, school-process variables, and the influence of significant others, seemed to be stronger for black males than for the other race-by-sex subgroups. Thomas's analysis is a complex one and drawing appropriate implications from the findings is difficult, but it does make clear that the educational attainment process does not operate in the same way for all groups in our society, and that while race differences now seem to be more consequential for college attendance than sex differences, equality between the sexes, particularly among whites, has not yet been achieved.

Conclusions

Social scientists generally agree that differences in the academic achievement patterns of females and males are the result of a combination of physiological, psychological, and sociological factors, although they disagree about the relative weight of different factors and the way in which they are related to each other. That is, sex differences seem to combine explanations from both cells 1 and 2 of Exhibit 2–1, although the way in which they operate to affect academic achievement may itself be affected by characteristics of the learner's environment, both in and outside of the school. While each sex tends to outperform the other in some areas and at some phases of the life cycle, there is no evidence of significant differences in total or average intelligence. Among a host of specific types of intellectual and personality development, only visual-spatial aptitude, mathematical aptitude, verbal aptitude, and aggression/activity appear to be based upon genetic or innate sex differences, and even these traits can be manipulated experimentally or enhanced through training.

There is little doubt that success in the student role is related to the way children are socialized to their sex role. While there is a trend in Western societies toward equitable child-rearing practices, parents of both sexes treat their sons and daughters differently in certain respects. The area of greatest differentiation is in very specifically sex-typed behavior, even though there is growing evidence that child-rearing techniques that emphasize "sex-appropriate" behavior are detrimental to high intellectual achievement, especially for girls. In general, parents are more resistant to "feminine" interests and behavior in sons than to "masculine" interests and behavior in daughters.

It also appears that societal expectations and the way in which tasks are assigned to males and females affect their sex-role behavior and their ultimate achievements. Anthropologists have found that in societies in which "feminine" work, such as looking after small children, is more equitably assigned to the two sexes, there is less aggressive behavior by boys and fewer behavioral differences between boys and girls. In societies in which independence is encouraged in both sexes, the performance differences between boys and girls on even sex-linked tasks (for example, tasks requiring visual-spatial skills) are less than in societies in which child-rearing practices are more restrictive and the treatment of girls and boys is more differential.

The structure of the student role and the educational system in general is in some important respects incongruent with sex-role expectations and performance, *for both boys and girls.* For boys, the feminine atmosphere of the school and the emphasis upon obedience and conformity, instead of upon more active learning, overshadows their first years in school, and they do not catch up with the girls in performance until the clear linkages of academic achievement with occupational and other kinds of adult success make school and learning more relevant. For girls, intellectual interests and potentialities are increasingly repressed as they come to represent unfeminine competitiveness.

The past decade has seen important changes in the position of women and in the relations between the sexes. A major goal of the women's movement is a full redefinition of sex roles, which will, it is argued, increase intellectual independence and reduce anxiety about competition among girls and, at the same time, widen the range of educational options for boys. Passage of Title IX of the Educational Amendment of 1972, which ruled that sexist practices are illegal in American public schools, and documentation of the extent of existing inequalities (from the absence of female role models in textbooks to the uneven distribution of sports equipment and training to boys and girls) have already led to changes in school curricula and resource distribution. The gap between the proportions of females and males earning higher educational degrees is narrowing, although sex differences in those obtaining the highest degrees as well as the highest occupational positions and incomes are still substantial, and different racial or ethnic subgroups within each sex still experience the educational process very differently. Whether the new trends will succeed in making sex roles more congruent with the student role, and whether changes will be extensive enough to have any real impact upon learning, remains to be seen.

Notes

1. My use of the word *sex* will include both the physiological and behavioral aspects of male-female differences. For the sake of simplicity, I have not distinguished between sex and *gender,* which is used in much of the recent literature (not always consistently) to refer to behavioral role differences.

2. Maccoby and Jacklin point out that many of the apparent differences between males and females may reflect biases in the research techniques used and the reporting of findings. They found instances in which a commonly believed sex difference is confirmed when ratings by parents, teachers, or other observers are used, but is not confirmed when simple frequency counts of relatively unambiguous categories of behavior are tallied in the course of direct observation (Maccoby and Jacklin, 1974: 7). Another problem is that results showing no difference between boys and girls on some characteristic or outcome are less likely to be reported in the literature than results showing a significant difference, so that the literature as a whole gives a misleading picture of the number and magnitude of sex differences.

3. In the relaxed situation, the test administrator affected a conspicuously easy-going manner, introducing himself as a graduate student who simply wanted to "try out" some tests on them. In the aroused condition, the administrator introduced himself and the tests in a brisk, formal manner, and told the subjects that the tests measured both their general level of intelligence and their capacity for leadership.

Individual Abilities   Chapter 6

American children are given IQ tests, American adults are impressed (or depressed) by the results, and children are treated accordingly. This means that a high IQ score, like a white skin, will be an asset even if IQ itself is no more intrinsically important than skin color.   Christopher Jencks

No one has yet produced any evidence based on a properly controlled study to show that representative samples of Negro and white children can be equalized in intellectual ability through statistical control of environment and education.
A. R. Jensen

Individual potential is one of the most unmarketable properties if the child acquires no means for its development, or if no means exist for measuring it objectively.   Martin Deutsch

To teach rigor while preserving imagination is an unsolved challenge to education.   R. W. Gerard

The view of the child formulated in Chapter 1 postulated that one characteristic that almost all children have in common is a curiosity about their environment and a desire to master it. The chapters immediately preceding have shown, however, that children differ greatly in their ability to translate this apparently universal motive into a capacity to learn in a formal educational setting, and that a child's family resources and experiences contribute to such differences. In this chapter, we shall consider another type of individual differentiation, that of individual abilities. Although it seems reasonable, indeed self-evident, that those children with the greatest mental abilities will be most successful at school, neither the source of innate ability differences nor the processes by which they are nurtured and channeled into actual learning are fully understood.

First, the distinction between ability and achievement is not clear cut. This is partly because "pure" ability is virtually impossible to abstract, even in a very young child, from the life experiences that may have nurtured or failed to nurture talents. Ability tests have been challenged on the grounds that they do not control for external influences, but this is probably an unreasonable demand. Indeed, it is probably impossible to construct a test of pure cognitive ability, or any other kind of ability, that is valid in any society or subculture. (For further discussion of this issue, see Hurn, 1978: Chapter 5.) Some scholars feel that what distinguishes ability tests from achievement tests is not the presence or absence of external influence but the nature of the influence.

> Intelligence tests must now be thought of as samples of learning based on general experiences. A child's score may be thought of as an indication of the richness of the milieu in which he functions and the extent to which he has been able to profit from that milieu. In contradistinction, school achievement tests assume deliberate instruction oriented to the outcomes measured in the tests. (Stodolsky and Lesser, 1967: 548)

In addition to distinguishing between ability and achievement, it is also important to distinguish between the ability itself and the test used to measure it. So-called intelligence tests do not measure actual intelligence, but rather they give a sampling of responses or behaviors that are believed to reflect intelligence. Thus in following the discussion in this chapter, it will be important to keep in mind the differences between: (1) the mental ability itself; (2) performance or score on the test being used as a measure of (1); and (3) performance on academic tasks or tests (academic achievement).

Second, mental ability is multidimensional, a composite of a number of different talents that are differentially related to success in conventional learning tasks and only some of which have been subjected to rigorous psychological scrutiny. In Project Talent, an extensive survey conducted during the early 1960s for the purpose of estimating the range and levels of ability among American high school students, each subject in a national sample took two full days of tests measuring over fifty different kinds of abilities and information (Flanagan *et al.*, 1962). The mental ability most strongly related to academic achievement is intelligence, which has come to be used almost interchangeably with IQ score. There are, however, many different IQ tests. Furthermore, behavioral scientists are coming to believe that most IQ tests measure only one kind of intelligence.

Finally, while measured intelligence is the best single predictor of scholastic performance, it does not explain everything. Even if the estimated upper limit is the true one, there is still a lot of difference to be explained by other factors. (Even if intelligence accounted for 100 percent of the performance *variation* among students, other variables might affect the level for performance of *all* students in a given class or school.) Moreover, while students cannot perform above their ability levels, they can and often do perform well below them. And there is also the possibility that the relationship between ability and performance in one social context might not be the same in another.

The meaning and measurement of ability and its relationship to achievement have been the subject of much recent controversy. Ability tests and testing have been accused of perpetuating—perhaps even producing—the gaps in achievement between advantaged and disadvantaged children. For example, the National Advisory Committee on Mexican-American Education has called for a halt to ability testing in the public schools, charging that all tests now in use discriminate against bilingual children. A case initiated in the San Francisco Bay area on behalf of a group of black children (Larry P. *et al.* versus Wilson Riles *et al.*) charged that these children had been misplaced in classes for the mentally retarded because the Wechsler Intelligence Scale, the test used for diagnosis and placement, discriminated against minority children.[1] A scholarly article aimed at clearing up the confusion about intelligence and its measurement (Jensen, 1969) instead unloosed a flood of controversy, carried on in newspapers and news magazines as well as in professional journals, which has still, a decade later, not abated.

The controversy over Jensen's paper is of sociological interest in itself, illustrating some of the dynamic features of the school's environment to be discussed in Chapter 12. In this chapter, we shall examine Jensen's paper and other pieces of research in terms of what they say about the sociology of mental ability, in particular the social factors that contribute to the development and use of mental ability. We shall first focus upon intelligence, since it is the ability most strongly related to success in school, and since the twin problems of accurate measurement and understanding of origins are well illustrated in the current arguments over intelligence testing. Then we shall consider rather more briefly two other aspects or types of individual ability that have sociological ramifications. One is cognitive style, or the way a student approaches and attacks a learning task; the other is creativity, or the extent to which he or she handles learning tasks in a novel or imaginative fashion.

Measurement of Intelligence

Although IQ has come to be almost synonymous with the term *intelligence,* the IQ test is a relatively recent invention. (Binet and Simon's Metrical Scale of Intelligence, the ancestor of present-day IQ tests, was devised in 1905.) IQ tests vary in content and design, but all of the tests currently in wide use contain items having to do with the recognition, retention, and manipulation of verbal and numerical symbols, which have been found to be strongly related to each other both within and between tests. Perhaps the most accurate way to describe what it is that IQ tests measure is to say it is the capacity for abstract reasoning and problem solving. When the tests are administered on a group basis, or when individuals' responses are scored against the averages or norms of some larger population, an individual's score also indicates his or her aptitude for, or likelihood of success in, traditional school subjects.

It should also be noted that an IQ is a measure of *relative* brightness; an individual's intelligence "quotient" is obtained by dividing his *mental* age (that is, the age in the general population at which his score is the statistical average) by his *chronological* age, and then multiplying by 100 to eliminate decimal points.[2] The particular score established as the norm for a given age depends, of course, upon the population or class of subjects upon which the test is standardized. Since most IQ tests have been standardized on groups containing high proportions of middle-class subjects, their validity as accurate indicators of the intelligence of low-SES children, or children from non-English–speaking homes has been justifiably questioned. Thus while the tests do not themselves *cause* the initial discrepancies between students (as the attacks of certain social scientists and ethnic groups have implied), by reflecting the lack of learning opportunities caused by poverty and discrimination, they are in a sense unfair to disadvantaged groups. Moreover, to the extent that test scores are used to place children in school tracks or programs, they themselves may lead to subsequent differences in academic achievement.

Like school achievement, IQ scores are related to social background. The relationship between IQ and socioeconomic status is a worldwide phenomenon, documented by an extensive crosscultural literature. IQ scores are also related to ethnicity. For example, differences averaging about fifteen points have been found in a number of statistical comparisons between black and white school children (Persell, 1977: 75).

While individual IQ scores are relatively stable (more stable, for example, than electrocardiogram or basal metabolism readings), they are not fixed, and some of the shifts over time are in predictable directions. Children's IQ scores tend to move closer to those of their natural parents, regardless of whether or not they are rasied by them (Jensen, 1969; Scarr and Weinberg, 1976). The scores of children in very poor urban schools tend to decrease the longer they stay in school. As Paul Goodman bitterly noted, the education in many New York City schools "succeeded in making the children significantly stupider year by year" (Goodman, 1960: 79). In fact, an individual's test score can be affected by a host of psychological and sociological factors; in a review of the literature on ability testing, Goslin (1966) identified eighteen such variables. In addition to inherited or innate factors, Goslin discusses the effects of *personality characteristics,* such as achievement motivation, interest in the test content or problems, and level of anxiety; *background factors,* such as cultural background, and schooling and other previous educational experiences, including previous experience with similar tests; the *social situation* in which the test is given, including the pnysical setting and the behavior of the tester; and chance or *random variation,* including luck in guessing at the answers to unfamiliar questions, and clerical errors in administrating or marking the test.

That disadvantaged children can often raise their scores dramatically if the test is administered in a friendly atmosphere where they are both expected and helped to do well is illustrated in the following description of some experiments by Haggard.

> Haggard reasoned that although deprived children may have taken many IQ tests, they really did not know how to take these tests properly: they lacked meaningful,

directed practice. They also lacked motivation, and their relationship to the examiner was typically distant and beset by fears.

Haggard decided to control each of these factors. He gave both deprived and non-deprived children three one-hour training periods in taking IQ tests. These practice periods included careful explanation of what was involved in each of the different types of problems found on the IQ tests. The explanations were given in words that were familiar to both groups. Haggard also offered special rewards for doing well, and he trained his examiners to be responsive to the deprived children as well as to the middle class youngsters, thus greatly enhancing the rapport.

Under these conditions the IQ's of the disadvantaged children improved sharply. *This occurred with only three hours of practice.* And it occurred even on the old IQ tests with the middle-class-biased items. Apparently more important than the content of the test items was the attitude of the children toward the test situation and the examiner. (Riessman, 1962: 53. See also Persell, 1977: Chapter 5)

The effects of many of the variables identified in Goslin's review are probably interactive or cumulative. Thus the setting in which the test is administered not only affects performance directly but can also affect attitudes (desire to succeed, test anxiety, and so on) that in turn affect performance. For example, the studies of n Achievement reported in Chapter 5 showed that, for boys at least, achievement motivation could be changed by manipulation of the test atmosphere.

The increased criticism of school-testing programs has led to attempts to develop "culture-free" tests, which do not depend upon verbal facility or life experiences that middle-class, white children as a group are more likely to have had. There are to date few serious alternatives to the classical IQ test, and the findings of research based on them are mixed. On the positive side, the author of one culture-free test, based upon matching random forms (thus eliminating not only the factor of language but also the geometric shapes that are perhaps more familiar to middle-class than to lower-class children), found that the scores were closely correlated with standard IQ scores for a sample of middle-class, white children but not for a comparable sample of low-income, black children (Rosenberg, 1966). Furthermore, the difference between the average scores on the new test for the two groups was negligible. On the negative side, other researchers have found that minority children score even lower on culture-free tests than they do on conventional IQ tests, and the results of such tests generally have not been found to be strongly correlated with school achievement. One critic concluded that while culture-free tests may be useful in certain situations and for certain diagnostic purposes, they are unsatisfactory substitutes for verbal-based tests, because

> the items usually employed are themselves subject to particular environmental experiences. A circle in one place may be associated with the sun, in another with a copper coin, in still another with a wheel. . . . Pictures, in the long run, are just symbols, and these may be as difficult to understand and recognize as words. . . . Nonverbal, even more than verbal tests, need to be related to particular environments and, from a practical point of view, are both limited in range and difficult to contrive.

Finally, many performance items when increased in difficulty tend to become measures of special abilities rather than having any significant correlation with over-all measures of intelligence. . . . Copying a diamond is a good test at the 7-year level, but whether a child of 12 can reproduce a complicated design has little to do with his general intelligence and represents at most a special ability.

(Miller, 1967: 75)

Another kind of new test is the "culturally specific" test, which does not try to eliminate cultural influences but instead to identify and capitalize on the type of information and experiences to which minority children have been exposed. For example, Robert Williams, a black scholar who successfully resisted his high school counselor's advice to forget college and "take up a trade," and a group of associates at Washington University in St. Louis have developed a series of culture-specific tests for black children, including a general intelligence test that uses words and expressions that are familiar to blacks. Williams's test includes items like the following:

1. *Alley apple*
   (a) Brick
   (b) Piece of fruit
   (c) Dog
   (d) Horse
2. *Get it together*
   (a) To go to jail
   (b) To do something
   (c) Cordially invite
   (d) Corrupt
3. *Jump sharp*
   (a) Well dressed
   (b) Angry
   (c) Bitter
   (d) Get the point

Preliminary research with this test has indicated that white students score on the average higher than black students on standard IQ tests, but that black students score on the average higher than white students on Williams's Black Intelligence Test, and that the gap between average black and white scores is greater on the latter than the former test. Correlations between scores on the Black Intelligence Test and a standard achievement test (California Achievement Test) were low. The distribution of scores on the Black Achievement Test, unlike the bell-shaped distribution found on most standardized tests, tends to be asymmetrical for both blacks and whites. That is, there is usually a large number of high scores and a small number of low scores for black students, a small number of high scores and a large number of low scores for white students, instead of a large number of middling scores and a small number of high and low scores.

By attempting to assess what a particular subgroup of children have actually learned, tests like Williams's Black Intelligence Test represent a different approach to intelligence testing. While critics have argued that Williams's test is too "easy" for black students, and that it is not a good predictor of conventional academic skills and success, Williams defends his approach by saying that it disproves the assumption that black children are not capable of learning, and that if they can learn in one environment, as his tests demonstrate, they can *if properly taught* learn in another (Williams, 1972 and 1975. Wright and Isenstein, 1977, contains a discussion of the rationale and substance of culture-specific tests and an extensive bibliography of the published work of Williams).

Origin of Intelligence

Almost all biological and behavioral scientists agree that the intelligence of any individual is a combination of genetic mechanisms established at birth and the environmental influences experienced during childhood. Environmental influences can be both physical (say, adequacy of diet) and social (the way a child is treated by others). The argument is over the *relative* contribution of heredity and environment. Throughout most of the 1960s, the trend in the behavioral sciences was to play down the former and play up the latter. The Stodolsky and Lesser passage quoted earlier in this chapter illustrates the experiential view of intelligence (at least of measured intelligence) and some reviews estimated the genetic component of intelligence as less than fifty percent (for instance, Mayr, 1967) as compared to Jensen's estimate of about eighty percent.

A major proponent of the power of the learner's environment and the potentialities of environmental manipulation is J. M. Hunt, whose influential work *Intelligence and Experience* (1961) synthesizes psychological and neuropsychological research on intelligence and discusses the implications of work in the area of information processing using electronic computers. Hunt dismisses the view of genetically fixed inherited capacity destined to develop in a biologically predetermined fashion. He argues that both the initial establishment and the subsequent development of the child's mental capacities are the result of interaction between hereditary potential and experiences in the outside world, the child's "encounter with the environment," as Hunt puts it.

Hunt marshals evidence in support of his view from studies of humans and nonhumans. He also cites research on the intellectually damaging effects of deprived environments upon children, including on the one hand extremely isolated environments (such as isolated farms or canal boats), and on the other hand environments where there may be many other children but too few adults and resources to provide environmental stimulation (such as orphanages). That such children have consistently lower measured intelligence seems to result from a combination of (1) lower intelligence among people who abandon or isolate children or who have extremely large families (the very poor) and (2) an environment in which there are relatively few adults and/or the available adults have relatively little time to spend with each child (in orphanages or large families where all the adults must work).

The implications of this view of intellectual origins and development are great. As Hunt summarizes:

> It is no longer unreasonable to consider that it might be feasible to discover ways to govern the encounters that children have with their environments, especially during the early years of their development, to achieve a substantially higher adult level of intellectual capacity. Moreover, inasmuch as the optimum rate of intellectual development would mean also self-directing interest and curiosity and genuine plea-

sure in intellectual activity, promoting intellectual development properly need imply nothing like the grim urgency which has been associated with "pushing" children. (Hunt, 1961: 363)

Hunt does, however, caution that constructing educational environments that maximized each child's intellectual potential would probably increase rather than decrease individual differences in performance, and the first major argument in Jensen's paper is that behavioral scientists have, for a variety of professional, sociopolitical, and ideological reasons, underestimated both the great spread in natural intelligence and the impact of genetic factors, to the detriment of educational theory and policy making. "The belief in the almost infinite plasticity of intelligence, the ostrich-like denial of biological factors in individual differences, and the slighting of the role of genetics in the study of intelligence can only hinder investigation and understanding of the conditions, processes, and limits through which the social environment influences human behavior" (Jensen, 1969: 29).[3]

Like Hunt, Jensen cites evidence from studies of selectively bred laboratory animals, but he uses the same data to argue that the ability of rats to behave "intelligently" (to get through mazes quickly without making errors) can be markedly influenced by selective breeding, and that the dull and bright rats do not respond in the same way to the same kinds of environmental manipulation—that is, how the animals respond to their environment depends upon their genetic constitution (Jensen, 1969: 40–41).

Jensen's evidence on human intelligence is drawn heavily from studies of kinship IQ correlations. For example, the correlation between IQ scores of natural siblings reared apart is considerably higher than that of unrelated children reared together in the same home and not a great deal lower than the correlation for siblings reared together. Identical twins have the highest correlations of any sibling combinations. The correlation between the IQ scores of children with those of their natural parents increases steadily over time to a value of about .50 between ages five and six, "and this is true whether the child is reared by his parents or not" (Jensen, 1969: 48–52).

Jensen argues that one cannot deduce from studies of extremely isolated or deprived children that large increases in IQ can generally be induced by environmental enrichment. Unlike the extremely isolated child, urban poor children in general are free to move about in their environment and to interact with great numbers of people. (As we saw in Chapter 3, the problem of the urban ghetto is not lack of stimulation but lack of articulation between the home and neighborhood experiences and life in school.) This important difference is reflected in test score differences between extremely isolated children and children of the urban poor generally. The latter tend to show a slight gain in IQ after their first few months in school, but unlike children brought from isolated life situations this initial gain is soon lost, after which there is a gradual but continuous decline in IQ throughout the remaining years of schooling. Thus Jensen is pessimistic about the chances of producing large and permanent increases in the IQ scores of poor children by means of environmental manipulation (Jensen, 1969: 59–60).

If this had been the sum of Jensen's paper, it probably would have attracted little attention outside of scholarly circles. After all, both Hunt and Jensen conceptualize intelligence as formed by a combination of genetic factors and environmental experiences; they differ mainly in the relative weight they assign to these two influences and in the extent to which they believe environmental effects can be meaningfully manipulated. Both sides of the debate have been based upon interpretation of data from small and rather special samples (orphans, twins), and there is no way of knowing whether the cases that have come to the attention of social scientists are typical of even the special subgroups of children that they represent. The best one can say is that we still lack the evidence to decide conclusively which side of the argument is closer to the truth.

Jensen, however, moved on to argue, as the passage quoted at the beginning of this chapter indicates, that the lower IQ scores of disadvantaged racial-ethnic and socioeconomic *groups* could also involve genetic as well as environmental components—that heredity is a major factor in explaining IQ differences *between* as well as *within* social groups. One of the arguments for a genetic explanation of the relationship between SES and IQ is that of "assortive mating," which claims that young people tend to select dates and mates not only from similar social backgrounds (which, given the strong relationship between SES and IQ, tends to bring together persons of relatively similar intelligence), but also of similar IQ (bright people being attracted to other bright people). While this seems true among certain groups in our society (among university students and graduates), the extensiveness of such a pattern is simply not known. An even more circuitous argument is based upon the correlation between intelligence and occupational status. The educational and occupational systems operate as "screening" mechanisms, and over the generations, individuals get "sorted" into occupational and status categories commensurate with their abilities. It is, argues Jensen, "most unlikely that groups differing in SES would not also differ, on the average, in their genetic endowment of intelligence" (Jensen, 1969: 75).

Jensen's empirical claim for hereditary racial differences seems to rest upon the fact that no one has yet established *statistical* equality of white and black IQ scores, even when the variables that are supposed to "explain" the differences (such as, inequalities in income or in educational level or quality) are controlled. In Jensen's view, the hypothesis that "the lower average intelligence and scholastic performance of Negro children could involve not only environmental, but also genetic, factors," is consistent with the "preponderance of the evidence," although he realizes that such a hypothesis is "anathema to many social scientists" (Jensen, 1969: 82–83).

That such a view is "anathema" is an understatement in view of the clamor that has risen in response to Jensen's paper. The more dispassionate arguments against innate interracial ability differences usually point out that while interracial comparisons of mean IQ scores consistently have shown that white children on the average score higher than comparable samples of black children, there is considerable overlap in the IQ distributions of the two groups. A few blacks will score higher than almost all Caucasians, and many blacks will score higher than most Caucasians (Pettigrew, 1964: Chapter 5). Indeed, Jensen points out that in no group is there a sizable proportion of children with IQ scores below 75, or the "educability" level. Individual differences *within* any racial group greatly exceed between-group differences.

Jensen's claims have been further weakened by recent revelations that many of the major studies on which he based his claims contain serious methodological errors and some are actually fraudulent. Re-examination of the original sources by Kamin (1974) and Green (1976) revealed that nearly all were seriously biased or suffered from weaknesses in research design and procedures, ranging from inadequate measurement of IQ (for example, in some studies of children raised by foster or adoptive parents, the IQ of natural or adoptive parents was inferred from the social status of the household rather than measured directly; in other studies, the authors failed even to report how IQ was measured) to incorrect computations of correlations between parent and child test scores. Even more shocking, Kamin unearthed fairly convincing evidence that Sir Cyril Burt, a prominent British psychologist whose research on the effects of heredity on intelligence was considered by many to be the classic work on the subject, had altered and even fabricated data in order to support his assertions about the intellectual inferiority of slum children, Jews, Irish, and females![4]

The core of the argument, however, is that there really is no way to test Jensen's hypothesis (or its reverse) in our society. A true test of innate intelligence must compare subjects and groups of equivalent backgrounds, a requirement that simply cannot be met in a society in which there is a high level of racial segregation and discrimination and gross differential poverty between racial groups (see Pettigrew, 1966; Pettigrew also argues that the effect of "pure race" on intelligence cannot be tested in America because of the high proportion of American blacks of mixed blood). One can, with the available evidence, construct an equally strong explanation of between-group difference in IQ scores based upon differences in child-rearing and other socialization factors, since we know that the way children are treated both within and outside the family does differ by race and socioeconomic status (see Chapters 3 and 4).

In sum, one can conclude only that differences in measured intelligence do exist both within and between cultural subgroups; that the within-group differences are greater than the between-group differences; that the extent to which differences are genetic as opposed to environmental in origin is still unknown, but that genetic effects would seem to explain more of the within-group than of the between-group differences.

Finally, Jensen turns to the question asked in the title of his paper—can intelligence be raised substantially by intervention in the child's environment? Jensen's answer is no, given the high genetic component of intelligence. He draws two kinds of implications from his answer: one seems unduly pessimistic because it misses the basic point about society's needs and the schools' functions; the other offers a sensible sequence of strategic priorities.

On the pessimistic side, Jensen comments that, "while you can teach almost anyone to play chess, or the piano, or to conduct an orchestra, or to write prose,

112 Part Two The Student

you cannot teach everyone to be a . . . Paderewski, a Toscanini, or a Bernard Shaw'' (Jensen, 1969: 76). Granted that neither our patterns of reproduction nor our available modes of environmental intervention have to date produced a large supply of geniuses, the more important part of Jensen's observation seems to be the first. He himself admits that in no cultural subgroup are there many children below the educability level. Even among the most socially disadvantaged, most children are capable of learning the basic skills required by the educational and occupational world.[5] Jensen is also worried that our rapidly automating technological society is pushing up the mental ability requirement too rapidly, but this does not cancel out the argument that many children would be *capable* of learning much more than they do if the school environment were redesigned to enable them to learn.

Jensen's other argument is that scholastic *achievement* is much less tied to genetic factors than is intelligence. Thus educational reform programs should be aimed at the first rather than the second.

> This means that there is potentially much more we can do to improve school performance through environmental means than we can do to change intelligence per se. Thus it seems likely that if compensatory education programs are to have a beneficial effect on achievement, it will be through their influence on motivation, values, and other environmentally conditioned habits that play an important part in scholastic performance, rather than through any marked direct influence on intelligence per se. The proper evaluation of such programs should therefore be sought in their effects on actual scholarship performance rather than in how much they raise the child's IQ. (Jensen, 1969: 59)

In a review of the compensatory programs that have been initiated in recent years, mainly under the aegis of the federal antipoverty program, Jensen concludes that the rew instances where the results have been truly encouraging have been in projects that focused upon teaching the specific skills that are linked to school learning rather than attempting all-round enrichment of the child's environment and experience. An example is the Bereiter-Engelman program at the University of Illinois, which is built upon brief but intensive periods of drill in language, reading, and arithmetic skills, using almost militaristic procedures that demand a high and continuous level of participation from all the children. The now-famous opening sentence in Jensen's paper—"Compensatory education has been tried and it apparently has failed"—is not only inflammatory, but also misleading. Jensen's statement does not mean that compensatory education *cannot* succeed, but rather that most of the programs to date have focused upon the wrong things.[6]

Cognitive Style

It is now clear that intelligence is far from a unidimensional concept, even when one is concerned only with the kind of intelligence required by formal schooling. Research conducted during the last two decades has also indicated that intelligence per se should be distinguished from (a) *cognitive style,* or the mode by which an individual attacks an intellectual task, and (b) *creativity,* or the quality of inventiveness and imagination with which an individual handles ideas. During the 1960s, research on cognitive style distinguished between *analytic-cognitive* or *analytic-descriptive* styles and *relational* styles of thinking. Tests of cognitive style typically involved a series of figure-sorting tasks where, for example, the subject was asked to say which pictures out of a set were most alike and how he or she came to this decision. A student using an analytic style would tend to group pictures on the basis of some shared physical attribute—a lamppost, door, or hammer are all "hard" objects; a radio, television, and telephone all "make noise." By contrast, a student using a relational mode of thinking would group objects in terms of their meaning or functional relationship to each other. For example, a comb, lipstick, pocketbook, and door might be grouped together under the conceptual umbrella of "getting ready to go out." In the relational mode, no single object is an example of the label that envelopes it; each has meaning only in connection with other objects in the set.

Work by Jerome Kagan and his associates (1963) and by Rosalie Cohen (1968) indicated that conventional school tasks and standardized tests favored students who used analytic-cognitive modes of conceptualization. In Cohen's opinion, "so discrepant are the analytic and relational frames of reference that a pupil whose preferred mode of cognitive organization is emphatically relational is unlikely to be rewarded in the school setting, either socially or by grades, regardless of his native abilities, and even if his information repertoire and background of experience are adequate" (Cohen, 1968: 4–5). In fact, a child who has high intelligence or other abilities but a relational cognitive style may be in a particularly unhappy position since his or her talents are not of a sort that allow him or her to play the student role successfully, and Cohen speculated that a disproportionate number of behavior as well as learning problems come from children who do not approach classroom tasks with the cognitive style "approved" by the school system.

Creativity

Intelligence can also be distinguished from the dimension of creativity, which is the ability to produce new or novel ideas—or linkage between ideas, insights, and solutions—as opposed to the logical selection and combination of cognitive components. While the precise definition of creativity is still a matter of debate among scholars in the field, most concepts of creativity include the following indices:

1. *flow*. The creative person produces a relatively large number of reactions or products within a given time.
2. *originality*. The creative person produces ideas that occur with very low frequency in an average test population.
3. *flexibility*. The creative person can produce reactions or products in widely diverse categories or areas.
4. *relevance*. The ideas produced by the creative person are not absurd or redundant. (Gilford, 1967)

Although behavioral scientists have long felt that creativity and intelligence are different psychological dimensions, proof of such differentiation rests upon developing a set of creativity-assessment devices, parallel to the IQ tests of intelligence, that are highly interrelated among themselves but are independent of or from measures of other mental abilities.[7] Most creativity tests judge the extent to which an individual *differs* from or exceeds some group norm or standard. One kind of task is to name all the uses one can think of for some common object (for instance, a key, shoe, chair, or newspaper). Responses are judged both for quantity and originality. Another procedure is to give a simple ambiguous stimulus and, again, to judge the number and uniqueness of the responses: for example, for a triangle with three circles around it, "three mice eating a piece of cheese" was a unique response, while "three people sitting around a table" was not; for two half-circles over a straight line, "two haystacks on a flying carpet" was a unique response, "two igloos" was not (Wallach and Kogan, 1967: 40). Another technique is to analyze children's own stories or drawings on the basis of originality of theme and execution.

The first major published studies of creativity in children (Getzels and Jackson, 1962; Wallach and Kogan, 1965 and 1967) identified children on both creativity and intelligence, made some comparisons between them, and drew some conclusions about how differing combinations of these two mental dimensions relate to success in school. The sample for the Getzels and Jackson study consisted of over five hundred students, the upper six grades of one private school. The major portion of their reports is a comparison of students who scored high on creativity but not on IQ with students who scored high on IQ but not on creativity (cells b and c respectively of Exhibit 6–1).[8] Data consisted of responses to a series of ability, achievement, and attitude tests. The creativity battery included measures of the ability to devise mathematical problems, to compose endings for incomplete stories, to think up word definitions, and to imagine uses for an object. Some of the students' own stories and pictures were also analyzed for theme and originality. In addition, the parents of some of the subjects were questioned.

The researchers found that the high-creativity and high-IQ students differed on a number of attitudinal and family experience variables. First, the parents of the latter were more "vigilant" about their children's behavior, their academic performance, and their choice of friends. They also tended to be more critical of their children and of the education the school was providing. The qualities they especially valued were the conventional (and visible) virtues of cleanliness, good manners, and studiousness. In contrast, the parents of the high-creativity students focused less on the conventional virtues, more on such things as the child's "openness to experience" and "interests and enthusiasm for life" (Getzels and Jackson, 1962: 68–75).

Second, while both groups of students agreed on the types of personal characteristics that would contribute to success in school and in later life, only the high-IQ group wanted these characteristics for themselves. Subjects were asked to rank thirteen hypothetical children, each exemplifying a desirable personal

Exhibit 6-1
Combinations of Mental Characteristics Used in Creativity Studies

		Intelligence	
		High	**Low**
Creativity	**High**	a	b
	Low	c	d

quality (for instance, one child was described as the brightest student in the school, another as the best athlete, another as having outstanding social skills), in three ways—as to (1) which would be the most successful in adult life; (2) which ones their teachers would like best; and (3) which they themselves would like to be like. The rankings of the high-IQ and high-creativity groups were almost identical for the first two categories: that is, the two groups agreed on what qualities are valued by adults. There were, however, differences in responses to the third category:

> For the high IQ students the relationship between the qualities they value for themselves and those they believe lead to "success" as adults is quite close. That is, these students appear to be highly success oriented. For the high creativity students the relationship between the qualities *they* value and those they believe lead to "success" as adults is virtually *nil*. These students appear *not* to be highly success oriented (at least not by conventional standards of adult success). (Getzels and Jackson, 1962: 35)

Third, the in-school experiences and behavior of the two types of students differed. Both groups had high achievement motivation and high actual achievement, suggesting either that IQ tests do measure something other than pure scholastic aptitude, or that the highly creative student has other qualities that compensate for a lesser amount of "pure" intelligence. They differ, however, in their approach to intellectual tasks. By comparison with their high-IQ classmates, the high-creativity students' work was characterized by a certain playfulness. Their stories were "significantly higher than the high IQ adolescents' in *stimulus-free themes, unexpected endings, humor, incongruities, and playfulness* and showed a marked tendency toward more *violence*" (Getzels and Jackson, 1962: 38). The less methodical, more playful approach of these children may also explain another empirical finding—the teachers in this school preferred the high-IQ to the high-creativity students (Getzels and Jackson, 1962: 33).

The "playful" component of creativity is even more strongly emphasized by Wallach and Kogan. They deduced (1) from the number of references made to "playing with ideas," "letting things happen," "freedom of expression," and the like in memoirs and interviews with writers, scientists, and other highly creative individuals, and (2) from the inability to separate creativity from IQ when it is measured in a test-like situation, that creativity, "if it is to reveal itself most clearly, requires a frame of reference which is relatively free from the coercion of time limits and relatively free from stress of knowing that one's behavior is under close evaluation'' (Wallach and Kogan, 1965a: 24). Thus, as researchers, they took great pains to construct a "permissive" atmosphere for the administration of their research instruments. The administrators got to know the children, by observing and playing with them before the actual testing; subjects were tested individually rather than in groups; the tasks were introduced as part of a study of children's games for the purpose of developing new games that children would like, *not* as a test or as anything directly related to their regular school work, and there was no time limit on any of the procedures.

The 151 children in Wallach and Kogan's samples were all fifth graders, the entire fifth-grade population of one suburban, New England public school system. Thus they were younger than the subjects of the Getzels and Jackson study, but like them were mainly of middle-class background (the 6 percent of the children's fathers who did not have professional or managerial occupations were nearly all in upper-level, blue-collar occupations—electricians or carpenters).

The ten creativity indicators—a uniqueness and a productivity measure for each of five types of association tasks (including naming uses for common objects and responses to ambiguous doodle pictures)—were found to be highly intercorrelated and to have only low correlations with intelligence. Thus Wallach and Kogan succeeded, where Getzels and Jackson did not, in producing a clear distinction between measures of the two concepts. The Wallach and Kogan study is also an extension of Getzel and Jackson's work in that they compared children in all four cells of Exhibit 6–1.

Exhibit 6–2 summarizes the results of an analysis of the classroom behavior of the four subgroups of female subjects. (The behavior variables were derived from a series of nine rating scales completed during a two-week observation period preceding the administration of the creativity tasks by two judges who worked independently both of each other and of the administrators of the other tests and tasks. For a full discussion of the scales and the rating procedures, see Wallach and Kogan, 1965a: 35–38.) As Exhibit 6–2 indicates, children high in creativity *and* intelligence combined academic bent with successful peer relationships. They displayed the "highest level of self-confidence, the least tendency toward deprecation of oneself and one's work, the strongest tendency to seek out others for companionship, the strongest tendency to be sought by others, the highest levels of attention span and concentration for academic work" (Wallach and Kogan 1965b: 115). The only negative aspect of their behavior was a tendency to engage in "disruptive" behavior (in particular, attention-seeking acts such as speaking out of turn or making noise), a tendency that in the authors' opinion is congruent with their positive self-image and high (and healthy) level of interest. As they put it, "It's as if they are bursting through the typical behavioral molds that the society has constructed" (Wallach and Kogan, 1967: 41).

Examination of the other three cells of Exhibit 6–2 shows that

> those high in creativity but low in intelligence, in contrast, were the most cautious and hesitant of all the groups, the least confident, the most self-deprecatory, the least sought after by others, the least able to concentrate and maintain attention, and

Exhibit 6-2

Girls' Classroom Behavior by Intelligence and Creativity Levels

		Intelligence	
		High	**Low**
Creativity	**High**	Self-evaluation: high Concentration and attention span: high Tendency to seek and be sought by peers: high Disruptive behavior: high	Self-evaluation: low Concentration and attention span: low Tendency to seek and be sought by peers: low Disruptive behavior: high
	Low	Self-evaluation: high Concentration and attention span: high Tendency to seek and be sought by peers: low on seeking, high on being sought Disruptive behavior: low	Self-evaluation: medium Concentration and attention span: low Tendency to seek and be sought by peers: medium Disruptive behavior: low to medium

Adapted from findings in Wallach and Kogan, 1965a and 1965b.

in addition they were quite avoidant of others. The one characteristic they shared with the high-high group was the presence of disruptive behavior. Turning next to the group low in both creativity and intelligence, these girls were more confident and self-assured, less hesitant, and more extroverted socially than were the high creativity–low intelligence girls. Finally, the group of high intelligence but low creativity was least likely to engage in disruptive behavior, was reasonably hesitant about expressing opinions, was sought out socially by others but tended not to seek out others in return, and was high in attention span and concentration. In sum, the high creativity–low intelligence group seems to be the maximally disadvantaged group in the classroom, and the high intelligence–low creativity group seems to be characterized by a basic reserve and an unwillingness to take chances. (Wallach and Kogan, 1965b: 115–116)

For boys, the relationship between the *intelligence* dimension and classroom behavior was similar to the girls' pattern, but creativity had no observable behavioral consequences (Wallach and Kogan, 1965a: 89–94). Although their data do not explain these sex differences, the authors speculate that they may be a function of the differential role expectations explored in the previous chapter. Since achievement is highly valued in boys (and the boys in this sample were more achievement oriented than the girls), the intelligence needed to perform well in classroom tasks was all that was needed for approval and self-confidence.

However, a further analysis that brought in the additional dimension of cognitive style (using Kagan's basic test) showed that adding this mental variable did not affect the girls' results in any consistent way but that it did bring out an effect of creativity among boys that did not show up when only intelligence and creativity were controlled. The highly creative boys seemed able to switch rather flexibly among the different cognitive modes. By contrast, boys high on intelligence but low on creativity concentrated on the "conceptual common elements" (the analytic mode) and displayed an "avoidance" of thematic-relational categorizing, and boys low on both dimensions seemed "locked" into relational modes of responding and relatively incapable of analytical thinking (Wallach and Kogan, 1965a: Chapter 4). Thus the most general implications of Wallach and Kogan's research are: (1) that one can design appropriate learning programs for children only by taking into account the combination of their abilities and modes of thinking; and (2) that boys and girls respond to the classroom and to intellectual stimuli differently, which may be explained by "differential normative expectations for boys and girls in the achievement and affiliation areas" (Wallach and Kogan, 1965a: 94).

Recently, efforts to cultivate creative thinking, particularly among disadvantaged students, have been initiated by some Israeli social scientists working both in elementary schools and in the informal educational framework of an experimental summer camp for sixth and seventh graders (Goor and Sommerfeld, 1975; Goor and Rapaport, 1977). Building upon earlier findings of the playful or gamelike quality of much creative behavior, Goor and Rapaport developed a set of games that require a high level of abstract and hypothetical thinking. The games include a variation of the brainstorming process, a game called "Visits from Outer Space" that has children examine and describe familiar items by trying to look at them as if they were totally unknown; and a game of medium displacement or transformation, the object of which is to express the feeling and information received by one sense by means of another sense—for example, to express with play dough (sensation of touch) a concept of noise, such as a waterfall (sensation of hearing).

Comparison of children who were in the experimental creativity-cultivation programs with children in matched control groups indicated statistically significant differences on several measures of creativity, even several months after the experimental treatment. Goor also found some evidence that the disadvantaged children benefited more from the program than more privileged children, and he hypothesized that the obstacles to creativity are different for privileged and underprivileged children. The latter tend to go from one concrete example to another without going through an abstract phase in between, by comparison to more privileged children, who often move directly from concrete to abstract and remain there. Thus a cultivation program that requires abstract thinking in order to participate in an enjoyable activity may be especially beneficial to children whose typical thinking patterns do not nurture abstract thinking.

Research on actual creative achievements—for example, in music, art, science, writing, social activities, and so on—both in Israel and the United States, has indicated that students who engage in many creative activities score higher on creative-thinking tests, but they do not score higher on intelligence tests or get higher school grades. Creative-thinking test scores were most highly correlated with leadership, and science, art, and writing activities, less strongly correlated with creativity in the areas of drama or music (Milgram and Milgram, 1976; Wallach and Wing, 1969).

The Consequences of Testing

As ability tests have come to be more and more widely used for more and more purposes in our society, some educators and social scientists have become concerned not only with their validity—that is, the extent to which they are accurate measures of students' real aptitudes—but also with the consequences of testing even when the tests have been responsibly validated. As the quotation by Jencks at the beginning of this chapter indicates, test scores may have consequences for individuals' subsequent life opportunities whether or not they serve as relevant prerequisites. Several sociologists have noted that intelligence, as measured by IQ tests, has largely replaced noble blood, family background and upbringing, race, religion, and other characteristics that were formerly the major criteria for the ascription of status and the major determinants of success in life (Goslin, 1966: Chapter VIII; Hurn, 1978: Chapter 5). Goslin speculates about the likely effects upon the individual of continuous evaluation via standardized tests.

> His admission to college or his promotion in industry may depend upon his performance on an ability test. In addition, his perception of himself may be influenced by his score on the many tests to which he is likely to be exposed during his lifetime. The kind of instruction he gets in school, the opportunities for specialized training, the way he is treated by his peers, teachers, and parents, and in the long run, his chances for success in life may be altered by his performance on objective tests. (Goslin, 1966: 178)

Rationalizing failure is more difficult when it cannot be blamed on accident of birth, an unfair or corrupt government, or simply bad luck. And what happens to the self-image and academic motivation of individuals who are informed that they are of low ability? Critics worry that standardized tests have been adopted without sufficient investigation of their possible "side-effects" on individuals and society.

Radical sociologists would go even further. Bowles and Gintis argue that "I.Q.-ism" has become a crucial component of capitalist ideology, serving to legitimate the inequalities of the capitalist stratification system. From a reanalysis of U.S. Census and other national survey data on IQ, social-class background, and educational attainment, they conclude that while all three contribute independently to economic success, IQ is by far the least important. Despite the fact that few occupations actually require the cognitive skills measured by IQ tests, "I.Q.-ism" has been adopted by those in power, because it "is conducive to a general technocratic and meritocratic view of the stratification system that tends to legitimate these social relations, as well as its characteristic means of allocating individuals to various levels of the hierarchy." Moreover, it "operates to reconcile workers to their eventual economic positions" (Bowles and Gintis, 1977: 226).

While most sociologists are less willing to draw firm conclusions about the intentions of testers and the consequences of testing than the radical Marxists, who believe that intelligence testing is consciously used by those in power to help maintain the status quo, some recent trends indicate that concern is widespread. Within the last few years, a number of school systems, in this country and elsewhere, have modified their testing programs or abandoned them altogether. In Sweden, following extensive reform of the educational system in the 1950s and 1960s, standardized testing at the national level no longer exists. A marking system that covers the attitudes of students and their cooperation with teachers and other students as well as their level of accomplishment has replaced formal examinations at the elementary and secondary levels, and each municipality has autonomy to decide on the use of intelligence testing. Since the late 1960s the use of aptitude tests has decreased; what testing now occurs is mainly for diagnostic purposes, and different municipalities use different (usually several different) tests (Stenholm, 1970; Kjell Harnquist, personal communication). In the United States, a number of recent court decisions have ruled that assigning children (especially poor or minority children) to educational programs or tracks on the basis of standardized test scores violates the principle of equal educational opportunity.

A second trend is in the direction of giving students and their families more information about their test performance. Goslin, whose research on the sociology of ability testing has already been discussed, has also been instrumental in promoting research on the ethical and legal aspects of school record keeping, which ultimately led to federal legislation providing for parental access to official school records and prohibiting schools from releasing school records to third persons without the written permission of parents. Goslin and others are sensitive to the possible negative as well as positive consequences of this trend (see, for example, Goslin, 1969 and 1966: 179ff). But it does represent an important effort not only to understand the consequences of testing, but also to translate social science research into rational public policy.

Conclusions

Although explanations of learning based upon differences in individual mental abilities are classified in one cell of Exhibit 2–1 (Cell 1), the review of research in this chapter has indicated that individual ability is not a single dimension but rather a complex of dimensions, only some of which are linearly related to each other. Psychologists have given more attention to intelligence than to any other kind of mental ability, but few are satisfied with our present measuring instruments. A low score on an IQ test may reflect lack of interest in verbal and numerical symbols, lack of motivation to do well on tests, lack of practice in taking tests, and lack of real-life experiences related to the content of the tests, as well as a low level of natural intelligence, and it is often difficult to sort out which factors are operating in a particular case. While it seems clear that intelligence combines genetic and environmental components, neither the relative strength of the two nor the way in which one may affect or limit the power of the other has been decisively determined. And while intelligence, like school performance, is strongly related to the background variables of SES and race, the extent to which social subgroup differences are also genetically determined is also unknown, and interpretation of what empirical evidence exists is clouded by political and ideological biases.

What does seem clear is that a child's learning in school is not simply a function of his or her total or composite level of natural abilities. It is affected by the extent to which the particular combination of mental abilities he or she possesses meshes with the structure and expectations of the school. Thus children who have well-developed imaginations but low interest in or limited experience with verbal and numerical symbols, or children who analyze problems in their total relational context rather than in a logical, analytical fashion abstracted from their larger meaning are not likely to receive much encouragement from their teachers; on the contrary, they may be defined as stupid or troublemaking. To look at it another way, the conventional classroom is structured to build up ever-greater repertoires of factual information and analytic skills but not to encourage the "playful contemplation" that is conducive to creativity. The social structure and dynamics of the school will be the subject of Part Three of this book, after which we should be better able to determine the best interface between what the individual student brings with him or her to school and what he or she confronts upon arrival. In the final chapter of the book we shall consider some proposed changes in the structure of learning environments that might increase the productivity of certain kinds of children.

Children's learning is also dependent upon the extent to which their total experience outside of school has prepared them to play the student role in accordance with the expectations of school personnel. A synthesis of the findings of the past four chapters suggests, as indicated in Exhibit 6–3, that social background and experiences shape children's abilities to some degree (there is probably some reverse effect also, but the impact of children's ability upon the family itself is less well understood and is probably much smaller), which in turn affects their academic attitudes and performances, and that these variables have both interactive and independent effects upon school success. Whatever the exact contribution of hereditary, environmental, ability, and social background factors, children enter school with a tremendous range of difference in their facility to benefit from it.

Almost no one is fully satisfied with the design and utilization of the currently available measures of ability. But except for a small minority who believe in the feasibility of schools and societies with no gradations of talent and achievement, most people acknowledge that some form of sorting is inevitable, and few would wish to return to the sorting systems that prevailed in the past. As one thoughtful analysis of ability measurement concluded, in critiquing standardized tests and testing procedures it is useful to think about alternative ways of evaluating abilities and performance.

> It is worth remembering that some cures are worse than the disease, and that abandoning the use of criteria like test scores and credentials might lead to greater reliance on who one knows, how one looks, or where one comes from. Designing

Exhibit 6-3
Characteristics of Individual Students that Are Related to School Performance

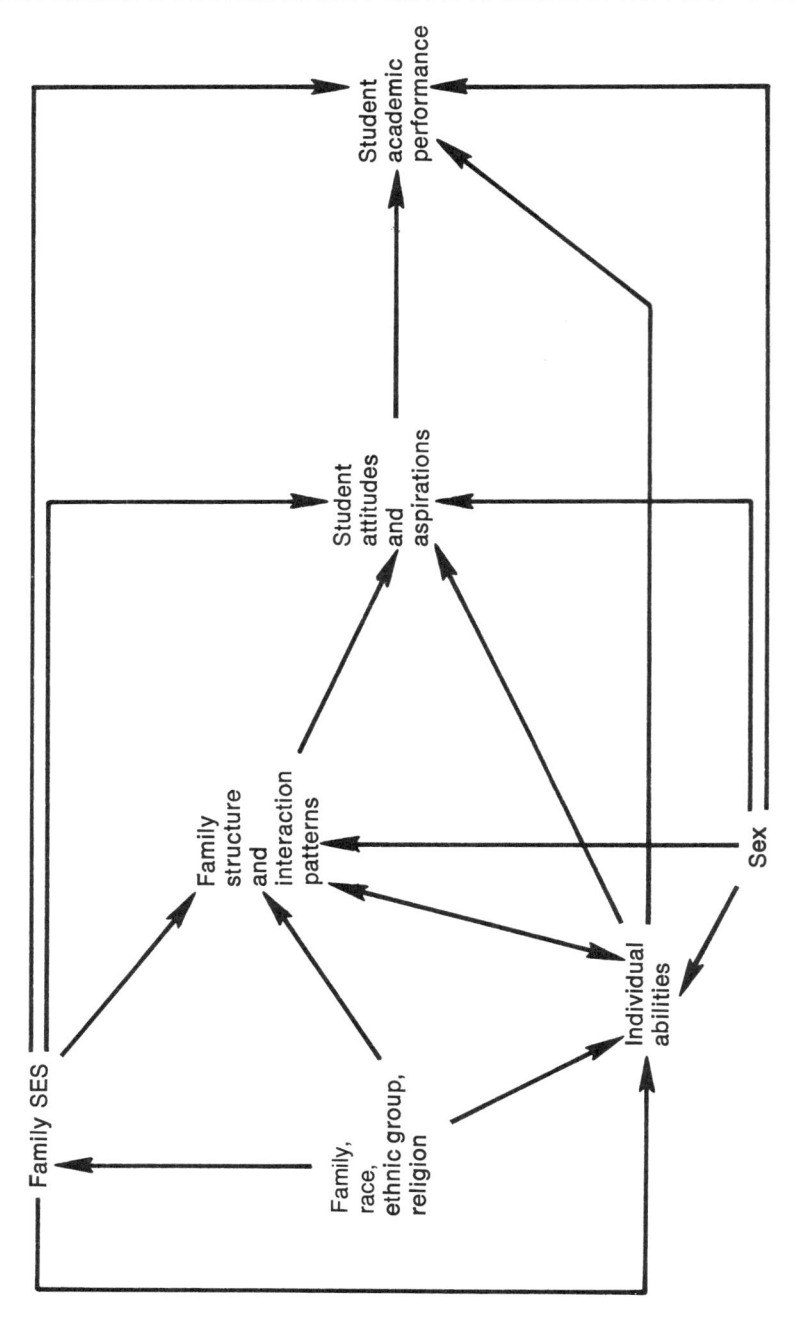

more rational and fair ways of allocating privilege—or perhaps of abolishing some forms of privilege altogether—will be a difficult and lengthy task. (Bane and Crouse, 1975: 11–12)

Notes

1. At the time of this writing, Larry P. v. Riles, although initiated in 1971, was still being debated in the California courts, and similar cases are scheduled for other United States cities. For a discussion, see Holden, 1978.

2. The use of a single number, the IQ score, like the group situation in which IQ tests are typically administered, is a fairly recent development. Testers in Binet's day usually worked with a single child, and Binet himself tested for many different facets of intelligence, using medical and family histories as well as standardized tests. For a study of ability testing in historical and sociological perspective, see Goslin, 1966.

3. This is also the view of some sociologists (for instance, Eckland, 1967), who have pointed to the necessity of integrating environmental and genetic principles in the study of intelligence. Like Jensen, Eckland feels an understanding of genetic factors is necessary in understanding social-class differences.

4. Intelligence testing has never been free from unsavory elements. Terman, who translated, published, and standardized the Binet test on American children, believed that Indians, Mexicans, and blacks were innately inferior. In his words: "Their dullness seems to be racial. Children of these groups should be segregated into special classes . . . they cannot master abstractions, but they can often be made efficient workers" (Terman, 1923: 123). As late as the 1930s, data on group differences were routinely interpreted as demonstrating the inferiority of particular immigrant groups (Hurn, 1978: 128). Burt's behavior is, however, particularly distressing, not only because of the virulent prejudice permeating his work, but also because of its recency and the multiple fraudulent research practices apparently used.

5. One educated guess is that over 90 percent of the children now in school are capable of mastering most subjects, given sufficient time and appropriate types of help (Bloom, 1968: 4).

6. On compensatory education programs, see also McDill et al., 1969.

7. There is also some evidence from biological research that creativity or imagination may have a different biological basis from more logical forms of mental ability and activity—that is, that creative thinking emanates from a separate territory of the brain and nervous system from reasoning and abstract thinking. One suggestive piece of evidence is that individuals with certain kinds of brain injuries may perform as well as previously on IQ tests but decline on tests requiring imagination. For a brief discussion of the biological basis of creativity, see Gerard, 1952.

8. It should be noted that while Getzels and Jackson focused upon the subjects who were high on only one of the two ability dimensions, such cases were in the minority. All of the creativity tests in the test batteries administered correlated significantly with IQ for the boys, all but one for the girls. In fact, the individual creativity test scores were as highly correlated with IQ as they were among themselves, a point taken by Wallach and Kogan as one of the starting points for their research and one of the reasons why they took special pains with the setting of their test administration.

PART THREE

The School

The School as a Social System   Chapter 7

Education being a social process, the school is simply that form of community life in which those agencies are concentrated that will be most effective in bringing the child to share in the inherited resources of the race, and to use his own powers for social ends.   John Dewey

A school may be viewed as a network of positions or statuses to which staff and pupils are allocated and in which they learn the norms which define their roles. These stem from the formal school structure or from subcultures within it.
          M. D. Shipman

A school is a complex system comprised of human behavior, organized in such a way as to perform certain functions within the structure of the society. This statement literally means that schools, at least to a sociologist, consist of the behavior or actions performed by human actors which are organized so as to produce certain specialized outputs for society and its members. It explicitly excludes the notion that schools may be regarded as buildings and grounds or as collections of biological human beings.   Frederick Bates and Virginia Murray

Schools are a mixture of bureaucratic and professional systems—and are not functioning very well as either.   Sanford Dornbusch

In this part of the book, we shall study the structure and dynamics of the school as a social system and as a learning environment. Schools are large and complex social organizations, which makes them both a source of interest and a source of frustration to sociologists. Because schools are both large scale (encompassing the activities of hundreds, sometimes thousands, of people) and of relatively long duration (while new schools are being built all the time, many have been in existence longer than the lifetime of their oldest members), no researcher can actually "observe" an entire school. There are too many things going on for too long a period of time. Imagine, for example, that you could actually see and hear everything that went on in every room of a single high school for one second. It would be difficult if not impossible to make sense of even that minute portion of a school's "lifetime."

The Sociologist's View of the School

Because we cannot directly experience schools as total entities, we must operate on the basis of conceptions. The quotations at the beginning of this chapter are a sampling of conceptions of the school proposed by or adopted by educational sociologists. Since Dewey, it has been fashionable to think of the school as a small community, ideally with some continuity between the learning experiences in school and those in the larger society (Dewey, 1928: 416ff). More recently, Katz, in a paper entitled "The School as a Complex Social Organization" (1964), pointed out that schools, like most complex organizations, are not self-sufficient communities but rather specialized structures serving special functions and tightly interlocked with other structures. The special function of the school, according to Katz, is to prepare children for active participation in adult activities. Thus it must allow enough independent action to ensure adequate performance of adult activities without constant supervision, but it must be ever alert to activities, organizations, and opinions that are potentially dangerous to the carrying out of this function. (For instance, serious questioning of the "American way of life." See also Zeigler and Peck, 1970.)

Schools as Institutions

Some conceptualizations of the school are based upon comparisons with other types of institutions. For example, schools have been compared with prisons, mental hospitals, and other *involuntary* institutions, where a large group of "clients" are serviced by a smaller group of employees of the institution, some of them professionals. Because the services provided have not in many cases been requested by the client, a central problem of involuntary institutions is maintenance of order and control. For this purpose, the institution staff may develop elaborate rules and monitoring systems. In the opinion of John Holt: "What is most shocking and horrifying about public education today is that in almost all schools the children are treated, most of the time, like convicts in jail. Like black men in South Africa, they cannot move without written permission" (Holt, 1969: 134–135). Obviously, such comparisons can be taken only so far. One important difference between most schools and most involuntary institutions is that the latter are likely also to be total institutions, so that all of the clients' activities take place within the boundaries of the institution. The comparison does, however, clarify the nature of the authority problems of service institutions like the school, in which persons in one set or category of roles do their work *for* persons in another set or category of roles, usually without taking very much into account the wishes of those who are serviced. As one analyst puts it:

One aspect of the institutional organization of activity is a division of authority, a set of shared understandings specifying the amount and kind of control each kind of person involved in the institution is to have over others; who is allowed to do what, and who may give orders to whom. This authority is subject to stresses and possible change to the degree that participants ignore the shared understandings and refuse to operate in terms of them. A chronic feature of service institutions is the indifference or ignorance of the client with regard to the authority system set up by institutional functionaries; this stems from the fact that he looks at the institution's operation from other perspectives and with other interests. In addition to the problems of authority which arise in the internal life of any organization, the service institution's functionaries must deal with such problems in the client relationship as well. One of their preoccupations tends to be the maintenance of their authority definitions over those of clients, in order to assure a stable and congenial work setting. (Becker, 1968: 298. For a more recent study of schools as service organizations, see Wagenaar, 1978.)

Schools as Sets of Behavior

The third quotation at the beginning of this chapter is from a paper by Bates and Murray, who argue that an adequate conception of the school should (1) tell what are the basic elements of the school as a social object, (2) show how these elements are organized to comprise the whole, and (3) identify the boundaries of the school and its relationship to its environment. In their conceptualization, the basic element of schools, like that of all other complex formal organizations, consists not of persons or of physical structures but of *behavior,* or more specifically,

> the behavior of a large number of actors organized into groups that are joined together by an authority structure, and by a network of relationships through which information, resources and partially finished projects flow from one group to another. (Bates and Murray, 1975: 26.)

The boundaries of the school are behavioral, not geographic. To put it another way, school-related behavior (for example, doing homework or grading papers) is part of the school as a social system, whether or not it takes place in the school building. Conversely, behavior that is not relevant to a school role is not part of the school system, even if it occurs on the school grounds (for example, two boys continuing on the school playground a fight begun in their home neighborhood). Bates and Murray point out that much of what occurs on school grounds is actually a part of other behavior systems, while at the same time, the school "spills over past the confines of the campus and occurs wherever school roles are performed or where people interact as members of schools groups" (Bates and Murray, 1975: 32).

Schools as Bureaucracies

Schools have often been cited by sociologists as examples of bureaucratic systems (for an excellent general discussion of schools as bureaucratic organizations, see Parelius and Parelius, 1978: Chapters 4 and 5). The conceptualization of the evolution of bureaucratic structure was one of the major contributions of

Max Weber, the great German sociologist and contemporary of Durkheim. In a series of voluminous studies of civilizations ranging from ancient China through medieval Europe to modern Prussia, Weber traced the evolution from societies in which the social order was based upon strong personal ties, to societies in which social stability was based upon general rules applied impersonally to all. Bureaucracy, according to Weber's conceptualization, "has a 'rational' character: rules, means, ends, and matter-of-factness dominate its bearing" (Gerth and Mills, 1958: 244). While Weber found traces of bureaucractic forms of organization as far back as ancient Egypt and China, its main development occurred in seventeenth- and eighteenth-century France, Prussia, and Russia, as the ruling monarchies moved out of feudalism toward more rationally organized, routinized forms of rule. By the nineteenth century, the bureaucratic form was applied to the newly emerging industrial organizations as well as to government, and since that time, bureaucratization has spread to all forms of social life.

In the patrimonial societies of the ancient Near East, medieval Europe, and China from the seventh century until modern times, education was the privilege of a small group, who were often perceived as possessing magical powers along with their official positions. The focus of formal education was upon learning the rules of "correct" behavior—including respect for and obedience to elders and superiors—rather than upon the acquisition of practically useful knowledge (the latter was incorporated into the training of other persons at lower levels of the society). Examinations tested whether the candidate was thoroughly familiar with the classical literature and had acquired ways of thought and a code of conduct based on the classics.

In the feudal societies of Europe, elite education emphasized the heroic virtues and sense of honor. These often were acquired through participation in ritualistic games such as tournaments—an early form of "learning by doing." The feudal virtues stressed, in Weber's view, a "studied opposition to the matter-of-fact attitude and to business routine."

In industrial and industrializing societies, advancement, both within and outside of the educational system, is via merit (in particular, by performance on examinations or by acquiring diplomas or certificates) rather than via social position or privilege. Scientific and technical expertise is more highly valued than knowledge of classical literature and manners. "The expert, not the cultivated man or the hero is the educational ideal of a bureaucratic age" (Weber, 1958: 240ff). As in patrimonial China, social status depends upon both educational qualifications and governmental office; but the criteria for success in the bureaucratic system are technical rather than humanistic.[1]

The structural specifics of the bureaucratic model of the school were spelled out in greater detail in later sociological analyses, in particular in Bidwell's analysis of the school as a formal organization. Bidwell points to the following characteristics of modern school systems that are consistent with the bureaucratic model:

1. a functional division of labor (for instance, the allocation of instructional and coordinative tasks to the roles of teacher and administrator)

2. the definition of staff roles as offices, that is, in terms of recruitment according to merit and competence, legally based tenure, functional specificity of performance, and universalistic, affectively neutral interaction with clients
3. a hierarchical ordering of offices, providing an authority structure based on the legally defined and circumscribed power of officers and regularized lines of communication
4. operation according to rules of procedure, which set limits to the discretionary performance of officers by specifying both the aims and modes of official action (Bidwell, 1965: 974)

Bidwell also concludes, however, that on each characteristic the school situation represents a modification of the pure bureaucratic model. As we shall see in the next chapter, recruitment and training of teachers differ from other professions, partly because there is no comprehensive body of knowledge and skills that all teachers can be taught and on which they can be evaluated. The affectively neutral or impersonal relationships characteristic of bureaucratic interaction certainly do not characterize most nursery school and elementary school classrooms. And the self-contained classroom within which many teachers operate permits more discretion and more diversity of procedures than the ideal-typical bureaucratic setting. Finally, empirical studies have revealed considerable variation among schools in the extent to which they adhere to the bureaucratic model. For example, in a study of St. Louis elementary and secondary schools, which will be discussed in more detail later in this chapter, Moeller (1968) was able to select schools located from one end to the other on an index of bureaucratization based upon the following eight characteristics: (1) uniform course of study, (2) communication through established channels, (3) uniform hiring and firing procedures, (4) secure tenure for nonteaching personnel, (5) explicit statement of school policies, (6) clearly delimited areas of responsibility, (7) specific lines of authority, and (8) standard salary policies for new teachers.

The hierarchical ordering of offices in the school is indicated in Exhibit 7–1. The pyramid form was chosen in preference to the organization chart form, commonly used to illustrate the structure of bureaucratic institutions, because, while it oversimplifies in certain respects, it shows the relative quantitative strength as well as the relative positions of the roles. The role hierarchy begins with a single or small set of administrative roles at the top of the pyramid, moves down through several sets of adult roles, each set larger than the one just above it, to the majority group of students at the base. Not included in Exhibit 7–1 are clerical and custodial roles, which have to do with the organizational and physical maintenance rather than the educational functions of the school. (For a description of this vertically arranged hierarchy in a single high school, see Cusick, 1973.)

The remainder of this chapter will be devoted to a discussion of the roles comprising the school educational system. Since the teacher role will be considered in detail in the context of the classroom situation (in Chapter 8), and the student role considered both in Chapter 8 and in an entire chapter devoted to the student

Exhibit 7–1
The Role Structure of the School

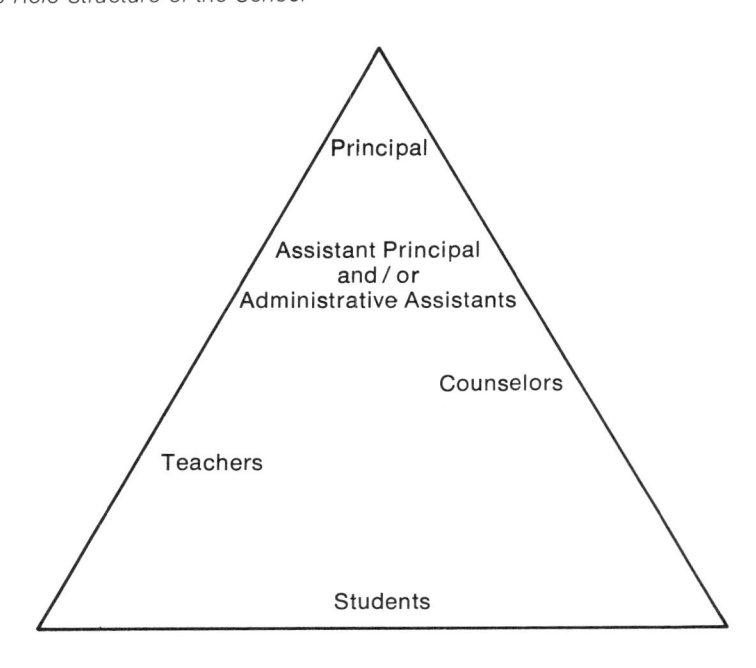

```
                    Principal
              Assistant Principal
                   and / or
            Administrative Assistants
                              Counselors
         Teachers

                    Students
```

peer group (Chapter 11), we shall here focus upon the positions of teacher and student in the role hierarchy of the school as a social system.

The Principal

At the top of the role hierarchy is the principal, the "boss" of the school. His or her duties encompass the general management of the school and its instructional program, dealing with students and teachers, and maintaining relations with social groups and systems outside of the school, both professional (superiors in the "central office") and nonprofessional (parents and community-interest groups). Seymour Sarason, who as Director of the Yale Psycho-Educational Clinic was involved in a long-term research-consultation project in the New Haven public schools, concluded that although the principal role is a pivotal one, relating both to the school as a social system and to life in the classroom, "neither by previous experience nor formal training nor the processes of selection is the principal prepared for the requirements of leadership and the inevitable conflicts and problems that beset a leader" (Sarason, 1971: 131). Principals are recruited almost exclusively from the teaching ranks, and it is commonly held that without sustained experience in managing a classroom, one can understand neither the specific goals and problems of the classroom teacher nor the general goals and problems of the school as a system. Sarason argues that, on the contrary, years of working with children in the small, autonomous world of the self-contained classroom provides little preparation for the visibility and accessibility of the principal's office and the varied and complex relationships in which the occupant of the office must engage. That the principal is under a great deal of pressure because of the broad scope of the role is a recurring theme of the National Principalship Study, a survey of principals, their administrative superiors, and a sample of teachers from 490 elementary and secondary schools in forty-one large American cities, conducted by Neal Gross and a large group of Harvard research colleagues. Data were collected in four-hour interviews, supplemented with extensive written questionnaires. At least half of the principal respondents reported exposure to each of forty potential conflict items in the questionnaire, with the conflicting demands of teachers and parents being the greatest source of pressures. Over half said they worked an average of two or more nights a week in addition to their regular workday.

Further evidence of conflicting pressures is presented in a study of Oregon principals (McAbee, 1958) that compares respondents' actual use of their time with their opinions on how their time *should* be spent. On the average, the 204 principals in the sample thought they should spend about 13 percent of their time on routine office work; in fact, they spent an average of 22.5 percent of their time at this type of task. Conversely, the type of activity to which they felt they should devote the most time—supervision of teachers and improvement of instruction, 22 percent—actually received about half that much time. In other words, practical realities force many principals to allocate their time in a way that is inconsistent with their own role expectations.

Although nearly all principals are former teachers, they do not constitute a representative sampling of teachers. Although they are similar to teachers as a whole in socioeconomic origins and religious affiliation, they are more likely to be male (about half the elementary principals in the National Principalship sample, as compared with less than one-fifth of the teachers. A study by the National Association of Secondary School Principals showed that in the mid-1970s, 93 percent of all U.S. high school principals were men, up from 89 percent in 1965). They are also more likely to be older, with more years of teaching experience, and to be white (and teachers themselves are more likely to be white than their students). In the National Principalship Study all eight schools with all-white faculties had white principals; all eight schools with all nonwhite faculties had nonwhite principals; nearly all of the fourteen nonwhite principals were in schools where over 80 percent of the teachers were nonwhite; and all of the nonwhite principals were in lower-SES schools.

Do the characteristics and behavior of the principal have any impact on student productivity? In the National Principalship Study, a measure of principal efficiency, the EPL (Executive Professional Leadership), was computed from the ratings given to each principal by a subsample of the teachers in his or her school on eighteen kinds of behavior that included: giving teachers the feeling that their work is an important activity, getting teachers to upgrade their performance standards in their classes, and maximizing the different skills found in the faculty.

The data analysis showed a strong positive correlation between the EPL scores and teacher morale, which was in turn related to teacher performance. (Items in the Teacher Performance Scale included the estimated percentage of coteachers who "do textbook teaching only," who "do everything possible to motivate their students," and who "try new teaching methods.") The relationship between principal's adequacy and teachers' performance, both as defined by the teachers, virtually disappeared when teacher morale was controlled, suggesting that teacher morale may intervene and account for the relationship between EPL and teachers' professional performance.

Student performance in this study was measured by teacher perception of the overall achievement level in the school, including estimates of the percentage of the student body who were or were not mastering subject matter and skills, displaying interest in academic achievement, and working up to their intellectual capacities. Gross and Herriott found that the relationship between principal and student behaviors was initially smaller than those between principal and teacher measures, and that it decreased with the addition of every control variable. Further analyses, indicated that for any level of principal's EPL and parental income level, the latter always explained a much greater amount of the variation in student behavior, and that the EPL variable had a consistent relationship with academic performance only in the lowest income schools (where, presumably, weak parental influence by another adult role). The relationships of student academic performance with the two teacher variables were, on the other hand, fairly substantial (.35 with teacher performance and .39 with teacher morale, *after* removing the effects of students' family income).

What the analysis as a whole suggests is a chain type of relationships within the school, in keeping with the hierarchical position of the roles. While the principal's behavior has little direct effect upon students' academic performance when other variables are controlled, "both teachers' performance and morale *may* serve as links in a causal chain between the EPL of principals and the performance of their pupils" (Gross and Herriott, 1965: 57). To put it another way, the principal's impact upon student behavior is not a function of his or her interpersonal relations with the students themselves, but rather of his or her relationships with the teachers, who do have a direct impact upon student performance and whose behavior is affected by their confidence in and interpersonal relationships with their principal.

A recent, in-depth study of twenty-two elementary schools participating in a national evaluation whose purpose was to identify school factors related to school success in raising reading and math achievement of disadvantaged and low-achieving students found consistent relationships between a school's success and some aspects of school management (Wellisch *et al.*, 1978). A school was classified as successful if at least two grades gained in national percentile standing in at least one of the two subject areas and at least one grade gained in the other subject area. Data on each school were collected by two-person teams, who administered questionnaires and interviews to principals and teachers, as well as recorded observations in the field.

Three characteristics of principals were examined: (1) how strongly administrators felt about instruction, (2) whether they communicated their ideas concerning instruction, and (3) the extent to which they assumed responsibility for instruction. On each of these characteristics and on an index of administrative leadership combining the three, there were statistically significant differences between the nine schools classified as successful and the thirteen classified as nonsuccessful. The successful schools were also more likely to be characterized by coordinated instructional programs and by a distinct emphasis upon academic standards (for example, not automatically promoting students who did not meet academic standards). In sum, the successful schools were more likely to be led by principals

> who felt strongly about instruction and assumed relatively more responsibility for instruction-related tasks such as selecting basic instructional materials and planning and evaluating programs for the entire school. These leadership qualities were recognized and reported by teachers, which no doubt reflects the fact that effective administrators also communicated their views concerning instruction to teachers. (Wellisch et al., 1978: 219)

The Teachers

Henry Adams is credited with saying that no one can be a teacher for ten years and remain fit for anything else. Since Adam's time a number of works have dealt with the dilemmas of teacher status. Considerable research has been done on the kind of person who goes into teaching. Most studies indicate that teachers tend to be of predominantly middle-American family background, to be disproportionately female and white, and to have less outstanding academic records in college than students going into other professions (for a profile of teachers' backgrounds, see, for example, Brookover and Erickson, 1975: Chapter 9). This means that there is general teacher-student status congruency in schools of middle-range SES, but that teachers in schools of high SES are apt to be of lower status than their pupils, and teachers in low-SES schools are apt to be of higher status than their pupils (although teachers in higher-SES schools were also of slightly higher social origins than teachers in lower-SES schools). There is also a tendency for the proportion of nonwhite students to exceed the proportion of nonwhite teachers, but as in the case of SES, the incongruency is greatest at the lowest-SES schools. Thus schools with a high proportion of students from low-SES families may have some rather special problems with respect to the teacher-student relationship.

The relatively low status of teachers in the school-role hierarchy gives them little control over their working conditions.

> They have little control over the subjects to be taught; the materials to be used; the criteria for deciding who should be admitted, retained, and graduated . . . the qualifications for teacher training; the forms to be used in reporting pupil progress; school boundary lines and the criteria for permitting students to attend; and other matters that affect teaching. (Corwin, 1965: 241)

The teacher's relationship with the principal is an ambiguous one. On the one hand, the teacher is dependent upon the principal and/or other administrators in much the same way as the student is dependent upon the teacher—as judge (the principal is generally in charge of teacher evaluation) and dispenser of rewards and punishments (assignment to classes and recommendations for retention and promotion). On the other hand, teachers as a group have a direct effect upon the principal's behavior.

> Although the teachers are subordinate to the principal in the organization, they wield powerful sanctions. A principal who fails to meet the expectations of a majority of his teachers may find his authority severely undermined, if not openly flouted. Many teachers have tenure and can be dismissed or transferred only with difficulty. . . . At the secondary level the teacher is also a specialist in subject matter, often in an area unfamiliar to the principal. Lacking control in technical matters, the principal's authority is weakened and circumscribed. The "technical freedom" may exist even at the elementary level, since many elementary school principals have not taught at this level . . .
>
> An additional element of strength in the teacher's position is the definition of his role as a professional one. The control over professionals in a formal organization is a delicate matter, even more so than the control over technical specialists. To the extent that the principal accepts the teacher as a professional person, he must also accept restrictions on his own authority. (Dodd, 1965: 3.12–3.13)

The imbalance of power and influence in the teacher-principal relationship is hardly conducive to free and frank interpersonal communication, and Sarason noted a tendency to deal with this imbalance by minimizing contact. In the several New Haven elementary schools in which he observed, Sarason found that the average frequency of appearance of the principal in a classroom during a two-week period was between one and two times, with the duration of such appearances between two and ten minutes. In high schools, such visits were even rarer. In a majority of cases, there was no subsequent communication after a visit, and even when there was communication, few teachers stated that the communication was helpful (Sarason, 1971: 126).

Examination of the reward system for teachers reveals that teachers are for the most part not rewarded for increasing their students' learning. Pay raises are given for years of service rather than evidence of student improvement, or for obtaining additional course credits at a teachers' college or university department of education (shown in the Coleman report to be relatively unrelated to student in-school achievement). Teachers who experiment with new teaching materials usually do so on their own time and are seldom rewarded for even successful results. Of course, the reward of greater interest or achievement among their students can be a powerful inducement for many teachers, but the point is that the school system provides no formal means of recognizing this kind of activity. In fact, teachers who substitute materials of their own for the regular syllabus run the risk of being reprimanded or even losing their jobs, as the recent memoirs of several classroom teachers testify (Holt, 1964; Kohl, 1967; Herndon, 1968). A sociologist who was a participant-observer in a high school concluded that schools had little use for teachers who were either very scholarly or very critical, and that the social structure of schools places as many constraints upon teachers as upon students. "If a teacher wants to be different, there are a large number of barriers to obstruct him. And even those that begin their teaching careers by wanting to become different may become discouraged, accept the organizational constraints as unavoidable, even necessary, and let those demands define their behavior" (Cusick, 1973: 39).

During the past decade, the efforts of American teachers to improve their working conditions and job security have also been adversely affected by socioeconomic conditions in the larger society, in particular by the economic recession and the declining birth rate. By 1976, the supply of newly qualified teachers exceeded demand by about eighty thousand (National Center for Education Statistics, 1978: 177), an imbalance that put teaching in the category of a declining occupation and undoubtedly contributes to feelings of stress among individual teachers.

In Part Two, we saw that a sense of control of one's destiny was an important factor in a student's self-image and academic success. Moeller's study, introduced earlier in this chapter, focuses upon the relationship between the extent of school bureaucratization and the teacher's sense of ability to influence the organizational forces that shape his or her occupational destiny. Moeller's hypothesis is that "the general level of sense of power in a school system varies inversely to the degree of bureaucratization in that system" (Moeller, 1968: 238).

The study sample consisted of twenty elementary and twenty secondary teachers from each of twenty selected school systems in the St. Louis metropolitan area. Each of the twenty schools was rated by several judges on the eight characteristics listed on page 131 of this chapter, and each was given a bureaucratization score based upon how many of these eight characteristics applied. The teachers' sense of power was measured by a six-item scale based upon responses to statements like the following: "In the school system where I work, a teacher has little to say about important system-wide policies relating to teaching."

The empirical results showed no support for Moeller's original hypothesis. Contrary to his expectations, teachers in bureaucratic systems tested significantly higher in sense of power. In an effort to understand these unexpected findings, Moeller examined the effects of some other variables upon sense of control. Regardless of the structure of the school system, strong sense of control was positively related to: having a position of authority within the school; having organizational ties outside school but within the profession (say, membership in a teachers' union); coming from a family with relatively high occupational status; being male; and having taught more than three years. It was negatively related to working in a school system whose superintendent exercised restrictive or oppressive authority.

An additional variable that was related to sense of control and also interactively related to the degree-of-bureaucratization variable was *particularism* in the administrator-teacher relationship, defined as the extent to which school officials interacted with teachers in a personal, as opposed to an impartial, manner.

Particularism was more prevalent in low bureaucratic systems, but teachers in highly bureaucratized systems who *did* have strong personal ties with administrators tested significantly higher in sense of power than those without such ties, while there was no such relationship in the low bureaucratic systems. As the author sees it, in a nonbureaucratic system, close, informal relationships are more common and nearly everyone has access to the administrators: "This, in effect, tends to devalue this avenue, for if everyone has access, then all should benefit equally" (Moeller, 1968: 249).

The final portion of Moeller's paper is devoted to interpreting the unexpected finding that the apparently more rigid policy of the bureaucratic school enhances rather than reduces the teacher's sense of control. He concludes that one of his original assumptions about the bureaucracy dimension was incorrect; while he perceived low bureaucratization as promoting the personal and professional autonomy of the teacher, these teachers saw it as reflecting a lack of order and predictability.

> Without the stabilizing benefit of a comprehensive and uniform written set of rules for the school system, many decisions arise for which adequate policy is unavailable. This, it would seem, leads teachers in the low bureaucratic systems to be uncertain as to such decisions and the element of unpredictability inherent in the system tends to abrogate their sense of power . . .
>
> In systems characterized by firm policy, we may postulate that teachers' knowledge of that policy is, in itself, a form of power. When policy is applicable to all, then any individual who knows the rules by which the system is governed is able to predict how any particular situation will be handled. This factor enables the teachers in the bureaucratic school systems, by the expedient of learning the rules, to anticipate how the administration will act in most problems confronting it. More importantly, knowledge of policy enables teachers to know the most effective course of action to take in order to influence the policy-maker. (Moeller, 1968: 248–249)

This theme is echoed in a study of 115 new teachers in a large California school district (Edgar and Warren, 1969), which found that while autonomy was desired in some areas (curriculum content and teaching methods), a common source of dissatisfaction was lack of sufficient administrative structure and guidance in such areas as discipline and clerical tasks.

> It is further concluded that the usual unitary approach to the study of "autonomy" may be misleading and that the distinction between active and inert tasks, delegation versus direction, authority rights and legitimacy feelings are more promising research tools than the broader and ambiguous concepts of professionalism and bureaucracy. (Edgar and Warren, 1969: 399)

It should be noted that neither of these studies includes any measures of student performance. While we are making an assumption that teacher sense of control is related to classroom performance and thus to student learning (an assumption that is to some degree supported by the Gross and Herriott model), this assumption is not directly tested in the Moeller or the Edgar-Warren study.

Perhaps not surprisingly, turnover rates within the occupation of teaching are high. Besides leaving teaching altogether, two alternative strategies for dealing with the strains and inconsistencies of the teacher's role are the formation of informal faculty peer groups within the school and involvement in formal professional teachers' organizations and activities outside of the school. Teacher colleague groups have so far received little systematic research attention, although participant observers in schools have often described the faculty room as a refuge for teachers whenever they can escape from their classrooms, where they can engage in activities, such as smoking and drinking coffee, that are generally forbidden elsewhere in the school, and gossip about students and school personnel not present.[2] While a faculty room is an almost universal feature of American schools, some observers question whether it symbolizes any real degree of teacher solidarity. They claim that public school teachers "are characterized less by solidarity and viable colleague controls than by isolation from colleagues and sentiments favoring personal autonomy in the classroom," a consequence of a "fragmentary work structure that minimizes formal and informal interaction with fellow teachers" (Bidwell, 1969: 1252). Definite conclusions about the nature and strength of teacher peer groups must, however, wait upon further empirical research.

The second alternative is participation in formal teachers' organizations. The last few years have been marked by increased unionization of educational personnel, with bargaining arrangements that determine benefits, policies, and practices at the level of an entire school system. Membership in the National Education Association is now over two million, and the combined membership of the National Education Association and the American Federation of Teachers is greater than membership in either the Teamsters' or the Auto Workers' unions (National Center for Education Statistics, 1978: 180). Militant forms of collective behavior have also increased markedly. Until 1966, there were fewer than ten work stoppages a year, involving no more than twenty thousand teachers. Beginning in 1966, the number of stoppages, the number of teachers involved, and the amount of time involved in strikes jumped sharply, reaching a high of 218 stoppages involving 182,000 teachers in 1975 (National Center for Education Statistics, 1978: 182).

Whether increased teacher activism and increased organization across school boundaries will have positive effects upon teachers' classroom competence is still an unanswered question. Proponents of unionization argue that by improving the working conditions and image of teaching and giving teachers a greater share in making the decisions about how schools are run, unionization will both improve the performance of persons already in the profession and attract more able teachers in the future. It is difficult to evaluate this argument in the absence of more empirical evidence. For example, an annotated bibliography of over two hundred references on teacher unionization and educational negotiation (Murphy, 1973) includes no studies linking increased professionalism and activism with changes in classroom behavior. Other observers have predicted that to the extent that collective behavior by teachers focuses on higher salaries, shorter working hours, and other benefits to themselves, its impact upon learning will be slight, and it may have negative effects upon the public image of teachers as hard-working people selflessly dedicated to children's best interests. It may also lead to higher expectations for teacher performance and more rigorous public scrutiny of the results (Lortie, 1975: Chapter 9). Recent demands for teacher and school accountability seem a trend in this direction.

Special Services Personnel

A relatively new and still ambiguous role in many schools is that played by counselors and other special-services personnel. During one week, Sarason counted ninety-three different people not counting the regular full-time staff who performed some special service in a single New Haven school.

> School psychologists, psychiatrists, and social workers, remedial reading teachers, speech and hearing specialists, special class supervisors, curriculum supervisors, representatives from different social agencies, a wide assortment of volunteers, class mothers, teachers' aides—these are only some of the special services that are represented in a school. . . . The fact that so many different people come into the schools bears witness to at least two things: there are problems in the school, and the usual personnel cannot, or have not been able to, resolve them. (Sarason, 1971: 127)

Some of these personnel are full-time employees of a school or school system, others are brought in on a temporary or part-time basis. The largest group of full-time persons are counselors, now over thirty-two thousand in number, whose training and credentials are generally different from those of regular classroom teachers. The role is of interest here because it seems to be emerging as the authority for defining the child's capacities, deciding whether or not his or her achievement and behavior are satisfactory, and determining his or her educational, and even occupational future (including what course of study to follow, whether to apply for college, what careers to aim for). The growing power of the counselor with respect to differentiating the student population is a consequence of two trends:

the increasing complexity of the larger society, which means among other things that families no longer can provide occupational training, or even appropriate advice. Lower-SES parents can seldom guide even a talented child along the tortuous path to upward mobility, and, to a growing degree, being middle-SES no longer assures automatic acceptance into the more prestigious educational and occupational positions

the increasing specialization within the school, such that differentiation of students is no longer done via informal decisions of the principal and teachers but is a separate task assigned to a special role

The major proponents of this view of the counselor are Cicourel and Kitsuse (1963), who claim that parental status and peer group climate are no longer the only major determinants of student aspirations and achievements, and that "the distribution of students in such categories as college-qualified and non-college-qualified is to a large extent characteristic of the administrative organization of the high school and therefore can be explained in terms of that organization" (Cicourel and Kitsuse, 1963: 6–7). In the upper-income suburban school studied by Cicourel and Kitsuse, the counselors were responsible not only for administering standard ability and achievement tests, but also for deciding whether a student was achieving at a satisfactory level and what education program he or she should be assigned in the future. In the substantial number of cases in which there was discrepancy between tested ability and school achievement, the counselor had to make a judgment about the student's achievement type. From the data gathered in interviews with students and counselors, the authors conclude that these judgments were typically made under pressure of time and were weighted by the counselor's own biases. For example, out of a sample of eighty students, all but one classified by the counselor in the brightest achievement category also were indentified by the counselor as being in the highest social class attending the school. As the authors conclude:

> Our materials suggest that the counselor's achievement-type classification of students is a product of a subtle fusion of "rational" and common-sense judgment. Belonging to the "in-group" may be given greater weight than grade-point average in classifying a student as an "excellent" student, or "getting into a lot of trouble" may be more important than "performing up to ability level" in deciding that a student is an "underachiever." (Cicourel and Kitsuse, 1963: 71)

Although the counselor is gaining ever more power over the lives of students, there is also evidence that counseling services are not distributed equitably to the student body. Studies by Armor (1969) and by Weinberg and Skager (1966) showed a relationship between the extent of utilization of career guidance services by high school students and their family and school status. Students from middle- and upper-SES families, students in college preparatory courses, and students with high extracurricular participation were more likely to have discussed their future plans with a counselor; virtually none of the students who were from the lowest-status families or who admitted to having been in some kind of trouble with the law had discussed their problems or plans with a counselor. Thus, "counselors are seeing, generally, the students who need help less. For counseling programs established on a self-referral basis, the students who may require assistance most may be using the facilities least" (Armor, 1969: 132). The fact that counselors were not communicating effectively with many students also was indicated by the large number of students who planned to go on to college but were not in the college prep program and/or were in the lower quarter of their class academically. Moreover, the proportion of students in this category did not substantially decrease if the student had gone to see a counselor (McNeely and Buck, 1967). In sum, there is a discrepancy between reality and aspiration for many students, and counselors do not seem to be clarifying the situation for many such students.[3]

The proliferation of part-time specialists not only makes school organization charts more complicated, but may also be a source of additional tension and conflict for both principals and teachers. The very presence of outside experts is evidence that the regular staff cannot "do the job" themselves. At the same time they are perceived as transients, whose expertise does not include the intimate knowledge of a school and its occupants supposedly possessed by the full-time personnel. The presence of outsiders may cause further strains in the already uneasy relationship between principal and teachers. The nature of most problems referred to specialists involves them with classroom teachers, they are defined as having expertise not possessed by the principal, yet the latter is ultimately responsible for what goes on in the school and the success and failure of its students. Sarason observed that: "Messy triangular relationships are by no means infrequent, and it is not unusual for the teacher to feel caught in the cross-fire" (Sarason, 1971: 128).

The Students

Since there will be a detailed consideration of the student role and the student peer group in later chapters, here we shall only review the characteristics of the student body that describe its position in the total school role structure.

First, although students constitute the majority group in the school, they are at the bottom of the role hierarchy, and they are the only members of the system who have no choice about being there—at least until the legal school-leaving age, which is set by adults.

Second, although students are the school's "clients," and the major school decisions are made on the grounds of "the welfare of the students," they have little say in these decisions. What is "good" for students is "defined by the adults (teacher, principal, or parent), and fulfillment of the student's expectations is not a necessary part of his welfare" (Dodd, 1965: 3.12).

Third, the increased role specialization in schools, which has produced new staff roles in addition to making the traditional ones more "professionalized," probably has contributed to increased separation of students from staff, and also may have intensified the development of distinct student peer groups with their own activities and norms, which are not always congruent with those of the formal learning system.

While students are often referred to as a kind of undifferentiated mass, in most Western school systems students are differentiated both vertically (by age) and horizontally (usually by ability). As we saw in Chapter 1, age grouping in schools is a fairly recent phenomenon. Joseph Kett, a social historian who has studied the changing structure of American schools and changing norms pertaining to childhood and youth, found that until well into the nineteenth century, schools were often located in barns or private homes with students of all ages and achievement levels mixed together. Kett traces the emergence in the nineteenth century of a new "culture of childhood," which "demanded a segregation of children from adults in asylum-like institutions called schools," although he notes that the process of age gradation was "not altogether smooth; in the 1880s the Boston school superintendent still found it necessary to complain about the large number of 16- and 17-year olds still in grammar school. But by then, their presence was recognized as anomalous" (Kett, 1976: 222).

The current vertical organization of American schools, with its division into preschool, elementary school, junior and senior high school, and higher education has been criticized on the grounds that it fosters age segregation among students, that it forces children of very different abilities and interests to work at the same activities and at the same pace, and that the transitions from one level to the next are often difficult. Individualized instruction is in part a response to the fact that "there are very few fourth-grade children in a so-called fourth-grade class when a fourth-grade child is defined as one who achieves at fourth-grade level in all subjects at approximately the mid-point of the school year" (Goodlad, 1966: 34). The conventional elementary, junior high, senior high structure is being broken down in many school districts by court-ordered desegregation programs that group all students in the district who are in two or three contiguous classes (for example, all fifth and sixth graders or all ninth and tenth graders) in a single school. Such reorganizations are changing the social class and ethnic composition of many schools, but may at the same time be reinforcing age grouping and age segregation. The effects of two different modes of vertical organization (K–8 schools and K–6 schools with associated junior high schools) on the transition into seventh grade were recently studied by Blyth, Simmons, and Bush (1978), who found that seventh graders in the K–8 systems, by comparison with those who went on to a junior high, appeared to be less academically oriented, more influenced by their peers (since they dated more), more likely to be robbed, assaulted, or otherwise victimized by other students in their school, and more eager to be with their class friends. However, they also "became increasingly more positive about themselves, participated more in activities, and felt less anonymous in their school environment" than seventh graders who went into a junior high (Blyth, Simmons, and Bush, 1978: 159).

Ability tracking, the major mode of *horizontal* differentiation within schools, is strongly correlated with students' race and SES. It has been criticized because there is little evidence of learning gains associated with tracking, and because it produces a stratification system with stigmatizing effects for those at the lower levels. A study of the antecedents and consequences of curriculum tracking, using longitudinal survey data from a national sample of students contacted in the ninth, eleventh, and twelfth grades, concluded that tracking affects educational aspirations and achievement, and that in a variety of ways, "sorting processes within high school may substantially affect later socioeconomic attainments" (Alexander, Cook and McDill, 1978: 62).

Research by Rosenbaum (1975) indicates that even within a single school students in different tracks may have very different experiences and develop very different views about school and about themselves. In a high school with a socially homogeneous student population (about 80 percent from white, lower-middle- or working-class families) and a highly stratified tracking system, Rosenbaum found a strong relationship between track and IQ change that was independent of the initial level of IQ and of sex, social class, teacher recommendation, and SCAT (School and College Ability Test) verbal and math scores. As Rosenbaum sees it, tracking is both a form of stratification and a form of socialization of individuals relative to the group as a whole. His interpretation is that college tracks lead to *differentiating* processes, in which students are encouraged to be self-directed and to give expression to their interests and abilities, while noncollege tracks lead to *homogenizing* processes, in which students are offered a narrower range of courses and opportunities (in school and after graduation), less is expected of them by teachers, and their class peers are less stimulating intellectually and motivationally. Rosenbaum's findings suggest that different socialization processes occur in the upper and lower tracks, so that students of otherwise similar characteristics come to feel differently about themselves and their school experience.

Unfortunately, changes in either the vertical or horizontal organization of schools are seldom based upon empirical research on the impacts of alternative arrangement on students, including how they cope with transitions from one school to another.

Conclusions

In this part of the book (Chapters 7 through 11) we shall examine explanations for differences in learning based upon the characteristics of schools and their component elements, that is, the cells in the right-hand column of Exhibit 2–1.

In this chapter, we have tried to describe the school as sociologists conceptualize it, as a complex formal organization and behavior system. Like bureaucratic structures in general, the school has a hierarchical role structure. Like other service institutions, the school has a more-or-less continuous problem of capturing and maintaining the involvement of its large group of clients (the students) and of maintaining discipline—although this is often under the guise of what is good for the student.

At the top of the hierarchy are the principals, who usually come to this role by way of teacher education and classroom experience but who are not typical of teachers in general. They are both superordinate to and dependent upon the teachers in their schools, and their impact upon students is mainly indirect, through the direct effect of their personalities and behavior upon teacher morale and competence.

The teachers' position in the school is an inconsistent one. On the one hand, they are in sole command of the classroom; on the other hand, they lack the salary, prestige, and decision-making power of many other professionals. Teachers' lack of autonomy and their discontent with their position may partially explain what often seems to be an overemphasis upon classroom authority and resistance to any new teaching methods that appear to threaten such authority. (Of course, these are also explained by the schoolwide focus upon the control aspects of system maintenance, to the extent that teachers who are suspected of less-than-tight control of their classes are automatically defined as incompetent.)

In the 1960s, an entire literature grew up around the theme that students are exploited by the very institution that was designed to serve them (for example, the work of radical critics like Holt, Kohl, Kozol, Herndon, Dennison, and Farber). While this work is mainly evocative rather than grounded in systematic empirical research, its arguments are consistent with sociological research findings that the students' own interests and expectations have little force in shaping the organization and the curriculum of most schools. Moreover, their classification as successes or failures and the other decisions that most vitally affect their future lives are increasingly concentrated in the hands of specialists whose judgments often are made with limited information and time and are weighted heavily by social and personal biases. The proliferation of specialists may also add to the complexity of the principal and teacher roles and increase the conflicts between them.

In the next chapter, we shall focus upon the social structure of the classroom, where the business of learning is presumably carried out, and in subsequent chapters, we shall try to identify those characteristics of classrooms and of schools as a whole that explain their "productivity" or effectiveness as learning environments.

Notes

1. Excerpts from Weber's writing on education are included in the collection of his essays edited by Gerth and Mills (1958). A brief discussion of Weber's career and his conceptualization of bureaucracy can be found in Collins and Makowsky (1978).

2. To those familiar with the work of Irving Goffman, faculty room activities thus fall into the category of behavior that Goffman terms *backstage:* "The backstage language consists of reciprocal first-naming, co-operative decision-making, profanity, open sexual remarks, elaborate griping, smoking, rough informal dress, 'sloppy' sitting and standing posture, use of dialect or substandard speech, mumbling and shouting, playful aggressivity and 'kidding,' inconsiderateness for the other in minor but potentially symbolic acts, minor physical self-involvements such as humming, whistling, chewing, nibbling, belching, and flatulence. The frontstage behavior language can be taken as the absence (and in some sense the opposite) of this. In general, then, backstage conduct is one which allows minor acts which might easily be taken as symbolic of intimacy and disrespect for others present" (Goffman, 1959: 128).

3. Armor suggests that counselor effectiveness may be hampered by the fact that the professional role was developed, in the early part of this century, "before the institutionalization and codification of the knowledge base." He would include in this base "detailed knowledge of the occupational structure and of the special requirements for each vocation," tools for the "assessment of such individual characteristics as may be required for each vocation (or class of vocations)," and, more recently, familiarity with colleges and their requirements (Armor, 1969: 45).

Classroom Role Structure and Role Relationships
Chapter 8

Now, the class is a small society. It is therefore both natural and necessary that it have its own morality corresponding to its size, the character of its elements, and its function. Discipline is this morality. . . . On the other hand, the schoolroom society is much closer to the society of adults than it is to that of the family. For, aside from the fact that it is larger, the individuals—teachers and students—who make it up are not brought together by personal feelings or preferences but for altogether general and abstract reasons, that is to say, because of the social functions to be performed by the teacher, and the immature mental condition of the students. For all these reasons, the rule of the classroom cannot bend or give with the same flexibility as that of the family in all kinds and combinations of circumstances. It cannot accommodate itself to given temperaments. . . . It is a first initiation into the austerity of duty. Serious life has now begun. Emile Durkheim

Students have effects on the teacher, who in turn affects the learning of the student. Students have effects on each other; the informal social structure produces differential treatment of students by the teacher. Elizabeth Cohen

During the past decade, interest in the classroom as a social organization has gained impetus from a number of developments in the sociology of education. Two landmark studies, Philip Jackson's *Life in Classrooms* and Robert Dreeben's *On What Is Learned in School,* were published just over a decade ago, and in the intervening years there has been a substantial output of empirical research, using a variety of research techniques, on topics ranging from power relations to peer group interaction, teaching styles, physical arrangements, and classroom social climates.

Interest in research on the classroom has probably been stimulated by the disappointing results of several large-scale surveys on the effects of the school as a whole on student achievement, which led at least one sociologist to propose that "what transpires in the classroom is likely, on *a priori* grounds alone, to be a more salient unit than the school in cognitive development" (Richer, 1975: 388). Actually, some earlier research had already pointed in this direction. For example, in a carefully designed study of the effects of ability grouping upon academic and social success, comparisons of class-average test scores in three subjects showed that, with one exception, the differences between class averages *within* a given ability-grouping pattern were as great or greater than the mean differences *among different ability patterns,* and, moreover, that the between-class differences within individual schools were greater than the range among schools (Goldberg *et al.,* 1966: 61. The findings of this study will be discussed more fully in Chapter 9.) Likewise, in a reanalysis of data from the *Equality of Educational Opportunity* survey comparing the relative influence of desegregation at the level of the school and the classroom, McPartland found that

> it is desegregation at the classroom level which encompasses the factors having important influences on Negro student academic performance. No matter what the racial composition of the school, increases in Negro student achievement accompany increases in the proportion of their classmates who are white. The only students who appear to derive benefit from attendance at mostly white schools are those in predominantly white classes within the school. As far as differences in their achievement are concerned, the students in segregated classes may as well be in segregated schools as desegregated ones. (McPartland, 1967: 5)

Thus both the McPartland and the Goldberg *et al.* studies support the premise that the classroom is of central importance, although McPartland's analysis focuses upon the influence of the students' peers, "who form the immediate environment for an individual," while Goldberg notes two characteristics that vary from class to class: the *syntality* or group personality of the classroom unit and the teacher.

Sociological research on the classroom has also received impetus from radical critics like Holt, Kohl, Kozol, Herndon, and Dennison, who are not sociologists—who are in fact quite hostile to the social sciences as well as the educational "establishment." Based primarily on first-hand accounts of the authors' own classroom experiences, this body of work is highly descriptive, often polemical. However, by postulating as problematic features of school organization that have often been ignored or taken for granted by sociologists, the radical critics offer both a criticism of conventional theories of the classroom and some important insights into the learning process.

The Teacher Role

Teaching has been defined as a series of interactions between someone in the role of teacher and someone in the role of learner, with the explicit goal of changing the learner's cognitive or affective states (Bidwell, 1973). Until the last decade, research on the teacher role focused on the social backgrounds of teachers, with some consideration of the implications of teachers' status for their relationships with students, and largely unsuccessful attempts to identify the personal characteristics of teachers and the teaching styles that explained differential student achievement.

A great deal of effort was expended during the 1940s and early 1950s in devising scales to measure teacher effectiveness. (A number of these are described in reviews by Medley and Mitzel [1963] and Gordon and Adler [1963].) Most of these scales were developed in essentially the same way. Starting with a set of dimensions believed to be related to effectiveness, an observer visited classrooms for short intervals of time, coding the teacher's behavior with respect to the dimensions. Teachers were then designated as "good" or "poor" depending upon their classification on the scale.

Although the content of the scales varied considerably, they shared an almost total lack of relationship to any measure of student achievement. Aside from the ridiculous categories used in many scales (for instance, "good" teachers are more likely to smile and gesture but less likely to snap their fingers or stamp their feet than "poor" teachers), they are based upon a fallacy "which says it is possible to judge a teacher's skill by watching him teach," that an intelligent observer "can recognize good teaching when he sees it" (Medley and Mitzel, 1963: 257).

Among the most influential research studies during the 1940s and 1950s were those on leadership "style." Applied to education, the basic premise was that the teacher's quality as a leader, including how he or she sought to control the classroom situation, determined students' morale and performance. The pioneers in this research were Lewin, Lippitt, and their associates, who in the late 1930s began a series of experiments in which various leadership climates were artificially created.

In one of the best-known experiments, four members of Lewin's research staff were trained in the following three leadership styles:

authoritarian. The general group goals, specific activities, and procedures for carrying them out are all dictated by the leader. However, the leader remains aloof from active participation except when demonstrating or assigning tasks.

democratic. All policies, activities, and work procedures are decided upon by the group as a whole. The leader takes an active part and tries to be a regular group member in spirit without doing too much of the work.

laissez-faire. There is complete freedom for group or individual decision making, with a minimum of participation by the leader.

Each staff member was assigned to a club of ten-year-old boys, ostensibly to direct a variety of craft activities. In addition to selecting the groups so that they were initially comparable in the distribution of several personal and social characteristics, "the factor of personality differences in the boys was controlled by having each group pass through autocracy and then democracy, or vice versa. The factor of leader's personality was controlled by having each of the leaders play the role of autocrat and the role of democratic leader at least once.'' Thus, "every six weeks each group had a new leader with a different technique of leadership, each club having three leaders during the course of the five months of the experimental series'' (Lewin *et al.*, 1939: 271–272, 298).

Discussions of the results of these experiments usually emphasize the higher levels of satisfaction and "group-mindedness" and the lower levels of aggression in the democratic groups (Lewin *et al.*, 1939: White and Lippitt, 1962). Less often reported is the finding that the quality of work produced was greater in the autocratic setting, although activity in this setting requires the presence of the leader—when the autocratic type of leader left the room, output tended to drop off. It is also an interesting and little reported finding that productivity in the laissez-faire setting, in which there was little formal structure and members were free to do as they pleased, went up in the absence of the leader. The authors attributed this to an observed tendency for one of the boys to assume a leadership role when the adult leader was absent. In sum, students may be happier and feel more positive toward the teacher and the other members of the group in a setting in which the adult acts essentially as one of the group and in which decisions are made via group discussion, but they may produce more when their leader tells them what to do and how to do it. And certain learning tasks may be handled effectively by giving students very little direction, forcing them to organize the situation themselves.

Experimental studies testing the Lewin thesis in classroom situations indicate that (1) student productivity is not always greater, or as great, in democratic or "student-centered" classes; and (2) many students feel dissatisfied or anxious in this kind of setting. One review of forty-nine studies reported contradictory results; eleven found greater learning in student-centered groups, thirteen reported no difference, and eight found teacher-centered groups superior (Gordon and Adler, 1963). Another analysis of thirty-four such studies (Stern, 1962) found that of the eighteen in which student reaction was measured, nine were predominantly favorable, four unfavorable, and five mixed. Only two of the studies showed greater gains in cognitive knowledge of the subject matter in the democratic classes, as compared to five in which the cognitive gains were significantly less; in the rest of the studies there was no significant difference between the two types of classes. Some research based on the California F (authoritarianism) scale indicated that the type of student with high authoritarian needs is especially uncomfortable in an informal, equalitarian classroom atmosphere (Stern, 1962: 692–697).

If one can draw any conclusions from the mass of studies carried out during the past twenty-five years, they seem to be limited to the following:

there is no one best type of teacher or teaching for all students, probably not even one best way to teach any given student all subjects

the focus of research should be upon the two-way interpersonal ties and interaction between teacher and student, as opposed to trying to deduce the components of effective teaching by studying the teacher alone some improvement in student performance as well as in the quality of student-teacher relationships might be produced by systematic efforts to match teachers more closely to the types of students and courses that fit their values, needs, and style of teaching

full understanding of effective teacher behavior depends upon a comprehensive theory of the classroom as a social system

More recent research on the teacher role has attempted to identify the distinctive components of teaching as a professional role and the ways in which teacher role behavior is shaped by the design of the educational system.

First, unlike law, medicine, and most other professions, teaching does not have a coherent body of expertise that can be translated into occupational guidelines. Thus, much teaching has an improvisatory quality. A study of fifty teachers identified by their principals as highly successful revealed that these teachers made little use of objective measures of achievement for evidence of their teaching effectiveness, but depended upon often fleeting behavioral cues from students to tell them how well they were doing their jobs (Jackson, 1968: 126).

Second, teaching differs from the more prestigious professions in its patterns of recruitment, training, and career mobility. Because it is an easy-entry but limited-mobility profession, teaching attracts a disproportionate number of late-deciding males for whom it provides a fallback occupation when other plans fail to materialize, and a disproportionate number of females who plan to work for brief or irregular intervals or to combine work with marriage and household responsibilities. Teaching is primarily rewarded not with prestige or financial gain but with psychological gratification, salary increases are generally based upon time on the job and accumulation of course credits rather than "productivity," and career advancement requires the teacher to leave classroom teaching and go into administrative work (Lortie, 1971, 1975; Dreeben, 1970: Chapter 6).

Third, teaching combines intensive and virtually continuous interaction with students and virtual isolation from peers and other adults. Classrooms are crowded places with lots of talk (Jackson estimated that elementary teachers engage in as many as a thousand interpersonal exchanges per day). At the same time, teaching is lonely work compared to occupations with peer work groups and highly developed networks of collegial relationships. Teachers work separately from each other, and while they may talk shop in the teacher's lounge, they learn very little by direct observation about what their colleagues are doing and how well they are doing it (Warren, 1975; Dreeben, 1970: Chapter 3; Sarason, 1971). Thus, "each teacher becomes, in a sense, a solitary craftsman, inventing on his own hook procedures and ways of working that have already been perfected by his colleague down the hall" (Jackson, 1971: 29). Besides preventing the development of strong collegial bonds, the isolation of the classroom may insulate teachers from social-control mechanisms. A study of classrooms in German and American elementary schools (Warren, 1973) concluded that while the classroom was not an impregnable sanctuary, teachers were sheltered from intervention by parents and other citizens as well as from regular observation and evaluation by their superiors.

The Teacher-Student Relationship

Half a century ago, John Dewey asked: "Why is it, in spite of the fact that teaching by pouring in, learning by passive absorption, are universally condemned, that they are still intrenched in practice?" (Dewey, 1928: 46). Philip Jackson (1968) concluded that the three distinguishing features of classroom life are "crowds, praise, and power," and that the most useful quality for a student to possess is patience. By comparison with the teacher role, the student role is characterized by passivity. The "good" student listens to the teacher, follows instructions, does not disturb the class, and is otherwise receptive to *being taught*.

Sociologists have noted that the typical teacher-student relationship is an imbalanced or asymmetrical one. The teacher and student roles differ in:

degree of volunteerism. As Dreeben (1973) points out, teachers are affiliated with schools by hiring, students by conscription.

degree of activity versus passivity. The "good student" role calls for more docility and patience than initiative and self-responsibility (Jackson, 1968; Flanders, 1970). Moore identifies the following role perspectives as available in the classroom: agent, patient, reciprocator, and referee, and argues that teachers monopolize the active roles, leaving the child "to be patient to the acts of agency of the teacher" (Moore, 1969: 586).

power or authority. Teachers are superordinate to students by virtue of their age, training, and control of classroom resources (including rewards and punishments), and one of the most important things students learn in school is how to deal with impersonal authority (Jackson, 1968 and 1971; B. Bloom, 1976).

In the classical view of the classroom, such asymmetries are both inevitable and appropriate. Durkheim claimed that the teacher role was characterized by an "indisputable authority" based upon the teacher's age and a certain moral authority attached to the vocation of teaching. The teacher-student relationship brought together two populations of unequal culture; the teacher was imbued with civilization, the students were subjects to be civilized. Recent research by social historians indicates that at least through the nineteenth century, American schools were designed on a Durkheimian model of order, although the classroom teacher's moral authority was often maintained by corporal punishment and humiliation rather than by the spontaneous acquiescence of students (Finkelstein, 1975).

Durkheim's view of the teacher-student relationship is no longer widely held. Today many sociologists would agree with Dreeben that "when there are substantial inequalities of power between those in authority and those not, and when some number of subordinates are present while preferring to be elsewhere, compliance can become a serious issue, particularly when those in authority do not have at their disposal adequate inducements to make *voluntary* compliance possible" (Dreeben, 1973: 459). The structural defects inherent in the teacher-student relationship were pointed out in Waller's *Sociology of Teaching*, published in 1932 but still one of the most vivid analyses of the social structure of schools.

> The teacher represents the established social order in the school, and his interest is in maintaining that order, whereas pupils have only a negative interest in that feudal superstructure. Teacher and pupil confront each other with attitudes from which the underlying hostility can never be altogether removed. Pupils are the material in which teachers are supposed to produce results. Pupils are human beings striving to realize themselves in their own spontaneous manner, striving to produce their own results in their own way. Each of these hostile parties stands in the way of the other; insofar as the aims of either are realized, it is at the sacrifice of the aims of the other.
>
> Authority is on the side of the teacher. The teacher nearly always wins. In fact, he must win, or he cannot remain a teacher. . . . Conflict between teachers and students therefore passes to the second level. All the externals of conflict and of authority having been settled, the matter chiefly at issue is the meaning of these externals. Whatever the rules that the teacher lays down, the tendency of the pupils is to empty them of meaning. By mechanization of conformity, by "laughing off" the teacher or hating him out of all existence as a person, by taking refuge in self-initiated activities that are always just beyond the teacher's reach, students attempt to neutralize teacher control. (Waller, 1932: 195–196)

Considerable research supports Waller's contention that students are not without resources of their own for coping with the classroom power structure. One student strategy is simply to withdraw. A study in which the activities of high school students were monitored provides some empirical support for the claim of the radical analysts that students are not really "present" during a substantial portion of the time they are in school. A sample of seventy-eight high school students were equipped with electronic paging devices whose signals were scheduled to occur at random intervals during each two-hour period for a week. When signaled, the students recorded where they were, what they were doing, who they were with, and their feelings about the situation (including their degree of concentration). The results showed that the levels of boredom were markedly higher and the levels of concentration markedly lower in the classroom than in any of the other settings where the students spent their time. Indeed, the authors estimated that the students were, on the average, paying attention less than half of the time they were in the classroom (Csikszentmihalyi, Larson, and Prescott, 1977).

A different kind of student response to unwanted teacher demands is to interrupt the classroom proceedings and threaten the teacher-student status differential. Reported instances of violence have been increasing since the late 1960s, and public opinion polls indicate that classroom disorder is perceived by teachers and by students as a major problem (Bayh, 1975; Ritterband and Silberstein, 1973).

A variety of student maneuvers are analyzed in a pair of books by John Holt: *How Children Fail* (1964) and *How Children Learn* (1967). In the following passage, Holt describes the elaborate stratagems employed by one child who figured out that with a student-teacher ratio of over twenty to one, the teacher cannot focus very long on any one student.

> She also knows the teacher's strategy of asking questions of students who seem confused, or not paying attention. She therefore feels safe waving her hand in the air, as if she were bursting to tell the answer, whether she really knows it or not. When someone else answers correctly, she nods her head in emphatic agreement. Sometimes she even adds a comment, though her expression and tone of voice show that she feels this is risky. It is also interesting to note that she does not raise her hand unless there are at least half a dozen other hands up.
>
> Sometimes she gets called on. The question arose the other day, "What is half of forty-eight?" Her hand was up; in the tiniest whisper she said, "twenty-four." I asked her to repeat it. She said, loudly, "I said," then whispered, "twenty-four." I asked her to repeat it again, because many couldn't hear her. Her face showing tension, she said, very loudly, "I said that one half of forty-eight is . . ." and then, very softly, "twenty-four."
>
> Of course, this is a strategy that often pays off. A teacher who asks a question is tuned to the right answer, since it will tell him that his teaching is good and that he can go on to the next topic. (Holt, 1964: 12–13)

The teacher's position may indeed be more vulnerable than the disproportionate authority assigned to it would lead one to believe. As one researcher put it: "Regardless of what may be written into state law or school board regulations, the actual exercise of teacher authority is an uncertain, precarious enterprise" (Wegman, 1976: 77). In a study of high school classrooms, Wegman identified several areas of disciplinary concern, ranging from students' freedom to move about the classroom to the handling of wisecracks, where collective agreements between students and teachers must be reached, often only after extensive negotiation. In a study of classroom management, based upon data from kindergartens, high school classes, and children's summer camps, Kounin (1970) identified a number of teacher strategies that were positively related to student work involvement and negatively related to misbehavior. These included: (1) the teacher explicitly communicating to students that he or she knows what is going on and can identify and stop infractions; (2) attending to multiple intruding events without becoming overly immersed in any one; (3) maintaining a constantly changing flow of activities; and (4) managing recitations in a way that keeps students engaged (for example, by creating uncertainty about the order in which students will be called upon). Kounin also analyzed "desists," or teachers' strategies for stopping misbehavior, and the group effects of such disciplinary actions. He found that effects varied by setting—for example, desists based upon anger produced more effects among kindergartners than among high school students. Among the latter, Kounin found that student reactions to desists were related both to students' motivation to learn and their attitudes toward the teacher.

In sum, while the teacher and student roles are asymmetrical in many respects, most current conceptualizations of teacher-student interaction assume that students and teachers have mutual effects on each other. (This perspective is illustrated by the Cohen quotation at the beginning of this chapter.) Research indicates that teachers and students respond to the classroom role structure in a variety of ways, and that many teachers depend more upon their personal resources than their formal authority in order to gain compliance from students. There is anecdotal evidence that many teachers, especially at the elementary level, have devised ways to soften the dullness and harshness of the daily grind.[1] Alone with their own classes for most of the school day, teachers can if they choose deal with their students in a less impersonal way than the formal dictates of the role structure would indicate, and can also act as a buffer between the students and the more abrasive aspects of the formal school system.

Among the many aspects of teacher-student interaction that appear to affect students' academic attitudes and performance, two have been of special interest to sociologists during the past two decades. One concerns the exchange of *expectations* among teachers and students, and the effects of expectations upon subsequent performance. Research on expectancy effects is based upon the concept of the self-fulfilling prophecy, which is itself based upon a theorem set forth by one of the first American sociologists, W. I. Thomas: If individuals define situations as real, they are real in their consequences.[2] A second aspect of teacher-student interaction is *evaluation*. The continuous, public evaluation that characterizes classroom life has been noted by many observers, and some recent sociological research documents the relationship between the way in which students are evaluated and social background variables such as SES and ethnicity. In the next sections, we shall discuss research on these two topics.

Expectancy Effects

In the mid-1960s, Robert Rosenthal and Lenore Jacobson conducted an important experiment designed to test the proposition that within a given classroom, "those children from whom the teacher expected greater intellectual growth would show such greater growth." The setting for the study was an elementary school in an older section of San Francisco attended mainly by children from lower-SES, but not desperately poor families. About one-sixth of the school's 650 students were of Mexican parentage. Students were organized into three ability tracks, based mainly upon reading performance. The lowest track classes contained disproportionate numbers of Mexican-American and lowest-income children. Another characteristic of the school was the relatively high proportion of transfers; about 30 percent of the school population transferred in or out during a given year.

As is appropriate in a study based upon a single school, Rosenthal and Jacobson make no claims for the representativeness of their sample. Rather, by deliberately choosing a difficult sample—a school with a large proportion of students from subgroups whose school performance is normally lower than the population at large—they make the findings of a limited sample seem more convincing than they might otherwise be.

First, all children in grades one through six were given a nonverbal intelligence test, "disguised as a test designed to predict academic 'blooming' or intellectual gain." In each class about 20 percent of the students, *chosen by means of a table of random numbers,* were assigned to the "experimental" condition. "The names of these children were given to each teacher who was told that their scores on the 'test for intellectual blooming' indicated they would show unusual intellectual gains during the academic year.... The experimental treatment for these children, then, consisted of nothing more than being identified to their teachers as children who would show unusual intellectual gains" (Rosenthal and Jacobson, 1966: 115–116). Eight months later all the children were given the same test again.

Exhibit 8–1 shows the mean gain in IQ points for experiemental and control subjects at each grade level. For the school as a whole, the children from whom the teachers had been led to expect greater gain did show such gain (the difference between experimental and control group was statistically significant at the .02 level). This difference was greatest for the first and second graders; in fact, they accounted for most of the total difference, and the differences were nonexistent or even in the opposite direction for the older children.

In addition to grade level, Rosenthal and Jacobson controlled for ability track, sex, and ethnic group. The tendency was for the middle track—the more "average" children—to benefit most from the experimental treatment, but the differences were not statistically significant. Sex differences were similarly not large or clear. While girls who were expected to show an intellectual spurt had slightly greater gains in total IQ than boys similarly designated, the relationship was complicated in that girls were overrepresented in the higher ability track, and the sex differences were contingent upon the *types* of IQ. Rosenthal and Jacobson's summary of the findings involving subjects' sex was that "girls bloom more in the reasoning sphere of intellectual functioning when some kind of unspecified

Exhibit 8–1
Mean Gains in IQ
in Rosenthal and Jacobson's Experimental and Control Groups

	Controls		Experimentals				
Grade	M	σ	M	σ	Diff.	t	p†
1	12.0	16.6	27.4	12.5	15.4	2.97	.002
2	7.0	10.0	16.5	18.6	9.5	2.28	.02
3	5.0	11.9	5.0	9.3	0.0		
4	2.2	13.4	5.6	11.0	3.4		
5	17.5	13.1	17.4	17.8	−0.1		
6	10.7	10.0	10.0	6.5	−0.7		
Weighted M	8.4*	13.5	12.2**	15.0	3.8	2.15	.02

* Mean number of children per grade= 42.5
** Mean number of children per grade= 10.8
p† one-tailed
Source: From Rosenthal and Jacobson, 1966: 116.

blooming is expected of them. Furthermore, these gains are more likely to occur to a dramatic degree in the lower grades'' (Rosenthal and Jacobson, 1968: 81). In other words, high teacher expectations seem to allow children to increase their potential in the area that is not normally perceived as "natural" to their sex (reasoning for girls, verbal skills for boys), and the younger the child, the greater the chances of affecting these abilities (before the child has been rigidly socialized as to what is appropriate behavior for boys and girls—see Chapter 5).

Among the most interesting findings were those relating to ethnic groups:

> In total IQ, verbal IQ, and especially reasoning IQ, children of the minority group were more advantaged by favorable expectations than were the other children, though the differences were not statistically significant.
>
> For each of the Mexican children the magnitude of expectancy advantage was computed by subtracting from his or her IQ gain the IQ gain made by the children of the control group in his or her classroom. The resulting magnitudes of expectancy advantage were then correlated with the "Mexican-ness" of the children's faces. . . . For total IQ and reasoning IQ, those Mexican boys who looked more Mexican benefitted more from teachers' favorable expectations than did the Mexican boys who looked less Mexican. There is no clear explanation for these findings, but we can speculate that the teachers' pre-experimental expectancies of the more Mexican-looking boys' intellectual performance were probably lowest of all. These children may have had the most to gain by the introduction of a more favorable expectation into the minds of their teachers. (Rosenthal and Jacobson, 1968: 82)

In evaluating the results of Rosenthal and Jacobson's study, the first point is that while the findings are generally supportive of the study's hypothesis, the differences are neither consistently in the direction predicted nor are they very large. We have noted already that in Exhibit 8–1 the difference for the school as a whole is mainly accounted for by large differences in two of the six grades tested. The multivariate analysis suggests complex patterns of interaction among such variables as sex, ability level, ethnicity, and grade in school, with no consistent overall effect of teacher expectations upon all student subgroups. If one takes these various subgroups as replications of the basic experiment, one can say only that the hypothesis is supported in some but not all cases. It should also be noted that in almost all the cases where the difference between experimental and control subjects was significant, the differences were about half a standard deviation or less in magnitude. Such a difference is moderately substantial but not dramatic.

A second type of objection has to do with the authors' choice of measures. The dependent variable, performance on an intelligence test, can be criticized on the grounds that it was a single test and like all single tests limited in its range. It would have been useful to test also some of the more specific learning that took place. (Some data of this sort were undoubtedly available—for instance, results of standard achievement tests or grades in various subjects.)

Another objection about the dependent variable is procedural—that is, that in some cases, especially in the younger classes where the experimental treatment had the greatest effect, the post-test was given by the classroom teacher, who had been subjected to the experimental manipulation and who might thus, consciously or unconsciously, aid the children who were "supposed" to bloom. Rosenthal and Jacobson report that retest results in groups tested by their own teacher did not differ significantly from groups tested by a school administrator who did not know which children were in the experimental group, but still one would like to see further testing controlled for possible teacher effects on the postexperimental instruments (note that this in itself would constitute a further test of the basic Rosenthal-Jacobson hypothesis).

With respect to the experimental variable, the manipulation of the teachers' expectations is dramatic, and the random selection of bloomers by, in a sense, holding constant the idiosyncracies of individual students makes the point that this kind of treatment can produce results with virtually any kind of child and in the absence of any other stimuli to achieve. It does not, however, tell us anything about the normal selection process by which teachers come to hold different expectations for different students. A design alternative would be to manipulate the presentation of students to teachers. Given that certain kinds of children (white, middle-class, suburban) are preferred by many teachers, if one could coach students so that they more closely resembled those youngsters who are favored by the schools, this might lead to teachers responding to these students differently. The success of researchers in prepping children for IQ and achievement tests, job interviews, and so on, an example of which was described in Chapter 6, indicates that this kind of strategy may not be as difficult as it initially appears, that, indeed, it may be easier to change the attitudes and behavior of children than those of adult educators.

Some of the weaknesses in the data and its interpretation arise from the unavoidable limitations of any single-school study. Because the total number of subjects was only about 320, of whom only about 65 were in the experimental group, the researchers could say little about the characteristics of children who are most affected by rising expectations. The analysis controlling in turn for sex, ethnic group, and ability group indicated complex patterns of effect, and Rosenthal and Jacobson did attempt to gather some clues from detailed case studies of a small subsample of their subjects. However, in the absence of enough cases to hold constant a number of variables simultaneously, understanding of the pattern of relationships is impossible. Similarly, the limited number of *classes* (18) allows little analysis of the kinds of teachers or teaching that are most responsive to manipulation of expectations.

Finally, the authors themselves raise an important missing element. As they put it in the summary chapter of their book, "we can only speculate as to *how teachers brought about intellectual competence* simply by expecting it." A number of possibilities are suggested—paying more attention to these children, treating them in a pleasanter or more encouraging fashion, using new or different teaching techniques, evaluating them differently, demanding more of them. Even by "facial expression, posture, and perhaps by her touch, the teacher may have communicated to the children of the experimental group that she expected improved intellectual performance" (Rosenthal and Jacobson, 1968: 180; italics mine). Since Rosenthal and Jacobson neither observed in the classroom nor questioned teachers or students about classroom processes, they can only speculate about how attitudes were translated into actual classroom behavior.

Ever since the publication of *Pygmalion in the Classroom* (1968), there has been a proliferation of studies testing the self-fulfilling–prophecy hypothesis and attempting to explicate the process by which expectations are translated into behavioral changes. The results of empirical research have varied, depending partly upon the research design. For the most part, attempts to replicate the original Rosenthal and Jacobson design have produced few significant differences between these students and their other classmates (Mendels and Flanders, 1973; Finn, 1972; Braun, 1976).

More positive results have been obtained from studies in which teachers are given photographs of children (not their own students) and asked to rate their potential. In one such study of ninety-six teachers in four elementary schools, Harvey and Slatin (1975) found a strong relationship between the race and perceived SES of the children in the photos and the teachers' expectations for their academic success or failure, with white children and children of perceived high status more often chosen for success. The additional factor of physical attractiveness was incorporated into a study of similar design, based upon a large sample of teachers in over five hundred schools (Clifford and Walker, 1973). The attractiveness of the children in the photos was found to be significantly associated with teachers' expectancies about a child's intelligence, likely educational attainment, popularity with peers, and parents' interest in education.

A few studies have examined the actual classroom situation rather than manipulating teachers' expectations or asking them to make predictions about fictitious students, and have attempted to trace the sequential interaction between teachers and students that produces differential student performance. A case study by Rist (1970) followed a group of black children, taught by black teachers, from kindergarten through second grade. During the first eight days of their school life, the kindergarten children were assigned to three different tables, based upon the teacher's estimation of their learning potential. Rist noted that these assignments were often made in contradiction to reading readiness test scores, and regardless of test scores the lower social-class children were more likely to be placed at the "low" table. Children assigned to this table were also placed farthest from the teacher and thereafter received less attention than groups closer to the teacher. The sequence of differential teacher expectations, which led to group assignments, which in turn led to differential treatment, produced increasingly differential performance as the children advanced in school. By the second grade, none of the children who remained in the same class had moved up to a higher group, and the children at the back table were all poor readers who were socially labeled as "the Clowns."

Observation and interviews with teachers in four New York City schools (Leacock, 1969) produced evidence that teachers' expectations vary by the class and race of students. In a middle-income, white school, the children toward whom the teachers felt most positively had an average IQ score eleven points higher than those toward whom they felt negatively; by contrast, in a low-income, black school, the children about whom the teachers felt positively had an average IQ score almost ten points lower than those about whom they felt negatively.

In another study of sequential interaction between teachers and students (Brophy and Good, 1970), four teachers in a small Texas school district were asked to provide their own rankings of pupils' abilities, based upon their prior contacts with them. It was found that teachers consistently favored students rated as high achievers over those rated low in demanding and reinforcing quality performance. The teachers directed significantly more criticism toward those for whom they had low expectations and more praise toward the "highs"; they were also more persistent in eliciting responses from "highs" than "lows." Consistent with the interactive model proposed by the authors, the children who were rated as high achievers in first grade initiated increasingly more work-related contacts with their teachers and thus created more response opportunities for themselves.

While most of the research on expectation effects focuses on teacher expectancies for students, there is some experimental work that manipulates students' expectations for their own performance. A series of experiments by Doris Entwisle and her colleagues at Johns Hopkins University has demonstrated that children's expectations for *their own* performance can be raised experimentally by a suitable adult and that high expectations in one area also raise expectations in other unrelated areas (Entwisle *et al.*, 1974). One experiment involved a story-telling activity in which children were asked to supply missing words to story "skeletons." The experimental treatment put selected children in a one-to-one situation with an adult, who encouraged the child to make up a story and then responded positively to the child's performance. The experiments produced positive gains in expectations among all groups of children exposed to the experimental treatment, though its success with inner-city black children was generally greatest if black adults were used. In one integrated elementary school, white experimenters were able to raise expectations for both black and white children in mixed-race groups, a result that is, the authors say, "one of the few quantitative pieces of evidence of positive consequences of school integration" (Entwisle *et al.*, 1974: 11). In general, the experimental treatment was more effective with boys than girls, perhaps, the researchers concluded, because girls are accustomed to receiving praise and positive evaluation for their work.

Researchers at the Stanford Center for Interracial Cooperation, using a technique that they termed *expectation training,* prepared black children to become the teachers of white students in a series of demanding tasks, including learning a foreign language and building a radio transmitter. The competence of the black "teachers" was reinforced for all participants—for example, by showing videotapes in which black children spoke in a foreign language to an adult from that society who praised them for their skill. The expectation-training techniques have been tested in Israel as well as in the United States, and research has shown increases in equal-status behavior in interracial groups of children and young adolescents, but few differences between the effects of this technique and other experimental techniques for changing students' expectations and performance (Cohen, Lockheed, and Lohman, 1976).

While the experiments conducted at Johns Hopkins and Stanford demonstrated that students' attitudes and behavior can be changed in desirable directions, it is important to bear in mind that experimental manipulation may have negative as well as positive outcomes. For example, an experiment conducted by a third-grade teacher to inform her students about the consequences of discrimination showed how quickly feelings of inferiority and superiority can be induced—and reversed (Peters, 1971). The class was divided on the basis of eye color, and on the first day of the experiment, the teacher told the students that the brown-eyed children were superior—more intelligent, and thus worthy of more rights and privileges than the blue-eyed children. Peters reports that the children learned their new roles so quickly that by the end of the day, blue-eyed children were not only behaving awkwardly and disconsolately, but actually did poorly on their class work. Children of different eye color who had previously been friends now avoided each other, and incidents of bullying and even physical assaults on blue-eyed children by brown-eyed children were recorded. The following day the roles were reversed. Now it was announced that the blue-eyed students were superior. Again almost immediately the blue-eyed students, now identified as superior, behaved as though they were superior and actually outperformed their brown-eyed classmates. The teacher's observations reflected her concern over some of the results of her very effective experimental treatment.

> All of the children enjoyed being considered superior, and the feeling that they were had obviously pushed them to do better work than they had ever done before. But some of them took a savage delight in keeping the members of the "inferior" group in their place, in asserting their "superiority" in particularly nasty ways. . . . I was wholly unprepared for their lack of compassion for people they normally considered their best friends. (Peters, 1971: 37)

Evaluation of Classroom Performance

In most classrooms, the student is "bombarded with messages telling him how well he has done and (with a short inferential leap) how good he is" (Dreeben, 1968: 38). Longitudinal studies of school grades and test performance suggest that classroom evaluation processes operate over time to produce increasing differentiation between students but increasing consistency in the position of a given student in the achievement hierarchy (B. Bloom, 1976). Two explanations have been offered for this phenomenon. One explanation is that the student, interacting with the evaluation system, receives feedback from his or her performance on one task that affects the level of enthusiasm and confidence with which he or she approaches the next task, which in turn affects performance on that task, and so forth. In a given school year a student may be evaluated on as many as 150 learning tasks (many of which are of a sequential nature), and he or she comes to acquire an increasingly clear self-image, which shapes subsequent effort and performance (B. Bloom, 1976: 143–145).

A second explanation for the increasing consistency of performance by individual students is that after evaluating a student's performance on several tasks, the teacher reaches an opinion about that student's general competence, and any subsequent performances will be evaluated in terms of this general view. An empirical study testing this model (Finn, 1972) showed that teachers who read an essay that was attributed to a bright, high-achieving student tended to rate it higher than when the same essay was attributed to a student of low ability and achievement. The Brophy and Good research discussed earlier indicated that teachers not only demanded higher performances from the children for whom they had developed higher expectations, but were more prone to praise such performance when it occurred. Conversely, the same teachers were more likely to accept poor performance from low-expectation children, less likely to praise good performance when it did occur, and less persistent in eliciting correct responses from them.[3]

Several recent studies have attempted to determine how closely grades match students' actual competence and how accurately teachers communicate their evaluations to students. Some research data indicate that grades are often more closely correlated with students' conformity to classroom behavior standards than to their academic competency (Gravenberg and Collins, 1976; Brophy and Good, 1974). Some important work by Dornbusch presents evidence that the evaluation system does not operate equitably, and that racial-minority and lower social-class students are most likely to receive a distorted picture of their capabilities and performance. In a study of high schools in the San Francisco area with varying distributions of black, Spanish-surname, and Anglo students, Dornbusch found that the minority students, who were on the average not achieving at high levels, were more likely than their Anglo counterparts to see their teachers as friendly toward them, to claim that they were trying extremely hard in school, and to report that the work assigned was "just right" for them. High-achieving students, who were disproportionately from the majority racial group, were more likely to report that the work assigned in school was too difficult and to express anxiety about their own efforts and competency. As Dornbusch summarizes the results of his research:

> the academic standards and evaluation system found in the schools did affect the students' assessment of their effort and achievement. Low achievers, particularly black and Spanish-surname students, were allowed to delude themselves. This is not simply a result of fantasizing or tending to misinterpret evaluation of their performance. Combining all ethnic groups by schools, we still find the highest self-assessment of effort in the lowest achieving schools, lowest effort-engagement in those schools, and praise and warmth associated with lower achievement. Students in every ethnic group are allowed to misinterpret feedback on this level of effort and achievement, but the process is stronger among blacks and Spanish-surname students. Those groups are hurt most by this distorted system of evaluation. (Dornbusch, 1976: 16–17)

The evaluation system illustrates one more aspect of the asymmetry of the teacher and student roles. There have been, of course, a number of studies in which students rate their teachers but these are mainly research exercises and seldom have any effect upon the teacher's position in the school. Teachers are much less frequently evaluated than are students, almost never by their peers, and contact between teachers and their principals is "infrequent, rarely involves any sustained and direct observation of the teacher, and is usually unsatisfactory"

(Sarason, 1971: 35). Dornbusch's study found that teachers were not much more informed about the evaluation system than were students; 51 percent of the over five hundred teachers in the sample answered "no" to the question: "Do you have any idea of any criteria on which you are evaluated?" Dornbusch did find, however, that teachers whose classroom performance was more visible to colleagues and to principals (who worked in a teaching team or in a school with open-space architecture, for example) were more satisfied with the evaluations they received than teachers in self-contained classrooms, and he predicts, as does Lortie (1975: Chapter 9), that increasing pressures, from school boards and other organizations outside the school, for teacher accountability will produce the impetus toward teacher collegiality that the social organization of the traditional school has failed to provide.

Student-Student Relationships

The student peer group has always been considered, as one observer puts it, "the netherworld of the classroom" (Cohen, 1972). It is generally viewed with suspicion and some anxiety by teachers concerned with keeping classrooms "under control." Sociologists have noted that the classroom contains a number of peer status systems, some of which originate and are maintained quite independently of the formal organization of the classroom. They have postulated that some students influence other students' academic attitudes and behavior (in sociological terminology, some students serve as *reference groups* for others), but they have not so far identified very specifically the processes by which these influences operate. The aspect of student-student relationship that has received the most attention is students' feelings toward each other, as measured by a technique called *sociometric analysis*.

Sociometry, a field that is largely the creation of Moreno and his followers, attempts to measure the *tele relations*—the positive or negative attractions—among the members of a group. The basic data-gathering technique is to ask all members to tell which other members they feel most strongly about (like, dislike, respect, want to work with, and so forth) or to identify the ones with high and low status in the group (the most popular, the smartest, or the best leader). Sociometric analysis had a brief vogue in teacher education, and during the 1950s American teachers produced *sociograms* (diagrams consisting of circles, representing students, linked by arrowed lines, representing their likes and dislikes for each other) by the thousands. The basic postulate of the sociometry enthusiasts was:

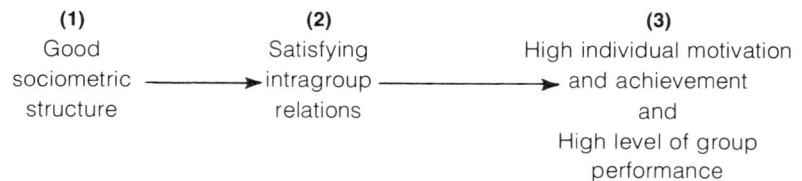

(1)	(2)	(3)
Good sociometric structure	⟶ Satisfying intragroup relations	⟶ High individual motivation and achievement and High level of group performance

The exact definition of "good" sociometric relations is not specified in the literature. Presumably, it includes a high rate of interpersonal contacts and no isolates or sharp cleavages between subgroups and identifiable leaders—since these are the kinds of things that are made visible by sociograms and matrices.[4]

The trouble with this formulation is that any empirical evidence that can be brought to bear on it—in particular findings from the field of industrial sociology on the factors contributing to worker productivity—indicate that it is not true. More specifically, studies of factory work groups suggest that while factor (1) does usually lead to factor (2), factor (3) does not necessarily follow. Reviewing some of his own and other researchers' studies of the electrical industry, Kahn (1956) found that some show direct, some inverse, and some no relationship, and he concludes that group-atmosphere measures are less powerful predictors than measures of individual goals and interests. His formulation is that a worker will have a high rate of production when he or she perceives high productivity as leading to or having some direct connection with his or her individual interests, providing there are no serious barriers.

Translated into educational terms, this would say that students "produce" when they see that it is in their interest to do so (when getting good grades is highly rewarded by their peers, or when they are committed to getting into college or some vocational field that requires a good school record), providing there are no obstacles that seem impassable (low ability or parents with low income). A sociometrically integrated class thus will assure a high level of academic productivity only if this group sets a standard of high productivity, that is, if academic excellence is to the interest of the group members. Otherwise, good group relations make no contribution to academic performance goals and may in fact work against such goals if the group is unified in its nonacceptance of achievement values. Probably, the effect of sociometric structure upon academic achievement is interactive with other features of classroom organization. For example, it may be more important in classes with an open communications pattern than in classes in which most communication is from teacher to student and little student-to-student communication is allowed. The reward structure is also a likely factor. The general point is that satisfying group feelings do not in themselves seem to produce high levels of learning.

There have been a number of attempts to relate individual students' sociometric status to their academic status. Most of the results are inconclusive, although there are a few studies showing that children tend to overselect children with higher academic status (McGinley and McGinley, 1970). There is also research showing negative correlations between sociometric status and minority group membership. For example, a study was done by Bartel, Bartel, and Grill (1973) in which black and white children from kindergarten through fourth grade in integrated schools were given a sixteen-item sociometric test. The test showed that while all children tended to select members of their own race on the positive items, both black and white children overselected blacks on the negative items. (The purpose of the work at the Center for Interracial Cooperation, mentioned above (Cohen, Lockheed and Lohman, 1976), is to make findings like these increasingly rare.)

Recent research has attempted to identify the major sources of peer status and to understand how they are related to each other and to classroom behavior. Cohen (1972) has identified the three major types of status as: societal status, based upon differences in sex, social class, race, and ethnicity; sociometric status, based upon bonds of interpersonal liking or attraction; and achievement status, based upon grades, ability grouping, or other academic ratings. Societal status has been found to be associated with activity rates in the classroom and with the other two types of status. Higher rates of classroom participation have been found among males, whites, and children from higher-status backgrounds (Katz, 1972; Brophy and Good, 1974; Leacock, 1969), although as we shall see in the next chapter, changes in the technology of the classroom can affect the participation levels of students of lower societal status.

Most legitimate peer group interaction in schools has been limited to extracurricular activities that rarely deal with the basic issues of classroom life (McPartland, 1977). One technique that has attracted the interest of educational reformers because it widens the range of student interaction is student tutoring. The basic idea of children teaching other children is not new. In some societies older students routinely look after younger ones and there is also a great deal of within-class collective group activity (for example, in the Russian schools described in Bronfenbrenner, 1970). Peer tutoring emerged informally in this country as a practical response to the personnel shortages in the one-room schoolhouse. During the peak years of civil rights activism in the 1960s, thousands of American students were involved in tutoring programs for minority group children, though much of this was conducted outside of schools and school hours.

In the tutoring projects developed during the last few years, most student tutors are of the same race and social class as their "students," and some have learning difficulties themselves (S. Bloom, 1976; Devin-Sheehan, Feldman, and Allen, 1976; Paolitto, 1976; Pine and Olesker, 1973). Most of these projects are small scale, and data on the results have been limited. One of the most extensive and carefully monitored projects was designed for a New York City antipoverty program and involved 240 student tutors and over 600 pupils randomly assigned to experimental (tutoring) and control (no tutoring) groups. Over one five-month period, children who were tutored gained 6.0 months in their reading skills, but their tutors gained 3.4 years (Gartner, Kohler, and Riessman, 1971: 22–25). The relatively greater benefits that seem to accrue to the tutor, a finding reported in a number of tutoring projects, may reflect the double strengthening of student-student bonds that characterizes the tutor role (that is, the relationship with "pupils" plus collegial bonds with fellow tutors).

An experiment at Penn State tested the feasibility and effectiveness of peer tutoring at the college level. Under the Penn State Pyramid Plan, much of the class work in psychology courses was carried out in small groups composed of six freshmen, six sophomores, two juniors who served as assistant leaders, and a senior group leader who had been trained by the departmental faculty. Comparison of test data collected from Pyramid classes and control classes showed that students in the former were higher on "knowledge of the field of psychology, scientific thinking, use of the library for scholarly reading, intellectual orientation, and resourcefulness in problem solving." In addition, a higher proportion of these students continued as psychology majors (McKeachie, 1962: 333). Despite the apparent effectiveness of peer-tutoring arrangements, and despite the financial pressures that force most institutions of higher education to rely upon the large lecture course as their major mode of teaching, use of the student peer group has received little systematic attention. Colleges and universities continue to use armies of graduate students to cover the discussion sections of large lecture courses (indeed, few universities could afford to operate without this source of cheap labor), but experiments like the Penn State Pyramid Plan are rare.

Conclusions

Philip Jackson, whose *Life in Classrooms* combines the author's own observations in elementary classrooms with a synthesis of other empirical studies on the classroom, concludes that the distinguishing features of classroom life are "crowds, praise, and power," and that the most useful quality a student can acquire is patience. The conventional classroom role structure is not conducive to the active involvement of most students in the learning process, but rather seems designed to promote distance and distrust between student and teacher.

Early studies of teachers and teaching techniques tended to segment the personal characteristics and behavior of the teacher from the other elements of the classroom situation, and about all one could conclude was that there is no "best" way to teach all students and subjects. More recent research indicates that although the teacher and student roles are asymmetrical, students have many strategies for resisting teachers' efforts to maintain classroom order and their own authority. Recent research also suggests that teachers' expectations can affect students' actual achievements, and that students' and teachers' aspirations and achievements can be raised by experimental manipulation of expectations. Evaluation of student performance does not, however, always reflect actual competence, and racial-minority and lower-status students are most likely to receive a distorted picture of their capabilities and performance.

Studies of classroom arrangements designed to make the student role more active and students more responsible for their own and other students' learning have produced generally positive results. The small amount of empirical research on alternative definitions of the student role probably reflects the way in which children and youth are viewed in our society (see Chapter 1). It may also reflect the nature of the classroom itself. In the next chapter we shall continue our examination of the classroom by turning our attention from its role structure to its dynamics as a small social system.

Notes

1. See, for example, Jackson, 1968: Chapter 4.

2. The self-fulfilling prophecy is most elegantly discussed in Robert Merton's essay by that name (Merton, 1957: 421–436).

3. These two explanations are based respectively on symbolic interactionist theory and dissonance theory.

4. See Gronlund, 1959: Chapter 7.

The Class as a Social System   Chapter 9

Only in schools do thirty or more people spend several hours each day literally side by side. Once we leave the classroom we seldom again are required to have contact with so many people for so long a time.   Philip Jackson

I think that what we need is not to touch up or modernize classrooms but rather to eliminate them. (Question from the audience: "Where would we learn?" Answer: "We'd manage.")   Jerry Farber

In this chapter, we shall turn from the internal role structure of the classroom to its workings as a social system. As the Jackson quotation suggests, the class is in some respects analogous to a crowd—in it, a fairly large number of individuals are in close physical proximity. This may explain partially why teachers often seem to be so obsessed with discipline and control, with not letting students get "out of hand." One way to maintain order in a crowd is to have a clear authority hierarchy with clearly institutionalized dominance and subordination. As we saw in the last two chapters, both the classroom and the school as a whole have a hierarchical role structure.

Another mechanism for maintaining order is to have a regular institutionalized sequence of events. As Jackson points out, one can enter a classroom almost anywhere in our country and recognize what is going on. This is because

there is a limited number of forms of classroom activity: seat work, teacher lecture or demonstration, oral recitation, and group discussion almost exhaust the repertoire. And most so-called educational innovations are really a variation, often disguised by technological gadgetry, of one of these basic tasks.

all activities are organized into a schedule—the pledge of allegiance is followed by reading at 8:30, which is followed by arithmetic at 9:00, which is followed by social studies. . . . The music teacher comes for an hour on Tuesday mornings, and the art teacher on Thursdays. And so on. There is an almost holy aura about the schedule, and it takes an event of crisis proportions to change it.

While the details and the order of events vary from one location to another, the basic structure of the "daily grind" is common to most. In addition to the rigidity of the schedule as a whole, each individual activity has its own rules—no loud talking during seat work, raise your hand to talk during discussion, keep your eyes on your own paper during tests. Note that the goal of much educational reform, including the free school and open classroom models, is to break up the ritualistic, cyclic quality of classroom life; in the latter by making a rich variety of materials and activities available from which the student can make a choice, and in the former by doing away with the schedule altogether and allowing the mass behavior of the crowd to develop freely—and occasionally to erupt.

In the following sections, we shall take up some of the factors that affect how the class operates as a learning environment: (1) class size, (2) the social composition of the class, (3) classroom technology, including recent technological innovations in teaching, (4) the communication structure, (5) the reward structure, and (6) the social climate.

Size

The variable of group size illustrates the tendency to cling to an established pedagogical view despite persistent lack of evidence to support it. One of the basic tenets of our educational system is the value of the small classroom. Any report on a school or school system includes statistics on class size, and educators frequently use a small student-teacher ratio as one of the factors explaining a good school system and a large ratio as an excuse for a poor one. In virtually all of the recent teacher strikes and other confrontations between militant teacher groups and school administrations, one of the demands is for smaller classes. From the teacher's point of view, smaller classes are an obvious convenience. Fewer students mean fewer papers and tests to grade, fewer individuals with whom to communicate, a smaller probability of a classroom getting "out of control," and so on. The relevant question here, however—and the grounds upon which demands for smaller classes ostensibly are made—is whether size is meaningfully related to learning efficiency.

Research in this area has not been characterized by a high level of sophistication or rigor (possibly related to the education profession's vested interest in small classes), and it does not establish the overall superiority of either large or small classes. A comprehensive survey of empirical studies of class size sponsored by the Educational Research Service indicated that certain kinds of students—those in the lower grades, disadvantaged children, and those with lower academic abilities—benefit from smaller classes, but only when their teachers adapt their teaching methods to a more intimate setting. The report concluded, however, that there did not appear to be any optimum class size, and there was no evidence that smaller classes per se would increase academic achievement (Porwell, 1978).

When one considers the size differences that can actually be compared in most schools, the lack of effect of class size is not really surprising. The reduction of a class from, say, thirty-five to thirty students does not require any basic changes in the way it is organized and conducted. A reduction to ten or fifteen might make a difference, but from a practical point of view, this class size is unlikely in most of our public schools, even if found to be significantly more effective.

What seems more likely is that size alone is not a strong determining factor but rather is related to *other* factors that affect classroom productivity. For example, if one compares classes in a well-to-do suburb with those in the central city, the latter probably will be larger in size but lower in academic achievement—an indirect relationship between size and performance. But if one compares urban and rural schools, the latter will probably have smaller classes and lower achievement. In other words, size may be a causal factor, but it can be understood only when considered simultaneously with other factors.

Another possibility is that size affects different aspects of group functioning in different ways. McKeachie suggests that the apparent lack of relationship between class size and productivity may be due to two effects working in opposite directions. On the one hand, increasing size increases the resources of a group (the total pool of information available and the opportunities for feedback). On the other hand, it diminishes the possibility of getting the maximum contribution from all members.

Although the size of a class as a whole is not susceptible to manipulation in most school systems, it is possible to break down a class of any size into a number of smaller subgroups. At the subgroup level, research in the small-groups area of school psychology offers clues about optimum group size.

One of the initial issues raised in small-groups research was whether a group of *any* size had advantages over the individual. To put it another way—do individuals working together solve problems or learn faster or better than they would working alone? The answer seems to depend upon the nature of the learning task. For example, in a fairly early study, Shaw (1932) found that groups were more efficient than individuals at problems that had a single correct answer, especially if the final answer depended upon reaching correct solutions at several intermediate stages. Shaw's interpretation was that someone in a group was likely to catch a member's errors, and that individuals were prevented from pursuing unprofitable lines of reasoning. Other experiments have shown group performance to be superior to individual performance on a variety of tasks, although there seems to be a ceiling on the complexity of problems that a group can handle well, and groups are relatively better at solving specific problems than at more creative tasks (for instance, better at solving problems and puzzles than at designing them). One study (Perlmutter et al., 1952) has indicated that individuals' productivity can be increased by placing them successively in group and individual situations; individuals who first had a group work experience performed better on a memorization task than individuals who did not have an initial group experience.

One might deduce from the above findings that increasing the size of the group would thereby increase problem-solving efficiency. However, a number of studies have shown little difference between groups of from two to five members, and in terms of "unit efficiency" (total time to reach a solution based upon the number of group members), Bales and Borgotta (1953) found a curvilinear rather than a linear relationship between size and efficiency. That is, there may be diminishing returns in simply increasing group size, and some research indicates that smaller groups perform better than larger ones on more abstract problems.

Increasing group size has a number of different ramifications bearing on group efficiency. Bales's research has pointed to increasing role differentiation with increasing size, with the leaders taking over an ever-greater share of the interaction. There is an extensive, though not consistent, literature on the unique characteristics of small groups of specific sizes, summarized in the following passage:

> The crucial transitions are those from one person to two, from two to three, from three to four, from four to seven, and from seven to nine. . . . The transition from one to two creates the basic unit of social behavior, the dyad. In a dyad there is interdependence, reciprocal behavior, and the necessity for accommodation to another person. The transition from two to three is significant because now there exists the possibility of an alliance between two members against the third one. The phenomena of control, cooperation *and* competition, and influence are produced by this transition. . . . The transition from three to four creates the possibility of two equal dyads or alliances, and this may perpetuate both the social unit and the problems of control. The significant feature of four is that an alliance between two members is not sufficient to gain control. . . . The jump from four to seven is crucial because just as individuals can form coalitions in the interest of control, so can groups. A seven-man group has the potential of splitting into two dyads and a triad. If the two dyads combine resources, they can gain some control over the larger triad. . . . Perfect symmetry with regard to all the processes we have described would be found in the nine-man group. Here there can exist three groups of three. This permits coalitions *within* a specified triad and coalitions *between* a pair of triads. (Weick, 1969: 24–25)

Thus, while teachers and school systems can probably do little to change the size of the class as a whole—and the available evidence shows that class size per se has little direct effect upon student learning—the small-groups literature offers a number of suggestions on optimum group size that could be used in subdividing a class for various learning activities.

Social Context

The conventional classroom contains one adult and multiple (usually twenty-five or more) students. The average American classroom is sex heterogeneous and age homogeneous. A few schools, mainly private, remain exclusively for boys or girls, but sex segregation in the classroom is a declining phenomenon (though as we saw in Chapter 5, boys and girls in the same class are often treated quite differently). By contrast, age homogeneity, which was not introduced into American schools until the mid-nineteenth century, is now firmly entrenched (Kett,

1974). As Dreeben (1968) points out, homogeneous age composition is important in two senses: (1) it provides a built-in standard for comparison, and (2) it puts each student "in the same boat" with others in terms of their basic social situation and the way they are treated by teachers. While homogeneity on any characteristic has some of the consequences noted by Dreeben, age homogeneity is unique in one respect. Students may share gender, race, or social class identity with some of their teachers, but all students are separated from all of their teachers by their membership in different age strata. This separation has a number of implications, among them that "classroom learning is primarily determined by teachers' perceived differences between children and adults, a fact that makes recognition of communalities almost impossible" (Sarason, 1971: 182).

Classrooms differ also in their degree of homogeneity with respect to race, ethnicity, SES, and academic ability or performance. Ability grouping, or homogeneity on the last named characteristic, continues to be a controversial issue, because it tends to be related to and to accentuate racial and social-class differences, and because a large body of research stretching over five decades has failed to establish conclusive evidence about the effects of grouping upon students' attitudes and achievement. A discussion of one carefully designed study will illustrate the difficulty of drawing firm conclusions about ability grouping.

The major objective of an experiment conducted in New York City schools by Goldberg and associates (1966) was to determine the extent to which students' achievement increments over two academic years were affected by:

their ability level

the presence or absence of gifted children in the class

the presence or absence of slow learners in the class

the ability range in the class

their relative position within a given ability pattern

The sample consisted of eighty-six classes organized into fifteen different patterns of ability level and spread. Tests measuring achievement in several subjects, plus attitudinal questionnaires, were given at the beginning of the fifth and end of the sixth grade, and mean increments were computed for each class in each area of achievement.[1] Thus the study is a rare example of a relatively long-term longitudinal study of a relatively large sample.

While the sample size is large, it is not representative of the children of this age group in New York. In an attempt to obtain schools with broad ability ranges, the researchers included only schools that listed four or more fourth graders with IQ scores of 130 or higher and that were willing to cooperate. The sample thus excluded most schools from the low-income areas of the city. Moreover, schools that met the minimum requirement for students at the high end of the ability continuum tended to contain few students at the *low* end; there were only 206 students at ability level E (with IQ scores below 100). As the authors themselves point out, "conclusions can only be generalized to similar populations, and probably have little relevance for schools with predominantly low socioeconomic status or non-white pupil populations" (Goldberg *et al.*, 1966: 152).

It also should be noted that the experimental manipulation consisted only of setting up fifth-grade sections according to specified grouping patterns. Beyond allotting time for pre- and posttesting, there was no attempt to control what went on in the classroom. Thus we do not know how teachers were assigned to the various classes, nor anything about the content of various courses, and the methods of teaching used during the period of the study.

To summarize some of the most important results of the study:

1. The presence of gifted children in a class had some upgrading effect upon the bright but not gifted students, less on the other students in the area of science. In social studies, the upgrading effect was on the less-able classmates. There were few effects in other subjects.
2. The presence of slow learners in a class does not appear to have any consistent effect.
3. Considering the *range* of ability within a class, the gifted students did best in a class of all gifted peers. Other students tended to do better in the broadest rather than narrowest range, but the overall differences were not large or consistent.
4. A student's *relative* ability position in a class had no consistent effect upon his or her test performance. "Neither for all three intermediate ability levels taken together or for each of them taken separately was any one position related to greater increments in all subjects" (Goldberg *et al.*, 1966: 56).
5. Comparisons of classes differing in range of ability (containing one, a few, or all ability levels) produced some statistically significant differences, but did not consistently favor broad or narrow patterns, and controlling for individual ability removed most of the significant differences. When each ability level was viewed in the separate subjects, with ability range also controlled, only eleven of the 105 comparisons were statistically significant, though nearly all favored a broad rather than a narrower range.
6. Differences between classes of the same ability distribution pattern were generally greater than differences between different ability patterns. (This was the finding reported at the beginning of Chapter 8—see also, Goldberg *et al.*, 1966: 57–58, and Table III–8.)

The findings as a whole indicate that ability grouping alone does not have a strong impact upon the performance of most students. The presence of extremely gifted students in a class does seem to have some positive effects upon their classmates, although these children themselves did their best work in classes of their ability equals. On the other hand, the presence of low-ability children, at least when they constitute a minority in a class, does not have a negative effect, a finding that speaks to the fear that racial integration and other kinds of school reorganization designed to assimilate low-SES children into middle-class schools will "pull down" the more able students.[2]

In a recent review of research on ability grouping, Richer obtained the following rather inconclusive tally: 167 studies favored homogeneous grouping, 44 studies favored heterogeneous grouping, and 193 studies showed no significant differences between homogeneous and heterogeneous grouping (Richer, 1976). Richer argues that the predominance of null findings may mean that the conditions necessary for the emergence of measurable effects have not been clearly identified, and he postulates that the effects of ability grouping depend upon the extent to which students compare themselves with students of higher ability levels—that is, use them as *reference groups* for themselves. Reference-group theory implies that the high-ability groups are salient units for the slower students, and Richer hypothesizes that this is most likely in smaller classes, with relatively few ability subgroups, and where the subgroups are clearly differentiated but not so dissimilar that students cannot identify with their peers in other groups. He also postulates that reference groups will be more likely as more classroom rewards are allocated on the basis of intellectual performance and the greater the perceived opportunity to move up to high groups. Finally, the more that ability group assignment is correlated with demographic factors, in particular race and SES, "the less likely are lower ranking persons to see upward mobility as possible and hence the less likely is normative reference-group taking" (Richer, 1976: 70).

Research generally indicates that the advantages, both academic and affective, of homogeneous grouping are felt mainly by high-ability students. They are the only ones who show consistently (though usually slightly) greater academic gains in homogeneous than in heterogeneous classes, and being in a high-ability group tends to inflate the self-esteem of its members. The other side of the coin is that children assigned to low groups tend to perform at a lower level than low-ability children in heterogeneous groups, and the stigma attached to low groups sometimes affects their self-esteem adversely (Esposito, 1973; McGinley and McGinley, 1970).

Classroom Technology[3]

Most classrooms consist of four walls with rows of desks or tables and chairs for the students and a single desk at the "front" of the room for the teacher. The modal classroom situation involves spatial containment and crowding. Primary school classrooms are generally larger than secondary school classrooms and allow more physical mobility within the classroom (some have space set aside for play activities) but less mobility outside (Sarason observed that kindergartens are so self-contained that they have their own bathrooms and one can spend a long time in the halls of a primary school without ever seeing a kindergartner).

Students are usually assigned to a specific seat for an entire school year, and several recent studies have shown that seating assignments both reflect teachers' attitudes toward students and affect students' actual classroom behavior. An analysis of thirty-six videotaped lessons in sixteen elementary classrooms (Adams and Biddle, 1970) revealed not only that most classroom talking was done by the teacher (a finding so common as to be almost a truism), but, more interestingly, that virtually all the students who did speak were located in a small, T-shaped zone consisting of three seats down the center of the room and the two front seats on either side of this center strip. Both the Rist and the Brophy and Good studies discussed earlier found that seating assignments were related to students' societal status and, ultimately, to their achievement status. In a dissertation project on physical and social distance in teacher-student relationships, Schwebel (1969) found that teachers often used seat assignment as a mode of classroom control; for example, placing children they judged disruptive in different parts of the room or next to "good" children (thus in effect deputizing the role of control agent to selected students). Regardless of the criteria used, those children placed in front seats were more attentive to classroom activities and were more positively evaluated by their teachers, their peers, and themselves.

During the 1960s a number of technological innovations were introduced in American classrooms, some developed in this country, others imported from abroad. We shall not attempt a systematic review here (see Silberman, 1970, for discussion of some of the more important innovations), but it is interesting to note that by the early 1970s most of these innovations had disappeared or changed almost beyond recognition. We shall consider only two that seem of relatively greater sociological interest because they consciously restructure the social organization of the classroom.

One such innovation is Moore's "responsive environment," a combination of spatial arrangements and equipment (including the widely publicized "talking typewriter") designed to be intrinsically attractive (*autotelic*), to allow freedom of movement and privacy from meddling adults, to be self-pacing, and to provide immediate feedback on the consequences of actions (Moore and Anderson, 1969). One of the many intriguing findings about the responsive environment is that the major appeal of the computerized typewriter seems to lie in the increased social interaction facilitated. In fact, Moore found that many of the impressive learning results occurred just as regularly when a child worked at a regular typewriter with a teacher beside him or her as when he or she used the computer-based equipment. In other words, the distinction between the technological and the social structural effects of a given innovation is not always clear;[4] in this case what seemed to matter to students was that their actions got responses.

Similarly, the set of arrangements and techniques comprising the open classroom, the most widely adopted technological innovation of the past decade, combines technological and social structural elements. The open classroom model calls for maximum flexibility in the use of physical space—the open education movement has, in fact, spawned a parallel open-space movement among school architects (Dreeben, 1973). Compared to traditional instruction, open education places fewer restrictions on student movement and interaction, provides more alternative activities, and gives students greater autonomy in deciding how they will use their time in school. The teacher assumes a complementary role, with less control over equipment, materials, assignments, pacing, and evaluation (Silberman, 1970; Barth, 1972; Epstein and McPartland, 1976).

The sociologically interesting questions about the open classroom, or any other technological innovation are: (a) whether it really is a technological innovation (that is, whether it really changes the nature and distribution of classroom resources); and (b) whether it has measurable effects upon the attitudes and behavior of students and/or teachers. Research to date indicates that the open classroom is a distinctive technology, that it does change the interaction patterns in the classroom, but that it does not have consistently positive effects upon student output. In a comparison of data obtained in sixty-two open and traditional classrooms in the United States and Britain, Walberg and Thomas (1972) found differences between the two types of classes, on factors ranging from individualism of instruction and evaluation to emotional climate and teacher collegial relationships, that were significantly greater than differences between different status levels and differences between the two countries. Teachers in open-space classrooms have reported more interaction with other teachers, greater autonomy and influence within the school, and more informal rewards (for example, more satisfying relationships with students), though they do not perceive their opportunities for career mobility increased in such schools (Cohen, 1973; Cohen and Bredo, 1975; Meyer et al., 1972).

A comparison of social networks in traditional and open classrooms indicated that students' interpersonal relationships were also affected by open classroom structure. While degree of clustering of friendships was similar in the two types of classrooms, the distribution of popularity was less hierarchical and more uniform in open than in traditional classrooms. Asymmetric relationships (for example, Child A chooses Child B but is not chosen by B) were found to occur less frequently in open classrooms, although children in traditional classrooms had, on the average, more friends (Hallinan, 1976). In a study of children's personal-space perceptions, in which third and fourth graders in two schools were provided with a cutout silhouette figure, representing themselves, and asked to place this figure where they would position themselves in relation to a series of other persons (best friend, not best friend, class bully, teacher, and adult visitor), Brody and Zimmerman (1975) found that students in open classrooms placed themselves closer to all these persons, and that they actually displayed closer "approach" behavior toward both children and adults in their classrooms.

Research evaluating the effects of open education on students' academic development has produced mixed results. In general, children in traditional classrooms outperform children in open classrooms on standard achievement tests; perhaps, suggests one researcher, because greater freedom does not necessarily motivate students to develop the skills needed for success on achievement tests (Wright, 1975: 461). A comparison of open or informal versus closed or formal classroom styles by a British researcher showed a consistent tendency for ten- to twelve-year-olds in the more traditional, formal settings to score higher on tests of reading ability, punctuation and sentence completion, mathematical comprehension, and computational skills. In some substantive areas, the gaps between formal and informal learning styles were greatest for the students of highest ability (Bennett, 1976). Wright's study reported no differences between open and traditional classes on tests of creativity, self-esteem, locus of control, and various measures of cognitive development, though children in open classrooms had higher scores on a measure of school anxiety (the author speculated that since testing and other formal evaluations are less common occurrences in open classrooms, they may produce more anxiety when they do occur). There is also evidence that some students—in particular, working-class children and children from minority racial groups—are more positively affected than others by open classrooms (Cockerham and Blevins, 1976; Richer, 1974).

One of the most extensive analyses of the effects of open classroom technology on the quality of school life utilized survey data from 7,200 students in thirty-nine elementary, middle, and high schools that differed significantly on a measure of school openness. A major finding of the study was that the openness of instruction had a greater impact on students' perceptions of the quality of student-teacher relations than on any other dimensions, including students' commitment to classwork and their overall satisfaction with school. The authors concluded that the open classroom "appears to involve a basic change of the school authority structure, but may not involve as much change in the social or task structure of schools" (Epstein and McPartland, 1976: iii).

A comment made by the authors of this report suggests why the open-classroom model has been so widely disseminated in this country, despite lack of evidence that it strengthens students' academic development. They note that students may prefer open classrooms because they are more like life outside of school, thus "reducing the sharp points of comparison between school and non-school which may cause some students in traditional classrooms to be resentful and discontented" (Epstein and McPartland, 1976: 5). Open-classroom technology is probably more congruent with contemporary American child-rearing practices—and thus produces fewer discontinuities between home and school—than the traditional classroom practices described in Jackson (1968) and Dreeben (1968). If, as Durkheim argued, schools reflect the societies in which they are located and are the places where societies recreate themselves in the young, the open classroom may be seen as an almost inevitable technological response to changes in the institutions outside of the school.

Communication

Since the goal of the formal learning system is to communicate information and skills, it is surprising how little systematic research has been done on the communications structure of classrooms. One thing known about classroom communication is that there is a lot of it. Jackson estimated from his own observations in several elementary classrooms that the teacher averages over two hundred interpersonal exchanges ever hour of every working day. However, as earlier noted, the only consistently active communicator in most classroom interaction is the teacher, and much of the communication is one way.

Exhibit 9–1
Communication Patterns in Bavelas and Leavitt Experiments

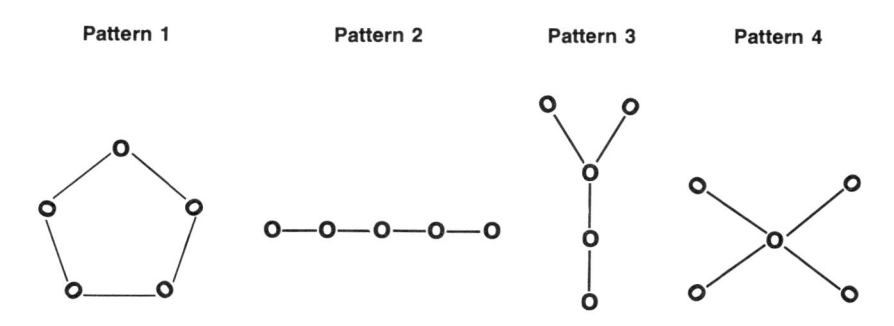

Pattern 1   Pattern 2   Pattern 3   Pattern 4

What systematic research there is on group communication is largely from the small-groups field of social psychology, in particular the work of Bavelas, Leavitt, and their colleagues. Although most of this work is with groups much smaller than normal classroom size—and would thus apply directly to discussion groups or other subgroups rather than to the class as a whole—it contains much that is relevant to a sociological theory of the classroom.

In a series of laboratory experiments in which the communication channels of five-person groups were controlled (the patterns are shown in Exhibit 9–1), both Bavelas and Leavitt found that communication patterns affected amount of activity, satisfaction, speed, and accuracy of performance on discovery problems on both the individual and group level.[5] On the group level, groups arranged to afford a high degree of "centrality" (pattern 4 in Exhibit 9–1) tended to organize quickly to solve the problem with relatively few errors, although the total amount of group activity and satisfaction were not necessarily high. Leavitt attributed this to the position of the leader, which served as a kind of central office for receiving, organizing, and dispatching messages. When centrality was more evenly distributed (pattern 1), there was more activity and overall satisfaction, but fewer error-free solutions of the puzzle.

At the individual level, individuals in central positions were more likely to become active, more likely to become group leaders, and more satisfied with their group and their job. By contrast, where one position is low in centrality relative to the others, subjects in these more peripheral positions were likely to become "dependent on the leader, accepting his dictates, filling a role that allows little opportunity for prestige, activity, or self-expression" (Leavitt, 1958: 563). Leavitt's summary of his own experiments would apply to both men's results:

> Patternwise, the picture formed by the results is of differences almost always in the order *circle, chain, Y, wheel* (or patterns 1,2,3,4, respectively in Exhibit 9–1).
>
> We may grossly characterize the kinds of differences that occur in this way: the circle, one extreme, is active, leaderless, unorganized, erratic, and yet is enjoyed by its members. The wheel, at the other extreme, is less active, has a distinct

leader, is well and stably organized, is less erratic, and yet is unsatisfying to most of its members. (Leavitt, 1958: 558)

To apply these findings to the school classroom, the communication structure of most classroom activities is an extension of pattern 4, with the teacher in the central position and most of the communication consisting of a series of one-to-one exchanges between teacher and student. Such a crude diagram covers up much of the relevant detail of actual classroom situations—for instance, whether the communication is one-way from teacher to student, whether the teacher simply asks questions and indicates whether students' answers are "correct," or whether there is anything like a true discussion between teacher and student. Even this oversimplified conceptualization, however, has suggestive implications. First, the typical classroom communication structure is the one that is least gratifying to all group members except the member in the central position, although it is in a sense the most well-organized structure (which may explain its appeal to teachers). Second, while this type of group was found to be most productive of correct answers to clearly structured tasks, this is really the result of the activity of the one central role—the productivity and contribution of other group members at the individual level was often greater in less organized types of structures where individuals were allowed to talk to members other than just the leader. Indeed, the highly centralized group seems to achieve its order and efficiency as a consequence of relatively passive behavior on the part of many members, a pattern that matches the typical classroom situation as described in the preceding chapter. To put it another way, in a highly centralized system in which most members can communicate only with the leader, the person holding this position may learn a lot and be satisfied with the position and with the group, but this very activity limits the learning opportunities of other individuals.

Finally, although their experiments were not designed to bear directly on this point, both researchers speculated on the question of the degree of insight encouraged in and nurtured by varying patterns of communication. While every group in the Leavitt tests succeeded in forming at least some of the puzzle shapes,

> the ability to restructure the problem, to give up the partial successes, varied widely from pattern to pattern. If the indications of the few experimental runs that have been made to date are any guide, both occurrence and utilization of insight will be found to drop rapidly as centrality is more and more highly localized. In one group, the individual to whom the necessary insight occurred was "ordered" by the emergent leader to "forget it." Losses of productive potential, in this way, are probably very common in most working groups, and must be enormous in society at large. (Bavelas, 1962: 681–682)

That is, once one moves beyond simple structured learning tasks to a more general understanding of some body of knowledge or to application of a skill or piece of information learned in one context to another context, more flexible classroom patterns that allow more communication among students may be more functional.

Classroom Reward Structure

The reward structure refers to the rules under which grades and other reinforcements are dispensed. A typology of reward structures developed by Michaels (1977) distinguishes among: (1) individual reward contingencies, in which the performance of each individual is compared with a previously established standard; (2) group contingencies, in which the performance of groups is compared with a standard, and rewards are allocated equally within each group; (3) individual competition, in which rewards are differentially allocated among individuals according to their performance relative to other individuals; and (4) group competition, in which rewards are differentially allocated among groups according to their relative performance, with rewards allocated equally within each group. McPartland (1977) points to an additional distinction between immediate and long-term rewards, pointing out that schools appear to be at a disadvantage compared to many other organizations in their ability to appeal mainly to the long-run interests of their members.

The reward structure of the typical classroom, a kind of compromise between the first and third types in Michaels's typology, has been blamed for many of the student failures. To many observers, the reward system of the classroom seems designed to produce anxiety, antagonism, and alienation in the teacher-student relationship. Three characteristics of the reward system are cited as especially nonfunctional in this respect:

the locus of rewards, which in most school systems is based upon grades. A dominant feature of grades is that they are external to the given learning activity. One carries out assignments in order to get a good grade or avoid a bad one, regardless of the intrinsic interest or usefulness of the activity involved. Such a locus obviously does not promote efforts to devise learning activities that are meaningful in themselves, nor does it make use of (nor trust) children's natural desire to know.

the structure of competition, which is mainly an individualistic contest for a scarce resource. High achievement by one student thus not only uses up or takes out of circulation one of a limited supply of good grades, but may punish the whole group by "raising the curve." Such a competitive structure discourages cooperative relationships among students and produces group sanctions against high achievement as a way of controlling the teacher's expectations.

the kind of student behavior that is encouraged. As Waller put it, the reward system fosters "docile assimilation and glib repetition," and discourages "fertile and rebellious creation." Those students who go along with the system for the sake of gaining its rewards concentrate on the kinds of behavior that are generally approved—say, reciting well and passing tests.

Critics have urged more frequent use of group reward structures, clearer reinforcement of appropriate behavior, and clearer separation of the motivational and evaluative components of the reward system (Spilerman, 1971; Slavin, 1977;

Stasz, 1975). As might be predicted, empirical research indicates that the outcomes of alternative reward structures reflect the level at which rewards are allocated. Thus individual academic achievement generally seems to be maximized by individual reward structures, individual competition in particular, while interpersonal collaboration and other group processes are facilitated by group reward structures that encourage or require cooperative task interaction (Bronfenbrenner, 1970; Johnson and Johnson, 1974; Michaels, 1977). There is some empirical evidence, parallel to findings from research on open classrooms, indicating that the academic performance of racial-minority children is improved in classrooms that emphasize cooperation and student interdependence, even when that reward structure does not seem to affect the academic performance of majority-group children (Lucker et al., 1976). There is also some evidence that a mixed reward structure may be more effective than any single type. Researchers at the Johns Hopkins Center for Social Organization of Schools have been able to induce improved academic performance as well as reduced time on tasks and higher motivation levels using a concurrent reward structure that organizes students into teams and alternates between individual and group reward contingencies (DeVries and Slavin, 1976; Edwards, DeVries, and Snyder, 1972).

Some sociologists have attempted to build mathematical models of school reward systems and to test them against empirical data. An example is Coleman's stochastic or conjectural model of "situations in which one person's achievement takes away from another's success, and in turn the other person discourages efforts leading to such achievement." Coleman contrasts this model with situations where one person's achievement *contributes* to another's goals, and where, in turn, group pressure supports the efforts leading to such achievement. In an interscholastic athletic contest, "the achievements of one school's athletes contribute to the goals of all the members of the team and even of the school, who in turn cheer their team and accord the athletes high status and give them numerous other rewards" (Coleman, 1962: 120). Empirical data on the ways in which students react to and cope with the reward system will be discussed in Chapter 11, on the peer group.

The most systematic attempt to change the classroom reward structure, and probably the most controversial educational development of the past two decades, is behavior modification. Behavior modification is both a theory and a strategy. It posits that the way to get children to learn is to restructure the environment so that they must change their behavior (or "learn") in order to gain the rewards of the system. A basic principle of behavior modification theory is that behavior can be changed in prespecified directions without extensive examination of the student's underlying motivations. Rather, the teacher or researcher programs the environment so that correct behavior is quickly reinforced, either by direct rewards, ranging from candy to praise, or by tokens that can be exchanged for desired rewards.

In an early classroom experiment the disruptive behavior of a hyperactive child was reduced as follows: for every ten seconds of nondisruptive behavior, the child was given one point. Accumulated points could be converted into pennies and candy that were shared with the child's classmates. That is, the reward structure made the entire peer group depend upon the individual "problem" child, which both increased their pressure upon him to change his behavior and prevented them from dismissing him as a pest with whom they did not have to identify.[6]

Some of the most promising experiments have been carried out in experimental classrooms at the Central Midwestern Regional Educational Laboratory (CEMREL). All are based upon a simple, cost-reward system in which plastic tokens are the major medium of exchange.

> A child who completes his arithmetic or reading may earn a dozen tokens, given one by one as he proceeds through the lessons. And at the end of the lesson period comes the reward.
>
> Often it is a movie. The price varies. For four tokens, a student can watch while sitting on the floor; for eight, he gets a chair; for 12 he can watch while sitting on the table. Perhaps the view is better from the table—anyway, the children almost always buy it if they have enough tokens. But if they dawdled so much that they earned fewer than four, they are "timed out" into the hall while the others see the movie. Throughout the morning, therefore, the children earn, then spend, then earn, then spend. . . .
>
> At the beginning the tokens are meaningless to the children; so to make them meaningful, we pair them with M&M candies, or something similar. As the child engages in the desired behavior (or a reasonable facsimile), the teacher gives him a "Thank you," an M&M, and a token. At first the children are motivated by the M&M's and have to be urged to hold on to the tokens; but then they find that the tokens can be used to buy admission to the movie, Playdoh, or other good things. The teacher tells them the price and asks them to count the tokens. Increasingly, the teacher "forgets" the M&M's. In two or three days the children get no candy, just the approval and the tokens. By then, they have learned.
>
> There are problems in maintaining a token exchange. Chidren become disinterested in certain reinforcers if they are used too fequently, and therefore in the tokens that buy them. For instance, young children will work very hard to save up tokens to play with Playdoh once a week: if they are offered Playdoh every day, the charm quickly fades. Some activities—snacks, movies, walks outdoors—are powerful enough to be used every day. (Hamblin *et at.*, 169: 21)

A substantial number of experiments have demonstrated that under such a system very young children can be taught to read, the verbal behavior of disadvantaged children can be enhanced, and changes in the behavior of hyperactive, aggressive, and autistic children can be brought about (Hamblin *et. al.*, 1971; Bandura, 1969). The key to successful learning lies in discovering the most effective type of schedule of reinforcers for the student involved. For example, the results of some experiments using verbal reinforcement indicated that reinforcers connoting praise— "good," "fine," and so on—produced the greatest improvements in performance among lower-SES children, while middle-class children were relatively more susceptible to reinforcers connoting correctness—for instance, "right" (Krasner and Ullman, 1965). Another requirement is to reward learning frequently enough to reinforce desired behavior but not so frequently as to satiate. Finally, for a behavior change to be permanent, it must be reinforced by the persons and groups with whom the child interacts regularly or uses as reference groups.

Critics of behavior modification object to the potential threat to individual freedom inherent in a technique that manipulates behavior so easily. They also worry about the long-term effectiveness of any learning approach that is dependent upon external rewards (which is not, in Moore's term, *autotelic*). There is in fact considerable evidence from psychological research that intrinsic and external motivations are mutually exclusive and nonadditive phenomena, and that while external rewards may enhance performance—at least in the short run—they may at the same time be detrimental to curiosity, autonomy, and discovery-based forms of learning (Deci, 1975). Such criticism can, of course, be leveled against *any* reward structure when participation in the system is not voluntary, and Hamblin argues that it is unethical as well as inefficient to design learning environments on the basis of educators' intellectual tastes rather than on the nature of children's learning mechanisms. If children learn more easily and effectively in an environment that "can be worked for material reinforcers," says Hamblin, why not allow them such an environment?

Classroom Social Climate

So far, we have been examining the various elements of classroom social structure and teaching technology. In this final section, we shall examine efforts to capture the full social essence or atmosphere of classrooms. The term used by sociologists to describe the overall social quality of a group or institution is social *climate*. Working from the almost commonsensical assumption that classroom climate has important effects on students' attitudes and performance, and from the less commonsensical assumption that the important features of the classroom as a learning environment can be described in terms of the combined attitudes or behaviors of the individuals comprising the class, social scientists have developed a host of measurement devices.[7] As we shall see, the climate measures developed to date have been only partially successful in capturing the full complexity of the classroom—or even its most salient aspects.

Classroom climate measures are of two general types. One type is based upon systematic observational techniques, by which the researcher attempts to record and classify "all" the classroom interaction during given periods of time. The second type is based upon information gathered from all class members, usually by self-report questionnaires, about their own attitudes and their perceptions of the behavior and attitudes of their classmates and teachers.

Climate Measures Based on Observation

Observational instrumentation has been dominated by the work of Flanders, whose Interaction Analysis Categories (FIAC) is the single most-often-used instrument for observing classroom behavior. Flanders's basic measure consists of ten categories of communication behavior, which are listed and described in Ex-

Exhibit 9–2
Flanders's Interaction Analysis Categories (FIAC)

TEACHER TALK
Indirect Influence

1.* Accepts Feeling: accepts and clarifies the feeling tone of the students in a nonthreatening manner. Feelings may be positive or negative. Predicting or recalling feelings are included.
2.* Praises or Encourages: praises or encourages student action or behavior. Jokes that release tension, not at the expense of another individual, nodding head or saying, "um hm? or "go on" are included.
3.* Accepts or Uses Ideas of Student: clarifying, building, or developing ideas suggested by a student. As teacher brings more of his or her own ideas into play, shift to category five.
4.* Asks Questions: asking a question about content or procedure with intent that a student answer.

Direct Influence

5* Lecturing: giving facts or opinions about content or procedure; expressing his or her own ideas, asking rhetorical questions.
6.* Giving Directions: directions, commands, or orders with which a student is expected to comply.
7.* Criticizing or Justifying Authority: statements intended to change student behavior from nonacceptable to acceptable pattern; bawling someone out; stating why the teacher is doing what he or she is doing; extreme self-reference.

STUDENT TALK

8.* Student Talk–Response: talk by students in response to teacher. Teacher initiates the contact or solicits student statement.
9.* Student Talk–Initiation: talk by students that they initiate. If "calling on" student is only to indicate who may talk next, observer must decide whether student wanted to talk. If he or she did, use this category.

10.* Silence or Confusion: pauses, short periods of silence, and periods of confusion in which communication cannot be understood by the observer.

*There is no scale implied by these numbers. Each number is classificatory; it designates a particular kind of communication event. To write these numbers down during observation is to enumerate, not to judge a position on a scale.
Source: From Flanders, 1960: Appendix F.

hibit 9–2. Seven of the categories are for various kinds of teacher talk, two are for student talk, and one for pauses, short periods of silence, or simultaneous talk by several people. The interaction is recorded by classroom observers who write down at three-second intervals the category that best describes the event(s) completed in that interval. The data thus consist of a list of numbers, which represent the sequence of events in the class.[8]

In a pair of experiments, the first a pretest for the second, Flanders tested a set of hypotheses interrelating the variables of teacher influence, student perception of teacher behavior, student dependence, and student learning. (A fifth variable having to do with the clarity of the task as perceived by the students was dropped from the second experiment after the pretest revealed no significant differences among respondents to the questions asked.) His general hypothesis was that student learning will be greatest when the teacher's influence is relatively indirect, although the strength of the relationship will vary with the students' own dependency needs.

The subjects for Flanders's study were eighth graders from a number of Minneapolis–St. Paul junior high schools. In the pretest, a laboratory experiment, subjects were assigned to groups of twenty each, balanced for sex and IQ distribution. Each group was taught a lesson in either math or social studies by a trained member of the research team, using teaching styles that varied on directness of influence and goal clarity.

The posttest covered the same two content areas. However, here the population sampled was *classrooms* (rather than individual students of different types). The sampling procedure was quite complex but can be summarized roughly as follows: all students in thirty-eight math and thirty-seven social studies classes whose teachers had earlier indicated willingness to participate in the project filled out questionnaires about the kinds of social patterns existing in their classes. Class averages were calculated, and the eight classes in each subject ranking highest in teacher direct influence and the eight ranking highest in indirect influence were designated for use in the study.

The teachers designated as highest on direct and indirect teaching style taught a two-week unit to their regular classes. Teachers were free to use the materials prepared as they wished, but the units were more or less the same in all classes. During the two weeks, trained observers in the classroom recorded the interaction using the FIAC scheme. All students were given pre- and posttests measuring the other major study variables.

On the basis of the observation, the teachers were classified on a simple "I/D ratio," which consisted of the total number of tallies in categories 1 through 3 divided by the total in categories 6 and 7 (see Exhibit 9–2). Categories 4 and 5 initially were included in the calculation of the I/D ratio, but later were eliminated in order to make the figure "more independent of the subject matter being taught." (Note that the I/D ratio also served as a kind of validator of the students' perception measure, which was used to select the classes for the study.)

The first experiment provided some but not very strong support for Flanders's hypotheses. In the geometry sessions, there was a consistent tendency for indirect teacher influence to be related to higher student performance, but the relationship was statistically significant only for students of average IQ (students were divided into three IQ categories) and for those who were most dependent. In the social studies sessions, however, there were no significant effects of teacher influence, goal clarity, or any of the other variables. The data also indicated some trends toward lower levels of dependency resulting from the indirect teaching situation, but the results were not statistically significant.

Exhibit 9–3
Means and Variance of Adjusted Final Test by IQ Group

	Teacher Style	Intelligence		N	Adjusted Final Test	
		IQ Group	Mean IQ		Mean	Variance
Social Studies	Indirect N = 7	High	124.7	59	38.7	13.3
		Average	110.9	91	36.3	20.5
		Low	94.8	33	33.0	38.2
		All	112.4	183	36.4	34.2
	Direct N = 8	High	123.3	38	35.7	18.9
		Average	109.2	101	33.8	31.2
		Low	93.8	59	31.1	38.4
		All	107.3	198	33.4	33.4
Mathematics	Indirect N = 7	High	122.1	51	31.3	44.7
		Average	106.9	100	28.9	38.7
		Low	93.1	33	24.2	30.0
		All	108.7	184	28.7	43.5
	Direct N = 9	High	122.9	42	29.3	40.1
		Average	107.1	77	27.3	38.8
		Low	91.6	60	23.3	23.7
		All	105.6	179	26.4	38.8

From Flanders, 1960: 90.

The second year's field experiment, using a larger sample and revised research instruments and scoring system, produced more substantial support for Flanders's predicted interrelationships. Exhibit 9–3 shows that in general, students in classes whose teachers had a high proportion of indirect relative to direct acts gain more than classes whose teachers had more direct teaching styles. In the top half of Exhibit 9–3

> the achievement of the seven indirect classes is compared with the eight direct classes for social studies. The difference between a mean of 36.4 and 33.4 is significant beyond the 0.01 level. . . . [Similarly in the bottom half of the table] the difference between the mathematics means of the seven indirect and nine direct classes shows superior achievement in the indirect classes.
>
> In those mathematics and social studies classrooms in which the teacher had a higher I/D ratio, the students scored significantly higher on a measure of achievement controlled for initial ability. There is no evidence to support the notion that students of above average, average, or below average IQ respond differently to direct and indirect influence. (Flanders, 1960: 89)

In a further analysis comparing only the five most direct with the five most indirect classes, this relationship was even more pronounced, although here the above-average students were the ones most affected by teaching style (a finding at variance with the results of the pretest). In addition to showing higher achievement, the students in the indirect classes tended to have more favorable attitudes toward the class.

One important prediction that was somewhat supported by the first experiment but not by the second was that students scoring high on the dependence proneness test would react differently to patterns of direct and indirect influence. There were no differences in achievement means between students with high- and low-dependence scores in either subject or either type of influence.

A more-or-less unanticipated finding was that *all* teachers used a great amount of direct influence. The difference was that "indirect" teachers were more likely to differentiate their type of influence in terms of the type of task or the stage within the two-week unit. That is, they were more flexible in their use of influence.

The great strength of Flanders's study is that it is based upon extensive but systematic observation of actual classroom behavior (not simply watching the teacher teach, but relating teacher behavior to the characteristics of the students and the learning tasks) and that the instrument for classifying the teacher's behavior was based upon a thorough review of previous work and a relatively sophisticated model of group behavior. The study is also unique in that the researchers tested their hypotheses in both a laboratory and a field setting.

The basic FIAC was developed during the early 1960s, but during the past decade Flanders and his associates have created a number of elaborations and variations of the original ten-category scale, have conducted empirical research relating the scale to student outcomes, and have attempted to utilize research findings to improve teacher education (Flanders, 1970). However, as in the case of the Rosenthal and Jacobson experiment on expectancy effects, replications of Flanders's studies by researchers not associated with him have not always supported his hypotheses. While Flanders's own experiments showed fairly consistent relationships between indirect teaching styles and positive student outcomes, studies by other researchers using the FIAC have shown considerably less consistent results (Nielsen and Kirk, 1974; Dunkin and Biddle, 1974).

Climate Measures Based on Questionnaire Data

Climate measures based upon self-report questionnaires also examine teaching style, but they are, by comparison with most observational scales, more concerned with the expectations and sanctions that organize classroom life, that is, with the kinds of behavior expected of students and what happens when they do or do not meet expectations. Many of these measures were influenced by Murray's Need-Press Model, published in 1938, which postulates that students' perceptions of the pressures and demands of their environment—which Murray terms *environmental press*—are the crucial elements of social climate. An example is the High School Characteristics Index (HSCI) developed by Stern, Stein, and Bloom (1956), which consists of a set of thirty environmental press scales of ten items each. The items, which are statements with which the respondent can agree or disagree, describe daily activities in the school and impressions of and attitudes about school policies and procedures. One statement, for example, is: "You need permission to do anything around here." The thirty press scales have such intriguing titles as Abasement, Adaptability, Affiliation, and Aggression.

Among the most important measures developed in the last decade is Walberg's Learning Environment Inventory (LEI), which is based upon a theoretical model of the class as a social system that posits that classroom climate is related to the classroom role structure and students' personality needs, and that all three, both jointly and independently, affect classroom behavior including learning. The LEI consists of about one hundred items. On each item, the respondent is asked to indicate on a four-point scale (Strongly Agree, Agree, Disagree, Strongly Disagree) how well that item describes his or her class. Responses to sets of seven similar items were averaged to give scores on a number of dimensions of subscales. Exhibit 9–4 shows the subscales in the LEI and a sample of items from each scale.

Empirical research by Walberg and his associates has indicated that classroom climate, as measured by the Learning Environment Inventory, can be predicted from a number of antecedent and concurrent variables. For example, classes in which students had positive or high scores on a series of personality tests tended to have high scores on the Goal Direction and Democracy subscales and low scores on the Disorganization and Apathy subscales. The greater the proportion of girls in a class the higher the class score on the Satisfaction Scale and the lower

Exhibit 9–4
Walberg's Learning Environment Inventory*

Subscale Title	Sample Item
Apathy	Members of the class don't care what the class does.
Cliqueness	Certain students work only with their close friends.
Cohesiveness	Members of the class are personal friends.
Competitiveness	Students compete to see who can do the best work.
Democracy	Class decisions tend to be made by all the students.
Difficulty	Students are constantly challenged.
Disorganization	The class is disorganized.
Diversity	The class divides its efforts among several purposes.
Environment	The books and equipment students need or want are easily available to them in the classroom.
Favoritism	Only the good students are given special projects.
Formality	Students are asked to follow a complicated set of rules.
Friction	Certain students are considered uncooperative.
Goal Direction	The objectives of the class are specific.
Intimacy	Members of the class are personal friends.
Satisfaction	Students are well satisfied with the work of the class.
Speed	The class has difficulty keeping up with its assigned work.

*Information compiled from Walberg, 1969, and Anderson and Walberg, 1974. Slightly different combinations of subscales are used in various studies by Walberg and his associates.

the class score on unfavorable scales such as Apathy. Walberg's own research has also shown positive relationships between various kinds of student learning and the scales for Cohesiveness, Environment, and Satisfaction, and negative relationships between learning and the Friction, Cliqueness, Disorganization, and Apathy scales, although the findings differed somewhat from one study to another. In addition, some research using the LEI suggests that different aspects of classroom climate may affect different students differently.

> Cliques, for example, seem to aid low-ability females, since for such females cliques are considered to be school-oriented. On the other hand, males of below-average ability form cliques which enable them to escape their responsibilites to the school and substitute for them peer group non-learning norms. Classroom intimacy, for another example, is positively related to learning for high-ability girls and has negative effects on learning for girls of lower ability. Other examples could be cited, but the main point is that classroom characteristics do affect learning and affect it differently depending on the students' characteristics. (Anderson, 1970: 150–151)

Conclusions

The classroom is a system characterized by the close physical proximity of its young members for long intervals of time and regulated by a relatively rigid authority pattern and schedule of activities, each of which has its own set of rules. While we are still far from a comprehensive, validated theory of the classroom, sociologists have during the past few years developed more sophisticated models that define and explain selected aspects of classroom structure and interaction. Most research now assumes that students and teachers have mutual effects on each other, that the sequence of interactive exchanges over time must be traced in order to understand the ultimate outcomes, and that a given classroom situation may be differentially perceived by and have different consequences for different individuals or subgroups. As one pair of observers put it: "One student's 'open' environment may be another's 'chaotic' one, resulting in different learning consequences" (Nielsen and Kirk, 1974: 68).

Class size and student achievement are not related, at least not in a simple, linear fashion for the size range normally found in our public schools. There are similarly, no clear-cut relationships between ability grouping and achievement. The presence of very gifted students may raise the performance of their classmates, though the gifted themselves seem to achieve at their highest levels in homogeneous classes. The presence of slow learners does not have any clearly negative effects upon other students.

The highly centralized communication system found in most classrooms may be satisfying to the person in the central position (usually the teacher). It is also an orderly system and an efficient way of reaching "correct" answers to well-defined problems, but less centralized structures are more conducive to the involvement of additional group members and encourage greater independence from the leader.

Classroom climate is a complex and multidimensional concept, difficult to capture empirically whether one attempts to measure it via observation or self-report questionnaire. There is some empirical evidence of effects of climate upon student attitudes and achievements, though research by the authors of a given climate measure tends to show stronger and more consistent relationships with student learning than replications by researchers not involved in the development of the instrument used. Theoretical work in this area may be hampered by certain partially ideological hangovers from the past. For example, the emphasis upon "warm" and "democratic" climates resulting from Deweian educational philosophy and Lewin and Lippitt's influential work on children's groups has persisted, despite substantial empirical evidence that pleasant, student-centered classrooms are not necessarily productive of student achievement—and may in fact produce the opposite.

The extent to which classroom social organization has changed, or can be made to change, has been of concern to sociologists as well as to educators. The 1960s were a time of unusual optimism about the possibilities of significant educational reform, but by the beginning of the 1970s many analysts felt that any substantial change at the classroom level would require changes in the basic structure of educational institutions and of society itself. Noting the capacity of teachers to convert teaching innovations into conventional classroom practices, scholars like Dreeben and Jackson remained dubious that any new research findings or technological inventions would have a revolutionary impact on the practice of teaching.

While the reformist spirit of the 1960s may be largely dissipated, there does seem to be evidence of some basic and long-term changes in the social organization of classrooms, in the direction of greater activism of the student role, more flexibility in the use of classroom time and space, more direct reward structures, and more interaction and cooperation among students and teachers. Partly in response to the radical critics and partly as a consequence of technological and social structural innovations such as team teaching, the open classroom, and teaching strategies based upon behavior modification theory, life in school does seem to be changing in ways that make it more congruent with children's experiences and treatment outside of school.

Notes

1. This reliance upon mean increments as indicators of learning or attitude change may introduce biases in interpretation, because for classes or subgroups that started out at a high level further increments are harder than for groups with lower initial scores.

2. Note, however, that Goldberg's findings caution against a simplistic interpretation. In their sample, only the most gifted—those with IQ scores of 130 or higher—produce an upgrading effect in a heterogeneous class. This, in addition to the wide interclass variations found within a given school and ability pattern, indicate that it is not enough simply to place culturally deprived children in schools with higher-status age mates. It is how and

in what number they are assimilated into a new learning environment that determine subsequent academic progress.

3. The research in this section is based upon the type of sociological explanation covered in cell 8 of Exhibit 2–1 in Chapter 2—that is, those aspects of the classroom as a physical environment that have impact on its social organization.

4. See Exhibit 2–1, cells 7 versus 8.

5. In a typical experiment, the task was to solve a puzzle in which fifteen pieces had to be arranged to form five squares. In another, subjects were given cards with a number of different symbols, the task being to determine the one symbol common to all cards. In both experiments, subjects were allowed to communicate only via written messages, according to the particular communication structure assigned. Some of the experiments used a specially designed circular table, at which subjects are separated from each other by vertical partitions, with slots between pairs of subjects who were allowed to communicate with each other.

6. This experiment and others incorporating behavior modification techniques are discussed in Krasner and Ullman, 1965 and 1966.

7. Over a hundred measures of classroom climate have been published within the past decade (Dunkin and Biddle, 1974: Chapter 5).

8. For a full description of the measure and the observer procedures, see Flanders, 1960: Appendix F. Flanders's measure is based upon a more elaborate and general scheme for the analysis of interaction in small groups developed by Bales and his colleagues at the Harvard Social Relations Laboratory—see, for example, Bales, 1952.

Effectiveness of the School   Chapter 10

At the heart of the controversies surrounding public education is the strongly held belief that schools should have a "positive impact" on their clientele.
William Spady

The hypothesis is rather compelling that qualitative differences in the schools themselves account for much, if not all, of the variation in academic and vocational achievement between one school and another.   H. S. Dyer

Schools bring little influence to bear on a child's development that is independent of his background and general school context.
James S. Coleman, Ernest Q. Campbell, et al.

To me, the most intriguing problem for future research is the apparent contradiction between survey data which seems to suggest that educational experiences have made little difference in students' lives and the participants' subjective feeling that a particular experience has been very important to them.
Christopher Jencks

Ever since the publication of *Equality of Educational Opportunity* in 1966, researchers and educators have been grappling with its rather distressing implication that schools per se have little independent influence upon children's intellectual achievements. The results of the survey are difficult to present concisely, since the analysis includes a host of dependent and independent variables. It is, moreover, carried out upon a sample broken down into a number of subgroups, by race, age, geographical region, and so on. The set of variables showing the strongest relationship to verbal ability scores, the major indicant of student achievement used in the report, are factors of the social composition of the student body—for example, the proportion who are in a college prep curriculum, the proportion who are white, and the proportion who have encyclopedias in their homes. Only a small amount of achievement variance is accounted for explicitly by variations in physical facilities and curriculum (say, enriched curriculum, foreign language programs, libraries, or science labs). Some teacher characteristics—race, verbal scores, and attitudes toward integration—are related to the achievement of some categories of students, but such characteristics as experience, academic degree, student-teacher ratio, and the availability of counselors are not correlated. In summarizing these results, the authors conclude that schools have little independent effect upon children, and, moreover, "that this very lack of an independent effect means that the inequalities imposed on children by their home, neighborhood, and peer environment are carried along to become the inequalities with which they confront adult life at the end of school" (Coleman, Campbell, *et al.*, 1966: 325).

How does one evaluate the effectiveness of a school? In Chapters 8 and 9, we have seen the difficulties of developing valid measures to describe a single classroom, even though at the classroom level we are limited to a relatively small group of students who are about the same age and engaged in studying a given course or curriculum with one or a few teachers. At the level of the school as a whole, the complexities of conceptualization, measurement, and analysis are intensified.

A host of school characteristics have been postulated as affecting school productivity. In order to organize the discussion in this chapter, we shall group the independent variables as follows: (1) characteristics of the students in a school, including their numbers, their family background, their abilities and their attitudes; (2) characteristics of the school staff, including their numbers, training, and experience; and (3) physical or nonhuman resources, including both those that directly convey the information or skills to be taught (for example, books, maps, laboratory materials, and audio-visual aids) and those that structure the learning environment spatially and temporally (for example, the physical plant, classroom furniture, clocks, and bells).

Although any research design depends upon the researcher's resources as well as the particular questions he or she wants to answer, one can identify some general research strategies for analyzing school effectiveness. The studies to be discussed in this chapter generally follow one of the following strategies:

Strategy 1: Designate one variable (or a small set of variables) that affects student performance. Draw a sample of schools that differ on this variable and compare them on some measure(s) of academic performance.

Strategy 2: Gather data on a large number of variables in multiple schools. Use multivariate analysis procedures to determine which variables are most strongly related to academic performance and whether various independent variables are themselves interrelated.

Strategy 3: Select a sample of schools that vary on overall academic performance—for example, schools that have produced high academic achievement or improvement and schools that have produced low achievement or minimal or no improvement. Compare these schools on selected school characteristics.

Strategy 4: Construct mathematical models of the relationships between educational "inputs" and "outputs," and test these models against empirical data.

Characteristics of Students

Interest in students as school "resources" has increased in recent years with mounting evidence that a given student's educational performance is at least partly explained by the characteristics of the student body of the school he or she attends. Among the most important student resource variables are *demographic* variables (the numbers of students who constitute a school's population and the distribution of various attributes among the student body) and *attitudinal* variables (students' aspirations and their attitudes toward school and learning).

School Size

The sheer number of individuals comprising a school's student body became a national issue with the publication of Conant's report on the American high school (1959), and its plea for the large, "comprehensive" high school. Conant based his plea upon the greater opportunities for differentiation in the larger school—the point being that a school with a graduating class of fewer than one hundred cannot offer an adequate program for all kinds of students (including nonacademic training for the less gifted as well as advanced courses in mathematics, science, and foreign languages for the brightest 15 to 20 percent). Conant, however, offered no empirical support for his contention—say, in the form of comparisons between large and small schools on measures of academic output.

By contrast, studies by Barker and associates at the University of Kansas that compared thirteen Kansas high schools, ranging from 35 to almost 2,300 in size, favor the smaller schools. The general finding of the Barker studies was that students in smaller schools and communities participated on the average in more nonclass "behavior settings" and held more responsible positions in these settings. (The authors defend their choice of extracurricular activities on technical grounds—the difficulties of assessing motivation and involvement in activities where attendance and participation are not voluntary—and on the grounds that the great amount of students' energies invested in extracurricular activities and the schools' extensive support of them put such activities within the boundaries of the total educational process.)

The bits of data on academic activity in these schools suggest, however, that the academic and nonacademic structures of a school are not necessarily parallel. There were, for example, fewer different kinds of subjects offered in the smaller schools, although these were the schools that provided richer extracurricular environments. And in a comparison of twenty-eight juniors from small schools with twenty-eight selected from the large schools, all with IQ scores above 110 and of the same sex, it was found that the total class enrollments for the bright students were higher in the small schools, but that this higher average was accounted for mainly by nonacademic electives such as music, home economics, and shop. The students from small schools were actually taking fewer academic courses (Barker et al., 1962: appendix 12.1). Another finding is that more students in the small schools had taken some kind of musical instruction, but that the large schools contained higher proportions of students who could be considered expert in some area of music. The authors interpret these findings as indicating greater and more varied academic "participation" by bright students in small schools. However, a different interpretation is also possible: that the small-school environment produces less motivation or pressure for the talented student to take the tough academic courses and to master a skill, such as playing a musical instrument, to the point of expertness.

A series of analyses of the Project Talent data collected in the early 1960s (Flanagan et al., 1962) revealed no consistent pattern of correlations between high school size (measured by number of seniors and average grade-level size as well as total school size) and a variety of school outcome measures (including achievement test scores, dropout rates, and proportion of seniors going on to college). A survey of almost a hundred studies conducted during the 1950s and 1960s also found no overall effects of school size, except where large schools offered more courses (Hechinger, 1977). A 1976 analysis by the State University of New York and a 1975 study by the Federal Reserve Bank of Philadelphia on factors affecting learning in that city's schools (Summers and Wolfe, 1975) both generally favored smaller schools, but it is not clear from these analyses whether achievement in the larger schools was poorer because of their size or because the largest schools are most often located in big cities with high proportions of students from disadvantaged families. In general, research that focuses solely or mainly on the variable of student body size (Strategy 1) has not shown strong correlations between size and academic achievement.

In sum, while there may be some optimum size ranges for elementary and secondary schools, they have not been identified in research to date. As is the case at the classroom level, size per se does not seem to affect academic performance directly.[1]

Social Context

A mode of analysis that has aroused considerable interest among sociologists in recent years is the study of "contextual" effects, an analysis that examines the extent to which an individual's attitudes and behavior are explained by the proportions of the total group who have given attributes. Contextual effects, like the effects of ability grouping within the classroom we examined in Chapter 9, are often postulated in terms of reference-group theory—that is, it is hypothesized that students respond to the norms, performance standards, and rewards that are salient to the student body of which they are members, or to certain other students who serve as role models. The basic technique in contextual analysis consists of combining the attributes of all the members of a social group or system to form a single measure by which the individual members may be identified. The variables that have been most often used in contextual analyses of schools are the demographic factors of SES composition and racial composition.

Among the first sociologists to examine contextual effects on learning was Alan Wilson, two of whose studies will be discussed here. Both studies use contextual variables based upon background attributes, although one is concerned with the effect of a single contextual variable upon student aspirations (Strategy 1); the other, with the independent and joint effects of two such variables, plus some additional independent variables, upon test scores (Strategy 2).

In the first of the two Wilson studies, conducted in the late 1950s, eight high schools in the San Francisco–Oakland Bay area were classified into three groups according to the SES of the students' parents. That is, the combined SES characteristics of the student body as a whole were conceived as forming part of the climate or context of the school for a given student. Group A schools contained high proportions of students whose parents ranked high in occupational and educational status; Group B schools had relatively fewer families in the higher categories, and Group C schools had the fewest.

The question Wilson wanted to answer was whether differences in school social context influenced the educational aspirations of boys from varying social strata. "Concretely, are the sons of manual workers more likely to adhere to middle-class values and have high educational aspirations if they attend a predominantly middle-class school, and conversely, are the aspirations of the sons of professionals more modest if they attend a predominantly working-class school?" (Wilson, 1959: 837). The empirical findings indicated that the answer is yes: 80 percent of the students in the Group A schools, 57 percent in the Group B schools, and only 38 percent in the Group C schools had college plans. Moreover, while the status of a student's parents did have an independent effect upon educational aspirations (children of professional parents were more likely to have college plans than children of manual workers), this family effect was modified by the dominant class character of the school's student body. Thus 93 percent of the sons of professionals in the Group A schools wanted to go to college, compared to less than two-thirds of the sons of professionals in the Group C schools; similarly, more than half of the sons of manual workers in the Group A schools planned to go on to college, compared to one-third in the Group C schools.

Wilson found similar relationships when he used the father's education and the mother's education as the independent variables, and also when he used academic grades as the dependent variable. In each case the combined attributes of the student body, which in Wilson's conceptualization produced the student norms, had a clear, consistent effect upon students' educational aspirations and performance—an effect in addition to students' individual family origins.

The second Wilson study (1967), carried out under contract with the U.S. Commission on Civil Rights, considers both the racial and socioeconomic context of schools. Again the sample is from the San Francisco Bay area, but ranges from elementary through high school. A major portion of the study is devoted to a comparison of the effects of school and neighborhood context upon the academic achievement of black and white children at different age levels. School composition is measured by the proportion of students who were black and the proportion who were of the lower class—or lower SES (whose family heads were unskilled laborers, domestics, unemployed, or welfare recipients). The neighborhood context measure was analogous to the school measure, except that the unit was the "enumeration district" in which the student's family lived. *Enumeration district* is a concept adopted from the 1960 census breakdowns and consists of a small geographic area of about two hundred households.

Examination of the mean reading-achievement scores for the sixth graders in the sample, controlling for one independent variable at a time, indicated that the greatest differences were produced by school context; the mean reading level of the sixth graders who had attended primary schools with populations of less than 10 percent lower-SES children was 7.4, compared with a mean of 4.9 for children in schools where a majority of their classmates were of lower SES. This was a greater difference than that produced by neighborhood context, or by individual family status or race (the mean reading scores of black and white sixth graders were 5.0 and 6.7, respectively).

The univariate comparisons do not, however, take into account the fact that many of these variables are themselves interrelated (for example, black students tend to live in predominantly black neighborhoods and to attend predominantly black schools). The multivariate analysis controlling simultaneously for school context, neighborhood context, individual SES, race, ability, parental supervision, and home atmosphere (number of objects in the home) showed that except for primary school mental maturity the greatest amount of variance in reading scores was explained by the social class composition of the primary school. Moreover, neither the *racial* composition of the school nor the racial *or* class composition of the *neighborhood* had any independent effect on school performance over and above the social-class composition of the school.

These findings have considerable significance for educational theory and policy.

> Our continuing reservation about the relevance of proposals to alter the demographic composition of schools is the question as to whether continuing residential segregation might structure the effective environment of students so that their integration in schools makes no difference. These data are inconsistent with this reservation. On the contrary, these data suggest that the effect of neighborhood segregation upon achievement is entirely through the resulting segregation of neighborhood schools on social class lines. Restructuring the composition of schools, even in the absence of residential rearrangements, can be expected to have an effect upon the academic achievement of students . . .
>
> Finally, the racial composition of the elementary school does not have any independent effect, over and above the social-class composition of the school, upon achievement. (Wilson, 1967: 180–181)

More recent research conveys more skepticism about the amount of variance in student outcomes that can be directly attributed to socio-economic context. Hauser's review of previous studies and his own analysis of data from the Wisconsin Study indicate that there is some relationship between SES composition and academic achievements and aspirations, but that it is relatively small when such important variables as students' IQ scores are controlled (Hauser, 1971 and 1974). From a reanalysis of EEO and Project Talent data, Jencks and his associates conclude that middle-class high schools have contradictory effects on students.

> On the one hand, they increase a student's chances of making college-oriented friends. This raises the probability that the student will go to college. On the other hand, middle-class high schools have higher academic standards than working-class high schools. This means that if a student at any given ability level enters a middle-class school, he is likely to rank lower in his class than if he enters a working-class school. . . . we would expect a student's chances of attending college to be greatest if he attended a high school where the other students had high aspirations but low test scores. . . . We would not expect his chances of attending college to be affected much either way if he entered a high school where the other students had both high test scores and high aspirations, or where they had both low test scores and low aspirations. Since most schools fall into one of the two latter categories we would not expect social composition to have much impact in most cases. (Jencks *et al.*, 1972: 152–153)

Finally, research indicates that SES contextual effects may themselves be dependent upon other factors. In particular, the racial and SES composition of most schools are correlated, so that minority students are disproportionately concentrated in lower-SES neighborhoods and schools and are thus more likely than whites to be subject to adverse contextual effects.

Research on racial composition (in most cases the minority group studied is blacks) indicates: (1) that the proportion of racial minority enrollment in a school is inversely related to student academic achievement, although the strength of the relationship tends to diminish at the higher grade levels; (2) that minority students' achievement tends to be higher in schools with a high proportion of white students, though only when white and nonwhite students are in the same classes (in fact, when black students are tracked into segregated classes in desegregated high schools, their performance suffers more than if they were in racially segregated schools); but (3) that the *aspirations* of black students tend to be higher in all or predominantly black schools than in schools with a majority of white students (Bargen and Walberg, 1974; St. John, 1975: McPartland, 1967; Spady, 1976). Spady interprets the latter finding in terms of comparative reference-group processes, by which even high-ability black students in integrated schools may not be receiving positive feedback on their efforts because of the tough competition. Thus,

> they see themselves as less capable of being high achievers than their white peers. . . . Able blacks in predominantly black schools, on the other hand, are more likely

to find themselves near the top of the class and apparently adjust their college attainment chances accordingly. They may lack a realistic perspective on how their objective achievement level compares with that of other ninth graders in other schools, however, and their aspirations may appear inflated or unrealistic. (Spady, 1967: 210. Spady's interpretation is consistent with the empirical findings of Dornbusch's study of inequities in school evaluation systems, discussed in Chapter 8.)

In sum, SES and racial context, which are themselves related, do seem to have some independent relationship with students' achievements and aspirations, but they are mediated by other characteristics of students and their schools. Moreover, the positive effects of being in a school with high proportions of high status and/or academically oriented students may be partly offset by the negative effects on many individuals' relative performance and their sense of competence.

Social Climate

Students' achievements and aspirations may be affected not only by the demographic characteristics of the student body of their school, but also by the social climate formed by their attitudes and values—as Spady puts it, by the "collective orientations" of the student body that "may stimulate or thwart individual students' interest in academic endeavor" (Spady, 1976: 204). Measures of classroom social climate were discussed in the preceding chapter, and here we shall consider measures that combine the attitudes and values of the entire student body of a school, or some meaningful portion of it.

Perhaps the most sophisticated and carefully controlled analysis of school value climate is the study by McDill, Meyers, and Rigsby (1969 and 1973) introduced in Chapter 2. The goal of the study was to explain why some schools are more productive than others. Thus McDill and his colleagues drew up a sample to study the dependent variable, selecting schools that differed in aggregate academic performance and comparing them on a number of individual and school characteristics (Strategy 3).

The sample was designed to maximize geographical spread and variation on multiple school characteristics. Ten pairs of high schools from eight states were chosen so that each pair was from the same state, but one school in each pair had a distinctly higher record of academic performance than the other. A three-stage sampling procedure was used: first, ranking all U.S. high schools in terms of their numbers of National Merit Scholars and the proportion of graduates who subsequently obtained Ph.D.'s as a rough measure of "academic productivity"; next, "selecting from the larger pool of institutions a limited number which varied on several demographic and social characteristics" (for instance, size, SES, and ethnic composition of the school and of the community it served). The final choice was made after obtaining—from alumni and educators familiar with their educational programs—additional information on the schools selected in the first two stages.

As we saw in Chapter 2, the procedure used to obtain the climate measures was a factor analysis of thirty-nine school characteristics. Some characteristics were based upon a single questionnaire item (say, the percentage of students in a school who say it is extremely important to get high grades). Others were a composite of several items, many of them adaptations of scales of environmental press, as described in Chapter 9. From the factor analysis of these single- and multiple-item characteristics, six constructs or factors emerged, each of which contained a number of characteristics that grouped together statistically and substantively. McDill titled the six factors as follows:

1. *Academic Emulation:* the degree to which academic excellence is valued by the student body. (This factor is the most important of the six statistically, accounting for a greater proportion of the total variance in achievement than any of the others.)
2. *Student Perception of Intellectualism-Estheticism:* the degree to which acquisition of knowledge is valued.
3. *Cohesive and Egalitarian Estheticism:* the extent to which the student social system emphasizes intellectual criteria for status as opposed to family background or other ascribed criteria. This factor also taps the degree of social integration among students.
4. *Scientism:* the degree of scientific interest and emphasis in the school.
5. *Humanistic Excellence:* parallel to factor 4, but focusing upon art, humanities, social studies, and current social issues.
6. *Academically Oriented Student Status System:* the extent to which intellectual and academic performance is rewarded by student peers as compared to rewards for participation in extracurricular activities.

Although the development of the school climate measures was of interest in itself, the real purpose of the study was to measure the effects of such dimensions upon student productivity relative to other characteristics, including the SES composition of the school. The data analysis showed a positive relationship between high scores on each of the six climate dimensions and students' math achievement scores, and between this achievement measure and high SES context. In terms of *relative* effects, each of the climate dimensions except factor 4 was more strongly related to achievement than was SES, with factor 1 having an especially strong relationship. Each of the climate dimensions continued to exert an effect in the expected direction even when the individual factors of scholastic ability, personal values, family status, and the school SES context were controlled simultaneously. By contrast, the original effect of SES context almost disappeared when IQ scores and individual SES were controlled. Thus McDill and his associates, contrary to Wilson, conclude that "the SES context of the school does not adequately reflect the shared norms and motivations of students and teachers and that direct measures of school climate should be employed in contextual research whenever feasible" (McDill and Rigsby, 1973: 88).

A regression analysis of the effects upon math achievement of the climate dimensions, father's education, and student's individual academic values and ability indicated that individual ability explains the greatest amount of variation, with father's education and own values having about equal weight. None of the school climate dimensions accounts for a large proportion of the variation in achievement, but each makes some contribution toward explaining this variation beyond that jointly explained by the other three variables (all of which already have been shown in much previous research to be correlated with academic performance). Academic emulation has the strongest independent effect of the six climate measures, and is apparently the most comprehensive indicator of the academic quality of the school.

McDill's analysis also included correlations of math scores with a number of formal school characteristics deriving from the economic resources of the community, including teachers' starting salaries and per-pupil expenditure. McDill found these correlations to be negligible or negative, a result congruent with the conclusion of *Equality of Educational Opportunity*.

In summary, the results of this very thorough analysis support the existence of school effects independent of the personal characteristics of the student body (either on individuals or aggregates). They also suggest something about the way in which schools as learning environments produce or fail to produce achievement. "More specifically, the findings lead to the tentative conclusion that in those schools where academic competition, intellectualism and subject-matter competence are emphasized and rewarded by faculty and student bodies, individual students tend to conform to the scholastic norms of the majority and achieve at a higher level" (McDill *et al.*, 1967: 199). Such schools are more likely to contain high proportions of students from advantaged families, but, concludes McDill, the value climate that builds up in a high school comes to exert an influence above and beyond what would be predicted on the basis of student-body characteristics alone.

McDill's work has in turn been tested and expanded by Brookover and his associates, who examined the social and psychological factors related to achievement in a sample of Michigan elementary schools. Factor analysis of responses from students produced four factors concerning student perceptions of: (1) the present evaluations and expectations of teachers and others in the school social system, (2) the future evaluations and expectations of others, (3) the level of feelings of futility permeating the school social system, and (4) the academic achievement norms existing in the school. Six meaningful factors emerged from the analysis of teachers' responses: (1) present evaluations and expectations, (2) future evaluations and expectations, (3) perception of parent and student "push" for educational achievement, (4) their own push of individual students, (5) feelings of job satisfaction, and (6) perception of student academic "improvability" (Brookover and Schneider, 1975).

Characteristics of Teachers

The second major human resource in schools is teachers, and much of the past decade's debate about school effectiveness has been about whether the quantity and quality of teachers as an aggregate have significant impact upon students' achievement.

Teacher quantity is generally measured in terms of average class size—that is, not just the total number of teachers in a given school or school district, but the number of teachers in relation to the number of students. As we have seen, class size has not been found to be consistently related to overall student achievement, although smaller classes do seem to benefit certain kinds of children, in particular low achievers, when teachers adapt their teaching styles to the smaller class size.

Teacher quality is generally measured by amount of education (usually number of formal college credits or degrees), experience, or some combination of the two. For example, in Bargen and Walberg's evaluation of Chicago public schools, each school was given a teacher-quality score that was the sum of (a) the mean number of years of teaching experience of the entire school faculty plus (b) the mean number of higher educational degrees, with each individual teacher being given a score of one for a B.A. degree, two for an M.A. degree, and three for an M.A. plus at least thirty-six additional hours of course credits. From their analysis of the Chicago data, Bargen and Walberg concluded that higher student achievement is partially determined by teacher quality, although over time the strength of the relationship between achievement and teacher quality declines while the strength of the relationship between present achievement and achievement in earlier grades increases.

Researchers disagree about the importance of teacher quality as measured by previous experience and training. A review of the literature by Averch *et al.* (1977) found, like Bargen and Walberg, fairly consistent positive relationships between student achievement and teacher experience, with stronger relationships for math, science, and social studies than for verbal or reading achievement. But reviews by Lau (1978) and Hechinger (1977) reported less consistent positive relationships, and the latter also found that the advantages of teacher experience began to diminish after about five years. The finding of the Coleman Report, which sparked much of the debate on teacher quality, was that with the exception of scores on verbal-ability tests teacher qualifications did not generally have as much effect as student characteristics on student achievement, but that teacher experience did benefit racial-minority students more than white students. In fact, Coleman and his coauthors qualify their general conclusion that schools have little independent effects upon children by pointing out that the degree of impact is different for different groups. Thus:

> improving the school of a minority pupil will increase his achievement more than will improving the school of a white child. Similarly, the average minority pupil's achievement will suffer more in a school of low quality than will the average white pupil's. In short, white, and to a lesser extent Oriental Americans, are less affected one way or the other by the quality of their schools than are minority pupils. This indicates that it is for the most disadvantaged children that improvements in school quality will make the most difference in achievement. (Coleman et al., 1966: 21)

Spady, drawing a similar conclusion, suggests that the achievement of high-status children may depend more upon "differences in the level of assistance and stimulation they receive at home, whereas lower SES students must depend mainly on the school for help" (Spady, 1976: 193).

The study of the Philadelphia schools, supported by the Federal Reserve Bank of Philadelphia (Summers and Wolfe, 1975), found that the effects of teacher experience depended upon the students and the subject being taught. For example, low-achieving students tended to do better in classes of twenty-seven or fewer, with younger and less experienced teachers (who perhaps had not yet developed negative expectations for pupils), and with a relatively large number of high achievers in their classes. The interaction between student abilities and teacher experience also varied by subject matter and the age level of the students.

> In elementary school, length of experience has a very different impact on high- and low-achieving pupils. High-achieving pupils do best with more experienced teachers, but these teachers lower the learning growth of low achievers—these students do best with new, relatively inexperienced teachers, who, perhaps, have an undampened enthusiasm for teaching those who find it hard to learn. In junior high school, a very experienced English teacher is particularly effective with high-ability students, but [teacher] experience of ten or more years helps all students. The pattern of effectiveness for math teachers is somewhat different: Math teachers with three to nine years of experience are particularly effective, but math teachers with more than ten years of experience actually have a negative effect on learning math. This latter effect arises, most likely, because these teachers received pre-Sputnik training. They are teaching the New Math, though they were not originally trained to teach it. (Summers and Wolfe, 1975: 12)

The findings thus indicate that school resources are more effective when they are targeted to the types of students who will benefit most.

Another possible component of teacher quality is teachers' earning power, although teacher salaries represent an investment made by school systems as well as a characteristic of teachers themselves. A study of Michigan schools for the purpose of identifying the distinguishing features of "outstanding" schools, found that such schools had a higher than average proportion of teachers earning more than eleven thousand dollars (Klitgaard and Hall, 1973). Bargen and Walberg's (1974) review of studies done mainly in the 1960s or early 1970s found a number of cases in which there was a positive relationship between teachers' salaries and some measure of student achievement and only one case in which there was a negative relationship, but Hechinger's (1977) review found more studies in which there was no relationship or the findings were ambiguous than studies in which teacher salaries were related to student performance.

Critics of *Equality of Educational Opportunity* have argued that Coleman's heavy dependence upon regression analysis, in which the order of controlling the variables affects the size of the coefficients obtained, led to an underestimate of the effects of school investments. Moreover, when two independent variables in a multiple regression analysis are themselves related, as are students' social background and school resources (including teacher quality), controlling for the first will reduce the correlation of the second with the dependent variable—that is, reduce the amount of the variance it "explains." As one critic points out: "By choosing to control first for social-background factors the authors of the Report inadvertently biased its analysis against finding school resources to be an important determinant of scholastic achievement'' (Bowles, 1968: 93). Bowles reanalyzed some of the data, reversing the order in which the school resources and social-class coefficients were computed, and found much stronger relationships between achievement and teachers' salaries, teachers' verbal ability, and class size than Coleman and his colleagues had reported. For example: "the amount of variance in achievement scores of twelfth grade Negro students explained by the variable 'teachers' verbal ability' more than doubles if this variable is brought into the analysis first, rather than after the social background variables." Bowles thus claims that "contrary to the Coleman conclusion, significant gains in Negro students' achievement levels can be made by directing additional resources to their education" (Bowles, 1968: 92, 94).[2]

What conclusions should be drawn from the confusing array of often discrepant findings about teacher qualification? Blanket claims that teachers don't make any difference are clearly unwarranted, but it is far from clear *how* they make a difference or how one can identify the kinds of teachers most likely to make a difference. Spady, whose thoughtful review of research on the impact of school resources was a major reference for this chapter, suggests that both educators and researchers may not have been paying attention to the most important aspects of teacher quality. They have, says Spady, been "too conscious of measuring formal course credits and degree attainments rather than the teacher's ongoing engagement in expertise-enhancing activities" (Spady, 1976: 201. He points, for example, to some research indicating benefits to lower-SES, white students from the verbal ability and the *recent* educational experiences of their teachers). Spady feels that

> school systems that give priority to formal teacher credentials and plant and program facilities may be handicapping their students' achievement as compared with those that concentrate on more able and better paid staff. The wisest resource allocations may be those that purchase able (as distinct from experienced) teachers rather than formal credentials, curriculum materials, or modern facilities. (Spady, 1976: 195)

Nonhuman Resources

Before the *Equality of Educational Opportunity* survey, it was widely believed that one of the major sources of educational inequality lay in the differences in the physical facilities of the schools attended by advantaged and disadvantaged children, and that greater equity could be attained by increasing the material resources available to disadvantaged schools. One of the surprising findings of the survey was that the schools attended by majority and minority students did not differ markedly on such criteria as age of school buildings, number of makeshift rooms, or number of special resources such as auditoriums, cafeterias, gymnasiums, and athletic fields. The areas in which the schools of minority pupils showed the most consistent deficiencies appeared to be those most directly related to academic activities—for example, they tended to have fewer physics laboratories, fewer textbooks and library books per student, less elaborate testing programs, and fewer academically related extracurricular activities (fewer school newspapers, chess clubs, or debating teams, but not fewer hobby clubs or social dances). However, few of the differences are large, and in most cases regional differences between schools are greater than minority-majority racial differences (Coleman, Campbell et al., 1966: 66-122).

What little subsequent research has been done on this topic generally confirms the EEO findings. Hechinger reports no evidence of direct effects of physical resources on learning, and a comparative analysis of nine English secondary schools indicated that the more successful schools (assessed in terms of attendance rates, delinquency rates, proportions of students going on for further education after school-leaving age of sixteen, and subsequent employment patterns) were situated in older and less "adequate" buildings (Reynolds, 1977). Summers and Wolfe conclude that

> *the general physical facilities of schools* do not make much difference, one way or another, to students' learning. Whether the pupil had more or less playground space, more or less crowded science labs, a new or old school building, or a building rated higher or lower in general physical condition, does not seem to matter much when it comes to achievement test scores. However, there may well be benefits from better facilities which are not reflected in these data. Some facilities may be far more important in imparting specialized knowledge than they are in imparting the knowledge tested on the general achievement scores we looked at. Further, good facilities may be important in attracting good teachers, and improving teachers' motivations. (Summers and Wolfe, 1975: 15)

The available research suggests that students' achievement is more immediately affected by the characteristics and attitude orientations of the other people around them in the school than by the technological or physical aspects of the school environment, and that educational decision makers would be well advised to adopt budgetary strategies that would increase investments in human relative to nonhuman or material resources. It is important to remember though that the amount of rigorous sociological investigation of the effects of school physical facilities is still very small, and that there is virtually no empirical evidence on students' actual exposure to and utilization of either the human or nonhuman resources provided for them.

It is possible that various physical resources, like various aspects of teacher quality, affect different students differently, and the Bowles critique of the Coleman Report underscores how difficult it is to estimate the true effects of investment in school facilities and personnel. While school expenditures are partly a reflection of socioeconomic factors, which are strongly associated with achievement, the relationship is complicated by variations in income level, cost of living and other economic factors, and by variations in the proportion of the education budget that is really available for programs and materials specifically oriented to raising the achievement level of special subgroups of students. For example, although the per-pupil expenditure is often relatively high in the inner-city school systems, a much larger amount must be spent on the upkeep of old buildings and replacement of equipment due to age or vandalism. The rigidity of school budgets, moreover, often means that individual principals and teachers have little to say about what is bought. In some cities, a given sum is allocated to each school for each category of materials, which may be spent only on that category. Thus, a school overstocked with textbooks cannot use "textbook money" to buy, say, audio-visual equipment, let alone to change the relative proportion of the budget invested in human versus nonhuman resources.

One of the few nonhuman school resources that has been found to be rather strongly related to student achievement is *time*, or the amount of exposure to instruction. Time inputs have been measured in a number of ways, from length of school day or school year to number of terms or years of study of a particular subject to school attendance rates and amounts of homework assigned.[3] Jencks's analysis found that the length of the school day was the only school policy or resource that had a statistically significant relation to attainment in both the EEO and the Project Talent samples. The Federal Reserve Bank study of the Philadelphia schools reported that at every level investigated, from sixth through twelfth grade, learning growth of individual students was positively related to proportion of days attended and negatively related to unexcused absences and lateness (Summers and Wolfe, 1975: 9). One of the most consistent findings of the crosscultural comparisons of achievement constituting the IEA (International Project for the Evaluation of Educational Achievement, to be discussed more fully in Chapter 13) is that in all of the participating countries student exposure, as measured by attendance, length of time of study, and quantity of homework, was positively related to cognitive achievements in mathematics, science, reading comprehension, foreign languages, and social studies (Lau, 1978). Certain aspects of schooling quantity are, of course, indicators of school investments as well as a characteristic of students.

The most detailed analyses of student-exposure effects to date are by Wiley (1974 and 1976), who argues that conclusions about the ineffectiveness of schools are often based upon inadequate conceptualizations of effectiveness. We should, says Wiley, be asking not how effective are schools, but how effective is a particular quantity of schooling for a particular student. Using data from the Detroit schools in the *Educational Opportunity* survey, Wiley tested the hypothesis that the total amount of active learning time on a particular subject is the most important determinant of students' achievement on that subject. One set of calculations showed that

> in terms of typical gains in achievement over a year's period . . . in schools where students receive twenty-four percent more schooling, they will increase their average gain in reading comprehension by two-thirds and their gains in mathematics and verbal skills by more than one-third. These tremendous effects indicate that the amount of schooling a child receives is a highly relevant factor for his achievement. (Wiley, 1974: 8)

Replications of Wiley's basic study by other researchers (for example, Karweit, 1976a) have not produced such striking results as Wiley's, partly because no available data sets exist on which researchers can test the entire range of the achievement-attendance relationship, partly because of difficulties in measuring "active learning time." Given, for example, the great variations in classroom control, discussed in Chapters 8 and 9, sheer quantity of exposure to a subject is probably not equivalent to active student learning. Cusick's participant-observation study of a high school provides dramatic anecdotal evidence of the large amount of time in which students are engaged in "waiting, engaging in some sort of spectatorship, interacting with their friends, or dealing with some maintenance matter, such as with lockers, passes, coming, or going," and the small amount of time in which they are engaged "to any significant degree in anything that could even remotely be called academic activity" (Cusick, 1973: 47). Indeed, he estimates that many students at the school spent as little as an hour a day actively involved in academic subject matter. Wiley points out, however, that quantity of schooling is one of the variables most readily manipulable by educational policy, and it is ironic that evidence of the importance of student time inputs is emerging just as many school systems, for budgetary and other reasons, are shortening the school day in various ways.

Perhaps the most direct evidence of exposure effects comes from studies of the fortunately rare instances when children are deprived of schooling altogether. A particularly depressing example is the sharp drop in all areas of achievement, as measured by the Stanford Achievement tests, among the black children whose school careers were discontinued by the closing of the Prince Edward, Virginia, public schools from 1959 to 1963 (Green and Hofmann, 1965). Although the reintroduction of schooling in 1963 produced slight improvements in academic skills, the low overall achievement at the time of the last testing indicated that the "lost years" without formal education could not be made up.

Some Methodological Issues

In the latter part of Chapter 2, we discussed some of the basic problems in making causal inferences about the factors that are related to academic achievement. As a number of studies discussed in this chapter have indicated, there are special problems in designing research to evaluate the effectiveness of schools as total entities or social systems.

One problem is the selection problem or the problem of *multicollinearity* (lack of independence) between student background and school environment factors. That is, "better" schools tend to be located in higher-income neighborhoods, attended by children from higher-status families, and staffed by higher-"quality" teachers, and this lack of independence between background and school variables tends to create a statistical bias against attributing student outcome differences to school resources. The longer students stay in school, the more difficult it becomes to distinguish between the two kinds of effects, and there are to date no "statistical tricks that will solve the problem in nonexperimental studies of student background variables being confounded with school differences" (McPartland *et al.*, 1976: 10).

A second problem is connected with the time factor, also introduced in Chapter 2. McPartland and his colleagues distinguish between short- and long-term effects of schooling (for example, between immediate outcomes such as achievement test scores and later life consequences such as occupational attainments and participation in political and social roles) and note that sociological research has tended to focus upon the first of the two. While it is seldom feasible to study cumulative school effects over a long period of time, McPartland and his colleagues speculate that even if short-term school effects are small, it is possible that

> a sizeable impact of school differences would become evident if certain contrasts coninued over many years.
>
> [Moreover], a reasonable explanation for why family or neighborhood effects are small is that a student is exposed to a consistent environment for the first variables but not for the second. The inconsistency of the school environment becomes obvious when we observe that the average student may have an exceptional teacher one year and poor one the next. (McPartland *et al.*, 1976: 5-6)

Interest in the long-term effects of schooling does seem to be growing. For example, while short-term benefits of integrated education are difficult to document, a comparative analysis of 1,600 *adult* blacks revealed a number of differences between those who had and had not attended racially integrated schools on a number of educational, intellectual, attitudinal, occupational, and economic outcomes (Crain, 1970 and 1971. For a more general analysis of the enduring effects of education, see Hyman *et al.*, 1975).

Partly as a consequence of the rather discouraging results of much research on school effectiveness, researchers have sought more systematic ways to identify and measure the major kinds of school effects and to describe the relationships between independent and dependent variables. Part of the effort has taken the form of attempts to construct statistical models of these relationships, to be tested against empirical data (Strategy 4; as described on page 193; this is the approach taken in Wiley's research on quantity of schooling).

Systems Analysis

Attempts were made during the 1960s to apply to educational problems the concepts and techniques of *systems analysis,* a methodology developed by mathematicians, economists, and engineers working particularly in the area of defense for comparing the relative costs and benefits of alternative resource allocations (for example, of various combinations of weapon systems or of different methods of organizing and supplying armed service personnel). Systems-analysis enthusiasts argued that most school budgets failed to show the real educational output of schools.

> Many things learned, presumably in school, can be and are being measured, and we should consider the results of these measurements in our model building. Even in those important and great areas of the child's mind where we cannot or do not measure, we can at least make a judgment as to the presence of these factors in each model. . . . *The point is that the building of models, the gathering of data, and the assignment of values bring us face to face with problems in such a way as to help us to make better judgments.* (Mauch, 1962: 160)

Systems analysis has so far had little impact on the field of the sociology of education. (One of the few published studies based on the technique, by Burkhead, will be discussed in Chapter 12.) One reason is that systems analysis depends upon being able to specify what constitutes a satisfactory output, and as we have seen, this is still difficult to do in connection with schooling. Moreover, the input is typically limited to variables that can be clearly quantified, preferably in terms of dollar costs. As one critic summarized the problem, the educational system is much more complicated than any system yet devised by the military, and we lack the understanding of its component parts assumed by a technique like systems analysis (Oettinger, 1968).

Production Function Analysis

A relatively new entry to the field of educational model building is educational *production functions,* a technique that borrows from econometric estimates of production processes in industry. The orientation of this approach is suggested in the following discussion by an economist of the technological and behavioral features that distinguish the educational production process.

> From the technological point of view, educational production differs from a more conventional production in at least four respects. First, educational production is typically a multiple-output process. Second, time is an essential element . . . unlike agriculture, educational outputs are not point outputs but typically consist of a time profile of educational achievement or knowledge. . . . Third, the raw material in educational production (the student), unlike other raw materials, is not completely passive. It reacts and responds to the actions of the educational producers. Finally, educational production is characterized by at least two types of externalities. The first is a public goods externality, which arises because some inputs, for example, teacher lecturing time, can contribute to the production of educational outputs in a whole class of students simultaneously. . . . The second is a peer group externality which may be said to exist if an individual student's ability and will to learn depends on the ability and will to learn of his or her classmates, so that the individual cognitive achievement of a student is correlated with the cognitive achievements of the whole class.
>
> From the behavioral point of view, there are two major differences. First, educational producers, unlike a more conventional producer, cannot be assumed to maximize profits and/or minimize costs or even to maximize utility. Second, control of quantities of inputs to the educational production process is not vested in a single manager. Instead, it is diffused among administrators, teachers, parents, and even students . . . [each of whom] has some degree of control over the outputs and inputs and tries to further his or her own objective, taking into account the actions of the others. (Lau, 1978: 3–4)

The Summers and Wolfe study discussed earlier in this chapter used production function estimates. A second study using this technique is by Levin (1976), who conceptualizes total educational output as consisting of multiple components—including students' motivation and attitudes (in particular, their sense of efficacy or fate control), and parental expectations, as well as student achievement—each of which constitutes an input to the educational process as well as an outcome of it. Thus Levin constructed his model in the form of a set of four simultaneous equations, solving for the interrelations of the four dependent variables as well as the effects of such independent variables as individual abilities, family background, school time inputs, peer characteristics, and community influences. The data used to estimate this system were derived from the sixth-grade subsample of that much-used data source, the *Equality of Educational Opportunity* survey. While acknowledging the speculative nature of his interpretations of the results, Levin points to the possible significance of the large coefficient for students' attitudes, compared to the coefficients for such family variables as family size, suggesting that

> educational programs that focus on student attitudes may be able to compensate for "disadvantages" in socioeconomic background. Indeed, this tentative interpretation argues against the simplistic observations of some social philosophers that educational programs cannot compensate for such background deficiencies, since these background factors now appear to have much of their direct effects not on achievement, but on attitude and, *through* attitude, on achievement. (Levin, 1976: 285)

Conclusions

The basic question raised in this chapter is whether schools have significant independent effects on students' achievement, or to put it another way, whether the performance of a given student or group of students would be any different if that student or students attended a different school.

The most useful research on school effectiveness examines the cumulative and relative effects of a variety of school characteristics. Single-variable analyses, such as studies of school size, have been inconclusive, and it seems unlikely that any single dimension of a system as complex as a school will explain much of the variance in its outcomes. The *Equality of Educational Opportunity* survey, while provoking strong criticism from many sides, has provided a rich data source for multivariate analysis of school effects as well as ideas that have challenged our thinking about the fairness of our educational system—in particular, the implications of the finding that disadvantaged children are especially susceptible to the quality of the schools they attend. Recent adaptations of model-building techniques developed in other disciplines, such as systems analysis and production function estimation, have, by forcing researchers to define and measure their variables more precisely, enabled them to make better predictions and to draw more causal implications from their findings.

The most powerful predictors of student achievement that have emerged from multivariate analyses are the composition and climate of the student body, and to a lesser degree of the teaching staff. A school that contains a high proportion of high-status, academically oriented students and teachers who exert pressure on students to achieve appears likely to create a climate in which actual achievement is enhanced. The measurement of teacher quality is still crude—attitudes and behavior may matter much more than the formal credentials that are used in most research on teacher quality—and different students appear to benefit from different kinds of teachers. Even with the limited knowledge now available, a number of responsible researchers are convinced that hiring able teachers is the best investment a school system can make. In an analogy to medical research, which also argues for more controlled research on teacher effects, Walberg and Bargen point out that

> like the cancer-smoking correlation, the scientific case for teacher qualities cannot be made without experiments. Yet, even in the face of non-causal evidence, the prudent man reconsiders smoking, and the just society reconsiders the distribution of effective educational resources. (Walberg and Bargen, 1974: 237)

The impact of school resources, including financial expenditures, is still debatable. The conclusion of the *Equality of Educational Opportunity* study was that economic factors have little effect, but this has been contradicted by earlier studies and by subsequent reanalysis of the EEO data. The strength of economic factors seems to depend upon what actual indicators are used and the order in which they are brought into a multivariate analysis. Moreover, the strength is hard to determine precisely because resources are interrelated with other factors related to achievement—they tend to be unequally distributed among schools, and schools with the greatest financial and other resources are at the same time likely to be high on the other variables related to academic success.

American schools differ on so many dimensions that it is difficult to identify the specific variables that both differentiate schools and contribute to academic achievement—which may explain the conclusion reached by many social scientists that "no measurable school resource or policy shows a consistent relationship to schools' effectiveness in boasting student achievement" (Jencks *et al.*, 1972: 96). What seems to matter most to a given student's level of accomplishment in school is who he or she interacts with there. It also looks as though there are trade-offs of school effects on student outcomes. For example, a mixed demographic composition of students and staff may enhance the academic performance of at least some students but have negative impact on some students' aspirations and satisfaction with school life. Or a school organization that maximizes student involvement in decision making may enhance creativity and satisfaction with school life but not cognitive learning, which is more likely to be increased by increased time inputs. But there is probably no school structure that maximizes all desirable outcomes.

Notes

1. Size may, however, be related to nonacademic student outcomes. For example, a study of school structural influences on student-interaction patterns (Karweit, 1976b) found that large student bodies tended to depress participation in and cohesion of friendship and esteem networks, possibly because of the increased anonymity and decreased visibility for students in larger schools.

2. The implications of Bowles's reanalysis also are applicable to the regression analysis used in the second of the two Wilson studies. The relative effects of SES and racial context might have been different if the order in which these coefficients were computed had been different.

3. I am grateful to Harry Bredemeier for pointing out that exposure to learning can also be perceived as a student characteristic or resource, in particular the extent to which students pay attention, show respect, exert effort, and display appreciation to their teachers. Bargen and Walbert (1974) found that the further Chicago students progressed in school, the more of the variance in their present achievement was explained by achievements in earlier grades. While this tendency may be partially explained by interaction and expectation processes that contribute to increasing consistency in the evaluation of individual students' performance (discussed in Chapter 8), it also suggests that student investments of time and energy are cumulative in effect and that increased investments may have positive long-term effects.

The Adolescent Society Revisited CHAPTER 11

At Madison Junior High School, if you cooperated with the teacher and did your homework, you were a "kook." At Levi Junior High School, if you don't cooperate with the teacher and don't do your homework, you are a "kook." . . . At Madison we asked a question, "Are you going to college?" At Brighton the question always is "What college are you going to?" . . .

What the pupils are learning from one another is probably just as important as what they are learning from the teachers. This is what I refer to as the hidden curriculum. It involves such things as how to think about themselves, how to think about other people, and how to get along with them. It involves such things as values, codes, and styles of behavior.   U.S. Commission on Civil Rights

Having invented the adolescent, society has been faced with two major problems: how and where to accommodate him in the social structure, and how to make his behavior accord with the specifications.   F. Musgrove

Society no longer depends on young people for anything in particular (unless it be as soldiers) and has been forced to create for them a succession of contrived roles and institutions not tightly woven into the community and structure. In a gradual way the change has been going on for centuries, but in the twentieth century the revolution in the economic and social position of youth has virtually moved to completion.   Joseph Kett

In 1961 a landmark study in the sociology of education, James Coleman's *The Adolescent Society,* was published. For almost two decades this study has served as a point of reference for debate and research about the social structure of the high school and the role of adolescents and youth in society. Thus, we shall begin this chapter on the special problems of adolescence and education with a review of the major themes of *The Adolescent Society,* then turn to a consideration of the sociological implications drawn from it and the subsequent research stimulated by it.

The major thesis of *The Adolescent Society* is that there exists a strong student peer culture that is separate from, and often at variance with, the values and goals of adult society. Coleman sees the emergence of this culture as an almost inevitable consequence of our complex, highly industrialized society, in which the family is losing more and more of the functions that formerly made it a self-sufficient socioeconomic unit as well as the major source of emotional support and solidarity. In contrast to the family, the school has acquired more functions, both an extension of formal learning tasks (since there is more to be learned in a highly technical society young people spend more years in school) and added responsibility for the teaching of values and morals—a function that used to be shared by the family and the church. As a formal institution, however, the school cannot provide the diffuse support and the particularistic treatment with which the family could infuse education. As a consequence, the student is "forced inward toward his own age group, made to carry out his whole social life with others his own age. With his fellows, he comes to constitute a small society, one that has most of its important interaction *within* itself, and maintains only a few threads of connection with the outside adult society" (Coleman, 1961: 3).

This conception of the youth-student within the learning system and the larger society is not unique to Coleman's work. A theoretical paper by Talcott Parsons, also written in the early 1960s, analyzes youth culture as a response to strains in contemporary American society produced by massive changes in the structure of society without parallel adjustments in basic value patterns (which still stress active mastery of one's environment). Rising levels of expectations for children are combined with increased autonomy resulting from permissive child-rearing practices and progressive educational methods. As a consequence, there is a kind of "duality" of orientation among the young: on the one hand, an almost compulsive independence, a touchiness with respect to any adult expectations and demands; on the other hand, an equally compulsive conformity and loyalty to the peer group, with very literal observation of group norms and intolerance of deviance (Parsons, 1962).

While much of Parsons's (and Coleman's) argument would apply to Western industrial nations other than the United States, Parsons makes no claims for wider applicability. One of the most extensive studies of the formation of age groups in general and youth groups in particular is Eisenstadt's massive comparison of anthropological materials from primitive, historical, and modern societies, *From Generation to Generation*, which classifies the underlying value orientations of total societies and subgroups within them. Eisenstadt finds no society in which groupings of children are absent. "In all societies, children are drawn together for various reasons, play together—often at being adults—and thus learn the various types and rules of cooperative behavior and some universalistic norms" (Eisenstadt, 1956: 46). Similarly, the existence of adolescent groups seems to be universal, forming a transition group oriented toward the ultimate attainment of full adult status within the society. But the form and function that such groups take differ greatly. In modern industrial societies characterized by an emphasis upon achievement and regulated by "universalistic" criteria (that is, the individual is evaluated according to his or her own worth, by general or "universalistic" standards, rather than upon his or her position in a given family or some other basic societal unit), the youth group becomes more significant in the life of the adolescent and at the same time more isolated from the rest of society. This explains the "strong emotional interdependence and intensive mutual identification" in such groups—and also explains how such groups can "become nuclei of various rebellious and deviant movements and activities" (Eisenstadt, 1956: 227–228).

The implications of crosscultural differences for the structure of formal learning systems will be discussed more fully in Chapter 13. The point here is that the structure and value orientations of the larger society define the position of youth and affect the nature of their relationships with their peers within as well as outside of school. And in societies like our own, the strength of the student peer group and its separation from other societal institutions is a response not only to the general value orientations of the larger society but also to the lack of fully institutionalized functions for the young within the productive life of their communities.

Coleman's Major Findings

The important elements of the high school system that are analyzed by Coleman are diagrammed in Exhibit 11–1. Coleman's study describes the content of adolescent values and attitudes (A), the way individuals' values and attitudes combine to form the value climate of a school (B), and the way in which the peer group, broken down into various subgroups varying in function and prestige (D) and operating within the context of the school (B and C), affects the performance of the individual students (E), and also reflects back upon their attitudes and aspirations (A).

The empirical data that Coleman used to support his argument of a separate and increasingly powerful peer influence come from the following sequence of questions:

> Let's say that you had always wanted to belong to a particular club in school, and then finally you were asked to join. But then you found out that your parents didn't approve of the group. Do you think you would
> _____ definitely join anyway
> _____ probably join
> _____ probably not join
> _____ definitely not join
>
> What if your parents approved, but the teacher you like most disapproved of the group. Would you
> _____ definitely join anyway
> _____ probably join
> _____ probably not join
> _____ definitely not join

Exhibit 11–1
Components of the High School Peer Culture

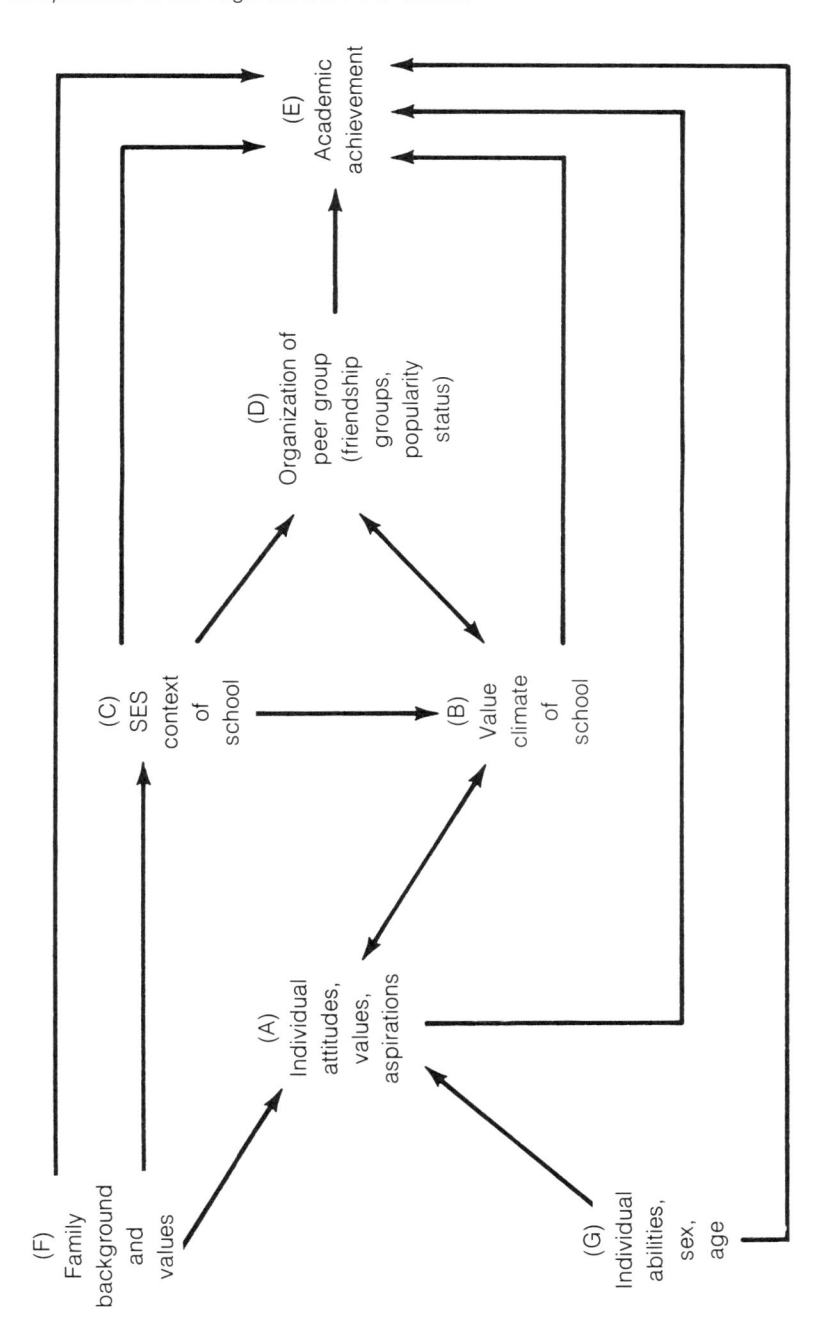

(A) Individual attitudes, values, aspirations
(B) Value climate of school
(C) SES context of school
(D) Organization of peer group (friendship groups, popularity status)
(E) Academic achievement
(F) Family background and values
(G) Individual abilities, sex, age

What if your parents and teachers approved of the group, but by joining the club you would break with your closest friend, who wasn't asked to join? Would you
_____ definitely join anyway
_____ probably join
_____ probably not join
_____ definitely not join

Which one of these things would be hardest for you to take—your parents' disapproval, your teacher's disapproval, or breaking with your friend?
_____ parents' disapproval
_____ teacher's disapproval
_____ breaking with friend

In response to the last question in the sequence, Coleman found that while the largest percentage indicated parental disapproval as hardest to take, this was a bare majority (54 percent for boys, 52 percent for girls), and only about 10 percent higher than the proportion most concerned with their friend's reaction (43 percent for both boys and girls), with teacher disapproval amounting to only a small minority. As Coleman interprets these data: "The balance between parents and friends indicated the extent of the state of transition that adolescents experience—leaving one family, but not yet in another, they consequently look both forward to their peers and backward to their parents" (Coleman, 1961: 5).

Student responses to questions about their interests and favorite activities showed a deep concern about acceptance by peers and engaging in shared activities with them. Favored activities included dating, talking on the telephone, being in the same class, and eating together with friends in school, and "hanging around together" or just "being with the group" outside of school. Esteem is gained by a combination of friendliness and popularity, an attractive appearance, physical and social maturity, and possession of skills and objects (cars, clothes, music, and so forth) valued by the culture. It is interesting to note that the latter are typically perceived as giving the owner an aura of sophistication, although the particular form they take is such as to set students apart from the adult world (for instance, rock music, teen styles in hair and clothes). Moreover, says Coleman, the attributes and activities most valued by students are discrepant with the central goals of the school as a formal learning system. As in his argument for the existence of powerful peer-group pressures, Coleman's argument for the discrepancy between peer-group and school-system goals is based upon a small set of questions that posit a basic dilemma that the respondent must resolve. In this case it is a choice of roles within the school system, and the basic question is:

If you could be remembered here at school for one of the three things below, which one would you want it to be?
Boys: _____ Brilliant student
_____ Athletic star
_____ Most popular
Girls: _____ Brilliant student
_____ Leader in activities
_____ Most popular

The responses, collected at the beginning and end of the school year, indicated that

> for boys, not only is the athletic star's image more attractive at the beginning of the school year; the boys move even slightly further in that direction—at the expense of the popularity image—over the period of the school year.
> The girls are somewhat similar: at the beginning of the school year, the activities leader and most popular are about equally attractive images, both more often mentioned than the brilliant student. By spring, the activities leader image has gained slightly in attractiveness, at the expense of both the brilliant student and the most popular. These shifts, of course, are quite small, and there are differences from school to school, as later chapters will indicate. Nevertheless, the point is clear; the image of athletic star is most attractive for boys; the images of activities leader and most popular are more attractive to girls than brilliant student. (Coleman, 1961: 30)

A parallel question asking which of the three kinds of ideal-type student they would like most to *date* revealed that the brilliant student, especially the brilliant girl student, fares poorly, and that the proportion of respondents naming the brilliant student as a dating choice declined even further during the course of the school year.

As he continues his search for an explanation of the low commitment to the basic goals of the school system, Coleman finds that when students were asked to speculate upon their *parents'* preferences for them, more thought their parents would be very proud of them if they made the basketball or cheerleading team than if they were chosen by a science teacher to act as his or her assistant. "Thus, even the rewards a child gains from his parents may help reinforce the values of the adolescent culture—not because his parents hold these same values but because parents want their children to be successful and esteemed by their peers" (Coleman, 1961: 34).

Obviously related to what individual students want for themselves is the question of what gives an individual status with his or her peers (D in Exhibit 11–1). Coleman asked two kinds of questions about status: (1) an open-ended question, "What does it take to get in with the leading crowd in this school?"[1] and (2) a pair of questions asking respondents to rank the following six items in terms of their importance in making a student popular with their own sex and with the opposite sex:

Coming from the right family

Leader in activities

Having a nice car (for girls: clothes)

High grades, honor roll

Being an athletic star (for girls: being a cheerleader)

Being in the leading crowd

For both sexes the emphasis was upon having a good personality, good looks, and good clothes. Averaging the rankings given to the lists of items showed that athletics was of primary importance in making a boy popular, with being in the leading crowd first in importance for girls and second for boys. Getting good grades was relatively unimportant for boys and even less so for girls, though it is worth noting that it is perceived as relatively more valuable for popularity with one's own sex. For girls especially, academic success is seen as contributing little to and possibly even detracting from popularity with the opposite sex. As we noted in Chapter 5, the tremendous importance of popularity with boys focuses the attention of many girls upon projecting an image of personal attractiveness, and personal attractiveness requires not appearing to care too much about academic success.

A major interest of Coleman's, and a major methodological and substantive contribution of *The Adolescent Society,* is the measurement of school value climates. As Coleman sees it, the attitudes of students at a given school form an important component of its social environment, and he wanted to show how they influenced individual students' status, attitudes, and achievement. The climate measure for each school in the sample is based upon the average rankings to the question of what it took to get to be important and looked up to by peers—the same question that was used to determine the components of individual popularity, but now combined and averaged within each school to get a composite index for the school as a social system. Coleman thus was able to locate each school in his sample in terms of its relative (that is, relative to the other schools) emphasis upon the three dimensions of scholastic achievement, family background, and athletic achievement (popularity and being a cheerleader for the girls).[2]

When Coleman compared the responses of students who received the greatest number of sociometric choices from their peers with the picture of the peer culture as a whole that he had already obtained, he found that no matter what the unique value climate of a school, the male elite was more oriented to the athletic image. In every school, boys identified as athletic stars received more sociometric status than those identified as top scholars, although the athlete-scholar usually received most of all, and the scholar who was not an athlete still received more choices than boys who were neither scholars nor athletes. Boys who were athletes or scholars or both made up almost half of the male leading crowds, although they constituted only about 12 percent of the total population of the schools (Coleman, 1961: 148–149).

The elites were less favorable to the brilliant-student value than the nonelites, although at the same time they tended to have higher grades than the student body as a whole.[3] Between-school comparisons revealed another interesting pattern, however; this was that the relative academic superiority of students in the leading crowd reflected the relative status of good grades in their schools. In schools in which the value climate incorporated a relatively high valuation of the brilliant student, elite students did even better relative to others (the standard deviation between grade averages for the leading crowd and for the total student body was greater); in schools with the lowest relative valuation of the brilliant student, the gap was smaller.[4] Although Coleman pointed out that his findings do not establish whether the grades of the leading crowds were a "source, consequence, or merely confirmation of the status system and its rewards for scholastic achievement," they do suggest a linkage between the value climate of a school and the level of scholastic performance of its students.[5]

The elites were also less adult oriented than the rest of the student body. In the hypothetical decision about whether or not to join a club that their parents did not approve of, it was found that boys and girls identified as being in their school's leading crowd were even less likely than others to say that their parents' disapproval would be hardest to take (Coleman, 1961: 6). They were, on the other hand, more school oriented than the nonelites, although their commitment to the school was of a special sort. In yet another set of questions positing a conflict between various reference groups, this one having to do with attending a school pep rally or going riding with friends, the high-status students were more likely to choose the rally.[6] They were, however, even *less* oriented than the student body as a whole toward doing what teachers wanted. As Coleman puts it, the elites are "selective in their overchoice of school-related activities."

Finally, Coleman's data throw light on the relationship between family status and peer status. Although there is a tendency toward control by the students from middle-class, relatively well-educated families, the strength of the effect of an individual student's family status upon his or her school status is mediated by the SES composition of the school he or she attends (the effects of components F and C upon D). This relationship is clarified by comparing two extreme cases, both schools in fairly homogeneous communities but at the opposite ends of the SES continuum (component C). At one extreme is Newlawn, "where students from well-educated families are very scarce," and where "they are scarcer yet among the leading crowd." At the other extreme, in Executive Heights, where most students are from well-educated families, middle-class students dominate the leading crowd. Coleman's conclusion:

> The leading crowd of a school, and thus the norms which that crowd sets, is more than merely a reflection of the student body, with extra middle-class students thrown in. The leading crowd tends to accentuate those very background characteristics already dominant, whether they be upper- or lower-class. A boy or girl in such a system, then, finds it governed by an elite whose backgrounds exemplify, in the extreme, those of the dominant population group. In particular, a working-class boy or girl will be most left out in an upper-middle class school, least so in a school with few middle-class students. (Coleman, 1961: 109)

The Adolescent Society has had strong supporters and vehement critics. Indeed, one mark of its importance is the number of critiques and subsequent research studies that it has stimulated. During the 1960s, a number of social scientists attempted to test or replicate specific aspects of the model indicated in Exhibit 11–1; in the 1970s, research has branched out to consider the location of youth within the total life cycle and the linkages of youth culture with the larger society. By comparison with the earlier research, the work of the past decade is more likely to be based upon historical or crosscultural comparisons, less likely to apply only to the contemporary United States situation.

The studies to be discussed in the following sections will be grouped in terms of their general location in Exhibit 11-1, including:

studies that focus upon the conceptualization, measurement, and effects of value climate (B)

studies that focus upon the organization of the peer group (D), including the breakdown into friendship groups, cliques, elites, and other subgroups, and the way in which peer status is related to academic achievement

studies that focus upon the *process* by which the peer group, influenced by individual and contextual factors, facilitates or hinders academic productivity (the linkages between A, B, C, D, and E)

studies that compare the strength of peer influence relative to that of parents and other possible reference groups, including the conditions under which and the areas in which peer influences are especially strong

(Note that a few of these studies antedate *The Adolescent Society,* showing how Coleman's work incorporates or reflects some earlier work on social system structure and operation in general and schools in particular.)

Further Studies of Value Climate

As we saw in the last chapter, not all researchers acknowledge the existence of value climates as social "facts" separate from the combined personal characteristics of the individual system members. The McDill study discussed there is one of a number designed not only to refine certain of the techniques introduced in *The Adolescent Society,* but also to test the hypothesis of the reality of an independent normative climate. In support of this hypothesis, McDill and his colleagues found clusters of items pertaining to composite student valuation of academic excellence that accounted for a certain proportion of the variation in students' mathematics achievement even when (1) their *individual* abilities, values, and socioeconomic status and (2) the SES *composition* of the school were held constant.

Although McDill developed multiple indices or factors of intellectual valuation, and each factor consisted of multiple items, his conceptualization of the value-climate measure was essentially the same as Coleman's—a simple averaging of responses for a given school, with each student's response given equal weight. Other research has been directed toward developing more elaborate concepts and measures. One early study that offers some interesting insights into the nature of value climate is the Bennington College study (itself an influential and much-debated piece of research). The work of Newcomb and others in connection with this very atypical girls' college suggests that climate may be established and/or heavily influenced by certain subgroups within the total system. The original "tone" of Bennington was set by the New Deal, liberal attitudes of the faculty with respect to the controversial public issues of the time. Even after the college was in full operation, its atmosphere was influenced predominantly by the faculty and by those students who had internalized the faculty values (although many of those students came from families with conservative political and social views). For certain subgroups (entering freshmen), the perceived attitudes and expectations of the faculty, rather than the actual, often conservative, values of their immediate peers, provided the major point of reference—and the freshmen who adopted faculty attitudes were the ones who tended to be named by their classmates as "most worthy to represent the college."

At the same time, there was evidence that this influence was limited in range and time. For example, 62 percent of the freshmen voted for the Republican candidate in a mock election, and a follow-up study of a portion of the original sample indicated that for most students the liberal outlook was only temporary.

A more recent study of peer group influence at the college level, which supported some of the Bennington findings and also suggested further refinements of the measurement of climate, was conducted by Wallace (1965). When he compared the postgraduate aspirations of an entire freshman class of a midwestern college at three times during the school year, Wallace found that the proportion of freshmen wanting to go on to graduate or professional school rose at each subsequent measurement, bringing the freshman profile ever closer to the aspiration pattern of upper-classmen. Even with measures of previous academic achievement and future occupational ambition held constant, the aspiration climate created by the freshmen's older peers seemed to account for an appreciable amount of their aspiration change.

There were also some interesting interaction effects among the three factors. For example, peer influence seemed to be most powerful among those students with the *lowest* past academic achievement. Wallace interprets this finding as suggesting that "the rise in low academic rank freshmen's graduate school aspirations may have had more to do with their social attitudes toward, and experiences in, college than with their expectations of graduate school success" (Wallace, 1965: 384), and that the student who is weaker academically is also the one most likely to be susceptible to and to conform to peer group pressures. A similar pattern was found in connection with socioeconomic ambition, with a greater rise in postgraduate study aspirations expressed among freshmen who chose relatively low-status occupations when they entered college.

A major distinction of the Wallace study is in the conceptualization of peer group influence. Unlike the Coleman measure, the Wallace technique computes an "interpersonal environment" score for each student by having the student check all the names he or she recognizes from a list of the entire student body. For each student, the measure "estimates that part of the total student-body with which he had direct or indirect contact sufficient to remember the names of its members" (Wallace, 1965: 378). This technique assumes that in a system as large as that of most colleges, there are likely to be several peer groups, each holding different values. Thus a student who seems to be a deviant from the student culture may simply be deviating from the most visible or "leading" clique, but may be well integrated into his or her own subgroup. And even if one can distinguish a single-value—or dominant-value—climate, Wallace's conceptualization suggests that it may affect different students differentially, depending upon the other members of the system with whom they have contact.

In summary, carefully designed studies provide enough evidence to allow us to retain the hypothesis of the reality of climatic or contextual effects, although some studies described here have suggested that the composition and influence of a school's value climate may not be exactly the same for all students. This leads us to the next set of studies, which have to do with internal differentiation within a given school.

The Components and Consequences of Peer Status

To support his hypothesis of the importance of peer group influence upon academic performance, Coleman showed that students within a given school grouped themselves into subgroups that varied in status as well as in favored activities, and that the elites tended (1) to represent the dominant social background of their school's student body and (2) to hold the dominant values of the larger peer group and to perform well at the activities most valued by the student body as a whole.

A study that predated *The Adolescent Society* and that foreshadowed it in certain respects is Wayne Gordon's *The Social System of the High School* (1957). In contrast to Coleman's multiple-school survey, Gordon's study is an intensive analysis of a single, midwestern high school. The author was, moreover, a classroom teacher and the director of guidance at the school for ten years. Although he supplemented his regular contacts and day-to-day observations with some quite structured interviews and questionnaires, his presence in the school already was established when he began the formal study, and thus he was able to be a participant observer without introducing the usual bias of this role.

Gordon's general goal was "to develop a general framework for the analysis of adolescent behavior in the high school and to explore the crucial relationship between the social status and the behavior of adolescents" (Gordon, 1957: xi). His model described the adolescent's social system as composed of three subsystems. First was the "formal scheme of things," the curriculum, course work, teachers, rules, grades, and other aspects of school as a formal learning institution. Second was a "semiformal set of sponsored organizations and activities," including athletics and clubs. Gordon saw these as arranged on a hierarchy of prestige, and among his research devices was a questionnaire in which students rated student organizations and the various positions within them. Third was the informal subsystem, the "half-world of usually non-recognized and non-approved cliques, factions, and fraternities." Like Coleman, Gordon measured interpersonal relations and peer status by asking students to designate which of their peers they liked best and held in the highest esteem, and he too carried out an extensive sociometric analysis of the entire student body.

Gordon's conclusions are very close to Coleman's. Success in nonacademic areas contributes more than scholastic achievement to status, although "students showed an upward trend toward the fulfillment of the expectations for grade achievement with each additional year in school," and "conformity to classroom expectations[7] ran a cycle through lower to upper grade levels in the order of a maximum conformity to a maximum nonconformity back toward increasing conformity among both boys and girls" (Gordon, 1957: 131). Successful participation in highly rated student activities—athletic teams, band, certain committees and clubs—is a better predictor of individual status. And the informal system of friendship groups and cliques is "especially powerful in controlling adolescent behavior, not only in such matters as dress and dating, but also in school achievement and deportment" (Gordon, 1957: viii).

A dissenting view of the relationship between academic achievement and peer status is registered in Turner's study of Los Angeles high schools. Turner agrees that a youth culture exists, but he argues that it is "segmented and ritualistic, not necessarily in conflict with other kinds of behavior looked upon favorably by the adult world," and that it "does not penetrate deeply enough to require that solidarity takes precedence over pursuits related to long-range success goals" (Turner, 1964: 146).

Turner's major variables are essentially the same as Gordon's—academic achievement, participation in school-sponsored extracurricular activities, and informal friendships with classmates—but while Gordon was interested in weighing the relative contribution of these three variables to an individual's overall status, Turner focuses upon the interrelation among the three. The differences in mode of analysis are indicated in the following diagram:

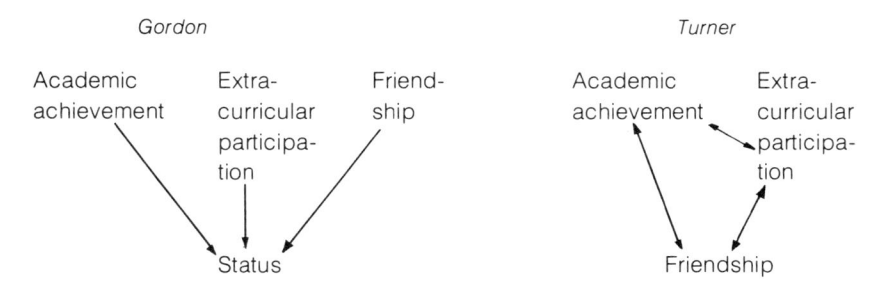

Gordon

Academic achievement Extracurricular participation Friendship
    ↘   ↓   ↙
                            Status

Turner

Academic achievement ⇄ Extracurricular participation
            ↘   ↗
            Friendship

Also in contrast to Gordon, who obtained his data on the first two variables from school records and student self-reports, Turner measured all three by sociometric questionnaire items; respondents were asked to name their classmates who best fitted the categories of "brain," "big wheel," and "desired friend."

The results of Turner's analysis showed positive correlations among the three ratings. To be named good at schoolwork was related to being named both as a "desired friend" and as a "big wheel," with the relationship slightly stronger for girls than boys. That academic success is *not* seen as unattractive is suggested by the finding that virtually no one reputed to be a "brain" was not also named as a "desired friend," although one could be named as a "desired friend" without being either a "brain" or a "wheel." While many students combined high "brain" with low "wheel" ratings, there were few cases of the reverse combination—low 'brain'–high "wheel." Turner attributes this to a possible halo effect, with "students overestimating the quality of school performance among their peer leaders," but he points out that "there could, however, be no halo effect unless students placed the same positive valuation upon both types of personal qualities." His conclusion is that his findings belie the notion of a youth culture "conspiracy" against academic excellence. On the contrary, individual students seem able to adhere to the central achievement values of the school while still enjoying the esteem of their peers, apparently embodying important peer standards while remaining somewhat detached from them (Turner, 1964: 153–154). Turner found, however, that the relationships among the three kinds of status he examined varied throughout the ten schools in his sample, suggesting that while status with one's peers does not necessarily detract from intellectual performance, and vice versa, the relationship depends also upon the social environment in which it occurs.

Processes of Peer Group Formation and Influence

We have seen that the particular subgroups to which students belong or with which they identify have an impact upon their behavior in school, although there seems to be no simple, direct correlation between academic achievement and other kinds of school status. We have not, however, said much about *how* students get themselves into one or another of the subgroups into which a student body divides itself and *what* happens within the peer group to affect students' attitudes and efforts.

Two studies document the impact of peer contact upon academic aspirations and performance. One is a study of some fourteen hundred male seniors in thirty North Carolina high schools, conducted by Campbell and Alexander (1965), that attempts to test the effects of interpersonal relations as formulated by Newcomb and the balance theorists[8] and to synthesize these effects with the structural or contextual effects formulated by Wilson and others, as described in the previous chapter. As part of a larger study, Campbell and Alexander collected three kinds of information about their subjects:

status, determined by the educational attainment of respondents' parents

friendship choices, obtained by asking each respondent, "What students here in school of your own sex do you go around with most often?"

educational aspirations, obtained by asking each respondent whether he or she wanted to and expected to go to college

The data obtained showed a clear consistency between the educational plans of individual respondents and the plans of the students they named as their best friends, even controlling for SES and regardless of whether the friends named reciprocated the sociometric choice. That is, a student at a given status level is more likely to have college aspirations and expectations, and actually to attend college, when his or her best friend also has college plans. The relationship was even stronger when the friendship choices were reciprocated (Alexander and Campbell, 1964).

The authors were, however, interested in testing not only the relevance of balance theory but also in comparing or synthesizing this model with the structural-contextual model, and in the second of their two papers they postulate a two-step model incorporating both processes. Respondents were scored (from 1 to 5) on each of three measures: their own status; their friends' status (the average of the fellow students named by the respondent); and their school status (the average status of all students in the school). Campbell and Alexander predict a positive correlation between the individual's aspiration and the status of both his or her school and friends. However, they also predict that school status and the tendency of individuals to choose friends of high status are related in themselves and that "the influence of friends may be an intervening variable that mediates the association between average school status and college expectations." More concretely, they expect the relationship between school status and college plans to disappear when friends' status is held constant, but the relationship between college plans and friends' status *not* to disappear when school status is held constant (Campbell and Alexander, 1965: 287).

The statistical computations relevant to these predictions are presented in Exhibit 11–2. Columns 1, 2, and 3 show the correlations between the various pairs of variables in the three-variable model. For example, column 1 shows that there

Exhibit 11–2
Correlations Among School Status, Friends' Status, and College Plans of High School Seniors—by Parental Educational Level

Parental Educational Level	School Status with College Plans (1)	Friends' Status with College Plans (2)	School Status with Friends' Status (3)	* (4)	** (5)	N (6)
Both parents—college	.10	.15	.49	.03	.12	172
One parent—college	.16	.29	.36	.06	.26	183
Both parents—high school	.15	.28	.50	.01	.24	147
One parent—high school	.07	.19	.34	.01	.18	178
Neither parent—high school	.14	.31	.40	.02	.28	295

Zero-Order Correlations: columns (1), (2), (3). Partial Correlations: columns (4), (5).

*School status with college plans, holding friends' status constant
**Friends' status with college plans, holding school status constant
Source: From Campbell and Alexander, 1965: 286.

is a slight positive correlation between average school status and college plans. The strongest two-variable relationship is between school status and friends' status (column 3): "persons at every status level are more likely to choose high-status friends when there are relatively large numbers of high-status persons in the system" (Campbell and Alexander, 1965: 287).

Columns 4 and 5, which show the relationships between pairs of variables with the third controlled, constitute the empirical test of the authors' predicted two-step model.

> Is there a relationship between school status and the college plans of individuals at each status level apart from the effects of interpersonal influence that are indicated by the status of friends? The answer to this question should be negative if our hypothesized two-step model is correct. In other words, we expect only negligible variation to be explained by school status when friendship status is held constant. The partial correlations presented in column (4) of the table show that this is precisely what occurs. By contrast, when school status is held constant, the relationship between college plans and friends' status remains strong, as revealed in the partial correlation in column (5). . . . These two sets of partial-correlation coefficients support the inference that the structural effects of school status are best conceived of as due to the interpersonal influences of an individual's significant others. (Campbell and Alexander, 1965: 287–288)

In summary, it is the interpersonal relationships with one's friends within the high school (D in Exhibit 11–1) that determine high or low academic aspirations, although the likelihood of having friends with a given set of attitudes toward school and learning is determined partially by the composition of the student body as a whole, which constitutes the pool from which one's friends may be drawn (column 3 in Exhibit 11–2).

The significance of direct contact with peers was also the theme of the study by McPartland discussed at the beginning of Chapter 8, although here peers are viewed in the role of classmates rather than friends. McPartland's analysis indicated that for children of racial-minority groups, the academic advantage of being in an integrated school depended upon *being in the same classes* with middle-class, majority-group students. That is, integration at the school level that does not include systematic means to prevent racial subdivision in different courses or academic tracks will not have much positive effect upon upgrading academic expectations and performance. Parallel to Campbell and Alexander's findings, McPartland's indicate that while the social (in this case racial) context of the school affects the likelihood of contact between students of different backgrounds, an individual student's academic gains are directly affected only by those students with whom he or she has direct interpersonal relations.

Intensive examinations of peer influence upon academic commitment were included in the studies of Vassar College students sponsored by the Mellon Foundation and directed by Nevitt Sanford (Sanford, 1962, and Bushnell, 1962). Questionnaire data and diaries (in which respondents recorded all their activities for several one-week periods) were collected from all students over a five-year interval. In addition, a sample drawn from one class was intensively interviewed and tested, an anthropologist was a kind of participant-observer of the student culture, and some studies of alumnae were conducted.

Sanford and his associates found peer group influences operating in much the same way as those described by Coleman. Although the pressures were more subtle, the fact that this was a residential school and that the girls spent a lot of time with roommates and other friends within the college made them even more intense. There was a distinct student culture, communicated largely via bull sessions and other informal interaction, although there were slightly differing emphases, attitudes, and life styles among different subgroups on the campus. These ranged from the "super-intellectuals" or "science-major types" to the sociability-oriented "debutantes" or "Yale weekend girls." The general theme of the student culture was pleasant campus life, with a minimum of individual soul-searching and interpersonal conflict, although the support of roommates and close friends was available to group members who were experiencing special strains, such as difficulty with a course or a professor, or a misunderstanding with a boy friend or with parents. Unlike their Bennington counterparts of an earlier era, most Vassar subgroups in the late 1950s resisted "acculturation" to faculty norms, not by rebelling against studying and achievement in general (good grades were, in fact, respected) but by refusing to be wholeheartedly committed to scholastic achievement at the cost of satisfactory social relations with peers. "If there is an ideal Vassar girl, she is the one who received consistently high grades without devoting her entire time to the endeavor. In fact, the emphasis on combining good marks with a reasonably full social life is so strong that some students who, in reality, have to work quite hard to maintain an impressive grade-point ratio will devote considerable effort to presenting an appearance of competency and freedom from academic harassment" (Bushnell, 1962: 507). Certain student norms—for instance, proscriptions against close relationships with professors or excessive amounts of study—helped to maintain the status quo that these students thought desirable. It is also interesting that the "scholar," one of several student types conceptualized by Sanford and a kind of clinical elaboration of Coleman's "brilliant student" role, tended to be found among girls who had suffered "early and persistent awkwardness in social relations with peers."

A study by Hughes, Becker, and Geer of student culture in a Kansas medical school acts as a kind of replication of the Vassar studies. Peer group effects showed up even more clearly in this setting because of the intense pressure placed on students by the formal requirements of medical training. The student culture was perceived to have two major functions: "first, to provide modes of adaptation that make the pressures of the school tolerable and not too upsetting to the individual student, and second, to provide support for patterns of behavior which, though they are in the interest of the students as they see it, may be at variance with what is desired by the faculty and administration" (Hughes *et al.*, 1962: 466). Thus, students reached informal agreements on what *all* of them would learn in preparation for exams, and informal norms directed which and how many case summaries out of the total assigned by professors would actually be completed and turned in.

One must, of course, be cautious in drawing generalizations about the learning system from studies of medical students or other near-adult students whose educational or occupational aspirations are stabilized. Such students "begin with similar interests, attitudes and goals; they are subjected to the same pressures—often intense ones—at the same time, and they work in close association with one another and in relative isolation from groups having different norms" (Sanford, 1962: 465). Although this setting provides the clearest possible view of the processes involved in the functioning of student groups, it leaves unanswered the applicability of this model to, say, the comprehensive high school. And we still know very little about the formation and influence of school peer groups among pre–high school students, although Hallinan's studies of the effects of classroom structure on the formation and stability of elementary school children's friendship patterns (Hallinan, 1976 and 1978, discussed in Chapter 8) begin to fill in this gap.

To round out our discussion of the internal structure of the school peer group, we shall turn to a study of subgroups that actively reject both the goals and the norms of the formal school system. Along with the culturally disadvantaged, the rebellious student provides a serious and growing dilemma for the schools, and the rebel is of particular relevance to this chapter since he or she is in some ways the "ideal type" of the adolescent society.

Like Gordon's study, Stinchcombe's *Rebellion in a High School* (1964) is an in-depth study of a single school, this one a predominantly working-class California school. The study also can be viewed as an elaboration of Coleman's point that the leading crowd of a school tends to accentuate the background characteristics and related norms that are already dominant, whether they are low-, middle-, or high-SES ones. Like the Newlawn school in Coleman's sample, the some sixteen hundred students at this school were mainly of working-class background (component C of Exhibit 11–1), and high proportions of the boys expected to become manual workers. One-fourth of them wished for higher occupational status than they expected to achieve.

A major finding of the study, however, is that it was not SES per se that determined whether a student was rebellious.[9] On the contrary, the data showed no statistical association between boys' social class and rebellion, a finding that, in Stinchcombe's opinion, "is sufficient to refute any theory which sees a direct, unconditional chain of causes from birth in a class to deviant behavior in high school. . . . Social class will be a central variable in the analysis . . . but its role in causing rebellion depends on complex intervening processes" (Stinchcombe, 1964: 86). The key intervening process is the student's perceived linkage or articulation between current school activities and perceived future status and activities. As Stinchcombe formulates it, rebellion is more related to status *prospects* than to status *origins*.[10]

The hypothesis that "high school rebellion, and expressive alienation, occurs when future status is not clearly related to present performance" is supported by the finding that the percentage of respondents exhibiting rebellious behavior is particularly high among: boys aiming toward the lower sectors of the labor market, boys aiming for middle-class occupations but taking vocational or other nonacademic courses, and girls fully committed to marriage without any curricular interest to tie current schoolwork with even a temporary future in the labor market. These were also the subgroups that most often reported spending little or no time on homework.

The lack of association between SES and rebellion was partly explained by the unusually open opportunity structure in this school. Although the community was predominantly working class, the school had a full college preparatory curriculum and the majority of its students in the college-prep course were working class. Such a situation is atypical and, as Stinchcombe admits, creates a rather different set of success strains than, say, a predominantly black slum school. Since lower-SES students were not blocked by lack of access to the training that could lead to social mobility, the rebel had to reject the notion of mobility itself.

The patterns formed by the data in this study underscore the need for looking at the multiple levels of the learning system in order to understand the relationship between any pair of components. They show that a strategy of simply introducing more middle-class orientations, or peers, into a school will not necessarily have the desired effect upon certain subgroups of students, in particular those for whom perceived articulation between school work and outside interests and commitments is lacking. Finally, Stinchcombe's study contributes a kind of conceptual model of a student type that is, according to some concerned observers, becoming more prevalent in our schools. Stinchcombe's rebel combines the attributes of "nonutilitarianism, negativism, short-run hedonism, and emphasis on group autonomy" with a simultaneous and strong identification with adult symbols. Rebels are, among other things, more interested in cars and more likely to own one, more likely to smoke and to claim smoking as a right than their nonrebellious peers. They are the ones most alienated from adult society at the same time that they highly value certain adult glamour symbols. In a sense, the rebel is the teenager who most purely personifies Coleman's adolescent society.

The Relative Strength of Peer Influence

A number of researchers have attempted to test Coleman's claim that the young increasingly are turning to one another, rather than to adults, for social cues and rewards. A study by Simpson of 917 boys in two white, Southern city high schools tested some alternative hypotheses explaining social mobility of working-class students. One hypothesis explains mobility as the result of parental influence; the other, as a consequence of anticipatory socialization into middle-class values by middle-class peers. Simpson's data, shown in Exhibit 11-3, indicate that both influences have an effect, although the first may be rather more important than the second. In both classes students high in parental and also peer influence were most likely to have high occupational aspirations (81.9 and 71.4 percent); and those with low influence from those sources were least likely to have high aspirations (30.1 and 25.6 percent). For working-class boys, the parental influence measure seemed to be the more powerful one.

Exhibit 11–3
Percent of Working-Class and Middle-Class Boys with High Occupational Aspirations, by Extent of Parental and Peer Influence

Working-Class

		Influence of Parents High	Influence of Parents Low
Influence of Peers	High	71.4 (28)	35.7 (70)
Influence of Peers	Low	55.6 (45)	25.6 (168)

Middle-Class

		Influence of Parents High	Influence of Parents Low
Influence of Peers	High	81.9 (94)	72.5 (109)
Influence of Peers	Low	78.0 (50)	30.1 (113)

Adapted from Simpson, 1962: 521.

Among the working-class boys high in peer influence, being high rather than low in parental influence brought the percentage of high-aspirers up from 35.7 per cent to twice this figure, 71.4 per cent; and among the working-class boys low in peer influence, high parental influence more than doubled the percentage of high aspirers, increasing it from 25.6 to 55.6 per cent. The effects of peer influence on working-class boys, with parental influence controlled, were substantially less than this. Among those high in parental influence, high peer influence increased the percentage of high-aspirers from 55.6 to 71.4. . . . The seemingly greater influence of parents than of peers is also evident when we compare the percentages of high-aspirers among working-class boys high in only one type of influence. Among those high in parental influence only, 55.6 per cent were high-aspirers, but this percentage dropped to 35.7 among those high in peer influence only. (Simpson, 1962: 521)

The corresponding differences for middle-class boys were slight (for example, compare 72.5 and 78.0 percent), indicating that the relative influence of parents and peers as defined by Simpson was roughly equivalent.

A study by Epperson of 619 third through sixth graders and 159 tenth through twelfth graders contained a critique and revision of the questions used by Coleman to measure relative parent-peer influence. As he points out, the wording of the question upon which Coleman draws his conclusion about the growing strength of peer influence (see page 216) equates *breaking* with a friend with *disapproval* of parents. Epperson asked the same questions but used the same words for all reference groups. He found that 80 percent of his high school sample said it would make them most unhappy if their *parents* did not like what they did

(Epperson, 1964: 94–95; note that Epperson's revision still retains the assumption of conflict between adult and peer reference groups, an assumption not made in all the other studies discussed here).

A second question raised by Epperson is whether the figures obtained by Coleman are to be interpreted as evidence of strong and emerging peer influence. In the absence of figures with which to compare them, it is difficult to evaluate the size of the percentages—except that the parent figures were larger. To meet this problem, Epperson included elementary as well as secondary students in his sample, and he reasoned that if the hypothesis of a distinct adolescent subculture was true, he should find "a decided difference between elementary and secondary school pupils in the degree to which they are concerned over the disapproval of their parents," with the relationship in the direction of lesser concern among the older students. His data showed that, on the contrary,

> secondary school pupils appear to be more, rather than less concerned about parental reactions. The elementary school pupils, however, appear to be more concerned over their teachers' disapproval, possibly because they spend more time with teachers than secondary school pupils spend with even their favorite teachers. Since opportunities for loyalties to develop are significantly different, these data provide no basis for saying that secondary school pupils are more estranged from adult culture. (Epperson, 1964: 95)

An important contribution of Epperson's study is the inclusion of preadolescent children. Epperson's conclusion—that, contrary to the fear of increasingly exclusive peer power, parental influence may be increased simultaneously in certain areas—could not have been drawn if he had not had comparative data from another age group.

In most of the 1960s research on peer versus parent influence, information on the latter was based upon students' reports of their parents' expectations. One exception is a study by Kandel and Lesser, in which data were collected from students in three high schools plus a subsample of their mothers. The authors found that "concordance," or agreement of respondents' educational expectations with their mother's expectations for them: (1) was stronger than concordance with best friends, in or outside of school, although those who agreed most with their mothers also tended to have high agreement with their friends; (2) held when a variety of factors, from social class to course in school, were controlled; and (3) seemed to be independent of family structure and even of the closeness of the mother–adolescent child relationship.

> Thus we take exception to the "hydraulic" view taken by many investigators regarding the relative influence of adults and peers which assumes that the greater the influence of the one, the less the influence of the other. Our data lead to another view: in critical areas, interactions with peers support the values of the parents.
>
> The assumption is commonly made that peers provide a deterrent to intellectual development and educational aspirations during adolescence. Our own data confirm that the climate of American high schools does not appear to reward intellectual achievement in school. But peers have less influence on adolescents than parents with regard to future educational goals. (Kandel and Lesser, 1969: 221–222)

Some additional insights and a crosscultural perspective on the parent versus peer issue are provided by a study of English students conducted by Musgrove, who collected questionnaire data from 778 boys and girls between the ages of nine and fifteen in two socially contrasted areas in the North Midlands. On questions asking respondents their preferred companions in a variety of activities and situations, Musgrove found that the proportion of choices for parents declined significantly each year except between ages ten and eleven, but that there was a relationship between the difficulty or seriousness of the activity and the choice of companion. For example, parents were more often chosen in a situation involving danger than as companions for a party, football game, or the movies. There were no relationships between responses to these questions and the IQ or SES of the respondents.

Analysis of responses to a set of social-distance scales showed, like Epperson's results, no support for the view that younger children are closer to adults than teenagers. The difference was that the youngest children in the sample tended to perceive the same social distance between self and parents as between self and peers, while the fourteen- and fifteen-year-olds placed their parents at a greater distance than their peers. That is, as one enters adolescence, one moves closer to peers without necessarily getting further away from parents.

A third set of questions, involving sentence-completion tasks (for instance, "Boys of my age can ___, Mothers can ___"), was given both to the students and to a subsample of their parents. The conclusion from these data was that even into adolescence students not only turn to parents on the more serious issues confronting them, but they also have a more positive image of adults than the adults have of them.

> The picture which adults had of teenagers was widely different from the picture that adolescents had of themselves. The adults' picture was overwhelmingly negative, with scarcely any reference to teenagers' increasing social and technical competence . . . 29 per cent were generally disapproving in their remarks, and only 15 per cent appear to have been generally approving.
>
> Although in some respects this study suggests important differences from American conditions, it is in line with those American investigations which have shown adolescents belittled by their elders, regarded as a separate, inferior, and even threatening population, exposed to contradictory expectations from the general body of adults, and consigned, as Hollingshead has said, to "an ill-defined no-man's land that lies between the protected dependency of childhood, where the parent is dominant, and the independent world of the adult, where the person is relatively free from parental controls." (Musgrove, 1964: 104–105)

Thus, Musgrove seems to say that even if a separate youth period and subculture is not real or necessary in itself, it is real in its consequences. If the larger society defines adolescence as distinct and problematic, this will have implications for the way students see themselves and the way they behave.[11]

Although the research was begun in the 1950s, one of the richest sources of data on the linkages between teenagers and their major groups is the information collected by a group of Rutgers University sociologists under the general direction of Matilda and John Riley. A sample of over twenty-five hundred high school students in eight predominantly middle-class New Jersey communities were questioned at two points in their high school careers, first in 1952 when they were ninth or tenth graders, a second time two years later. A battery of questionnaires covered topics such as: patterns of communication with a variety of communication objects; respondents self-image, present and future; and perceptions of the expectations of parents and peers concerning a wide range of attributes, skills, and activities. A follow-up study designed to study the continuing socialization of young adults involved tracing a subsample of the original respondents about ten years later. At the same time, a new study of students from the same New Jersey high schools was begun, and a subsample of students' parents were also questioned. We shall mention here only a few of the most significant findings.

Mothers and school friends, compared with fathers, teachers, siblings, and friends outside of school, were the most popular communication sources. On a list of ten topics, mother received the most or next to most choices on all but one topic, and friends in school received the most choices on half of the topics. Communication with fathers varied by topic—father was the person most often turned to for discussion of political questions, and was just behind mother on discussion of moral questions and school problems.

There was a clear pattern of specialization by topic. The topics high on parent communication included moral problems, school problems, and politics (the last the fathers' "specialty"). Communication with peers was low in all of these areas; their specialties included movies, whom to invite to a party, problems concerning the opposite sex, and "how you get along with the kids," all of which were rarely discussed with parents. Taking each topic individually, the Rutgers group found a negative relationship between the extent to which a topic was discussed with parents and the extent to which the same topic was discussed with peers. Graphs of response patterns revealed a clustering, which suggested an underlying structure of content specialization—one in which adolescent communication is directed predominantly to parents, another to peers. The first included the problems of present school work and educational plans for the future, as well as general moral decisions and problems; the second included things having to do with interpersonal relations, popularity, and status with peers.

Although there was a division of labor between the two major reference groups on individual topics, there was no relationship between overall communication with parents and peers. That is, students who talked with their parents on many topics were neither more nor less likely to have high total communication scores with their school friends. There was also very little change in communication scores or patterns in the two-year interval between the under- and upper-class high school years (Riley *et al.*, 1955).

Other important findings came from analysis of responses to a series of vignettes or brief descriptions of fictitious high school students, each embodying a particular value (say, academic achievement, good times, peer approval) found on the basis of preliminary interviewing to be of concern to adolescents (Riley *et al.*, 1961). Respondents were asked to rate each of the vignettes on the following questions:

Do I want to be just like them?

Do the well-liked kids in my grade want their friends to be like them?

Do my parents want me to be like them?

Would this help me later on when I am through school?

Comparison of responses to the whole set showed, for example, that the majority of respondents (79 percent of the boys, 83 percent of the girls) wanted to be like the following model:

> Paul and Miriam are good students. Although they are not bookworms or grinds, they get good marks because they spend quite a bit of time studying and are always "on the beam" when it comes to their work.

This was almost as many as identified with the peer-approval models of popularity and friendliness, and more than identified with the following:

> Dottie and Ed have a great deal of fun with their friends. They spend a lot of time with the gang, going out, studying, playing all kinds of games, and just hanging around together.

That is, the majority of these boys and girls wanted to be successful students. What they wanted to avoid was the appearance of being too outstanding or of being a "grind" (which the Coleman "brilliant student" may imply).

As a whole, the respondents did see their parents and peers as placing rather different valuation upon many of the attributes and activities encompassed in the vignettes. As might be expected, parents were perceived as placing relatively greater emphasis upon school and success, peers upon having a good time. Their own preferred image fell between their perceived expectations of these two reference groups, a pattern that the Rileys interpret as forming a bridge between the two, but which could also be interpreted as placing many students in a position of crosspressures or dissonance. The bridging view is supported by the additional finding that the expectations these students had for themselves *as adults* were different from the way they perceived themselves at the moment, and that the future expectations were, in fact, very close to perceived parental expectations. That is, while sensitive to the demands of current peer relationships and anxious to avoid the appearance of deviation from the approved adolescent image (for instance, spending an excessive amount of time and effort to get top grades), these students could at the same time distinguish between values relevant to their current—and temporary—adolescent status and those relevant to the roles they expected to play in the future.

While the original Rutgers data are now somewhat dated, the Rileys' basic conceptual model, as well as many of the important substantive findings, have been replicated in various ways: by the mid-sixties study of students in the same high schools, by a study of students in several Alabama and Georgia high schools (Brittain, 1963), and by a comparative study of United States and German adolescents (Johnson, 1976).

Many of the issues raised in this and the preceding section are summarized in a review of the literature on adolescent socialization by the coauthor of *Equality of*

Educational Opportunity and of the study comparing friends' status and school-status effects described earlier in this chapter.

While acknowledging the strains endemic to young people in a society in which youth as a group has a kind of "pseudo-independence" but no functional significance in the productive life of the larger society, Campbell (1969) contends that most adolescents get along remarkably well with their parents and continue to be substantially influenced by them. To bolster his argument, Campbell points out that many parents welcome rather than resist adolescent demands for independence and extension of loyalties to persons and groups outside the family. As we saw in Chapter 4—and will see again in Chapter 13—the parents of successful students are the ones most likely to encourage these tendencies, and "it seems reasonable to interpret most parent-adolescent conflict as occurring not because the direction of the adolescent's quest for greater independence is illegitimate but because perfect congruence in the speed and circumstances under which new forms of expression are tolerable is not achieved" (Campbell, 1969: 830). Campbell also points out that many aspects of youth culture—especially those that demonstrate physical prowess and skill in getting along with others—are positively sanctioned by adults. The athletic star and student-body president are heroes to their parents, teachers, and neighbors, as well as to their peers, and "the mother who complains that her daughter spends too much time on the telephone and receives multiple requests for dates is not nearly so pained as the mother who complains that her daughter reads books endlessly and hardly goes outside the house" (Campbell, 1969: 851). Campbell goes on to state that the "ecology of adolescent behavior functions to reduce the probability of head-on clashes." The young are skillful at avoidance tactics, and since many of their activities are not under adult surveillance, they can simply "not emit clear signals" to adults concerning behavior that might be disapproved (Campbell, 1969: 831).[12]

Finally, Campbell suggests that youth culture may fulfill an important function by virtue of being at variance with the goals of the school and adult world. During much of the school day, students are engaged in activities "that are defended far less for their intrinsic worth or gratification than because they are qualificatory to a desired state in adulthood," and outside of school they are constantly reminded that their usefulness to society is still potential. "In the midst of such themes of impermanence, preparation, and transition, the activities and value of peer culture have a very solid here-and-now quality about them" (Campbell, 1969: 843) that may help students to put up with the less satisfying aspects of school experience.

The high school world continues to intrigue sociologists, and while there has been a trend toward comparative, quantitative analyses testing various components of the Coleman model, case studies in which an individual researcher attempts to plumb the depths of high school culture and social structure continue to be published. During the past decade, for example, Cusick (1973) and Larkin (1979) have argued in support of Coleman's theme of the separation between the "official" school system of classes, teachers, grades, and routine, and the "extra-official" system of student groups and friendship-centered activities.

These recent studies suggest, however, that the adolescent society is in fact divided into a number of discrete social units (plus a rather disturbing number of student isolates who have little involvement in the school because they have no friends there), narrowly bounded by age, sex, socioeconomic status, and interests, with very little communication across clique boundaries. Cusick concludes that

> rather than a society or even a subculture, there is a fragmented series of interest groups revolving around specific items and past patterns of interaction. These groups may be the important social referent, not some mythical subculture or "adolescent society." . . . cross-communication among adolescents may be very limited, common activities and interests very rare, and . . . there may be no such thing as "all students." (Cusick, 1973: 161–162)

Youth and Society

One of the continuing controversies of the past two decades concerns the linkages of youth and youth culture with the larger society. Some of the basic themes introduced by Coleman in *The Adolescent Society* were developed further in a report he coauthored as chairman of the Panel on Youth of the President's Advisory Committee (1974). In this report, Coleman and his coauthors focus on the consequences of the extension of formal education and the exclusion of the young from the work place, arguing that keeping young people in positions of dependency and nonproductivity has resulted in the creation of a new stage in the life cycle—that of youth—which may now delay adulthood until the mid-twenties.

New insights into the position of youth have been provided from several areas of research that have developed rapidly during the past ten years or so. One source of insight comes from historical analyses of the changing perceptions and treatment of youth in this country and elsewhere. For example, Kett's analysis of changing patterns of age grouping indicates that young people's peer groups in early nineteenth-century American communities were typically characterized by a broader range of ages and less direct adult supervision—what Kett terms a "kind of promiscuous assemblage of ages"—than the age-homogeneous cliques and gangs found in today's suburbs (Panel on Youth, 1974: 12). He also concludes that while nineteenth-century adolescents were more likely to be fully incorporated into the economic life of adult society than their twentieth-century counterparts, this did not mean that relations between the generations were smooth. On the contrary, Kett feels that in a society in which most occupational tasks could be performed by an average teen-ager, young people "stood in a much more proximate and even menacing relationship to adults than they do now," and he hypothesizes that in general, "the more fully young people approximate equality in their economic relationship to adults, the more occasions for friction will arise" (Panel on Youth, 1974: 16, 17).

A second source of insight into the present position of young people is the newly emerging field of the sociology of age. The age structure of society, in particular the relative size of its constituent age *cohorts* (that is, all persons born in the same year, or near the same year, and aging together) affects individuals' experience of their lives, and social strains may result from imbalances between the size of cohorts and the number and nature of "openings" in the role structure of society (Ryder, 1965; Waring, 1975). Today's youth are members of the large "baby boom" cohort resulting from the period of high birth rate following World War II. Such large cohorts typically "create a 'people jam' at the entrances to the successive age grades they seek to occupy," in this case coinciding with increasing years spent in the role of student and delays in the achievement of full adult status (Waring, 1975: 242. See also Parsons and Platt, 1972). Thus the "new" phase in the life cycle postulated by Coleman and the Panel on Youth may be seen as the consequence of retardation of "cohort flow." By contrast, the marked drops in the birth rate that have characterized our society in recent years will produce relatively small youth cohorts in the not-too-distant future, leading some sociologists to predict labor shortages, pressures to shorten childhood and youth, and fewer tendencies toward deviance and "dropping out" among the young.

Indeed, Coleman's basic claim that the young are being increasingly excluded from the work place needs careful examination. The Panel on Youth data show that the actual decline in labor-force participation between 1960 and 1970 was only for boys; the proportion of girls increased both in school enrollment and in labor-force participation. Morever, the pattern for both sexes reflects a shift from going into full-time jobs before or at the end of high school to continuing in full-time education combined with a part-time job. The Panel views this trend as one that limits young people to "youth-type" or lowest entry-level jobs with little autonomy or opportunities for learning and advancement. But it could also be interpreted as allowing greater mobility and autonomy with respect to work over the long run.

Differences in work opportunities and the position of youth in the labor force are partly a function of society's stage of technological development as well as its ideological views. As one comparison between Chinese and American adolescent subcultures points out:

> In the advanced society fertiliser, D.D.T. and road construction equipment all reduce the amount of labour that little unskilled hands can do. The automobile removes the delivery boy on his bicycle from the local scene. Mechanised farm equipment replaces the afterschool "chores" of the farmer's son. The high school lad finds that his summer jobs have begun to disappear. Finally, the high school graduate finds that post-high school education is needed simply to gain a full-time position with more than a modest wage attached to it. To be sure, this development provides certain social benefits. The economy can forego larger and larger amounts of labour by teenagers. (Hickrod and Hickrod, 1965: 170–78)

The passage quoted above points to crosscultural comparisons as a third area of research from which insights on the position of American youth may be drawn. While crosscultural similarities and differences in educational patterns and outcomes will be the subject of Chapter 13, it is relevant to note here that the separation of contemporary youth from the mainstream of society is not inevitable, and that in some societies youth has been in the vanguard of major societal events and trends (see, for example, the discussion of youth activism in Maoist China, in Fan and Fan, 1975. Comparisons of the status and attitudes of youth in several different countries are contained in Boocock, 1974).

The Panel on Youth report tends to reflect what sociologists of age term a cohort-centric or age-biased view of the appropriate place of education and work in the lives of young people, in this case the biases of the middle-aged scholars who comprised the Panel. An analysis based upon a poll of young people themselves also acknowledges the impact of increased years of schooling, but interprets it rather differently.

> The current crop of high school students desires not only good jobs in terms of status, but also interesting and meaningful jobs that lead to self-fulfillment; and these young workers are the most disaffected part of the work force because they cannot find jobs that satisfy their requirements of challenge, growth, and self-fulfillment. . . .
>
> Significantly, the desire for jobs offering intrinsic rewards has increased over the past five years, even in the face of a tightening job market. (O'Toole, 1975: 31)

The report also tends to romanticize the situation of youth in the past. It is questionable whether rural youth of the American past, compelled to work long hours on the family farm, had many advantages over the full-time college student of today. However, there was in the past a real need for strong young workers, a need that no longer exists. The question then becomes how best to use the time and energies released from former kinds of work.

Conclusions

In this chapter we have examined the structure and dynamics of the peer group as it affects students' academic attitudes and achievement. The student peer group is in a sense both inside and outside the school. On the one hand, it is not part of the formal organization of the school, and it has its origins and carries on many of its activities outside of school. On the other hand, the preceding chapters have indicated that an important part of a student's learning environment consists of his or her fellow students, and that the composition and values of the student body are among the most important resources of any school.

Research testing Coleman's model of the adolescent society suggests that while a youth culture exists in this country (as indeed it does in virtually all industrialized societies), it is not a monolithic, all-inclusive phenomenon wholly at variance with the larger society. The studies we have examined here suggest that peer solidarity is a variable, affected by individual background (including SES, age, and sex), the school climate or context, and the nature of the surrounding environment. Several studies have also suggested that in many schools there may be more than one subculture, depending upon the breakdown of the student body into various cliques and subgroups.

With the exception of students who have rejected the basic goals of achievement and success, most young people use both parents and peers as reference groups. Parents are, in fact, more often turned to in connection with educational problems and plans, although the influence of peers in the academic area may operate to place limits upon investment in intellectual activities. Few students want to be known as "grinds," and they will often go out of their way to avoid giving the appearance of caring too much and trying too hard for good grades and other academic rewards.

It is also clear that youth culture is not a static phenomenon. While analyses that summarize a decade with a word or phrase (the "hedonism" of the 1950s, the "commitment" of the 1960s, the "me generation" of the 1970s) are suspect, thoughtful observers note the increasingly rapid rate of change in values and attitudes as well as the subcultural variations at any given point in time, and they worry that certain trends in our society as a whole (for example, increased racial segregation in large metropolitan areas) may divide students, even in the same school, into separate "subsocieties"—with a growing gulf between those who are reasonably compliant to the expectations of the learning system and who will move on through even higher levels of education, and those who actively rebel against the educational system or who withdraw from active engagement and simply mark time in school until they are old enough to drop out.

Ideally, research on peer group structure and influence should follow multiple cohorts longitudinally over time (for example, selecting a sample of thirteen-, sixteen-, and nineteen-year-olds and studying them at regular intervals for several years). The fifteen-year follow-up study of the *Adolescent Society* sample and the multiple follow-ups of Wisconsin Study and Project Talent subsamples all provide longitudinal data on a single cohort. These studies afford unusual opportunities to study the life-course patterns of persons born during the early 1940s in order to trace the impact of influences and events at one life stage upon developments in a subsequent life stage, and to explore the interrelationships of educational events and experiences with other major life events and experiences. It is important to keep in mind, however, that the experiences of any cohort and their reactions to these experiences are to some degree unique. (Being fifteen in 1955 is different from being fifteen in 1970 or 1980.) Thus the kinds of conclusions that can be drawn from these single-cohort studies, in the absence of comparisons with other cohorts, are limited.

Finally, learning approaches that utilize the power of the peer group are still rare. Peer-tutoring programs have demonstrated that making the student role more analagous to the teacher role can have positive effects on both tutors and tutored, but schools have not in general been very creative in this regard. Indeed, many aspects of school social structure, such as the reward structure, may be incongruent with important peer values. Thus searching for areas of agreement between youth and adult culture and for methods of learning that retain the structure and channel the energies of student friendship groups seems a fruitful kind of research.

Notes

1. The question of subdivisions of students in a given school into cliques, crowds, and so on—which may in some cases hold different values—will be taken up later in the chapter. Here it should be noted only that "in every school, most students saw a leading crowd, and were willing to say what it took to get into it" (Coleman, 1961: 36).

2. For a description of each school and its classification in this three-dimensional property-space, see Coleman, 1961: 92–96. Keep in mind that the relative position of the three dimensions *with respect to each other* was similar in all schools—in particular, being an athlete always outranked being a top student.

3. Measured in standard deviations above the school grade average.

4. This finding is consistent with findings from studies of leadership in general, which have shown that persons with high group status are the ones most cognizant of the goals and reward structure of the group and most likely to shape their own behavior around them. See, for example, Cartwright and Zander, 1962: Part 5.

5. Further evidence of such a relationship is indicated in the finding that the schools where good grades were most often mentioned as a criterion for being in the leading crowd were also the ones in which the IQ scores of students with the highest scholastic averages exceeded the school mean IQ by the greatest number of standard deviations. In other words, if the climate of the school supports scholastic achievement, the brightest students, like those in the leading crowd, are most likely to invest their energies in intellectual achievement. Conversely, where intellectualism is least valued, those with the most intellectual ability are more likely to channel their energies into other, more highly rewarded activities, leaving the top student role to be filled by students who have lesser ability and who are willing to work at a relatively unrewarded activity. In such schools, the adolescent subculture acts as a real deterrent to achievement among the most able (Coleman, 1961: 262–265).

6. An activity that personifies the ambiguous relationship between the teen society and the high school. Although held under school auspices, pep rallies really have nothing to do with the school's formal learning goals—or even with the physical education program per se.

7. Operationally defined as regular attendance and punctuality, and not having a record of disturbing or breaking the disciplinary rules of the classroom.

8. In barest outline, *balance theory* (also known as *consistency* or *dissonance theory,* although there are variations among the three) posits a condition of balance or consistency in a person when he or she perceives agreement among his or her attitudes or attributes or between his or her attitudes and those of another person. In the latter case, he or she is attracted to that person. Conversely, a condition of strain is produced when a person perceives discrepancies between his or her and another person's views, a strain that motivates him or her to remove this "imbalance" or dissonance—by changing his or her attitudes, by coming to perceive symmetry between his or her attitudes and the other person's, or by ceasing to be positively attracted to the other person. Newcomb, in his application of balance theory to his studies of college friendship patterns, hypothesizes that students who share common attitudes and interests, as well as physical proximity, are most likely to be attracted to one another and to group themselves together as a unit. And that the greater the number of attributes, attitudes, and activities shared by group members, and the

greater the extent to which such sharing sets the group apart from other groups, the greater will be the group's attraction for and influence upon its members (Newcomb, 1962).

9. Operationally defined by infractions of classroom rules that resulted in being sent out of class, or habitual absences or tardiness—the other side of the coin of Gordon's "conformity" measure.

10. Stinchcombe's focus upon future orientation rather than past status as the explanation for present behavior is echoed in Turner's hypothesis that boys from lower-class schools and neighborhoods were likely to display a "pattern of future orientation without anticipatory socialization" (Turner, 1964: 136). Such boys may value success and achievement, but they have not learned the student role well enough to attain them. Turner also found no strong correlations between differences in individual aspirations and differences in individual family background, but his explanation is that the important independent variable is the individual's larger social context, in particular the neighborhood in which the school is located.

11. A similar point is made in an American review published at about the same time as Musgrove's study: "in some instances the effects of visibility may well be to make the mythical stereotype based on it come true, owing to acceptance of a version of this stereotype by the very objects of the stereotyped perception" (Jahoda and Warren, 1965: 148).

12. This parallels Brittain's observation that adolescents "attempt to come to terms with parent-peer cross-pressures by simply not communicating with parents" (Brittain, 1963: 391).

PART FOUR

The School's Environment

Effects of the External Environment   Chapter 12

The things outside the schools matter even more than the things inside the schools, and govern and interpret the things inside.
M. E. Sadler (writing in 1900)

Were it not for their monopoly on educational opportunities for the poor, most big city school systems would probably go out of business.   Christopher Jencks

Deciding who gets to decide for a child should be approached with the queasy discomfort appropriate to all paternalisms. John Coons and Stephen Sugarman

Almost any day's newspapers bring reports of crises in the school's external environment. School board elections or school bond referenda polarize a community. Superintendents resign under fire from their boards or from community-interest groups. Teacher strikes close down entire school systems. Parents storm school board meetings demanding new schools, integrated schools, neighborhood schools, decentralized schools, or community-controlled schools. Indeed, in much of the frenzied activity the education of children seems all but forgotten, and the changes that do occur in the schools often seem to reflect a response to pressures rather than any overall educational philosophy.

In Part Three we attempted to identify factors within the school that have bearing on children's academic achievement. In this chapter we shall focus on factors *outside* of the school that may account for those differences in school structure and dynamics that are related to school effectiveness. To place the discussion in the context of the theoretical typology introduced in Chapter 2, this chapter will focus upon the lower left quarter of Exhibit 2–1 (cells 3 and 4). Part Two also examined outside-school explanations of learning but focused on the characteristics and socialization experiences of individual learners that were related to their academic success—that is, on cells 1 and 2. The right-hand side of Exhibit 2–1 was the subject of Part Three.

The major roles and systems that constitute the school's external social environment are shown in Exhibit 12-1, arranged to represent their general location with respect to the school and each other. The student body of a school is drawn from the families that constitute the general public. Thus, those members of the public most directly affected by school organization and effectiveness are school-aged children and their parents, although various other community-interest groups, such as taxpayer associations and civil rights activists, also attempt to influence school decision making. There has been considerable debate about the appropriate relationship between the public and the school, and some recent reforms have had the explicit purpose of allocating more choice and control to parents concerning the education of their children.

The governance of U.S. public schools is by a combination of professional and lay roles. Individual schools are grouped in school districts, political-educational units that are administered by a superintendent and staff, all of whom are part of the formal educational system though many do not teach or even encounter students and teachers very often. Not part of the professional system but legally responsible for school policy and governance, including the hiring of school personnel, are school boards, which consist of citizens elected or appointed for designated terms.

During the past decade, the influence of government, particularly at the higher levels, has been increasingly felt at the local levels of the educational system. Federal legislation, translated into practice by federal agencies like the U.S. Office of Education, has both increased the amount of federal money invested in education and attempted to decrease inequalities in the distribution of educational resources and opportunities. Court decisions have prodded educational decision makers to change the modes of financing public education and of assigning students and staff to various schools, and the courts have also ruled on the rights and obligations of parents, or particular subgroups of parents, with respect to the education of their children.

This then is the social arena in which various individuals, groups, and institutions interact with—and often clash with—each other over educational issues. Although much of the rhetoric on education still argues that schools are outside of—preferably *above*—politics, recent historical and political science scholarship makes it increasingly clear that the history of American schools can be read as a continuing series of political struggles between the various components shown in Exhibit 12-1 for control of the educational decision-making apparatus. (For an excellent application of this view to one large city school system, see Ravitch's (1974) study of two centuries of "school wars" in New York City. For a political science perspective on the political elements of the school system, see Wirt, 1975; Wirt and Kirst, 1972.)

Examination of trends in educational reforms and innovations also suggests that the target of change has shifted in recent years. The most widely discussed innovations of the 1960s—teaching machines, simulation games, team teaching, the open classroom—were essentially aimed at making the classroom, the student's immediate learning environment, more attractive and effective. By con-

Exhibit 12-1
The School's External Social Environment

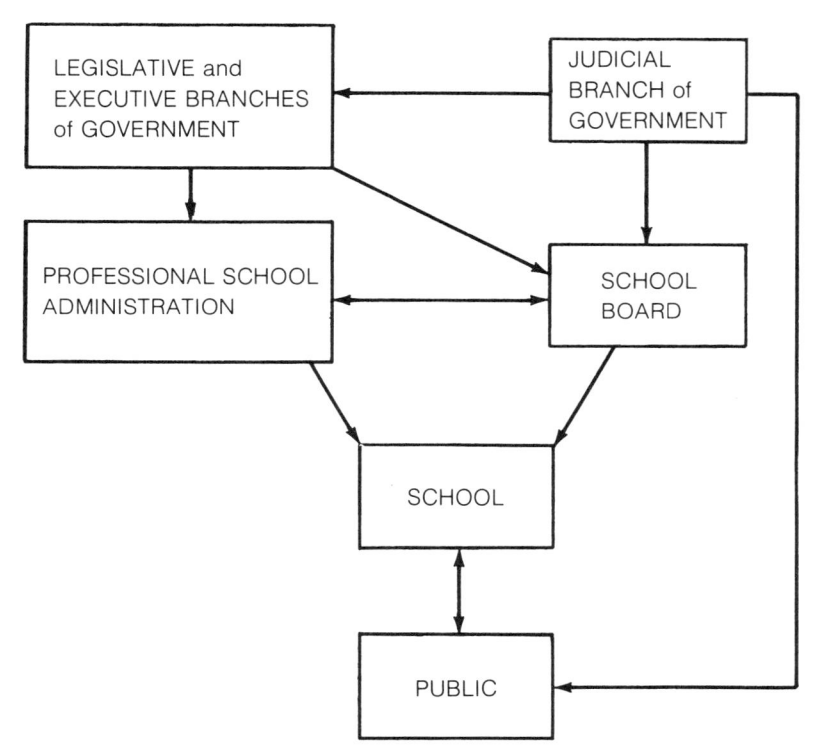

[Diagram: Legislative and Executive Branches of Government and Judicial Branch of Government both connect to Professional School Administration and School Board, which both lead to School, which connects to Public.]

trast, many of the reform strategies that have captured headlines in the past few years—open enrollment, busing, magnet schools, community control, and voucher plans—are based upon the assumption that children's experiences and performances *in* school can be improved by changes in the balance of power *outside*. Indeed, the core concepts that are used to justify or criticize recent proposals—equality, diversity, control, and choice themselves reflects shifts in the proposed locus of reform.

In the various sections of this chapter, we shall attempt to evaluate the impact of roles and institutions in the school's external environment (including the interactions among them) on the social structure and effectiveness of schools.

Professional Administration

To go outside of the school itself does not mean leaving the formal educational system. Individual schools are grouped in school districts, political-educational units directed by a superintendent and staff. In large districts, particularly in large cities, the professional staff takes the form of a complex hierarchical web of administrators and supervisors, curricular and other specialists, spilling out from the central office into a series of field offices. The growing size, power, and inertia of large-city educational bureaucracies has in recent years received much of the blame for the "troubles" in the schools.

Although they are formally dependent upon the school boards that hire, pay, and occasionally fire them, the professional managers tend to dominate school governance. Part of their strength lies in their sheer numbers and their job security. In New York City, for example, the Board of Education consists of nine people, all serving part-time without pay, while the bureaucracy of full-time administrators numbers over fifty-five hundred, about 10 percent of the total professional staff of the city's school system. Unlike business executives, school administrators below the level of superintendent seldom change employers; most have tenure and cannot be easily discharged. In such an unbalanced situation,

> unless the nine citizens are unusually able and active, they cannot begin to control the bureaucracy's behavior, nor can the superintendent they hire to direct the bureaucracy. In New York City and other places the superintendent has no power to appoint his own staff but must take only those who come from the ranks and who are seasoned in the system. (Sexton, 1967: 26)

In a comparative case study of six large-city school systems, Gittell and Hollander concluded that decision making was controlled by a small core of professionals, who successfully insulated themselves from public officials and organizations (on the grounds of freedom from "political interference") and from parents and other private citizens (on the grounds of lack of professional "expertise"). "The insulation of public education is twofold: bureaucratic centralization (or more accurately over-centralization) which is a product of size, reinforced by an ideological rationale of professionalization, which is a product of the vested interests of the educationists. The result is a static, internalized, isolated system which has been unable to respond to vastly changing needs and demands of large city populations" (Gittell and Hollander, 1968: 197). While some of the city systems in the sample were relatively less ossified than others, the authors found little empirical evidence of innovations in curriculum, teacher-recruitment procedures, or administrative organization in any. In a subsequent analysis, Gittell concluded that the role of the educational administrators in large, urban school systems supports Weber's theory of "the emergence of a specialized bureaucracy monopolizing power through its control of expertise" (Gittell, 1974: 46. Perceived professional expertise as a fundamental resource of superintendents is also discussed in Zeigler and Jennings, 1974: 150ff).

Most superintendents and other high-level administrators are white males in their late fifties and early sixties. In a study of decision making with respect to the school-integration issue, Crain (1968) found that most of the large-city superintendents for whom he could obtain background material were upwardly mobile men from small-town or rural backgrounds. Men who major in education, traditionally a "woman's field," tend to be of lower status than college men generally, and a man who rises to a superintendency usually has come a long way from his social as well as geographical origins. In Crain's view, the double strain—the inconsistencies between past and present status plus the conflicting demands of groups inside and outside the formal education system—result in a defensiveness about the schools and an intolerance of lay "interference," especially from groups who make aggressive demands for policy changes on grounds other than strictly educational ones (for instance, civil rights groups). In his study of school governance, *Who Runs Our Schools?*, Gross says of administrators:

> It takes a long time to get up there. And when you talk with these men, you get a curious feeling of inertia. You throw out an idea and the reaction is "It can't be done" or "Oh, we heard about that years ago." The man on top may want to make changes in the schools but he has to work through the structure and it may be very difficult. (Gross, 1965: 33)

Although much administrative behavior seems very remote from life in the classroom, a belief in the importance of the professional leadership appears to be widely held by social scientists as well as by the administrators themselves. For example, the contention of a former school superintendent and high federal official that "the local school administrator is the most significant individual in the lives of children and youth" (quoted in Sexton, 1967: 27) is matched by a sociologist's criticism of the Coleman Report for not examining the impact of professional leadership, on the grounds that "differences in the quality of school administration—holding pupil backgrounds constant—should account for as much of the difference in student achievement as does peer environment" (Dentler, 1966: 291). However, there has been little empirical research relating good measures of educational leadership to student outcomes.

One of the few comparative studies of resource allocation at the level of the school district shows a *negative* relationship between the relative size of the administrative staff and level of student achievement. In an analysis of data on 104 of the 178 K–12 public school districts in the State of Colorado, Bidwell and Kasarda found substantial evidence of the "importance of a district's relative investment in teachers for its aggregate level of student achievement. As pupil-teacher ratios declined across districts, the two median achievement scores rose." Moreover, "the better qualified the certificated staff, the higher the levels of reading and mathematics achievement." Student achievement was *not*, however, positively correlated with the size of the administrative staff. On the contrary, "as administrative intensity rose, the achievement scores declined . . . so far as student achievement is concerned, administrative overhead mainly diverts human resources from teaching and from other staff functions related to instruction" (Bidwell and Kasarda, 1975: 65–66). That is, school bureaucratization may be a real if indirect impediment to student achievement.

Another way in which administrative decisions may have direct effects upon children's in-school experience is in assignments to special or alternative school programs. Citing recent litigation in which it was disclosed that large numbers of Chicano children were misclassified as mentally retarded, Coons and Sugarman

(1978) argue that under a budgetary and administrative system in which school districts are given subsidies for children who are identified as "special," the labeling of large numbers of children as retarded, learning disabled, or otherwise handicapped is a financial temptation as well as an administratively convenient way to remove hard-to-teach children from regular classrooms. Apropos of the recent trend toward labeling more children as learning disabled and hiring more special education teachers, Bidwell and Kasarda's analysis indicated that the presence of specialists had only weak effects on district levels of achievement. They concluded that it is well-qualified classroom teachers, not special education personnel, who make a difference in the aggregate level of achievement.

The School Board

The highest lay authority in the educational system is the school board, which is charged with the making of public school policy and with liaison between the school and the community. Unlike professional administrators, school board member is a declining role. As a result of the consolidation of school districts during the past half century, the number of school boards (now about 15,000) as well as the proportion of board members relative to teachers, administrators, and students has decreased markedly. A 1956 study gave the total number of United States school board members as about 200,000, while the comparable figure in a 1972 study was only 90,000; the ratio of board members to elementary and secondary students declined from 1/46 in 1932 to 1/300 in 1967 (Zeigler and Jennings, 1972; Sexton, 1967).

The great majority of school boards are elected on a nonpartisan basis. Compared to the central administrative office, turnover of school board membership is high, and most board members serve while they have children in the schools they are elected to govern. By comparison with the general public, board members are disproportionately white, male, middle-aged, high in education, occupation, and income, and well established in their local communities. In a comparison of data from a national sample of school boards with a cross-section sample of the American public in the late 1960s, Zeigler and Jennings (1974) found that 80 percent of the board members had lived in the community over fifteen years compared to half of the general sample, that 93 percent owned their own homes compared to two-thirds of the general public, and that 61 percent claimed to attend church weekly compared to 38 percent of the general public. Zeigler and Jennings also found that board members tended to differ from the general public on a number of controversial issues. They were more tolerant or liberal on some issues pertaining to basic civil liberties (for example, on prayers in schools and the federal role in school integration), but more conservative on the role of teachers (for example, they were less favorable toward a stronger voice for teachers and toward the right of teachers to strike), and they were more likely than the general public to say that the federal and state governments exercised too much control over local education.

Most sociological research on school boards focuses on the pathways to board membership (more often via achievement of high status in business or a profession accompanied by involvement in prestigious civic organizations or through activity in general political party work or some special-interest group than through direct participation in educational affairs), the "progressiveness" or innovativeness of boards or board members, and the struggles between boards and superintendents for control of the decision making on important issues. Most research indicates that the views of the superintendent tend to prevail in most board-superintendent conflicts, at least as long as the superintendent can convince the board of his or her expertise, and that the board acts mainly to legitimize the decisions made by the superintendent and his or her staff (Kerr, 1964; Zeigler and Jennings, 1974). The Crain study mentioned earlier in this chapter presents a rather different view. In all but one of the eight Northern and seven Southern school systems studied, the board rather than the superintendent made the major decisions about school desegregation, perhaps because desegregation is an issue on which the superintendent is not perceived as having greater or more legitimate expertise than the board members. Although Crain pictured the boards as relatively strong and active, he admitted that much school board action was a response to crisis and was taken in the absence of any guiding educational philosophy or policy.

> The typical school board is not closely knit. It ordinarily meets to handle the legal paperwork of the schools; at irregular intervals it makes specific decisions about a particular policy. But it can be thought of as making school policy only in a fire-fighting fashion. If an issue comes up, it acts; otherwise it does not. It may not take a position at all on some of the most fundamental issues of school policy, simply because those particular policies have not been made salient by community discussion. The result is that the school board members do not, either as individuals or as a group, have a highly articulated educational policy. Almost every time they oppose the superintendent, or the superintendent comes to them for guidance, the board has some difficulty making a decision. Every issue is different and every decision can take a good deal of time. (Crain, 1968: 125)

School boards may be the most invisible components of the educational system. While reports of stormy public sessions often appear in local news media, such occasions are in fact rare. Many boards do not hold any meetings open to the public, and of those that do, few report attendance of more than five "outsiders" at any meeting. While measures of progressiveness and professionalism devised by social scientists can sometimes distinguish variations among boards, most boards like most central offices are not innovative (Wirt and Kirst, 1972: Chapter 5; Sexton, 1967; Gross, 1965; Marilyn Johnson, personal communication). Finally and unfortunately, none of the available research on school boards relates the structure of boards or behavior of board members to student or school outcomes.

The Public

The public is the community served by a given school. During the 1960s a number of studies relating community characteristics to school outputs were published. For example Rogoff hypothesized that part of the differential achievement of children from the same kind of family background can be explained by community setting, through a process by which "the ecological environment leads to formal and informal arrangements within and outside the schools, affecting the educational attainment of residents" (Rogoff, 1961: 242). Using data collected by the Educational Testing Service, Rogoff classified the communities in which schools were located into nine categories based upon population size and relationship to a metropolitan area (small, independent towns of three sizes; suburbs of three sizes; and cities of three sizes). When she controlled for family SES (middle-class suburban children were compared with middle-class children in other kinds of communities) and corrected for school differences in retention rates, Rogoff found that the large, suburban high school came off best on both college aspirations and scholastic aptitude test scores. High schools in the largest cities produced about the same proportions of high aspirers and achievers as those in small towns. Thus, there was a relationship between the structure of the community and what went on in its schools, although the relationship was not a simple, linear one.

Turner's study of social mobility patterns among Los Angeles high school students reaches similar conclusions. The ten schools in Turner's sample were selected as a more-or-less representative sample of socioeconomic areas of the city by applying the Shevky index of social rank to census track data. Thus each school was characterized in terms of the total community in which it was located.

Turner found that differences in educational values and aspirations were related to the status of the neighborhood, a relationship that held when factors of *individual* SES, IQ, and peer group pressures were controlled.

> Schools that draw their students disproportionately from higher family backgrounds tend to be more middle class in values than the individual backgrounds warrant. Schools which draw their students disproportionately from lower family backgrounds are less middle class in values than the individual backgrounds of their students warrant. The impact of neighborhood . . . is to accentuate the predominant tendencies. (Turner, 1964: 104)

Turner rejected the notion that peer group pressures explain away or are the mechanism through which the neighborhood influences aspirations. Contrary to the common notion that the peer group in low-SES areas has a depressant effect upon the ambitions and performance of able individuals, students in low-SES neighborhoods were as likely as other students to prefer friends with reputations for academic performance. Whatever it is in such neighborhoods that lowers academic ambitions and achievement, it is not a uniform negative pressure from peers.

A study focusing upon the effect of community size was carried out with Canadian data by Boyle (1966). Beginning with a review of previous work (including Rogoff, Turner, and Wilson's), Boyle pointed out that although each study showed that a school's student-body composition had a considerable effect upon individual aspirations or performance, each also showed an external-environment effect, and that this effect was stronger in larger than in small communities.

Canada was chosen as the setting for Boyle's study because, unlike the United States, it has a highly centralized educational system, a structure that produces relative uniformity in standards and practices. By thus providing a kind of control for within-school differences that would not be possible in most American school systems, Boyle could be more confident that differences in output would be related to factors outside of the school.

The results indicated that even in a learning system designed to play down interschool differences, a student's place of residence still partially determined his or her school experience. Comparison of schools differing in SES composition, without taking into account their community environment, did show fewer differences than one would predict using United States data. There were slightly higher proportions of students in high-status schools planning on college, but almost no differences between medium-SES and low-SES schools. However, the introduction of community size (whether the school was located in or outside of a metropolitan area) changed the picture. Controlling for both SES context and community size showed that

> the relationship between community size and population composition is so pronounced that *all* of the high-status schools, but *none* of the low-status schools, were located in metropolitan areas. As a consequence, the only comparison possible among metropolitan schools is between high- and medium-status categories, while the only comparison possible between non-metropolitan schools is between medium- and low-status categories. Among the former, the effect of population composition is quite strong ($a_1 = 0.25$), while among the latter the effect is minimal ($a_1 = 0.01$). This finding is consistent with the interpretation that more centralized administration in Canada will discourage divergence among non-metropolitan high schools but that residential segregation in metropolitan areas will create even stronger pressures toward divergence. (Boyle, 1966: 636)

This relationship is reduced somewhat but does not disappear when scholastic ability (performance on province-wide examinations) is controlled. The ability variable is related to the other two, in that the highest-ability students are the ones more likely to attend high-status metropolitan schools.

Thus both the population composition and the location of a school affect academic output, but these two variables are themselves interactively related, so that the size of the SES contextual effect is dependent upon the structure of the larger community. A certain amount of self-selection of students is also likely, with the more able and ambitious more apt to attend some schools than to attend others. However, differences in societal structure in general as well as educational structure in particular necessitate caution in applying findings from one society to another.

The most extensive evidence on the effects of the external social environment is contained in Burkhead's study of two, large-city school systems and a sample of small ones. This study represents one of the few available examples of the application of systems analysis techniques to the problems of learning systems (see Chapter 10). Burkhead's model relates a variety of input variables (for example, personnel time, expenditures for buildings and materials); process variables (class and school size); and status variables (in particular the median family income of the area of the city in which a school is located) to a variety of output or dependent variables (in particular standardized test scores and dropout rates). While not all of the variables are strictly comparable from one city to another—illustrating the difficulty of doing comparative analysis in a large society without national standards and measures—the careful definition and large number of variables used justifies confidence in the results. Within each city, a regression analysis was done to see which of the independent variables explained the greatest portion of variation in outputs.

The major finding is that in all the cities in the sample, the external variable of community average income explained a great deal more of the variance in test scores than any of the within-school variables, such as expenditures or class size. In the two large cities, variance in student output was almost wholly explained by the school's socioeconomic environment. To put it in the cost-benefit language of systems analysis:

> in Chicago an increase in median family income of $1,000 from the mean is associated with an increase of 21 per cent in the proportion of students scoring average or better in 11th grade reading. In Atlanta an increase of $1,000 in median family income is associated with an 8.5 per cent improvement in 10th grade reading scores. (Burkhead, 1967: 88)

That this effect is a matter of the social context created by the residents of an area rather than of a simple translation of high income into a more "expensive" educational system is indicated by the lack of relationship between current expenditures and school outputs. Furthermore, an analysis of resource allocation patterns (comparing the expenditure for textbooks and other materials, staff, buildings, and so on among school attendance areas differing in median family income) produced a slight U-shaped curve. That is, expenditures were slightly higher in the lowest and highest income areas, dipping slightly in the middle.

Although median area income was the most powerful single predictor of student output in every community studied, there was a major division between large and small communities. For example, community income level accounted for 86 percent of the variance in eleventh-grade reading scores and IQ scores in Chicago, and 85 percent of the tenth-grade verbal scores in Atlanta, but only 45 percent of the twelfth-grade reading scores for the 206 small-town public schools taken from the Project Talent survey sample. Even taking into account differences in age or grade level or in the particular tests used in the different cities, the magnitude of the difference is clear, and it holds up consistently in every comparison between the two big cities and the sample of small ones. Income level alone has less impact, or less exclusive impact, in smaller communities than in large cities. This difference is partly explained by the different meaning of the income level variable for large and small communities.

> The deviations around the mean of family income are likely to be much greater in the smaller community than in the school attendance area of the large city. To make the data comparable it would be necessary to collect data on the family income, or other socioeconomic variables, for each student in the small community and thus to

analyze the effect of school resource allocation policies on the educational outcomes of students with a similar background. (Burkhead, 1967: 85)

Burkhead also admits that his output variables are probably affected by factors not included in his analysis, such as the educational and occupational opportunities in the surrounding area, and differences in school-leaving laws and practices.

A dissenting view of community effect was expressed in the second of the two Wilson studies discussed in Chapter 10. To recapitulate, Wilson found that although children who lived in primarily lower-SES and primarily black neighborhoods during their elementary school years did achieve lower test scores at the beginning of junior high, these differences disappeared in the multivariate analysis that controlled for *school* composition. Wilson concluded that "the effect of neighborhood segregation upon achievement is entirely through the resulting segregation of neighborhood schools on social-class lines" (Wilson, 1967: 180).

Re-examination of the Wilson study shows that it differs from the others in several aspects—not only in its conclusions. First, the subjects were relatively younger. Not only was Wilson's the only sample drawn from junior as well as senior high schools, but the analysis comparing the relative effects of neighborhood and other variables uses the effect of respondents' residence *during their primary school years* on their *sixth-grade* reading scores. This raises the possibility that neighborhood impact is different at different age levels, but the *direction* of differences in this case (less effect when children first enter school than later) is the reverse of what one would expect.

A difference that makes more sense substantively concerns the measure of community that is used. Unlike Turner and Burkhead's measure, which was based upon the SES of the total area served by the school (including both families who did and who did not have children in school), and Boyle and Rogoff's, who controlled for total community size and position with respect to the nearest large metropolitan area, Wilson's "neighborhood" consists of "the several blocks surrounding the home of each student—ignoring school boundaries" (Wilson, 1967: 180). That is, the first four studies all focus upon the overall climate and resources of the total area that supports a school, while the latter focuses upon the immediate surroundings of the individual students. The combined findings suggest that it is the total community environment that affects the productivity of the school as a whole. Although Rogoff's data did not deal directly with the processes by which structural differences between communities lead to differential school outputs, she speculates that there may be a combination of differential formal arrangements and resources—such as community cultural facilities and events—and informal mechanisms, such as normative climate and opportunities for informal socializing, that affect *all* members of the community to some extent regardless of age and status (Rogoff, 1961: 242–243). Burkhead's conclusions also suggested a number of things that could vary from one community to another that were not included in his regression equation.

If there is an influence of residence at the level of the small neighborhood that is independent of family effects, it is apparently offset by students' relationships with significant others within the school. Thus Turner's findings imply that if there is a peer group influence upon educational aspiration and performance, it operates within the school rather than in the neighborhood, a conclusion also reached by Wilson. "While peers may have an influence, it is their behavior in the school setting—not their generalized attitudes as expressed out of school—which we should focus upon to illuminate the process of influence" (Wilson, 1967: 181). A related point is that, although assignment to schools is still largely in the hands of the professional education bureaucracy and still most strongly determined by proximity of residence, some families *choose* their residence in accordance with their aspirations for their children's education. Lower-SES children who attend schools where the general social level is higher often have parents who are training them for upward mobility, like the families of the college-bound boys studied by Kahl (Chapter 4).

This complicated set of relationships is summarized in Exhibit 12–2, which shows that the community as a whole, but not the small primary neighborhood, affects both school context and student performance. The neighborhood is related to academic performance only insofar as it constitutes the environment for family life and attracts families who share personal characteristics and attitudes toward education. Conversely, the peer group influence works within the context of the school but not of the neighborhood (further support for the model of high schools as "adolescent societies").

Attitudes of the Public

While there is a great deal of ambivalence about the appropriate role of the public in educational affairs, it has generally been assumed that positive public opinion is necessary not only because financial support for school comes from taxpayers, but also because the climate of public opinion, communicated to students and teachers, "affects the conditions for education and therefore the quality of education delivered and received" (Subcommittee on Elementary, Secondary, and Vocational Education, 1977: 177).

Gallup Poll data on attitudes toward education indicates that Americans are divided in their views about the quality of the schools. For example, in a 1973 poll about a third of the national sample polled said that their overall attitude toward the public schools in their community had become more favorable in recent years, another third said that their attitude had become less favorable, and the other third reported no change in opinion. However, a majority (61 percent) of the total sample felt that children today got a better education than they themselves had received. And the more respondents knew at first hand about the public schools, the more favorable their views. Thus 42 percent of the respondents who were parents of public school students said that their attitudes were becoming more favorable compared to only 25 percent of those who had no children in school, and 69 percent of the public school parents felt their children's education was better than their own compared with 56 percent of the childless respondents (Elam, 1973: 155 and 170). Respondents queried in public opinion polls do, however, identify a number of areas of concern about the public schools. Since 1970, the three problems most frequently cited are: lack of discipline in schools,

Exhibit 12-2
Relationship of External Environmental Variables to School Structure and Climate and Student Performance

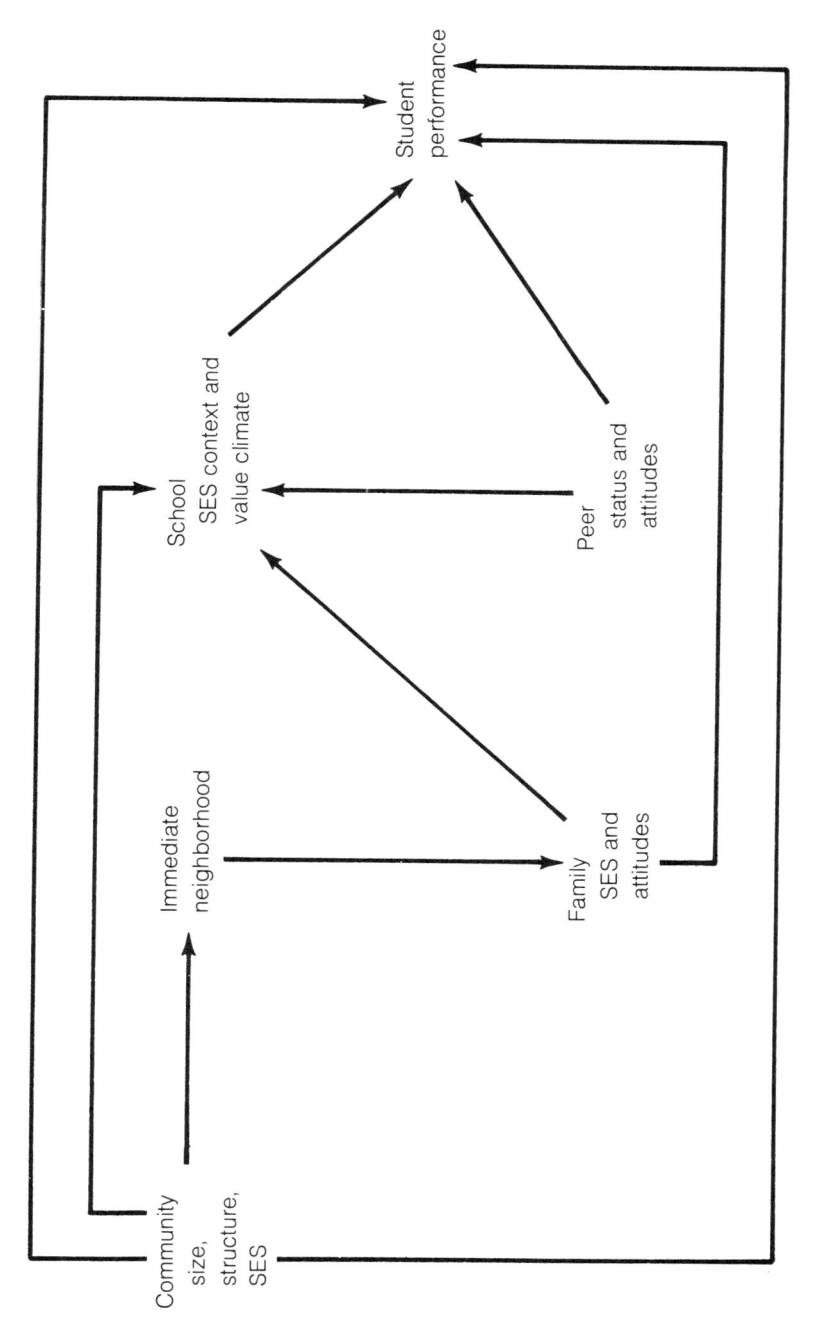

problems related to segregation and desegregation, and lack of financial support. By 1976, the problem of "poor curriculum" had joined financial problems in third place, and more than half the parents interviewed that year said that more attention should be devoted to teaching the basic skills (Subcommittee on Elementary, Secondary and Vocational Education, 1977).

While a number of hypotheses could be formulated concerning the effects of changes in public opinion upon school policy and ultimately upon students' experiences in school, and dissatisfaction with the quality of education seems to be a major motivation of members of the public who run for school boards, there is to date no empirical research testing the assumption that school effectiveness is affected, directly or indirectly, by the climate of opinion in the school's external environment.

Parents

As we have noted, parents are the members of the public most directly affected by school effectiveness, and we have also seen that they are somewhat more positive toward the schools than the general public. While we know a great deal about the effects of families upon individual children's academic success (Part Two), the direct effect of parents as a group upon the productivity of schools as social systems has received scant research attention. There are two conflicting hypotheses about the relationship between parental activity in school affairs and school outputs. One hypothesis predicts a positive relationship. Based upon a balance or dissonance theory model, this argument is that a high level of parental interest and involvement would be consonant with feelings of control of environment, and that parents who had such positive feelings would be most likely to communicate to their children the academic motivation and role-playing skills needed for school success. The alternative hypothesis, that parental activity is negatively related to school productivity, is based upon a model of role specialization. What teachers and schools need, runs this argument, is autonomy—release from the pressures of the external environment.

To date, these hypotheses have been supported more on the basis of personal biases than empirical evidence. What limited evidence there is favors the first model. The Gittell and Hollander study showed a relationship between indicants of community participation and educational innovativeness, although the link between innovativeness at the system level and actual student achievement was implied rather than documented. In an extension of his study of school-value climates, McDill added several community-level variables, and he found that the only one related to achievement was parental involvement in the schools. A simple scale of parental involvement was constructed from teachers' responses to the following three items:

> Most parents in this school are apathetic to school politics. (false)
>
> Parents of students here seem interested in their children's progress. (true)
>
> Parents often ask for appointments with teachers to discuss their children's school work. (true)

Each teacher was given an individual score from 0 to 3, and schools were ranked by the average of individual teacher scores. The index is admittedly crude, and it is based upon the perception of one subgroup in the learning system (parents) by another subgroup (teachers) that not only has a strong professional involvement but also a potentially biased view of the appropriate behavior of parents. Still the relationships of the scale with several measures of aspiration and achievement were consistently positive; Spearman rank order correlations with all but one of the six intellectual climate dimensions, with math achievement scores, and with college plans were all in the direction predicted and statistically significant. McDill found no effects on the achievement of a school as a whole from any of his measures of cultural and other facilities, although he points out that his information is only on the *availability* of such facilities and does not include any indication as to their utilization.

The National Principalship study indicated that the relationship between external participation and internal productivity may also be affected by overall quality of educational leadership. Dreeben and Gross (1965) found a positive correlation between parental involvement and both the involvement of teachers in key school decisions, as perceived by the principal, and the principal's skill in dealing with the community, as perceived by the teachers. If the educational administrator has skill in handling interpersonal relations generally, he or she may be able to handle a high level of activity by multiple subgroups, even when they are in conflict with each other. The findings of this study also indicated that high parental involvement was positively correlated with the SES level of the school, although neither the theoretical framework of the study nor the statistical analysis explains whether this is because families differ in their propensity to take an active role in school affairs, because schools are more receptive to the involvement of some parents than others, or because of some other process linking family involvement and school outcomes. It does suggest though that level of participation may be one of the intervening variables that explains the relationship between the socioeconomic level of a community and the output effectiveness of its schools.

A recent study by Wagenaar offers the strongest empirical evidence for the positive effects of involvement and support by community members. In a study of 135 elementary schools in one large midwestern city, Wagenaar (1978) found that internal structural variables, such as size, closeness of supervision, and standardization of rules and teaching practices were less strongly related to mean performance on standardized reading and mathematics tests than contextual variables, and of the latter, the most important was a dimension termed *permeability*, defined as the level of interaction between school personnel and community persons, and measured by a nine-item scale in which the school principals evaluated the amount of support given to the school by parents, the opportunities for parents to "sit down and discuss problems with the teacher," the percentage of parents and other citizens who attend school meetings, and so on. Wagenaar draws both theoretical and policy implications from his findings. Concerning the former, he notes that they contradict conventional theoretical analyses of service organization effectiveness, since they suggest that client involvement may be more important than internal structural variables (a conclusion that may also explain the generally ambiguous results of much of the school-effectiveness research described in Chapter 10). Concerning the implications for educational policy making, Wagenaar recommends that more attention be given to "improving the number, types, and levels of interaction, improving the communication between school and community, and utilizing community resources," and notes optimistically that "developments in this direction seem likely given public support for increased community involvement in schools" (Wagenaar, 1978: 621).

Thus, the empirical research to date indicates that parental activity and community involvement do not have harmful, and may have positive, effects upon school climate and performance within the school. A theoretical analysis of the possible mechanisms of coordination between bureaucratic organizations like the school and external primary groups like the family concludes that schools cannot afford either a complete "open door" or "closed door" policy in relation to parents, but must seek "some midpoint where limiting effects are minimized and complementary contributions of both organizational forms are maximized" (Litwak and Meyer, 1973: 429).

The Governmental Role in Education

The three principal types of educational reform to which the various branches of government have addressed themselves during the past twenty-five years are: (1) school desegregation; (2) a more equitable distribution of educational resources, including provision of additional resources for children defined as educationally deprived; and (3) reduction of the wide differences between and within states on expenditures for education by reducing reliance upon local property taxes as the sole or major source of school funds.

We shall not attempt to summarize even the major legislative and court actions pertaining to these issues,[1] but it should be noted that neither the feasibility nor the effectiveness of any major strategies developed to respond to these issues have been documented (we shall examine some of the arguments and evidence concerning school desegregation later in the chapter). Indeed, the impact of governmental policies and actions on student or school outcomes is even more difficult to evaluate than the effects of the other components of the external environment shown in Exhibit 12–1, because of the multiple branches and levels of government, many of which are far removed from the actual schooling process, and because of the frequent shifts and inconsistencies in policies and actions. There is, for example, no research that traces systematically the effects of a piece of legislation like the Elementary and Secondary Education Act of 1965 on the students it was designed to aid or that evaluates the extent to which the academic achievement of poor and minority children has been affected by the Civil Rights Act of 1964 or the 1974 Serrano *v.* Priest litigation on educational finance. One can identify the explicit intent of recent legislative and judicial decisions and some of the actual changes in the institutional arrangements of the school's external environment that they brought about—for example, an important feature of Title I of the Elementary and Secondary Education Act of 1965 was the requirement that parents of the children to be served by the new programs have a voice in how the money was to be spent, and the model of the parent advisory group that evolved was incorporated into grant-in-aid programs subsequently enacted in many states and municipalities. But the problems of urban school systems that the Act was intended to solve seem to have intensified rather than diminished during the decade and a half since its enactment, and the ultimate effects on students and schools of the programs it financed have yet to be specified. There is also some evidence that some governmental actions have unplanned and even unintended consequences (for example, that desegregation policies have in fact produced some of the very segregation they were designed to eliminate).

Another trend that can be noted is the increasing use of social science research as a basis for formulating public policy and deciding law suits in these areas. Levin (1976) warns of a number of problems inherent in this trend, pointing out that not only have social scientists not been able to trace the effects of particular educational strategies on either the academic success or the later life chances of individuals or groups, but that social science theories explaining the linkages are neither well developed nor consistent with each other, and, moreover, that the most powerful methodologies for testing alternative theories—that is, experimental approaches covering a fairly long segment of the student and poststudent years in the life cycle—are "politically and practically infeasible." Levin asserts, not entirely facetiously, that the types of social science evidence that will be received most favorably by the courts and other governmental bodies will have the following attributes: first, due to the image the layperson has of science and the current bias in favor of sophisticated empirical studies, like the Coleman Report, "acceptable" social science evidence "tends to be based upon complex, statistical methodologies that are generally beyond the experience and the competence of the court to question." Second, acceptable evidence "directly supports or refutes the matter under consideration." Because a court decision is ultimately an either-or decision, ambiguous research findings will be ignored; thus thoughtful analysis of competing hypotheses or strategies will be discouraged. Third, acceptable evidence is based upon theories that are "credible and understandable." For example, research based upon Marxian theory, however clear and competent it might be in other respects, would be poorly received in most U.S. courts, and strategies that show effects on outcomes that can be easily understood and monitored, such as cognitive test scores or order in the schools, are more acceptable than strategies that enhance happiness, sense of self, or noncognitive work characteristics such as respect for rules and dependability. Finally, evidence that is well received by courts or legislative bodies "implies a remedy that is readily within that [body's power] and is politically feasible." In sum, research results clearly favoring one educational strategy over another do not exist, and in their absence, "the evidence that does enter the courts or policy arena is considered and utilized on the basis of factors other than its scientific 'validity'" (Levin, 1976: 87–89).

Strategies for Change

Most recent proposals for educational reform have called for some kind of change in the distribution of power in the school's external environment. While specific innovations differ in purpose as well as design, the most influential proposals and experiments of the past decade have been designed to strengthen the school as a learning environment either by increasing *equality* in the distribution of educational resources and burdens or by increasing choice, including greater diversity of educational options (broader educational options) and greater freedom of choice among the options available.

The sheer volume of research and theorizing about educational equality versus inequality that has accumulated in recent years is evidenced by the fifty-four–page bibliography at the end of a recent review of the topic (Persell, 1977). A good deal of the literature consists of alternative definitions of equity, equality, and equality of educational opportunity, and attempts to link changes in the conceptualization of educational equality with changes in the structure and functions of the family, the occupational system, and the class structure.

A number of unresolved dilemmas remain. One is whether educational equality is to be conceived in terms of inputs or outcomes. In the first case, equality is achieved if the level of community investment in schools and the availability of school resources to students is equal, though there is still disagreement about whether equality of input requires all children to be exposed to the *same* curriculum or whether variations in courses and programs are allowed providing they meet some criteria of equal worth (itself a problem in definition). In the second case, equality is achieved only if the variations in educational achievements and attainments among children are eliminated or greatly reduced, though here there is disagreement about whether the same level of achievement must be reached by all children or by those of comparable abilities—that is, whether equality requires the elimination or reduction of the variance in the dependent variable of achievement, or whether variation is acceptable as long as it is not systematically correlated with specified independent variables such as race, family status, or sex, or as long as some minimal level of basic competencies is achieved by all students. (For more detailed discussion of these issues, see Coleman, 1968; Gordon, 1974; Miller, 1976; Bredemeier, 1978.)

Before considering some of the specific strategies proposed for decreasing the inequalities in our educational system, it should be noted that at least some analysts feel that the achievement of anything close to equality of outcomes would require measures more drastic than most Americans would find palatable. The report of the original planning conference for the National Institute of Education pointed out that given that children's success or failure in school is so strongly related to their family background, any serious proposals for equalizing academic achievement "must somehow prohibit the transference of social status from parent to child," which in turn raises some very difficult questions.

> If equality of educational opportunity indeed cannot be achieved except at the expense of the family, then shall we diminish the family? . . . If so, are we prepared

to provide for rearing our children by other means? Will the task be left to the schools, to which it already appears to be gradually falling? Do we tip the balance in favor of social disintegration when we help erode the institution most fundamental to the social orders of the past? We tinker not at the margins here but rather attempt to take into our hands one of the vital centers of the social structure. (Clark et al., 1971: 6)

Jencks, on the other hand, feels that cognitive achievement, at least as measured by test scores, probably could be equalized by the schools, but that this would require very tight control of the learning environment and, in all likelihood, withholding education from the most able students. He suggests, for example, providing only one or two years of schooling to very bright children, six years to children who are above average, and eighteen or more years to very slow learners.

The issue of choice really encompasses several subissues: (a) the amount of diversity or lack of it within and between schools in the public school system; (b) the extent to which parents can choose from among the schools or school programs that do exist; and (c) the amount of control or power that parents can bring to bear on the schools to provide the kind of learning environment they want for their children. A number of observers have pointed to the paradoxical combination of variety and sameness in American public schools. On the one hand, it is simply not the same experience to be a student in an affluent suburban school, a blue-collar suburban school, a rural school, and an urban ghetto school. The differences among the some eighteen thousand independent school districts in this country reflect not only the large gaps in community status and resources discussed earlier in this chapter, but also real ideologically based differences of opinion over educational goals and the best interests of children. On the other hand, in actual operation the majority of schools and school districts are similar in many important respects. This uniformity is conceptualized by Coons and Sugarman as follows:

> Explicitly the schools emphasize technology, uncontroversial information and skills . . . by and large the schools shun explicit treatment of controversial moral or political norms. Historically and currently they have striven with enthusiasm to produce "true Americans" by conditioning the children to the mind-set accepted in the larger—or at least local—society. . . . The similarities in the school's message are matched by the standardization of the setting in which it is delivered. Indeed, the most striking regularity is that of two dozen children sequestered five hours a day in the same room in the same building from September to June. . . . As we see it, the particular samenesses which characterize public education are chosen less often for their perceived educational advantage to the child than for other reasons—particularly for their unobtrusive harmony with majoritarian social and political standards. Their point is to forestall any political rocking of the school boat. (Coons and Sugarman, 1978: 42–43)

While it is clear that an important element of the inequality of our educational system is that many families—especially poor and minority families—do not have the choices that a few affluent families have, it is questionable whether strategies designed to maximize either equality or choice will have a similarly positive effect on the other. Coons and Sugarman argue that equality and choice are not incompatible—that, for example, the only stable and enduring kind of school integration is that brought about under conditions of choice (Coons and Sugarman, 1978: Chapter 7). The authors of the National Institute of Education planning document have reservations about such a claim. Comparing the substantially greater amount of choice available in American higher education than in primary and secondary education, they conclude that it is related to the greater internal differentiation of the former than the latter, and conclude that "for real choice there must be real alternatives." Yet they caution that

> varied schools raise the spectre of differential treatment and increased inequality. To be organizationally flexible and responsive to consumer choice brings the possibility that while some schools become seriously better some others will go from bad to worse. Clearly, the choice ought not to be near-infinite. (Clark et al., 1971: 11)

And in a mainly overlooked discussion of policy implications concluding his highly controversial study of "white flight," Coleman argues that no policy can give full weight to both equality and choice (which Coleman terms *liberty*), although he does propose a policy that would give some weight to both (Coleman, 1976).

The major concern of this chapter is the impact of institutional arrangements outside of the school on inside-school achievement. Thus, in the remainder of the chapter we shall discuss a few selected educational strategies (a) that are explicitly designed to improve students' learning by increasing equality or choice or both; and (b) about which there is at least some empirical research testing the effects of the innovation on students' attitudes and achievement.

School Desegregation: A Strategy For Reducing Inequality

Desegregation attempts to overcome the combined disadvantages of race and place by reassigning children so that the racial distribution in each school mirrors that of the larger society. Race has been and continues to be the most explosive subject of school-community relations, and large-scale desegregation efforts, particularly when accompanied by busing large numbers of children to school outside of their own neighborhoods, have been a chronic source of community conflict in the past decade.

Research on school desegregation has been disappointing in several respects. First, it has raised serious doubts about whether current U.S. policies have actually reduced racial segregation in meaningful ways. The controversy on this point reached a peak in the debate over Coleman's study of "white flight" (Coleman et al., 1975; Coleman, 1976),[2] which sparked quarrels not only over the measurement of crucial indicators and interpretation of empirical findings but also over the professional and personal integrity of the study's principal author. Using data collected by the U.S. Department of Health, Education and Welfare in 1968–1972 to monitor desegregation trends, Coleman found that by 1973 *de jure* desegregation (legally sanctioned desegregation) had been all but eliminated in the United States, and that segregation within school districts had been reduced, though there was considerable variation among regions (with considerable change in the Southeastern states but little in the Middle Atlantic and East North Central states. However, *de facto* segregation (segregation that is *not* legally sanctioned, including segregation that is legally prohibited as well as segregation for which there is neither legal approval nor disapproval) remained stubbornly resistant to reform, and Coleman's analysis indicated that in nearly every region of the country, there was actually an increase in segregation *between* school districts, particularly between large cities and their suburbs.

A third finding was that the "loss" of whites from central city school districts increased at the same time as the reduced segregation within districts, although this general finding was modified by four qualifications: (1) the loss of whites was greater in larger than in smaller cities; (2) the loss of whites was greater in cities with higher proportions of black residents; (3) the loss of whites was greater when there was a high disparity in racial composition between a city and neighboring suburbs; and (4) the loss of whites in a given city appeared to be a one-time effect, confined to the year of desegregation. From these findings, Coleman concluded that

> the present policies of school desegregation which focus wholly on within-district segregation exacerbate the already unstable ecology of our large cities. They are increasing, rather than reducing or reversing, the tendency for our large metropolitan areas to consist of black central cities and white suburbs. Thus their long-run effect is in a direction counter to their immediate and short-run effect of desegregating the city's schools. (Coleman, 1976: 12)

While much of the response to Coleman's study appeared to be grounded more in emotion or politics than in thoughtful weighing of the evidence, the more responsible critiques did raise two kinds of legitimate doubts about the analysis and the implications Coleman drew from it. First, some subsequent research produced alternative measures of both desegregation and white flight that may be more adequate than Coleman's. In particular, Rossell, a political scientist who supplemented the HEW data used by Coleman with pre–1967 data and case-study data that she collected directly from a number of Northern and Southern school districts, argued that one should distinguish between court-ordered desegregation and desegregation brought about by other factors (for example, black movement into formerly white neighborhoods); and that one should look at the movement out of central city areas by minority families as well as white families (she found, for example, that in San Francisco, black and Hispanic school-enrollment patterns changed more than white enrollment). Rossell's own conclusion was that desegregation created little or no white flight, even when it was court-ordered and implemented in large cities (Rossell, 1975). However, she did later acknowledge an "implementation year effect," parallel to the one-time effect reported by Coleman.

A second kind of critique is exemplified in research by Farley, a demographer at the University of Michigan Population Studies Center, who used data comparable to that used by Coleman but who interpreted the findings differently. While acknowledging that the data are consistent with the white flight hypothesis, Farley's argument is that they are also consistent with other hypotheses. In particular, "cities with a high proportion of blacks may have particularly unfavorable tax bases, may be losing employment, may be viewed by whites as dangerous, or may have an especially old stock of housing" (Farley, 1976: 17). In other words, what makes whites *or any families* leave poor, inner-city neighborhoods is the *combination* of factors that make these neighborhoods unattractive places to live, including but not limited to the enforced desegregation of the already overburdened school system.

The debate over the feasibility of desegregation in general and the effects of court-ordered busing in particular is far from over.[3] But whether or not one attributes declining white enrollment to our current desegregation tactics, these tactics have clearly not prevented the continued residential exodus that is leaving city school districts increasingly filled with children from the poorest minority families.

> Every major city in the nation has lost a large part of its white enrollment since 1968, when the first federal ethnic census was taken. Only five of the nation's 20 biggest school systems still have white majorities, and only nine of the 30 biggest. All except Miami have lost student population. . . . The result is that the big urban systems are largely nonwhite, and substantial proportions of their students are from poor families. In New York City, for example, 52 percent of the students are poor enough to be eligible for free lunches, and about a third are from welfare families.
>
> From 1968 to 1976, New York City lost nearly 30 percent of its white pupils and is now 70 percent nonwhite; Los Angeles lost 37 percent and is now 63 percent nonwhite; Chicago lost 40 percent and is now 75 percent nonwhite; Houston lost 45 percent and is now 66 percent nonwhite; Detroit lost 61 percent and is now 81 percent nonwhite; Philadelphia lost 25 percent and is now 68 percent nonwhite; Miami lost 27 percent and is now 59 percent nonwhite; Baltimore lost 41 percent and is now 75 percent nonwhite; Dallas lost 45 percent and is now 62 percent nonwhite; Cleveland lost 30 percent and is now 62 percent nonwhite; and Washington, D.C., lost 45 percent of its few white pupils and is now 96 percent nonwhite. These figures suggest that desegregation is going to be even harder to achieve in the future than it has been in the past. This abrupt demographic change is of particular concern because the schools have had the least success in educating precisely those children who now constitute the majority of their enrollment. (Ravitch, 1977: 13)

A second kind of disappointing finding is that while desegregation has not had any measurable negative effects on the achievement of majority children (a fear that provoked considerable resistance to school desegregation in the past), it has not had the strong and clear positive effects on minority children its proponents hoped to establish, nor has the achievement gap between poor, minority children and their more advantaged peers been noticeably narrowed. Local surveys, for example, Wilson's 1967 survey of Contra Costa County, California; St. John's 1969 and 1970 surveys of Pittsburgh ninth graders and Boston sixth graders, and Gerard and Miller's 1975 longitudinal study of Riverside, California, have generally found that black children in desegregated schools score slightly higher on achievement tests than blacks in all-black schools, but only when they attended schools with middle-class whites and when there is some level of meaningful integration within the school. Black students who move from black schools with a high proportion of students with high aspirations and achievement to desegregated schools with lesser standards, and black students who move to desegregated schools that were highly disrupted by the desegregation process or that have not enforced integration at the classroom level may not gain and may even fall back academically.

From a review of studies done up to the early 1970s, Jencks concluded that since most cognitive inequality is within rather than between racial groups, economic groups, and schools, any reduction in achievement variance brought about by desegregation would be quite small—he estimates about two or three points on most standard tests (Jencks *et al.*, 1972: 106). Following her empirical studies, St. John reviewed the design and findings of over 120 studies of the effects of desegregation on black and white students. She found no definitive positive findings about academic achievement, although there was some evidence that math achievement was related to desegregation and that the longer black students had experienced desegregated education, the greater their gains in arithmetic (St. John, 1975: Chapter 2). The pooled evidence indicated that the effects of desegregated schools on black children's self-concept and aspirations may be negative, at least in the short run, and that the effects on racial attitudes and friendship patterns are mixed, the results depending upon the design of a particular piece of research as well as the age of the subjects and the circumstances of desegregation. Acknowledging the limitations of the research available, St. John concluded that "the evidence of wide-ranging studies is in one respect clear: school desegregation per se has no unitary or invariable effect on children" (St. John, 1975: 121; similarly mixed results are reported in Levin, 1976).

A number of social scientists feel that we simply do not know enough about desegregation to decide whether it is feasible and effective. Crain (1976) argues that due to the time pressures of university life and the funding policies of public and private agencies, we lack the kinds of long-term comparative studies of alternative desegregation strategies that would enable educational decision makers to evaluate them responsibly. He points out that a large number of the studies included in St. John's review measured the impact of desegregation only over a one-year period, usually the first year of desegregation. We saw in Chapter 10 that Crain found in studying adult blacks to evaluate the long-term effects of racial desegregation that those who had attended integrated schools had higher aspirations and higher educational and occupational attainments. Crain's most recent work reviewed over one hundred studies that had previously been interpreted as showing no overall gains for minority students and concluded that three times as many studies showed positive achievement results as showed negative results, and moreover, that the positive studies tended to be methodologically stronger than the negative studies (Hawley and Levin, 1978).

Another weakness of the research on desegregation is that nearly all of it is of the "black box" variety, relating input and output measures without examining their interaction in the school situation. One of the few sociological analyses based upon actual observation of what takes place in desegregated classrooms is Rist's (1978) intensive case study of an upper-middle-class, white elementary school in Portland, Oregon, during its first year of a one-way desegregation plan. Rist found that the school personnel, inadequately prepared for the influx of children of a different race and social class (which they tended to confound), tried to treat the new arrivals as "invisible," ignoring the differences in skills and values that made it impossible for all but a few of the children to be easily assimilated into the ongoing school program. The black students were in fact subject to considerable pressure throughout the year and were often segregated within the classroom. Like Rist's earlier study of an all-black classroom, discussed in Chapter 8, this one is susceptible to observer bias and to the limited generalizability of one-person observational studies. His strong preference for "pluralist" over "assimilationist" desegregation models colors some of his interpretations (for example, he attributes the black parents' strong approval of the school's program to ignorance). But his findings are consistent with findings of more comparative research indicating that the positive effects of desegregation are only felt when integration occurs at the classroom level, and they suggest that rather major structural changes within the school are probably necessary to bring this about.

Magnet Schools: A Strategy for Increasing Racial Integration

As a consequence of the political backlash and the specter of white flight raised by compulsory desegregation, interest in plans to accomplish integration voluntarily has increased among educators as well as governmental policy makers. Magnet schools, so called because they attract rather than force students to attend, are based upon the assumption that high quality educational programs can induce students to attend school in "undesirable" neighborhoods, even when they are at some distance from the students' homes. At least a dozen cities have initiated or are planning magnet school programs, although unlike the other three strategies discussed in this section, magnet schools have received no specific governmental encouragement, in the form of subsidies, legislation, or court orders.

There has also been no systematic data collection about the programs that now exist. The best sociological analysis to date is a case study of one magnet school in the New Haven area by Rosenbaum and Presser (1978). The distinguishing feature of the magnet program, which was housed in a junior high that had previously had a reputation as a school with a poor educational climate, was that it was specifically and openly designed to attract talented students and to provide them with enriched specialized education in the area of their special talent, whether science, art, drama, or athletics. The school was not committed to any particular teaching approach other than a general innovativeness. Ability grouping was forbidden. Parental input was encouraged.

While the official goal of this school was to promote racial integration, there were important interracial differences from the beginning of the school's existence. First, recruitment was selective for blacks only; fearing that not enough white students would attend, the school admitted all who applied. Second, the "talent classes," which the planners expected to demonstrate racial equality, actually divided the students on racial grounds, because of the inequalities in their academic preparation. Thus, black students were overrepresented in the classes for dance, vocal music, and athletics, and underrepresented in the classes for math, science, and communication arts. Moreover, although all talents were claimed to be equally valued, in fact the teachers treated math and science talent students more respectfully than athletic talent students. Third, although tracking and ability grouping were explicitly prohibited by the school's plan, and students were assigned to racially balanced homeroom classes for all their nontalent subjects, these classes became internally differentiated over time, as the teachers assigned class work by difficulty level and the black students were disproportionately assigned lower difficulty work. Fourth, while the authors observed no incidents of violence or overt signs of dislike between the races, there was also no evidence of change in informal interaction patterns reflecting more interracial socializing or friendships. In selecting class representatives within each homeroom, black children nominated and voted for both black and white children, but white children nominated and voted only for whites. Observation of seating patterns in the lunchroom revealed that students usually ate with other students from their own or related talent classes (for example, math and science students sat together), and most of the black students ate at tables that were exclusively black.

The one striking integration success was in the area of music, art, and drama. According to the descriptions of these classes, the teachers encouraged students to interact with one another, disregarding race, and they readily responded. Thus black and white drama students would help each other memorize their lines, and art students cooperated on a number of group projects. The integration created within the classroom carried over to other activities; the only students who ate regularly in integrated clusters were from these classes. While unable to offer a clear causal explanation for the sharp differences between these classes and the academic classes like science and math, the authors speculate that the former may permit more cooperative work than the latter, and that they may attract different kinds of teachers.

> The teachers of these classes deserve a large amount of credit for these successes. They did not come easily; teachers put a great deal of effort and planning into making them happen. They avoided homogeneous groupings and divided their classes into heterogeneous, integrated work groups in which faster students could help those with difficulties. This procedure is more difficult, for it is difficult to coordinate small heterogeneous groups and keep them all working on productive activities. It also requires that a teacher prepare new curricula which students with different levels of skill can do together. (Rosenbaum and Presser, 1978: 178–179)

Rosenbaum and Presser's data also offer some interesting insights into the operation of expectations and the labeling processes discussed in Chapter 8, and suggest some qualifications of the Rosenthal and Jacobson hypothesis that positive expectations produce high achievement. The magnet school offered a natural experimental setting in which to test Rosenthal and Jacobson's hypothesis, since the school staff had "fantastically high expections, and, more important, uniformly high expectations for all students during the first weeks of school." Rosenbaum and Presser argue, however, that while these "fantasies" may have been useful in the beginning, contributing to the general climate of academic enthusiasm and commitment, they may have become a liability as

> reality began to intrude on people's perceptions, and an atmosphere of mediocrity began to supplant the initial feelings of specialness. Teachers began to comment that the students, supposed to be so incredibly bright, were not so gifted after all. . . . Most of the conversations in the teachers' room suggested that they had not expected reading and spelling difficulties from these children. (Rosenbaum and Presser, 1978: 171)

Apparently, when the teachers' high initial expectations were not met by the students' actual performance, their expectations were lowered and, moreover, became *differentiated for different students.* By the middle of the school year, the authors heard teachers'-room conversations in which it was argued that some of the students—usually black—did not "belong" in a school for the talented.

Rosenbaum and Presser concluded that a magnet program based on talent may succeed in integrating a school (the racial balance of the student body as a whole has been maintained) but not in achieving integration among and within its classes. Indeed, "a talent system based on previous academic achievement is likely to institutionalize and perpetuate . . . racial differences" (Rosenbaum and Presser, 1978: 168). Using talent as the criteria for admission raises other equity issues also. Students not admitted could be stigmatized, and a talent focus in one school could drain other schools of human and nonhuman resources (see Chapter 10). The Rosenbaum and Presser study does not provide information on this school's impact on other schools in the district. Of course, criteria other than talent might be used in choosing the student body of a magnet school, and evaluation of the model as a strategy for reducing educational inequality must await the results of other experiments.

Community-Controlled Schools: A Strategy For Increasing Parental Control and Administrative Accountability

Community control focuses upon activating a greater portion of the citizenry to involvement in their schools and making school staff and administrators more accessible and accountable to the public they serve. It is usually coupled with efforts to decentralize large city school systems. During the late 1960s pressures toward decentralization with community control came from spokespeople for minority group parents frustrated by the slow pace of racial desegregation and the treatment given to their children in the public schools.[4]

During this period, three groups of schools in New York City were designated community controlled. Each of these new districts had only between four and eight thousand students, compared with the average New York school district of thirty thousand, and each elected a local school board. In one of these new districts, the Intermediate School 201 district, a series of evaluation studies was carried out comparing student and school outcomes in the community-controlled schools with outcomes in a neighboring but centrally controlled school district. The results showed several statistically significant differences favoring the community-controlled schools (Guttentag, 1972).

Concerning academic achievement, the first and second graders in the IS–201 schools reached national norms in both reading and arithmetic, and the second and third graders in one IS–201 school with a special reading program were reading at nearly a full year above the national norm during a period when achievement norms in the city as a whole declined. Children who had been in the community-controlled schools for the full three years covered by the study had higher achievement scores than children in the district for a shorter period.

Studies of the school climate in the community-controlled schools and the comparison schools, using Stern's Organizational Climate scales (see Chapter 10), indicated that the climate in the IS–201 schools was characterized by high levels of intellectual activity, social action, individual responsibility, and open-mindedness. Although the comparison sample contained a higher proportion of middle-class schools and students,

> it was the IS–201 schools, with a lower-class population, which showed the stronger expressive climate and placed greater stress on intellectual matters, on achievement standards, and on personal dignity. In Stern's terms, the IS–201 schools had a press for achievement, change, tolerance, objectivity, and sensuality. This translates into a juicier, more vivid environment, one with more sights and sounds, one less repressively controlled. (Guttentag, 1972: 7–8)

Classroom observations, using Flanders's observational scheme described in Chapter 9, indicated that student-initiated talk was more often encouraged and students' ideas were more often accepted and used by teachers in the community-controlled than in the comparison schools.

The relative number of parents visiting the community-controlled schools was overwhelmingly greater than in the comparison district, and the visit was more likely to be an informal one initiated by the parents themselves simply to observe or help in a classroom, less likely to be a conference requested by school personnel to discuss a child's misbehavior. All schools in the IS–201 group had active afternoon, evening, and weekend centers open to community residents of all ages and interests, and several innovative programs were initiated by these schools, including a health program with a complete set of diagnostic examinations carried out in cooperation with nearby hospitals, medical schools, and colleges. No comparable programs or involvement existed in any of the neighboring centrally controlled schools.

Given the promising results of this one natural experiment in community control, the ultimate fate of the IS–201 district is depressing.

> It was swallowed up into a larger school district following a change in New York State law. This law created a weakened form of school decentralization throughout New York City. The law permitted elected boards, but these were stripped of the fiscal, personnel and curricular power which the experimental community controlled districts had assumed. . . . In the process of incorporation into the larger

district, all of IS-201's special programs were dismantled. Ironically, the district into which IS-201 was absorbed had served as the comparison school district in the studies just reported. (Guttentag, 1972: 17-18)

Clearly, successful efforts to shift the locus of decision-making power in the school's external environment will require political skills as well as ideological commitment and a model of change that meets sociological criteria of adequacy.

Education Vouchers: A Strategy for Increasing Parental Choice

Like community-controlled schools, voucher plans attempt to increase parental involvement in and control over their children's education, but while community control attempts to do this by improving the level of school-community relations in the child's neighborhood, voucher plans allow, indeed encourage, parents to "shop around" among all the schools in the district for the one that best suits their children's needs. Under such a system all parents of school-aged children would be issued vouchers to cover the cost of educating their children at schools, public or private, of their own choice. All vouchers would be worth the full payment of a child's education—thus the voucher model is defended by its advocates as a strategy for increasing equality as well as choice.

While the concept of educational vouchers can be traced back to Adam Smith in the eighteenth century, and it has been identified with scholars of as diverse ideological-political orientation as Milton Friedman, a conservative economist, and Christopher Jencks, a democratic socialist, its most recent manifestation was as part of the federal "war on poverty." In 1969, the Office of Economic Opportunity awarded a contract to Jencks to draw up a voucher plan that would contain safeguards against racial discrimination. The scheme developed by Jencks and his associates had the following features:

1. Any public or private school that fulfilled minimal requirements could participate in the plan and compete for students and their voucher money.
2. No participating school would charge more than the value of the voucher.
3. Any participating school must accept all applicants. Overselected schools would be required to fill half their vacancies by lot.
4. Children from low-income families would receive bonus or compensatory vouchers of somewhat higher cash value, to make them attractive to schools and to provide additional resources for their education.
5. Parents who were dissatisfied with the education their child was receiving could transfer the child to another school and the voucher money would move with the child.
6. Provision was made for a parent-student information system, and for a regulatory agency to monitor the advertising practices and selection procedures of participating schools, with authority to exclude schools for noncompliance with the requirements of the plan. (Stern et al., 1975; Doyle, 1977)

To date, the voucher model has had only a partial test. In Alum Rock, a lower-income district in San Jose, California, with a population about 55 percent

Mexican American, 12 percent black, and the rest Anglo, a five-year project began in 1972 that involved the establishment of forty educationally distinct mini-schools within six of the twenty-two elementary and middle schools in the district. Parents were provided with information about each mini-school and given a choice as to which of the schools to send their children. By 1977 the full district was involved, although the enrollment rules changed from guaranteeing parents their first choice to a first-come-first-served basis. Staff from mini-schools for which there was low demand were moved to schools with a greater demand. The Alum Rock project incorporated many of the components of the voucher model, though not the market competition that was an important part of the Jencks plan. Parental choice expanded during the period of the experiment along with increases in the numbers of schools and students involved, but private schools did not participate, teachers' job security was guaranteed (incompetent staff could be moved from one mini-school to another but not removed from the school system), and the project was subsidized by federal funds (the project is still in existence now that the federal grant has ended, but plans for the future are uncertain).

While thus only a limited test of the voucher model, the Alum Rock experiment has provided the only information available on its feasibility and effects. Certain initial fears—for example, that a voucher system would be hopelessly difficult to administer and that it would lead to greater racial segregation—were shown to be unfounded, at least in this particular setting. Preliminary analyses of data on students' attitudes and performance show predictable if not conclusive trends for the children in the more "traditional" classes and mini-schools to score higher on tests of basic academic skills, but lower on affective tests than students in the more innovative classes and mini-schools (Doyle, 1977). These findings are consistent with our observations in Part Three that intellectual achievement is a different dimension from happiness or satisfaction with one's schooling experience, and that teaching approaches that maximize one are unlikely to maximize the other.

The most unexpected findings concerned the response of parents and school personnel to the plan. Although voucher theory postulates parents as the active agents of change, forcing reluctant administrators and teachers to improve the quality of school programs,

> in Alum Rock, it was the teachers who took initiative in creating diverse new alternatives, while parents remained passive. Very few parents actually transferred their children to a new location in the first year. Although there was some switching between mini-schools in the same building, the general impression derived from the Rand report is that of fairly apathetic and passive parents, easily satisfied by the education their children were receiving, whose history of low participation in Alum Rock school affairs has been in no way disturbed. Thus, in response to a Rand questionnaire, 90 percent of parents thought the educational offerings in voucher schools were satisfactory, but 23 percent could not name their child's program and over half did not realize that the schools provide free transportation for children to voucher schools outside their neighborhood. . . . Voucher advocates seem to have overlooked the simple fact that it costs parents time and anxiety to become informed about schools and to make troubling decisions about the education of their

children. These costs may be higher in low-income families, especially when there is only one parent or both parents work. If capable decision-making by parents is to determine the quality of children's education, it is necessary to increase parental capacity to choose. (Stern *et al.*, 1975: 5-6)

Contrary to the theory, the initial support for the voucher plan came from the superintendent, who saw the federal money as a means of overcoming the serious financial problems in his district and as a means of promoting his own efforts toward decentralization. Likewise some teachers, particularly those with high levels of personal motivation and well-developed organizational skills, were among the most enthusiastic supporters of the project.

Overall, though, the voucher plan appears to be a strategy without strong support in any area of the school's external environment. Although federal funds were available for additional experiments, and several school districts have considered such an experiment, the Alum Rock project remains the only one that got past the planning stage. It is understandable that the voucher strategy, like the community-control strategy, would not be favorably received by administrators, school boards, and teachers' unions, since both strategies assume that the shortcomings in the present structure and operation of school systems call for a redistribution of power. However, unlike the IS-201 community school project, which was passionately supported by many parents, the voucher plan has failed to attract the constituency it was designed to benefit most. Public opinion polls showed a decline in support for vouchers from 1970 (Elam, 1973: 92-93). Opinion polls also indicate that what the public wants is not greater diversity in schools, but better schools of the sort that already exist, and the Alum Rock experiment indicated in addition that parents have such a strong preference for neighborhood schools that they will choose to send their children out of the neighborhood only if the outside alternatives are considerably more attractive. As one analyst perceives the weakness of the voucher strategy,

no one with any real power had any real incentive to try the voucher scheme.... The failure to obtain a large-scale voucher system is probably just an example of the proposition that when the costs of a project are perceived by a few active and politically powerful individuals and groups, and when the benefits are diffuse and not sharply perceived by any significant group or individual, a reform effort will fail. (Van Geel, 1978: 351-352)

Conclusions

Research on the school's external environment is very difficult to interpret in the context of this book, because the groups and institutions that comprise this environment are multiple, and some are at a considerable distance from the actual schooling process. Thus, the impact of the external environment involves a complex path of causal connections that have not been fully mapped by sociological theory let alone documented by empirical research. Two conclusions do seem to be justified from the research to date, however.

One is that it matters a lot *where* a child goes to school, since educational resources and burdens are unevenly distributed among schools and school districts.

The process by which community structure is associated with differential academic success is not clearly established—it is even *possible* that the relationship is spurious, though the combined results of several studies of community effects suggest a model something like Exhibit 12-2. They also imply that

> in large cities for a very great number of low-income children—perhaps for an increasing number—there is no reasonable expectation for an important improvement in the quality of education unless something dramatic is done to ameliorate the socioeconomic conditions of existence. This may require programs, public and private, on a scale which now looks nothing short of utopian. (Burkhead, 1967: 88-89)

Although Burkhead's study was completed over a decade ago, his comments are still depressingly timely, and it appears: (a) that the linkages of schools with their external environments have such a powerful effect upon schools and students that they must be a part of any comprehensive educational planning, and (b) that the solutions at this level that have any chance of raising the overall level of educational productivity will radically change school systems as we now know them.

The second conclusion is that, contrary to much of our educational ideology, schools are very much enmeshed in politics. As Gittell and Hollander put it, city schools, which now educate the majority of American children, "reflect the city in microcosm," and it is all but impossible to separate the educational and political goals of the various individuals, groups, and institutions that constitute the school's external environment. Recent critiques of the American educational system recognize that school administrators, school boards, parents, and other community interest groups are often in conflict with each other, and many call for shifts in the distribution of power among them.

Research on school superintendents and school board members indicates that they often differ in background and orientation from the groups they represent, and that both their job training and the often strong pressures on them make them wary of innovation. Indeed, some examinations of the inertia of big city educational bureaucracies and of the apparently unchecked growth of administrative staff relative to classroom teachers, students, and school board members conclude understandably that "the system *is* the problem."

Four strategies for improving school effectiveness by changing the school's external environment were examined. Desegregation, magnet schools, community-controlled schools, and voucher plans all attempt to increase equality and choice, although they emphasize different aspects of these goals. Of the four, only desegregation has been attempted on a large scale. The results have generally been more positive than negative, although integration at the classroom level, where its impact on attitudes and achievement is most direct, does not inevitably or easily follow desegregation at the school level, and the unsolved problem of residential segregation by race and social class that plagues all large metropolitan areas threatens to defeat efforts to maintain desegregated schools and school districts.

The other three strategies have been only partially tested, usually in short-lived experiments that differ from the original model in important respects. Again the results have been generally encouraging, but there are serious questions about the feasibility of adopting any of them on a large scale. In the case of community-controlled schools, an experiment that had impressive results in terms of student outcomes was a victim of political expediency, and voucher plans have failed to attract the support of any politically powerful individuals or groups. Magnet schools raise questions about the feasibility of maximizing both diversity and equality.

Finally, study of the school's external environment reminds us that in all educational reform, more is involved than simply raising test scores. Strategies for change also involve normative visions of the world. Thus school desegregation can be seen as a strategy for bringing about a fairer society—if one equates a fair society with the absence of racial separation—as well as strategy for raising the achievement levels of minority students. The reason why so many public policy decisions and community conflicts over educational issues seem "irrational" is that they reflect important underlying values and norms as well as evaluations of what will maximize academic achievement.

Notes

1. Such discussions can be found in Coons, Clune, and Sugarman, 1970; Wirt, 1975; Levin, 1976; Showell, 1976; Van Geel, 1978; and Lehne, 1978.

2. These references are to two of the several different versions of the research prepared by Coleman and his colleagues. For a chronological account of the various phases of the research and its reception, see Pettigrew and Green, 1976.

3. As this chapter was being completed a new study by David Armor, measuring white flight over a six-year period in twenty-three Northern and Southern cities, was announced in the mass media and has already produced counterresponse.

4. See Ravitch, 1974, for an analysis of alternating pressures toward centralization and decentralization in the New York City school system, as well as an account of the experiment with community-controlled schools.

Crosscultural Comparisons   Chapter 13

Educational practices are not phenomena that are isolated from one another; rather, for a given society, they are bound up in the same system all the parts of which contribute toward the same end: it is the system of education suitable to this country and this time. Each people has its own, as it has its own moral, religious, economic systems, etc. . . . Consequently, through comparison, by abstracting the similarities and eliminating the differences from them, one can certainly establish the generic types of education which correspond to the different types of societies.   Emile Durkheim

There must be a congruence between the purposes that society assigns to education and the purposes which have meaning for the persons who are the beneficiaries of that education.   Edmund Gordon

There is nothing wrong with the school as a social environment, except what is wrong with America.   Edgar Z. Friedenberg

In this final chapter dealing with substantive research findings we reach the outer limits of the learning system as it was mapped in Chapter 1. We shall consider here the relationship of the total society to its education system and the ultimate effect upon learning and achievement of that society's schools. The types of variables with which we shall be concerned are diagrammed in Exhibit 13–1. Following a consideration of some of the special problems of comparative educational research, we shall examine studies that identify the relevant characteristics of societies and their educational systems and that attempt to link the components of Exhibit 13–1.

Comparative education is an old and active subdivision of educational research, with an extensive literature and its own textbooks and journals. From a sociological point of view, however, it is a conceptually and methodologically

Exhibit 13-1
The Relationship of the Total Society and Its Learning System

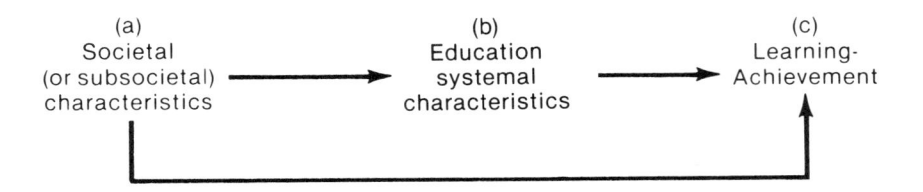

```
      (a)                    (b)                    (c)
    Societal            Education              Learning-
  (or subsocietal)  ─────►  systemal    ─────►  Achievement
  characteristics       characteristics              ▲
         │                                           │
         └───────────────────────────────────────────┘
```

underdeveloped field. As one sociologist puts it: "Although comparative education is rapidly growing in popularity, the field remains characterized by a 'buzzing confusion' regarding optimal strategies for its advancement as a scientific discipline." To date, its output consists "mainly of a large collection of concrete descriptions of the educational institutions of many nations, a growing but disjointed literature on the determinants of various educational activities, and a continuous flow of methodological discussions of the difficulties inherent in comparative research" (Livingstone, 1968: 11, 1).

What are the problems peculiar to crosscultural research? First, simply the logistics and the expense. Think, for example, of replicating the *Educational Opportunity* survey in other countries. To obtain an equivalent set of data in each country would multiply the cost—assuming that one could translate the concept of educational equality, as well as specific questions, into the terms of other societies. To economize by cutting down on the size of the sample or the scope of the measuring instruments would lower the likelihood of obtaining unbiased and truly comparable data.

The major difficulty is in ensuring comparability of data from one country to another. Categories of classification are often different. For example, not all countries have "comprehensive" high schools, and what constitutes a comprehensive school may differ from one country to another (Husen, 1967: Vol. II, 287). National school systems also differ not only in the structure or classification of schools and the content of the curriculum but in starting age and minimum school-leaving age and the proportion of the total population in school at various levels.

To assure the comparability of test materials, administrative instruction, and data-processing procedures when there are language differences is problematic. A final headache is that

> nearly all the sources of error are country-specific, and thus there is no possibility for randomization of errors. . . . In one study, it was said that the key-punching errors reflected differences in national character; Germany showed a total absence of random errors in key-punching; whenever an error occurred, it was a systematic error that appeared in all cards; in Italy the errors were scattered with apparent Latin abandon. Apocryphal though these stories may be, they point to the sobering fact that errors are highly correlated with country, and the cross-country comparisons on which such studies depend must be made warily. In the . . . [International Project

for the Evaluation of Educational Achievement], it was discovered too late for changing proofs that all the results reported for Finland were incorrect, due to poor communication—so the book carries a note at the front that is a solemn reminder of the special methodological problems of cross-national studies. (Coleman, 1969: 98)

Given the difficulties in executing and interpreting crosscultural studies, why bother with them? Apart from the pure interest of crosscultural comparisons, and the larger perspective they give on our own educational systems and problems, crosscultural comparisons are the only way we can answer certain questions, in particular the question of whether a relationship between a set of components in our own learning system is unique to that system and is explained by some characteristics of the larger society, or whether the relationship is characteristic of learning systems in general.

Relations Between Societies and Schools

One of the first sociologists to recognize and describe the relationship between a society and its schools was Durkheim. As the quotation at the beginning of this chapter indicates, Durkheim saw education as a social creation, as the means by which a society assured its own continuity by socializing the young in its own image. The components of the education system—which themselves "constitute perfectly defined facts and which have the same reality as other social facts" (Durkheim, 1956: 94)—are interrelated. They are interrelated internally, so that a given education system has unity and consistency, and also externally, so that the education system reflects a society's moral and intellectual values.

While Durkheim postulated a close relationship between the external and internal characteristics of a society's learning system, he did not spell out what he considered the crucial variables. Much of the literature on comparative education has been an attempt to specify these variables. Some sociologists believe that the way to understand a society's educational system is to understand how it is related to the other basic institutions of that society, in particular the family, the church, the state, and the economy. Certain historical periods have been characterized by the dominance of one of these basic institutions. In the Middle Ages in Europe, the church was dominant, but later the national state assumed major importance, with corresponding changes in the nature and structure of the schools, from the composition of the curriculum to the composition of the student body. In most modern industrialized societies the alliance between the state and the economy is close, and in communist-socialist societies, such as the U.S.S.R., Cuba, and the People's Republic of China, not only are the economic and educational systems under the aegis of state planning, but the schools are designed to be an instrument for economic development. Thus a majority of the students in Russian universities major in engineering and science; in the People's Republic of China many schools contain workshops and other schools are set up in factories, workshops, and communal farms (Havighurst, 1968; Carnoy and Wertheim, 1977; Leiner, 1974; Chen, 1974; Munro, 1971). There are few modern societies in which the family or the church is the dominant institution, although

Holland and Israel exemplify societies in which religious influences remain relatively strong. In Holland, both Protestant and Roman Catholic "voluntary" schools, as well as the schools established by public authorities, receive financial assistance from public funds; in Israel, parents have the choice of sending their children to state-financed religious or nonreligious schools (Havighurst, 1968; Chapter XII; Kleinberger, 1969).

Two decisions that must be made by any society are what subjects and skills are required for that society's maintenance and further development, and how many students are needed by—and can be supported by—the economy. Societies at a low level of industrial development can utilize only a small number of highly educated persons. "Under such conditions much of the effort of the schools and the external examining system is to find ways of rejecting the majority of students at various points in the educational system and to discover the talented few who are to be given advanced educational opportunity" (Bloom, 1968: 12). Highly developed nations, on the other hand, must find ways to increase the proportion of persons with secondary and higher education. In an economy that requires the range and complexity of skills required in the United States, investment in education may pay off at a greater rate than capital investment. In fact, it may be cheaper to educate nearly everyone at a given age level than to invest a great deal in the prediction and selection of talent. "The problem is no longer one of finding the few who can succeed. The basic problem is to determine how the largest proportion of the age group can learn effectively those skills and subject matter regarded as essential" (Bloom, 1968: 12).

Societies undergoing rapid social change or modernization have special problems in adapting the educational system to the human power needs in the other segments of the society. Developing nations often suffer shortages of persons with special kinds of learning (in engineering and other technical fields) and may have difficulty keeping persons with valuable skills once they have completed their education (as a result of "brain drains"). On the other hand, the institutional imbalances caused by rapid change may produce a temporary surplus of persons with higher levels of education. For example, although India suffers a shortage of persons trained in agriculture, technical fields, and the health professions, it has an excess of students in the classical academic courses of study, who cannot find work commensurate with their education. In India, the intense competition for the limited supply of degrees and diplomas of the sort required for desirable government and other white-collar positions explains the great amount of cheating on examinations endemic to some colleges. Those who fail constitute a pool of the discontented susceptible to the appeals of extremist political and social movements.

A sharp increase in the numbers or proportions of students at the higher levels may produce problems of adaptation for the students as well as for the society. In a paper on educational policy presented before a congressional committee on science and astronautics, Green (1970) cautioned:

> an increase in the social demand for formal education experienced as a sequential requirement in the lives of people, may be dysfunctional because in practice, it con-

stitutes an extraordinary extension of adolescence at precisely the time when people are maturing earlier. It means, among other things, the extended deferment of entrance upon meaningful work. . . . The result cannot help but be frustrating and indeed alienating in a society that has promised much to be gained from extended education and then has progressively deferred the reward. (Green, 1970: 6)

Stinchcombe's study of rebellious California students (discussed in Chapter 11) suggested that lack of perceived articulation between in-school learning and the requirements of future roles is a cause of poor academic performance and social alienation. Similar results were obtained in a study of Israeli high school students (Adler, 1967), which found that the major difference between dropouts and nondropouts was that the former were vague about their future plans and saw little likelihood of fulfilling their aspirations via their current course of study.

Overshadowing all other educational trends and all differences between societies and their educational systems, however, is the extremely rapid expansion of national educational systems that occurred throughout the world between 1950 and 1970, a phenomenon so distinct and so universal that John Meyer and others who have studied it refer to it as the "world educational revolution" (Meyer *et al.*, 1977). Data collected by the UNESCO Statistical Office indicate that the proportion of persons of the appropriate age group enrolled in elementary school jumped from 58 percent to 83 percent, and the proportion in secondary school jumped from 13 to 31 percent during this twenty-year period. While there were large enrollment gaps between richer and poorer countries, enrollments increased in nations at all levels of economic development. Thus secondary school enrollment increased from 21 percent to 46 percent in a set of countries classified as wealthy, while the comparable percentages for poor countries were 5 to 17 percent.

Meyer and his associates concluded from these trends that the growth of national educational systems was not explained by such factors as level of economic development and autonomy, political and social modernization, strength of national political cultures, or degree of ethnic heterogeneity, but rather by a "self-generating process based on the demographic characteristics of the school populations, independent of national economic, political, and social characteristics" (Meyer *et al.*, 1977: 247). That is, the worldwide expansion of education during this period was explained by properties of the contemporary world as a total "world system." Countries with widely differing political, social, and economic characteristics displayed similar patterns of growth, and differential rates of expansion between individual countries were explained by characteristics of the population and the organization of the educational system itself—for example, the size of the available "pool" of potential students, including the number of children of the appropriate age for a given level of schooling and the number of students graduating from the preceding level.

In support of their general hypothesis that with respect to educational development the world could be conceptualized as a single social system, "with an organizational and cultural milieu that penetrates all countries with common demands to increase education," Meyer *et al.*, offered the following arguments:

Development strategies vary across countries, but every national elite understands that the development process requires rational planning and technically trained personnel.... The expansion of education, then, may reflect convergence in the meaning and value of development despite differences in economic performance....

Second, an educated citizenry is a highly valued asset from all political perspectives.... In a world that emphasizes organizationally both citizenship and state authority (as, for example, in the United Nations), the expansion of education becomes convenient political shorthand for articulating a commitment to both goals.

Third, the contemporary world not only praises, but insists on "human progress."... The "new person" and the "new society"—Mao, Nyerere, Nkrumah, Castro, etc.—inevitably require more education.

Fourth, all of this occurs in a capitalist world economy in which "development" means success in economic competition. Elites that do not pursue the ends of economic and political development and education as a means to those ends, are likely to fall from power.... [Thus] elites vigorously promote education as a means of national mobilization. (Meyer *et al.*, 1977: 255)

The Structure of National Educational Systems

Although much of the comparative study of education has consisted of making detailed descriptions of the educational system of a single society, a few sociologists have attempted to develop typologies for the classification of multiple systems and to formulate hypotheses about the relationships between structural and outcome variables. One of the earliest typologies emerged from Turner's comparison of English and American schools. Starting from the assumption that the "accepted mode of upward mobility shapes the school system, directly and indirectly through its effects on the values which implement social control" (Turner, 1968: 219), Turner distinguished between "sponsored" and "contest" modes of mobility. Under the former, illustrated by English society and education, "elite recruits are chosen by the established elite or their agents, and elite status is *given* on the basis of some criteria of supposed merit and cannot be *taken* by any amount of effort or strategy. Upward mobility is like entry into a private club where each candidate must be 'sponsored' by one or more of the members" (Turner, 1968: 220). In contest mobility, characteristic of the American style, status is achieved through the individual's talents and efforts. Ideally, all members of the society have an opportunity to try for its prizes, and more than one strategy is available for obtaining them. Thus the American ideal (however much deviation there may be in actual practice) is to have within most schools a variety of courses of study as well as a cross-section of social class and ability.

Building upon Turner's dichotomy, Hopper (1977) argues that the structural properties of a society's educational system are reflected in the answers to four questions. First, *how* does educational selection occur? Hopper's scheme classifies educational systems on the degree of centralization and standardization of the total selection process. The educational systems of France, Sweden, and the U.S.S.R. are high on this dimension, those of the United States and Canada are low.

Second, *when* does the initial selection occur? Elitist systems, illustrated by those in France and England before recent reforms, are characterized by early formal differentiation and specialization, while egalitarian systems, such as Sweden and Canada's, specify that every citizen is entitled to the maximum amount of education, that selection should occur as late as possible, and that there should be a relatively small number of different educational routes or tracks.

Third, *who* should be selected? Borrowing from the terminology of Talcott Parsons, Hopper distinguishes between universalistic versus particularistic modes of selection—that is, the extent to which "society has a system of ascribed statuses on the basis of which certain diffuse skills and ascribed characteristics are likely to become unequally distributed" (high in particularistic systems), as opposed to an emphasis upon technical skills and achievement through merit as defined by generally accepted standards (high in universalistic systems). The availability of opportunities to learn valued skills is also higher in universalistic than particularistic systems (Hopper, 1977: 159).

Fourth, *why* should those who are selected be selected? Justification for selection of particular persons can be made in terms of the right of those selected on the basis of their diffuse skills and ascribed characteristics (aristocratic justification); in terms of the right of those selected on the basis of their efforts and technical skills and accomplishments (meritocratic justification); in terms of the society's "need" for people with diffuse skills and certain ascribed characteristics, so that it may be led by the most "suitable" persons (paternalistic justification); or in terms of society's "need" for identifying and training the most ambitious, energetic, and technically qualified persons (collectivistic justification).

Models of System Structure

One of the few systematic analyses of component *b* of Exhibit 13–1 was a theoretical model of the internal structure of national educational systems, based upon a review of the largely descriptive studies then available (Livingstone, 1968). Livingstone postulates the following as the basic "activities" that comprise any national learning system: (1) legal provisions; (2) financing; (3) staff development and maintenance; (4) educational research; (5) program control (or degree of centralization); (6) provision of educational facilities; (7) provision of auxiliary services; (8) instruction; (9) administration of students. By using these as the components or "focal systems" of his model, Livingstone formulates almost three hundred hypotheses about their interdependencies. Some of the major variables, which act as unifying themes organizing sets of hypotheses, are: enrollment (how many or what proportions of young people are in school); the number and types of different educational programs offered and at what point in their school career students must make a firm choice of specialty; the extent of centralization of the system (is there a national education ministry, and if so how great is its control over curriculum and the allocation of students); and the range and extensiveness of services offered beyond classroom teaching (say, guidance or financial aid). Here are some of the major hypotheses formulated around these themes, as paraphrased by this writer:

Enrollments at different levels of the education system are related; the greater the attendance rates at one level, the greater the rates at other levels.

The greater the enrollment rates at a given level: the more predominant are ability groupings of students and specialized subject teaching; the greater the basic education and formal training required of teachers and the higher the proportion of teachers who are formally qualified; the greater the number of teachers per school, but also the higher the ratio of administrators to teachers; the less the centralization, especially of program policy.

The greater the proportion of urban students at a given level: the greater the enrollment rates; the higher the educational expenditure (per capita and the proportion of the national income devoted to education) and the greater the proportion of public education expenditure allocated to special education; the greater the proportion of female students.

The greater the religious homogeneity of enrollment at a given level: the lower the educational expenditure; the lower the proportion of female students; the greater the proportion of students in private schools.

The greater the centralization in one area or activity of the system (say, program policy), the greater the centralization in another (say, guidance services or financial support). The greater the centralization, especially in program control, the greater the likelihood of external examinations to determine entrance to and graduation from schools or programs; the sooner the differentiation into specialized curriculum and the greater the proportion of students enrolled in vocational and other nonacademic programs; the lower the acceleration rate and the greater the degree of retardation at respective levels; the greater the proportions of secondary and higher level students receiving financial aid; the greater the proportion of rural students.

The longer the basic education program, or the later the differentiation into specialized curriculum: the smaller the proportion of the total school enrollment at the primary level and the higher the proportion pursuing advanced degrees; the greater the range and the more balanced the enrollments in higher level programs.

The greater the number of alternative curricula offered at elementary and secondary levels: the lower the enrollment rates within the compulsory age limits; the lower the proportion of students enrolled in strictly academic programs; the greater the likelihood of external examinations for admittance to or graduation from these programs.

Although most of Livingstone's hypotheses, like the majority of crosscultural studies, make comparisons only at the level of the educational system as a whole, he emphasizes that this is more a consequence of limited availability of data than of optimum research design. Subsequent empirical research, such as the IEA studies that will be discussed later in this chapter, allow comparisons within as well as between societies. Such research has supported Livingstone's general contention that "the educational systems of different nations are not internally homogeneous nor do they exhibit identical degrees of variation" (Livingstone, 1968: 7). Unfortunately, however, most of Livingstone's hypotheses have not been tested empirically.

Alternative Models

In recent years, American sociologists and educators have been attracted to the study of certain societies that seemed to offer fresh perspectives on our own most troublesome educational problems, despite—or perhaps because of—their very different ways of socializing and educating children. These include some societies in which American scholars have long been free to observe and conduct research and on which much has been published in English (for example, Israel, in particular the kibbutz model of child rearing and education), and other, mainly socialist, societies in which studies by Westerners have been very restricted (for example, the U.S.S.R., Cuba, and especially the People's Republic of China). Of particular interest to researchers are the natural experiments that have occurred in many of these societies in which a radical restructuring of the educational system was compressed into a relatively short time period—for example, the mass literacy campaign launched in Cuba after the revolution that brought Castro to power, and the closing down of the entire mainland Chinese educational system and its rebuilding in accordance with Maoist principles during the Cultural Revolution of the 1960s. Such instances represent, in the words of a Marxian analysis, "a moment when the school died and education lived," when "an extraordinary exchange of social techniques and knowledge, irreplaceable by the most modern and perfected pedagogical center, occurred" (Rossanda *et al.*, 1977: 655). In terms of our analysis in Chapter 12, they also represent an extreme impingement of the external environment on the school.

While there is much to be learned from the partially utopian experiments in educational reform that have been attempted in other societies, these experiments have provided especially rich information and insights on: the balance between individual versus group orientation in learning; the problems of integrating academic work and "productive" work; the incorporation of ideological or moral instruction into the school curriculum; and strategies for enhancing equity or equality in the educational system.

Individual versus Group Orientation. By contrast with the focus upon the development of individual personality and intellect that characterizes most schools in this country, the approved methods of child rearing and the structure of schools in Russia, China, and the Israeli kibbutz foster a commitment to the group and to society as a whole.

Although systematic study of Russian child-rearing and educational techniques is generally forbidden to Westerners, we are fortunate in the work of Urie Bronfenbrenner, who was given permission to travel in Russia in the late 1950s and whose knowledge of the Russian language enabled him to supplement the "official" information given to him with informal conversations in restaurants and stores. (For example, although in Bronfenbrenner's early trips, he was not allowed to visit Soviet elementary schools, he was able to compare the official teacher's manual given him with a conversation with three elementary teachers he met by chance in a restaurant.) According to his report, the process of "collective socialization" begins when the child enters school; the focus of evaluation is not upon the individual child but upon subgroups of students within the class. Competition is not eliminated—on the contrary, the use of competition as a motivating device is a crucial part of the design of Soviet schools—but it is at the level of the group rather than the individual. Even in the earliest grades,

> records are kept for each row from day to day for different types of tasks so that the young children can develop a concept of group excellence over time and over a variety of activities, including personal cleanliness, condition of notebooks, conduct in passing from one room to the other, quality of recitations in each subject matter, and so on. In these activities, considerable emphasis is placed on the externals of behavior in dress, manner, and speech. There must be no spots on shirt or collar, shoes must be shined, pupils must never pass by a teacher without stopping to give greeting, there must be no talking without permission, and the like. Great charts are kept in all the schools showing the performance of each row unit in every type of activity together with their total overall standing. "Who is best?" the charts ask, but the entries are not individuals but social units—rows, and later the "cells" of the communist youth organization which reaches down to the primary grades. (Bronfenbrenner, 1968: 61)

As the children grow older competition is initiated among classes, and then among schools, regions, and so on. At the same time, the source of evaluation is shifted from the teacher to the students themselves. Even in the first grade children act as monitors for some activities. Within the next few years they learn to evaluate themselves and their peers and to state their criticisms publicly.

Since Russia loosened some of its restrictions on travel, Bronfenbrenner has made nine return trips. His best-selling book, *Two Worlds of Childhood* (1970), is a comparison between family, school, and community environments of Russian and American children. In this book, Bronfenbrenner develops more extensively his theme that in each setting the Soviet child is a member of a collective group that emphasizes self-discipline and effort for the sake of the group, and that there is a congruency and unity of purpose from one setting to another. By contrast, the American child has greater independence from the group, which produces a spontaneity and expressiveness absent in Russian schools but that also may reflect an abdication of responsibility by the family, school, and community for the development of the young. Bronfenbrenner worries that in the absence of a clear ideology of child rearing and a clear commitment by adult institutions to guiding the child, socialization occurs more and more in the peer group (which, as we saw in Chapter 11, provides in addition a kind of protection from the stresses of the individualistic competition characteristic of American schools). If the current trends toward "affluent neglect" continue, says Bronfenbrenner, "we can anticipate increased alienation, indifference, antagonism and violence on the part of the younger generation in all segments of our society"; in sum, the "unmaking of the American child."

The preceding discussion also should make clear that the dimension of group orientation is not a simple one. While in Bronfenbrenner's terms, children in our society have a high degree of individualism and a low degree of "collectivity commitment," they are by other definitions very sensitive to the opinions and expectations of others. McClelland, for instance, found that high proportions of the American children he studied engage in group activities outside of school by comparison to, say, German children, who were more likely to engage in such individualistic activities as hiking, collecting stamps, or playing musical instruments (McClelland, 1961: 197ff.), and that through such activities they build up what seems to some observers an excessive sensitivity to the opinions of others. Bronfenbrenner's point is not that American children are lacking in group orientation but rather that in the absence of attention and systematic guidance from adult institutions, the child's "other-directedness" is virtually all toward age peers, and that he or she never develops a true commitment to the community or society as a whole.

Another experiment in collective living, which combines a theory of child rearing and education with a theory of economic organization, can be found in the kibbutzim and other cooperative settlements in Israel. Of course, the kibbutz is not representative of Israel as a whole—kibbutz schools enroll only about 5 percent of the nation's children—but its influence (both ideologically and as a source of national leaders) has been disproportionate to its quantitative strength. Among the distinctive features of the kibbutz educational system noted by Bruno Bettelheim, in a seven-week visit in 1964, were the following:

Children are reared apart from their natural parents, with a group of their age-peers. Most see their parents during daily visits, but the general responsibility for day-to-day care is assigned to trained "metapelets" or nurses.

All children receive the same education and the same preparation for school. Although the wide differences in individual ability are recognized, no child starts school at a disadvantage because of his social position. Similarly, students neither skip grades nor are held back because of their intellectual skills—the age-group stays together both in school and in the residence house throughout childhood and adolescence.

Academic learning is combined with "real" work in the kibbutz from the earliest years. Even young children help with the care of animals and in the maintenance of their residence house. "As the child grows older, he works more after-school hours at the farm or in the shop and is given ever more absorbing and responsible tasks" (Bettelheim, 1969: 49).

Children regularly see their parents and other adults, as well as older children, engaged in work that is understandable in itself and visibly meaningful to the life of the community.

Virtually all students stay in school to the end, because the usual reasons for dropping out are absent. Since the kibbutz is a communal society, there is no chance to earn money by leaving school. In the absence of TV and other forms of entertainment, and with all of his or her age-mates in school, there would be nothing for a dropout to do but sit in the children's house. Finally, the lack of individualistic competition in the classroom means that the classroom does not have to be a punishing experience for those less endowed intellectually.

In sum, "kibbutz education is so much a part of a common way of life, so embodies the youngsters' future aspirations that, however much they sometimes tire of learning, what they never feel is a split between them and the educational system" (Bettelheim, 1969: 50).

Most of the accounts of kibbutz life are rich in descriptive detail[1] but short on systematic data collection and analysis, and much of the interpretation of the effects of the educational system upon definite areas of academic achievement is biased by the authors' prior views on child rearing and/or the kibbutz and by lack of facility in the Hebrew language. One of the few behavioral scientists who has investigated the kibbutz modes of socialization with a tightly structured research design is Eifermann, whose large-scale study of children's games has indicated that the spontaneous behavior of school children reflects the collective orientation of the surrounding community. By comparison with children from other rural settlements, kibbutz children favored games that "demand cooperation toward the achievement of a common aim, but within an overall competitive framework," as opposed to games that are exclusively cooperative or that emphasize individualistic competition (Eifermann, 1969: 13). Although Eifermann's work to date has not related play behavior to academic behavior, it suggests a promising line of research.

In understanding the kind of education a child receives in a kibbutz, two important but often overlooked general characteristics should be noted. One is that, although the kibbutz modes of communal child rearing and educating have now taken on the aura of an ideology, their origins, as Bettelheim points out, were purely pragmatic. They were arrived at in a hasty and piecemeal fashion to allow a band of young pioneers to throw off the traces of their own childhood in European Jewish ghettoes and at the same time to survive in an underdeveloped land surrounded by enemies. In other words, the specific techniques of this very humane—and by many standards very effective—way of raising children did not evolve out of a general theory of child development, but rather the theory evolved gradually out of a series of improvisations implemented to meet the most pressing needs of the moment. A second general point is that a system that provides such a high level of integration among and cooperation between all its major institutions "can only exist where a consensus society is the universal ideal. This includes a far-reaching acceptance by the individual of the community's right to shape his own life and that of his children" (Bettelheim, 1969: 45–46).

By all accounts, the Chinese educational system has carried to an extreme the group orientation and societal control over the development of the individual student. Visitors' accounts routinely mention the theme of "serve the people" that permeates the school curriculum and classroom lectures and discussions at all levels of the educational system (Sidel, 1972; Kessen, 1975). Serving the people can take forms as varied as helping a classmate who has fallen behind in his or her school work, offering drinking water to drivers, conductors, and passengers at bus and train stops, and working extra hours on some community project.

Socialization to group life begins in the factory nursing rooms and commune nursery schools, which have proliferated in the past decade. The youngest children are taught to help each other at meal time and nap time, as well as to love China, Chairman Mao, and workers, peasants, and soldiers. Recent visitors to Chinese kindergartens have been impressed by the lack of aggressive and antisocial behavior, the absence of the kinds of toys, games, and other equipment that fill American nursery schools and kindergartens (many of which encourage solitary play and the development of individual skills), and the remarkable skill of the children in singing and dancing, usually in group performances that require high levels of concentration, physical coordination, and interpersonal cooperation. The impressions of one American visitor were summarized as follows:

> The Chinese, in the handling of their children, seem to expect good behavior, cooperation, and obedience, and in general, get it. Although they clearly recognize that there is a non-cooperative, hostile, aggressive side to man, they do not emphasize it. They emphasize the side they wish to promote. (Sidel, 1972: 188)

It is important to keep in mind, however, that virtually all of the evidence we have about recent developments in the Chinese educational system come from one of two sources: official documents that have been released to foreign news media or publishing companies[2]; and brief visits to schools and communities not selected by the visitors themselves by scholars who have very scant knowledge of the Chinese language, history, and culture. In addition, developments in the People's Republic of China since Mao's death have already brought about further changes in the educational system, before Western scholars have fully understood the earlier systems.

Academic versus Productive Work. As we saw in Chapter 11, a theme of much recent social criticism in this country is the growing exclusion of children and youth from the productive life of the community.

The work and study patterns of most Israeli youth are quite similar to their U.S. counterparts, with full entry into the labor force increasingly postponed as the years of formal education are increased and with occupational opportunity strongly related to social class background and the school tracking system. But Israel does offer some opportunities for work experience not available in this country. Utopian farming communities like the kibbutzim offer one such opportunity. Kibbutz children from the earliest ages make some kind of work contribution to their community, and by adolescence work has extended to a regular assignment in the community's fields, barns, or industry for several hours each afternoon. While the absence of adult "chaperonage" in adolescent residence homes still causes uneasiness among many Western visitors, at the same time, daily contact with persons of all ages and daily contribution of the productive labor of all ages ease the transitions in the life cycle.

Another unique Israeli institution is the army, in which young men and women serve immediately after high school and before being allowed to attend college. Men serve for three years, women for two. The army experience is an important phase in the life of Israeli youth.[3] Especially for male youth, it not only provides a testing ground but also serves as an integrating force counteracting the divisive aspects of the strongly tracked educational system.

> Military service gives the average Israeli youth the opportunity to share in a highly prestigious task while participating in a future-oriented and ethnically integrated youth culture whose values are mutual help, equality, and excellence. The Israeli army is therefore one of the most powerful correctives for the limitations of the educational system; it is an actively engaging and socially integrating experience which imparts to the young Israeli a strong sense of acceptance and participation. (Adler, 1973: 161)

While there are strong similarities as well as differences between the Israeli and American youth experience, China offers a far stronger contrast. Productive labor in China is the core activity binding all members of the society. Part-work, part-study programs are the model for all schools. Most of the schools visited by Westerners contained workshops where students not only learned technical skills but also engaged in productive labor. Assembling and packing toys, wrapping candy and fruit, punching out components and electroplating parts for oil filters, and wiring transistor parts were among the tasks observed by visitors (Committee of Concerned Asian Scholars, 1972; Kessen, 1975). In addition, many children and youth spend a month or more each year in agricultural or some other kind of productive labor. The purpose of work for students is ideological as well as practical. While the students are learning technical skills and making things that are actually used, they are also playing a part in building up their community and country.

While Chinese students have considerable opportunity to make use of their energies and idealism in activities that are recognized by the larger society, the choice of career or even of a student work assignment are not matters of individual choice. Young people are assigned to training and jobs by the government at the state or local level, and whole cohorts may be sent to work in a rural commune or to a factory in a distant part of the country. While some visitors report an apparently genuine, indeed almost religious fervor among youth peer groups working in rural communes, there are also reports of runaway youth roaming the streets of Peking and other large cities, supporting themselves by stealing and other delinquent activity. The feelings of a teen-ager who was refused permission to pursue her interest in medicine, even after scoring high in her academic examinations, are described in a book written by a young girl who escaped from mainland China. Her appeal to the local education bureau official produced a lecture on the need to submerge one's personal desires to the needs of China and its people: "I was then dismissed. At fourteen my life was fixed. I was to be an elementary-school teacher in three years and earn thirty-two yuan for the rest of my days. I would not have to wonder and plan for my future ever again" (San-san, 1964: 51).

It is ironic that in the United States most attempts to provide a meaningful work experience for students occur in communities designed for severely impoverished, disturbed, or delinquent children and youth. For example, in the Synanon communities, products of a highly controversial program designed to reshape the lives of former drug addicts, the Interface program for persons aged thirteen to eighteen facilitates the transition from adolescence to adulthood by transferring power and responsibility to the young, at work and elsewhere. The program includes four kinds of activities: academic activities, work experience, field trips, and time-off activities within Synanon. Young people are organized into groups that contain both sexes in the complete age range. Each group is divided in two, with half the group attending "massive dose" class sessions (three to four hours a day of one subject in class followed by an equal period of home study), while the other half hold down full-time jobs in the community. At the end of a given period of time—Synanon has experimented with periods varying from a week to a month—the roles are reversed: workers become scholars and the students take over the jobs.

Although Synanon is a far from typical American community, the experience does provide insights into the rewards and the difficulties of revising the work place to accommodate youth. For example, difficulties arose in getting department heads to place the youngsters in other than menial tasks and to treat them as responsible individuals. As one department head said, "Someone always wanted to put them in a ditch." On the other hand, some adults were very protective of their trainees, saving them from serving merely as errand runners and setting aside time for them to study during the work day and conferring regularly on their progress. Not only did the young feel more commitment to the adult community and more comfortable in their relationships with adults, but the morale and enthusiasm of some adult workers were raised by the presence of the young people (Mullen, 1973).

Ideological and Moral Instruction. In contrast to schooling in the past, the contemporary model of American education is religiously and politically neutral. Prayers and other religious exercises are forbidden in public (though not in private) schools, and recent sociology texts sometimes point to the difficulties of maintaining a sense of community and common purpose. Hurn, for example, believes that

> the ability of schools to transmit any consistent set of moral messages to the young has been impaired in recent decades. . . . Most obviously, the symbols of school solidarity have begun to disappear: school songs are sung less frequently, it is more difficult to get recruits for the school play or contributors to the school yearbook. The moral authority of the school to coerce students diminishes: students resent being told to cut their hair, to wear a particular style of dress, being forbidden to smoke or to leave the school premises during the school period. Such regulations, we have come to believe, are unnecessarily coercive. But the consequence of this decline in the authority of the school to coerce students is to move the school closer to a model of an educational service station and further away from the model of a solidary community with common values and ideals. (Hurn, 1978: 212)

On the other hand, some radical critics argue that American schools are permeated by implicit if not explicit moral training, which serves to inculcate the values of obedience, neatness, and promptness in working-class children and to prepare them to assume an adult status similar to that of their parents. Only at the college level and then only for some students do schools encourage critical thinking; most students are taught to accept without question the basic assumptions of the capitalistic system (Bowles and Gintis, 1976).

In Chinese and Israeli kibbutz schools, the ideological/moral component of the curriculum is explicit. The fundamental goal of Chinese education is, in Mao's words, to create a "well-educated worker imbued with both socialist consciousness and culture" (Mao, 1967: 92). Maoist educational philosophy, like kibbutz ideology, stresses the value of manual work and aims to bridge the chasm that in the past separated peasants and laborers from those who engaged in intellectual work. The following statement by the director of a Chinese middle school visited by an American team of child-development specialists contains several of the often-repeated themes in Chinese pedagogy.

> Formerly we put intellectual development first and kept a closed door. . . . The students did not know how the workers worked or how the peasants plowed the fields. Under Chairman Mao's revolutionary lines, we develop the children morally, intellectually, and physically. The students are educated to serve the people wholeheartedly. We also organize the students to take part in the class struggle and the struggle for scientific research; to learn from the workers, peasants, and soldiers; to combine theory with practice. (Kessen, 1975: 5)

Such a philosophy assumes a strong belief in the malleability and perfectability of human beings, and a deep faith in the ability of environmental (including educational) influences to produce desired values and attitudes in children (Munro, 1971a).

In both China and Israel, important moral-political education is provided by youth groups, independent of but closely correlated with the formal educational system and often based in schools. The Chinese Little Red Soldiers and Young Pioneers "enlighten children on communism and train them to be a new generation that loves the fatherland, the people, labor and science, that takes good care of public property, is healthy, active, courageous, honest and creative in spirit" (from a youth newspaper, quoted in Price, 1970: 229). Enrollment is optional, but observers estimate that at least 80 percent of students between ages seven and fifteen join. Members are organized in semimilitary fashion into squads, platoons, and brigades, and are identifiable by the red scarves they wear as symbols of membership. Activities range from group study of Maoist writings and discussions with older workers to tutoring children who have fallen behind in their school work and a wide range of community service projects.

Israeli youth movements, which originated in the 1930s and reached their climax in the 1940s, also have a strong collectivistic political orientation (which makes them similar to Chinese youth groups but distinguishes them from American youth organizations like the Scouts and 4-H clubs). Although there are eleven different movements, each with a different focus and source of support, all have an ideology based upon Zionism, ruralism, socialism, and asceticism. Special emphasis is laid on agricultural training, and graduates have founded or reinforced many kibbutzim and other pioneering settlements. The exact number of members is unknown—a recent estimate was something over two hundred thousand. In recent years, youth movements have been declining in prestige, momentum, and impact, as well as enrollment, but they still offer for a sizable minority of Israeli youth a means of taking an active part in building the society and an opportunity "to turn the tensions and anxieties of growing up in a new immigrant society toward collective goals and values" (Adler, 1973: 158).

Increasing Equality. Contrary to the claims of some Marxian theorists, educational inequalities are not uniquely characteristic of capitalistic societies, but can be found in socialist ones as well, including the ones discussed in this chapter. As one analysis puts it, educational inequality may "persist as long as capitalism survives, but the abolition of capitalism would hardly assure the emergence of a non-hierarchical school system" (Karabel and Halsey, 1977: 39). At the same time, some societies attach more value to equality than others, and the study of some other societies' efforts to enhance educational opportunity and equity provides a comparative framework for evaluating our own efforts.

Among the multiethnic societies that have a strong ideological commitment to equalitarianism, Israel has probably been the most innovative in educational research and experimentation. The mass immigration following the establishment of the state of Israel not only trebled the population in the first twelve years of independence, but also brought an influx of Jews from North Africa, Yemen, Iraq, Persia, India, and other African and Asian nations. These immigrants came to be referred to as Eastern or oriental Jews, as opposed to the Ashkenazi Jews of European origin, who were the founders of Zionism and the independent state of Israel. The large gap between European and Afro-Asian Jews on everything from family size and structure to educational attainment, occupational status, and income has been a major social-political issue since the beginning of the nation, because of Israel's explicit national commitment to equality.

According to Smilansky (1973), educational reform in Israel has passed through a series of stages: first, a "pioneering-voluntary" stage, in which teachers, social workers, nurses, and public officials invented programs and services in response to immediate—often emergency—needs; second, a "formal opportunity" stage, characterized by passage of a body of legislation guaranteeing equal opportunities for students of all ethnic backgrounds; third, a "compensatory" or enrichment stage, during which social scientific arguments against forcing a uniform schooling based upon European culture and norms on all children led to experimentation with a variety of special programs for disadvantaged students, often in ethnically segregated settings; and most recently, a concerted attempt to move beyond formal desegregation toward true ethnic integration in the schools.

The sheer number and variety of educational innovations tested during the past twenty-five years, both in and outside of schools, is impressive. While our discussion here cannot do justice to the Israeli achievements, the following innovations seem to merit special mention:[4]

a program, developed by Carl Frankenstein, to train teachers to recognize and correct faulty thinking patterns of disadvantaged students by systematic analysis of classroom dialogue

increasing the quantity of schooling for disadvantaged students by extending the school day, adding additional years of free education, and subsidizing education in boarding-school settings for substantial numbers of oriental students (note that this strategy is consistent with Wiley's findings on the effects of school quantity or time inputs, discussed in Chapter 10)

experimentation with a variety of informal educational frameworks, ranging from summer camps to streetcorner work with youth gangs, that emphasize autonomy and mutual respect and are based upon a symmetrical structure of interpersonal relationships that contrasts with the hierarchical structure of most formal classroom situations

a home-instruction project for preschool children, developed by Avima Lombard, that enlists and trains young nonprofessional women from low-income neighborhoods in the use of carefully programmed curriculum materials, who then teach the materials to mothers in the neighborhood, who in turn teach the material to their own children. This program is now sponsored by the Ministry of Education and involves over five thousand families throughout the country.

By contrast to the disappointing results of most American research on the effects of school desegregation, some Israeli research shows quite positive outcomes. The Nachlaot Integration Project involves an examination of the effects, separately and combined, of ethnic integration at the classroom level and an innovative activity-oriented teaching approach based upon the English open-classroom model. Children in five experimental elementary schools, matched with control schools in the same neighborhoods of Jerusalem, were followed for six years by a research team that used a variety of data-gathering instruments to measure both cognitive and noncognitive outcomes. Although the project is still in progress, the data analysis that has been completed indicates that lower-class children in settings that combine integration and classroom innovation achieved significantly better than children in nonintegrated settings. The performance of the middle-class children was essentially unaffected by integration (Klein and Eshel, 1976). These positive outcomes may be partially explained by the fact that the study was a long-term longitudinal one, that the researchers could control the experimental treatments, and that multiple methods of data gathering were used, thus avoiding the weaknesses of most American research.

While individual experiments like the Nachlaot project have produced promising results, Israel, like other nations, is far from the achievement of educational equality at the national level. In the early 1970s, an evaluation of Israeli elementary education, partially modeled on the *Equality of Educational Opportunity* survey in this country, was conducted with a nationwide sample of 17,700 students in about a hundred Jewish schools, plus a sample of students and schools in the Arab sector of Israel. (Before this study, virtually all research on the disadvantaged had focused upon oriental Jewish children; the problems and accomplishments of Arab education were all but invisible.)

The results of the survey, reported in Minkovich, Davis, and Bashi (1977), point to wide discrepancies in the distribution of educational resources and academic achievement by ethnic and social-class status and "generation in Israel" (that is, children whose parents were born in Israel tend to be at an educational advantage over children whose parents are immigrants, whatever their ethnic origins). Although the Ministry of Education has an official policy of "positive discrimination" in favor of disadvantaged students and schools, these advantages are mainly budgetary in nature and seem to be outweighed by other educational benefits possessed by advantaged schools (such as higher proportions of well-educated and experienced teachers and principals). Also despite official educational policy, Jewish schools tend to be segregated by ethnic and social-class background. The lower the socioeconomic status of an Afro-Asian student, the greater the probability that he or she will be in a class with few students of European background and that the latter will be of relatively lower SES; conversely, the higher the SES of an Ashkenazi student, the greater the probability that he or she will be in a class with few Afro-Asian students and that the latter will be of relatively high SES. Achievement test scores were strongly and consistently related with ethnic origin, SES, and generation in Israel, though in all subjects except language, a certain proportion of all subgroups failed to reach a "basic" level of competence (measured by a small subset of items on each test that indicated that a basic mastery of the subject had occurred). Integration tended to be positively correlated with achievement, though when SES variables and the "generation in Israel" variable were controlled in a multiple-regression analysis, the addition of school integration added almost nothing to the explained variance in achievement scores.

While it is difficult to compare achievement in Arab and Jewish schools because of differences in curriculum, the structure of the school system, and testing procedures, the data indicated that the average level of achievement in language is similar in Arab schools and Jewish schools overall, though it is somewhat higher than the average level for Afro-Asian students; the achievement levels in math are somewhat lower in Arab schools than in Jewish schools as a whole, though similar to average achievement in primarily Afro-Asian schools; and that achievement in geography and science are lower in Arab schools than in Jewish schools (where the average levels were also low enough to be of concern to the authors of the report).

Crosscultural Differences in Achievement

While the study of crosscultural variations in socialization and educational patterns is fascinating in itself, our ultimate objective is to determine whether differences in societies and their educational systems have impact on levels of educational achievement. Our best source of information on that topic is the set of studies comprising the International Project for the Evaluation of Educational Achievement (hereafter called the IEA), a gigantic international effort to assess the productivity of participating countries' educational systems and to identify differences in student characteristics, school characteristics, and teaching approaches that are related to differences in achievement both within and between countries.

The first phase of the IEA was a study of mathematics achievement in twelve countries,[5] based upon a sample of 132,775 students (between 2,500 and 38,000 in each country) and almost 19,000 teachers in over 5,000 schools. The results were published in two volumes, the first described the design and administration of the survey; the second was a compilation of its results. Mathematics was chosen as the first subject area to be investigated, because it presents fewer measurement problems than, say history or literature, and because "most countries represented are at present concerned with improving their scientific and technical education, at the basis of which lies the learning of mathematics" (Husen, 1967: Vol. I, 33).

The original goal was to test at two major turning points in the school career: (1) the last point at which all of an age group was still in full-time schooling (age thirteen, and (2) the preuniversity year. One problem was that although virtually all thirteen-year-olds were in school, they were not necessarily at the same level of the education ladder.

> The per cent of 13-year-olds who are not in the normal grade for 13-year-olds ranges from 1 per cent in one country to 29 per cent in another. As a result it was decided to test both populations, that is, all 13-year-olds (designated as Population 1a) and all pupils in the grade where the majority of 13-year-olds are (designated 1b). . . . To avoid disparity, it was agreed for this project that it would be the grade where the majority of the 13-year-old pupils were within 3 months of the end of the current school year.
>
> [Students in the pre-university year] . . . were divided into two target populations, that is, those students taking mathematics (designated population 3a) and those not (designated 3b).
>
> Between the 13-year-old level . . . and the pre-university year there are various major terminal points in the school systems. For example, the end of compulsory schooling is 14 years in Germany and 16 in Sweden; there are also major examination points such as 1er partie du baccalaureat in France or GCE "O" level in England. It was decided that countries could choose the population(s) they wished to test at these intermediate points in terms of their own plans for national investigations. (Husen, 1967: Vol. I, 45–46)

Having defined the target populations, the goal was to sample as many different schools with as few students per school as possible (to decrease the likelihood of bias due to the unique characteristics of individual schools).[6]

The problem of test construction was exacerbated by the linguistic and cultural differences among the participating countries. Nine different languages were used in the twelve countries sampled. After each national center prepared a report on the content and objectives of mathematical learning for students within the age range of the study, with suggested examples of appropriate test items, an international committee drew up an overall ''blueprint'' and a series of pretests that were tried out on small samples in three countries. The final test contained 174 items, mainly multiple choice, in ten separately prepared test booklets, graded in difficulty, with a time limit of one hour per booklet. In addition to the achievement tests, questionnaires were designed to measure students' perception of their school and their attitudes toward mathematics, school, learning in general, and the world around them.[7]

After administration, the test booklets were collected in national centers where responses were transferred onto punch cards or special sheets designed for the IBM 1230. These data were sent to the University of Chicago Computer Center for editing, sorting, filing, and most of the analysis. Desite the great care to ensure that materials arrived on time and in correct form, there were a number of small mistakes, as well as the boner, mentioned earlier, concerning the Finnish data.

The data analysis includes comparisons at both macro and micro levels. That is, as well as the comparisons between total or mean achievement scores among countries as a whole, there are *within*-country comparisons (for example, of achievement differences between students in comprehensive and specialized schools). An additional analysis compares subgroups of the total sample (for instance, the top 4 percent in each country).

The basic macro-level comparison, which shows the rough standing of each country in each of the four target populations, is summarized in Exhibit 13–2. The placement of each nation in the figure represents the deviation of that country's national mean from the grand mean of all countries. Especially noticeable are the overall good showings of Japan and Israel (although the latter had a very small sample and in only two of the four target populations) and the poor showing of the United States. Some countries displayed different performance patterns at the two different age levels. For example, France's deviation is below the overall mean at the thirteen-year-old level, when all the children in the age group are still in school, but rises toward the top after the school-leaving age apparently produces a more selective population in the schools.

The study found much variation in school-entry and leaving ages, with no clear relations with math achievement. The median entry age was six, and the countries in this category produced, *on the average*, higher test scores at age thirteen than at an entry age of five. Apparently the extra year of schooling in England and Scotland does not have a direct positive effect upon later mathematical competence. Of the two countries with an entry age of seven, one (Sweden) had as high a score as the median of the six-year-old entry group, while the other (Finland) had the lowest score of all (Husen, 1967: Vol. II, 77–78).

The findings on size are also ambiguous. Within the wide range of school sizes in the sample, the best test performance by most thirteen-year-olds was in schools with enrollments greater than eight hundred, although in a few types of schools small enrollments went with higher scores. For older students the evidence was contradictory, and at this age level national differences accounted for

298 Part Four The School's Environment

Exhibit 13–2
National Means Expressed as Deviations from the Grand Mean

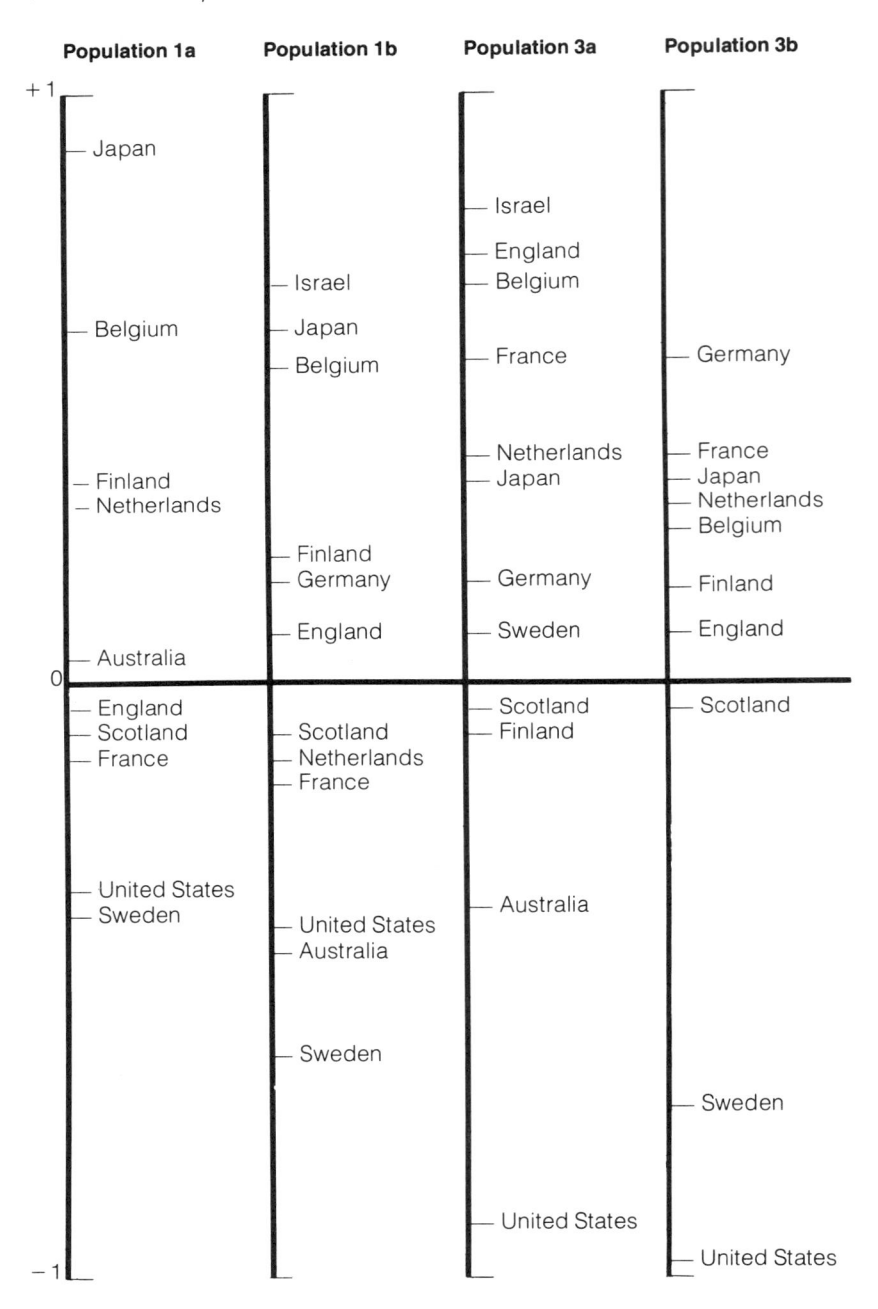

Population 1a	Population 1b	Population 3a	Population 3b
+1			
Japan			
		Israel	
		England	
	Israel	Belgium	
Belgium	Japan		Germany
	Belgium	France	
		Netherlands	France
Finland		Japan	Japan
Netherlands			Netherlands
	Finland		Belgium
	Germany	Germany	Finland
	England	Sweden	England
Australia			
0			
England	Scotland	Scotland	Scotland
Scotland	Netherlands	Finland	
France	France		
United States		Australia	
Sweden	United States		
	Australia		
	Sweden		
			Sweden
		United States	
−1			United States

Husen, 1967: Vol. ii, 27.

more of the variation than size of school. Classroom size ranged from means of twenty-four and twenty-five in Belgium and the Netherlands to forty-one in Japan. (The United States mean in this sample was twenty-nine.) On the national level, students in the countries with larger mean class size scored higher at the age-thirteen level, but this relationship was reversed at the preuniversity level. Within most countries there were no statistically significant differences in math scores among students in small, medium, and large classes. One interpretation suggested by the authors is that at the earlier age, when enrollments still include almost all children at that age, the best teachers often are assigned to the larger classes because they are thought better able to cope with them, but by the preuniversity year there is a tendency toward smaller classes for the more able and advanced students. At the later level, the class size variable is further complicated by "varying selection mechanisms affecting both the ability distribution and the social class composition of the classes" (Husen, 1967: Vol. II, 297). The general conclusion is the same one reached in Chapter 8: it is difficult to separate out the effects of class size from the effects of other variables, but merely reducing class size is not likely to increase achievement markedly.

A third system characteristic correlated with achievement was retentivity, or the proportion of the age group still in school at the terminal level. The general question here is whether "more means worse" in academic terms, whether an educational system that tries to keep high proportions of young people in school up to relatively high levels will sacrifice overall quality of education. Exhibit 13–3 synthesizes the IEA answers to this question. The countries are ranked according to the proportion of the total age group still in school at the preuniversity year, beginning with the most selective (or least retentive) system. As column two of Exhibit 13–3 shows, the average level of math performance was inversely related to the proportion of the age group still in school (the correlation between columns one and two is −.62). Thus more does seem to mean worse, in the sense that countries that retain a high percentage of students to this stage produce on the average lower standards of achievement than do the more elitist countries. However, when equal proportions of the total age group are compared, the results are quite different. These results are shown in column three. With one exception (Belgium, which has a four percent retentivity rate), the means go up when only the highest performance students are included, with the greatest increases in the countries with the highest retentivity rates. There are also changes in the relative standing of the countries.

> The rank correlation between the two sets of means is +.45. This indicates that one can predict only moderately well the mathematics performance of the upper 4 percent of the *age group in each country* from the mathematics performance of the students in full-time schooling. . . . Downward shifts occur in Belgium, which moves from third to seventh place; Germany, which moves from seventh to eleventh place; and Scotland, which moves from ninth to last place. Upward shifts occur in Japan, which moves from sixth to first place; Sweden, which moves from eighth to second place; and the United States, which moves from twelfth to ninth

Exhibit 13-3
Mathematics Test Scores by Retentivity Ranks

	(1) % Retentivity	(2) Mean Math Score Total Sample	(3) Mean Math Score Upper 4%
Belgium	4	34.6	34.6
Germany	4.7	28.8	31.5
England	5	35.2	39.4
France	5	33.4	37.0
Netherlands	5	31.9	34.7
Scotland	5.4	25.5	29.4
Israel	7	36.4	41.7
Finland	7	25.3	32.1
Japan	8	31.4	43.9
Australia	14	21.6	33.7
Sweden	16	27.3	43.7
United States	18	13.8	33.0

Adapted from Husen, 1967: Vol. II, 118 and 122.

> place. In general, those countries with the least restrictive policies as to who will continue in school show the greatest upward shifts, while those countries with stricter selection policies and practices show the greatest downward shifts . . .

The *range* of difference between high- and low-performance countries also decreases when only the most able students are compared: the range in column two is from 13.8 for the United States to 36.4 for Israel, a difference of 22.6 score points; in column three the mean score ranges from 29.4 for Scotland to 43.9 for Japan, a difference of only 14.5.

> This would support the proposition that countries do *not* differ considerably in the proportions of students talented in math, but that the differences in selection policies and practices cloud the picture. It is at least a feasible suggestion that the "cream" of mathematical talent is distributed equally over the various countries and that it is only the procedures for diluting the cream that vary from country to country.
>
> These findings can have important implications for educational policy and practice. The view that the lowering of selection barriers would lead to decline in achievement and, especially, a reduction in achievement among the cream of a nation's talent is questioned by these data. The results indicate that the most talented students continue to achieve at a high level, even when as much as 70 percent of the age group is enrolled in full-time schooling. (Husen, 1967: Vol. II, 122–123)

Another way to consider the retentivity issue is to select some level of test performance as an international "standard" and then to see what proportions of students in various countries achieve these scores or higher. The IEA data showed that the proportion of a total age group achieving a predetermined test score was positively related to the proportion still in school, suggesting that a country can increase its "total mathematical yield" by increasing its "intake" of students (Husen, 1967: Vol. II, 134).

A school-system characteristic also used as an independent variable was specialization—that is, whether a student attends a school that provides a single course of study (academic, vocational, or general) or a comprehensive school that provides a variety of courses. The authors' prediction was that the level of math achievement would be higher in the former than the latter. The data analysis was complicated and the findings disappointingly ambiguous. The problem of classifying schools in different countries in terms of a uniform measure of comprehensiveness has been pointed out already, and it appears that any conclusive interpretation of the data already collected waits upon a more adequate codification of this dimension. All that the authors could conclude from an extended comparison of different types of schools both within and between countries was that any initial advantage gained by students in specialized academic preparatory schools over their peers in more comprehensive schools is largely overcome by the preuniversity level. The presence of students with lower ability or students following general or vocational courses of study does not in itself have a negative effect upon those headed for universities. Moreover, nonacademic students in comprehensive schools seemed to do rather better than students following similar courses in separate schools (Husen, 1967: Vol. II, 101–102).

The effects upon achievement of two of the individual-student characteristics we have studied already are much clearer than the effects of school structural attributes. One individual characteristic is socioeconomic background. A regression analysis aimed at assessing the relative contribution of a number of different independent variables to the differences in test scores indicated that family background accounted for the greatest share of the variation (Husen, Vol. II, Chapter 6). For the thirteen-year-olds, the relationship between father's education and mathematics performance is significant in all cases (with the single exception of Finland in Population 1a). A similar relationship occurs between father's occupation and math scores. For the older students, on the other hand, the correlations are smaller and occasionally in the opposite direction (in Finland, Sweden, and Germany, the lower-SES students had higher test scores than the upper-SES students). This apparently reflects the fact that, except in the United States, the selection process is such that only the most able students in the lower-SES groups are still in school by the preuniversity year (Husen, 1967: Vol. II, 208–209).

The study provides replications of the sex differences that were the subject of Chapter 5. At every level and in most countries, boys were more interested in mathematics than girls and outperformed them. The exceptions were France and England, where the girls who were specializing in math (Population 3a) had higher interest scores than their male counterparts. "This may be understood in terms of these girls being so highly selected (almost six boys for every girl) that those girls admitted to mathematics specialization must be among the most highly motivated students'' (Husen, 1967: Vol. II, 258). Finally, achievement in mathematics on the national level was correlated with attitudes toward learning. In general, the countries with the highest average math scores were those in which the highest proportions of respondents

felt that mathematics was important to the future of human society

expressed liking for school and school learning (the least favorable attitudes were expressed by students from the United States, followed by the other English-speaking countries. Japanese students were most likely to express positive attitudes)

felt that human beings have effective control and mastery of their environment (Husen, 1967: Vol. II, 44–48).

A second wave of surveys extended the study to six additional subjects (science, literature, reading comprehension, English and French as foreign languages, and civics) and expanded the list of participating countries to twenty-one, though not all countries participated in all subject surveys. During this second phase, efforts were also made to expand the representation of less-developed nations, and Chile, India, Iran, and Thailand joined the roster. Seven volumes of findings plus some additional technical reports were published in the 1970s.[8]

In all subjects, the differences in average test scores between the relatively affluent, developed societies and the poorer, less-developed societies were very large. Although some of these differences might be explained by the cultural inappropriateness of some tests for some children, a more convincing hypothesis explaining the very low achievement of the poorer countries is the dual poverty-deprivation in students' environments both in- and outside of school. Not only do the poorer countries have less to spend on education, but many have experienced a crushing growth in enrollment in recent years (as indicated in the analysis by Meyer *et al.* discussed earlier in this chapter), which has further strained their already limited educational resources. Likewise, on all measures of home and community environment, from parents' education and income to access to books, television, and radio, the relative disadvantage of children in less-developed countries is huge.

By contrast, the differences in average test scores among the developed societies are not very great. When one compares students of the same age, grade level, and selectivity, ''one is hard pressed to guess successfully what a student's score will be from knowing his national citizenship'' (Inkeles, 1977: 156). While between-country differences do exist—for example, the science scores are somewhat higher in the Japanese and Hungarian samples than in other samples, and French language scores are somewhat higher for Rumania—no country has consistently higher or lower average scores in all subjects. Apparently, once a nation's educational system is over some kind of critical threshold, its overall educational efficiency is fairly similar to that of other nations at similar levels of development. Taken as a whole, the findings from the several subjects evaluated in the second phase counter the criticism of the American educational system that resulted from reports of the survey on math achievement—that is, that American students made a poor showing in international competition and that the weaknesses in our schools posed a threat to our national security.

The IEA findings do not rule out the existence of distinctive national or cultural factors that account for differential performance in various school subjects. For example, the authoritarian structure of traditional Japanese families and schools, and the dependence-training, group orientation, and fear of failure that seem to characterize Japanese socialization (Silberman, 1962; Benedict, 1946; Lebra, 1976) may explain the skill of Japanese students at mastering scientific facts and mathematical reasoning. But neither the IEA data nor the largely ethnographic research literature on Japanese character and culture provide a model of *how* particular modes of socialization operate to produce particular learning outcomes. Moreover, the same socialization patterns have also been hypothesized as producing the opposite learning outcomes. For example, John Holt and other radical critics have argued that American children fail to learn *because* the conventional classroom structure squelches autonomy and creativity and induces a fear of failure. The IEA analyses to date suggest that differences among the developed countries in the sample are better explained by differences in the distribution of resources—in particular by differences in time inputs—than by differences in national character or patterns of socialization.

Finally, the IEA findings indicate that the small effects of school "quality" relative to the overriding effects of family background that have been found in most American studies before and after the Coleman Report may not be generalizable to all societies. Coleman's conclusion that school resources make little or no contribution to academic achievement is probably applicable to societies in which all or almost all schools have adequate supplies of textbooks and writing materials, sufficient space for the size of the student body, and an adequate supply of adequately trained teachers, but until a society reaches a minimum level of economic security, it seems likely that "the poverty of resources in the school, itself a reflection of the poverty of resources available in the society at large, puts the students at a marked disadvantage in competition with those from more developed countries" (Inkeles, 1977: 167). Likewise, while the IEA data did indicate relationships between family background and academic achievement in all of the countries studied, the amount of test-score variance explained by home background factors varied considerably from one country to another. In Sweden and Australia, for example, these factors accounted for only half as much of the variance as they did in the United States sample. Sweden, like Israel and the People's Republic of China, has a national policy of reducing the correlation of school success with accidents of birth, and the IEA data suggest that the Swedes have already made progress toward this goal. The general point is that hypotheses that explain achievement in American schools—or the schools of any single society—may not be generalizable to other societies, and that crosscultural comparisons are the most direct way to correct faulty generalizations as well as research ethnocentrism.

Conclusions

If, as Durkheim postulated, schools reflect the larger society of which they are a part, one can only understand the educational system of any society by understanding the society itself, including the structure and interrelations of its most important institutions and the values and techniques by which children are socialized. A corollary of Durkheim's hypothesis is that if one wants to "do something" about the school system one must "do something" about other societal systems that interact with the educational system.

The data now available do not allow us to be very precise about the effects of crosscultural variables upon academic achievement and their interaction with other independent variables. There is a wealth of case study materials describing national education systems, past and present, and there are some crosscultural studies on the experiences of children outside of school that may affect their attitudes toward learning and their performance in formal educational settings. However, with the exception of the IEA, there are virtually no systematically conceived and conducted comparisons between sizable samples of students in a number of different societies. A few sociologists have attempted to develop typologies by which national systems can be classified on dimensions derived from sociological theory, but Husen's summary of the situation at the end of the first phase of the IEA—"we still have a long way to go before we will have crossnationally codified independent variables to describe the most important dimensions of school systems"—seems to describe the present state of conceptual development as well.

The evidence examined in this chapter has indicated that there are great differences between societies in what and how children learn, but that the major division is between the industrially developed, affluent societies of the world and the poor, developing ones. Indeed the substantial gap between rich and poor nations on all of the IEA survey results leads many analysts to the conclusion that the deficits caused by several environmental deprivations are beyond the capacities of the educational system to repair. And some critics, like Ivan Illich, feel that the costs of national educational systems in poor countries so outstrip the resources of such countries, and that the chances of poor countries "catching up" educationally to richer nations are so slim that compulsory education should be abolished altogether. On the other hand, nations at similar levels of economic development show similar overall levels of academic achievement, and the differences that do exist seem to be better explained by differential patterns of resource allocation than by any meaningful differences in national character or culture.

Crosscultural studies have replicated the finding in American studies that the status of children's families and the kinds of experiences they have in their homes have considerable impact on their success in school. However, the relative effects of home and school quality seem to differ from one society to another. The importance of additional school resources may be greater in developing nations than in developed ones, and the experience of at least a few societies suggests that the effects of family background may not be so overriding and irreversible as American research often implies.

Although there are worldwide trends toward increasing the equality of educational opportunities, in no society has the expansion of opportunities per se removed social class, ethnic, and gender differences in educational attainment. Instead expansion has occurred by a "filtering down" process whereby educational "demand" is satiated in the upper social strata before there is a great increase in noncompulsory school attendance by lower-status children. Some countries are making conspicuous efforts to change this pattern (for instance, Sweden, Israel, and the People's Republic of China), but nowhere do the schools overcome the inequalities with which children begin school.

Notes

1. In addition to Bettelheim's book, the best-known and most comprehensive accounts are Spiro, 1965, and Neubauer, 1965. For a bibliography of research on the kibbutz in English, see Shur, 1962.

2. For collections of official documents on education in communist China, see Fraser, 1965; and *Studies in Comparative Communism,* Volume 3, July/October 1970.

3. The army experience does not have quite the importance for females as for males. There is constant pressure from conservative religious factions to eliminate the women's army altogether, and women can be fairly easily excused from army service for religious or family reasons. There are also strong sex differences in the work performed, with females engaged disproportionately in teaching and office work.

4. For an excellent review of the major conceptions and trends in Israeli compensatory education, see Peleg and Adler, 1977. Recent research on school education is discussed in a special issue of *Megamot,* the major Israeli behavioral science journal (Volume XXIII, December 1977. English summaries of the papers are included). Recognition of the high quality of Israeli scholarship is evidenced by a grant in 1976 from the Ford Foundation to support work in this area by Israeli researchers.

5. Australia, Belgium, England, Federal Republic of Germany, Finland, France, Israel, Japan, Netherlands, Scotland, Sweden, and the United States.

6. For a full report on the sampling problems and procedures, see Volume I, Chapter 9. A detailed discussion and critique of the methodology by a scholar not connected with the IEA project is contained in Inkeles, 1977.

7. A full discussion of test construction can be found in Volume I, Chapter 5.

8. For references to the full set of IEA studies, see Inkeles 1977.

PART FIVE

Conclusion

Where We Are and Where We Are Going   Chapter 14

As we shall have more than one occasion to note, the evolution of education always lags very substantially behind the general evolution of society as a whole. We shall encounter new ideas spreading throughout the whole of society without palpably affecting the University corporation, without modifying either its course of study or its method of teaching. . . . Educational transformations are always the results and the symptom of the social transformations in terms of which they are to be explained. In order for a people to feel at any particular moment in time the need to change its education system, it is necessary that new ideas and needs have emerged for which the former system is no longer adequate. Emile Durkheim

The federal government has been initiating experiments and other research activities with schools for almost a decade. What is most noticeable is that schools have gotten worse during this period.   James S. Coleman

Nearly anything can happen in a place called a school.   Christopher Jencks

In Chapters 3 through 13 we examined a large body of empirical evidence organized by the level of the educational system to which it referred. In this final chapter we shall return to the questions raised and the theoretical and methodological alternatives posed in the first two chapters. To what extent does our evidence provide the "body of guiding ideas" we stated as our objective in Chapter 1? Are we closer to good theoretical models that explain the findings we have accumulated and identify the most important things we do not know? Can we specify the research strategies that will be most useful for testing our emerging theories of learning and for filling in the gaps in our information about learning environments and processes?

In Chapter 2 we argued that the major alternative explanations for differences in learning were: theories that explained learning differences by differences in the characteristics of the learners; theories that explained learning differences by differences in schools' external environments; and theories that explained learning differences by differences in the patterns of socialization and nurturance, the structural characteristics, and the technology of schools themselves (pages 18–21 and Exhibit 2–1). The general theoretical perspectives and the empirical research that have been most influential among sociologists have emphasized the importance of factors outside of the school—that is, explanations on the left side of Exhibit 2–1. Durkheim's insistence that the school is "only the image and reflection of society" is not only consistent with the conclusions of recent studies using sophisticated survey techniques, but also raised basic questions about the potentiality of schools as instruments of social reform that are still being debated by Jencks and others. Weber's model of bureaucratic structure, which he postulated as characteristic of all modern institutions but as originating in the governmental institutions of certain societies and only later permeating the educational system, is still the basis of much of the critical literature on American schools. And Marxian theory is the basis of a body of empirical research on schooling that posits the educational system as shaped and manipulated by elites who use the schools to justify their own privileges and to maintain the status quo.

Much of the empirical research published in recent years has emphasized the importance of external over internal factors. In studies like the *Equality of Educational Opportunity* survey, variables describing the background characteristics and home experiences of individual students and the composition of the school's student body explained more of the variance in achievement than did school facilities, characteristics of the teachers and curriculum, and other features of the school as a social system. Jencks concluded that the achievement differences between students in the same schools are generally far greater than the differences between the average student in one school and the average student in another. The Carnegie Council on Children, commissioned to evaluate the problems and prospects of the American family, concluded that the dominance of the family as an institution may be declining but that children's success in school is still very much a function of their family's position in society. In research at the community level, population characteristics such as SES and income levels have explained as much as 85 percent of the between-school variance on various measures of academic performance. Finally, crosscultural research has documented large differences in academic performance between the developed and developing nations of the world and has replicated the relationships between family status and educational attainment found in the United States, although the strength of family-quality effects relative to school-quality effects appears to differ quite markedly from one society to another. In sum, a large amount of research on the sociology of education can be summarized by Arnold Anderson's conclusion that schools modify but rarely transcend the influences of other institutions (Anderson, 1974).

While research documenting the effects of factors outside of schools seems to have dominated the sociology of education during the past decade, there has also been a revival of interest in studies of the schooling process, particularly at the classroom level. Sociological interest in the classroom undoubtedly received impetus from the work of radical critics like John Holt, James Herndon, Herbert Kohl, and Jonathan Kozol, whose work has decided shortcomings as sociological research, but who offer some important insights into school social processes as well as a criticism of the functionalist theoretical perspective (as represented by Parson's analysis of the classroom in 1959 and Dreeben's *On What Is Learned in School*), which has influenced almost all sociological thinking about the classroom since the 1950s.

Another impetus to research on schools and school effectiveness has come from the growing resistance of minority scholars to the labeling of minority children and the implication that minority culture and modes of child rearing are deficient. At the forefront of this resistance are Kenneth Clark and Ron Edmonds, who insist that the poorer academic records of poor black children are not explained by inadequacies in the children's families or general culture, but by the inadequacies of their schools and the many forms of cultural and racial inequities that they suffer. "Schools teach those they think they must and when they think they needn't they don't" (Edmonds, n.d.: 3), and the culture-of-poverty theory absolves educators from the responsibility to teach all children competently. Edmonds and colleagues at the Harvard Graduate School of Education have been involved in studies of effective schools that point to the significance of administrative policies and practices on the quality of classroom instruction and in turn on children's learning.[1] Clark's belief in the power of schools to overcome the disadvantages of poverty and prejudice is illustrated in his plan for reform of the Washington, D.C., public schools (Clark, 1972), although more recently he has expressed pessimism over the likelihood of such reforms ever being implemented.

During the past decade there has been an outpouring of sociological research on topics ranging from classroom power relations to peer group status and interaction, teaching styles, spatial arrangements, and classroom and school social climate. Influenced by interactionist theoretical perspectives (as opposed to earlier models that assumed unidirectional causal effects), most sociological research on learning now assumes that students and teachers have mutual effects on each other, that the sequence of interactive exchanges over time must be traced in order to understand the ultimate outcomes, and that a given classroom situation may be differentially perceived by and have different effects upon different individuals or subgroups. Recent research on the classroom has also revealed a number of ways in which social and technological structure can be (and has been) manipulated, although the actual effects of recent structural innovations—in particular the tendency toward more flexible, informal classroom structure, which has characterized American schools during the past decade—were not always anticipated and are not yet clearly understood. About all that can be concluded from the evaluation research to date is that the open classroom and other nontraditional learning environments may have a number of desirable effects upon interpersonal relationships, but that cognitive development and academic performance are not necessarily enhanced in such settings.

While much of the empirical evidence reviewed in this book is consistent with general themes developed by the classical theorists, a fully developed theory or theories explaining the causes of differential school learning does not yet exist. Indeed, much research has been justifiably criticized for simply correlating input and output measures without specifying causal relationships or even examining their interaction in the actual learning situation. This research approach is sometimes referred to as the "black box" model, because, as one pair of researchers describes it, "teaching goes in, and the student performance comes out, and no one really knows what goes on inside the box" (Dubin and Taveggia, 1968: 10). On the other hand, at least some of the evidence reviewed is based upon a "grounded theory" approach—that is, on watching and listening to students and teachers in everyday school situations.[2] Thus if the whole still eludes us, we seem to have at least pieces of a theoretical model, or links in the causal chain of relationships explaining learning differences. The following paragraphs will describe some of the links.

At the level of the individual learner, the work of Bernstein, Labov, Entwisle, and others who have studied sociolinguistic development suggests a causal chain whereby accidents of birth (in particular the social class into which a child is born) lead to differential patterns of socialization within the family (particularly with respect to the learning of language and role-playing skills). The closer the linguistic and behavior "codes" learned in the home mesh with those of the formal educational system, the greater the probability of the child's success in school.

At the level of the school, research by McDill, Coleman, and others suggests a model whereby the attributes and attitudes of the individual school members combine to produce a normative or value climate (though the process by which this happens has not been clearly specified), which in turn affects the nature of the interaction in the classroom and the aspirations and achievements of individual learners. Also within the school, learning or achievement levels can be increased by:

increasing the responsiveness of teachers (or nonhuman teaching resources) to students

redressing the asymmetries of the student-teacher relationship in the direction of making the student role more like the teacher role

providing more immediate and direct rewards for appropriate learning behavior, a higher ratio of rewards to punishments, and a mixture of individual- and group-reward contingencies

increasing the amount of direct student exposure to learning (this conclusion is reached from a synthesis of disparate findings such as the relationships found between achievement levels and: quantity of instruction and study time; student absentee rates; ratio of classroom teachers to administrative and special services personnel; and level of principal involvement and leadership in matters pertaining directly to classroom instruction)

At the level of the external environment, effects on learning seem to be mainly a function of the differential availability and commitment of resources to schools by communities and governmental agencies, although communities, like schools, may have value climates that encourage or discourage various forms of achievement. For example, communities in which the adults care very much about having winning football and basketball teams are likely to have high schools in which a high proportion of the most able students are more motivated to become athletic stars than brilliant students; and schools often gain a good or bad "reputation" because of the neighborhoods in which they are located. Some sociologists, like Meyer, have argued that the world itself now constitutes a social system, whose value system penetrates all nations and causes similar patterns of educational expansion regardless of differences between nations in political ideology and socioeconomic development.

Changing the Schools

Almost as soon as the school emerged as a distinct institution, people proposed ways of changing it. Utopian literature, from Plato's *Republic* to More's *Utopia*, and more recently Skinner's *Walden Two*, Huxley's *Island*, and a number of science fiction novels, contains many descriptions of the ideal education. While the details differ from one utopia to another, learning in most of them occurs in a pleasant, noninstitutional setting. Instruction tends to be informal, often in the form of games or simulations of adult activities that prepare the young to move into adulthood with a minimum of stress. Few have anything like a formal curriculum; grading is rejected as an insult to the learning process. Teachers are usually young and beautiful, always dedicated and effective, never harried or illprepared. Disorderly or apathetic students and bureaucratic administrators are notably absent.

While utopian novels offer them little in the way of feasible strategies for the reform of real life schools, sociologists have long been concerned with the extent to which the social organization of schools has changed, or can be made to change. The 1960s were a time of unusual creativity with respect to social structural innovations in schools, as evidenced by the large number and variety of alternative schools that were begun during these years. Although most of these pedagogical experiments were shortlived, their very existence provided sociologists with a rich source of data on the limits of possible variation in school social structure—as well as illustrating Robert Merton's Law of Human Society: Whatever is, is possible.[3] The reformist spirit of the 1960s has been largely dissipated by the sobering realization that none of the teaching innovations launched with such high hopes during that period offered a panacea for our enduring educational problems, and that solution of these problems probably called for investments of time, money, and other resources that were beyond the capacities of most school systems. However, efforts to redress educational inequities and failures have not ceased; they have if anything increased with the growth of the sociology of education as a major sociological subdivision. We shall mention here just a few of the more significant efforts.

Within the school, most recent reforms have focused upon "loosening" the social structure and physical space (that is, upon cells seven and eight of Exhibit 2–1), allowing students more freedom to move about, to interact with each other, and to decide themselves how they will spend their time in school. Recent technological changes have been more in the form of moving or removing constraining walls and furniture, less in the form of inventing new teaching devices that will revolutionize the learning process (as educators in the previous decade hoped that teaching machines, simulation games, and computer-based instruction might do). The unrestrained spontaneity that was the byword of the numerous but short-lived free schools based on the Summerhill model[4] has been replaced by what one might term the structured choice of the open-classroom model, where children are allowed to choose from a cafeteria of attractive but adult-designed learning activities and where group cooperation as well as individual achievement is encouraged and rewarded.

Few within-school reforms in this country focus on cells five and six of Exhibit 2–1, that is, on the way that students' mental and physical characteristics are developed by the school. While many critics decry the overemphasis on development of a narrow range of cognitive skills, and some argue for a return to some kind of moral education in the schools, few visualize schools in our society as having the broad responsibility for physical, moral, and intellectual development, within an ideological framework of service to the larger society, that is explicitly assigned to the schools in the People's Republic of China or the Israeli kibbutz. One of the few sociological models that focuses upon maximizing student growth is Bredemeier's "nurturance" model of schooling, which he contrasts to the sifting or classifying model that follows from functionalist theoretical assumptions.

> Conceived as nurturing structures, schools are more like horticultural stations that first sort plants into those that need one kind of treatment to maximize their growth and those that need another kind; and then tailor treatments to needs. The purpose of testing in such schools would be . . . to discover what had been the result of the interaction between the individual and his experience. What is commonly called "failure" on a test would be understood in very different terms; namely, as a signal that whatever had been the individual's experiences with a particular teaching style or pedagogical method or what not, they were not the experiences necessary to give him the qualities that would have resulted in a different score. . . . Tests in this context would be understood as being like tests for blood sugar in a *medical* setting, not a military recruitment or occupational placement setting. (Bredemeier, 1968: 21)

Bredemeier acknowledges that we are far from understanding the optimum techniques for nurturing students' intellectual and social growth—that "it is not at all clear what are, in the cultivation of human potentials, the educational analogies of fertilizer, nitrogen, water temperature, and so on." Thus schools themselves are conceived as laboratories or research institutes as well as training sites, where staff and students will be engaged in distinguishing among different pedagogical methods and matching them with student characteristics and needs.[5]

A second major approach to educational reform is to link the school more closely with the "outside world," in particular the home, the community, and the work place. Some of these reforms attempt to involve—some would say reinvolve—the family in educational activities with the child. Home-based or home-intervention programs are still in the experimental stages, and most such programs in this country are rather small-scale efforts to provide parents with materials on child development or toys and games to enhance children's physical and mental development. One of the few, fully developed, home-intervention models is the Israeli home-instruction program developed by Lombard (mentioned in Chapters 4 and 13), in which mothers in disadvantaged neighborhoods are trained in a highly structured, sequential program of instruction that they then teach to their own preschool children. While the learning effects of the program are still being evaluated, it has already been widely disseminated in many areas of Israel, and the data that have been analyzed indicate effects on parents, siblings, and the community at large, in addition to its intended impact on the preschool child. Lombard reports, for example, that even illiterate mothers have been spurred into learning the skills needed to teach their children, and the indigenous aides recruited to train the mothers now comprise a new paraprofessional group that has provided many lower-class women with opportunities for occupational mobility (Lombard, 1973).

Attempts to reduce the insulation of schools are more likely to focus on older students, often by way of greater attention to career education—for example, increasing the number or updating the substance of courses oriented toward helping students make informed career choices, exposing students to working adults, both in and outside of the classroom, or arranging work placements in local businesses and government agencies.

Probably the most comprehensive attempt to break down the barriers between the classroom and the community is the "school without walls," a model designed to maximize two-way interchanges between the school and its environment and to encourage learning not only from books but also more directly from people actually engaged in a particular subject or occupation. In the first two schools based on this model—the Parkway Program, begun in Philadelphia in 1969, and Metro, a Chicago school that opened a year later—a variety of individuals in addition to the regular faculty were brought in to teach about their particular field of expertise, and students went out into the community to seek information, instruction, and experience. The initial curriculum at Metro included:

a course on the newspaper, run by the *Chicago Sun Times,* during which students accompanied reporters on assignments

a course on dissent taught by the American Civil Liberties Union

a course on the ethnic and economic structure of the city, based upon student interviews with people on the streets of Chicago

a Spanish course in which students spent time conversing with residents of the city's Spanish-speaking communities

The most ardent supporters of the school-without-walls principle admit that the costs would be prohibitive for an entire school system and that probably it would not work with many students and teachers even if it were economically feasible. Neither of the first two tests of the model now exists in anything like its original form, and reports on the results—like reports on many experimental schools—describe the energy drain on the faculty as well as the heavy burden on other school and community resources (Center for New Schools, 1970).

An even more extreme view of eliminating the barriers between schools and their environments would eliminate compulsory education altogether. Ivan Illich, the author of widely read works on "deschooling" society (1970 and 1971), argues that not only can no nation afford a truly effective national education system, but that excessive faith in formal education perpetuates rather than eliminates social-caste systems, both within and between nations. Rather than continuing to pour ever more resources into formal educational systems, we should put our efforts into matching up individuals who want to learn a particular subject or skill with someone who will teach it to them, or organizing groups of individuals who wish to pursue some topic of common interest. Illich's published writings on deschooling society leave a number of questions unanswered, such as how his "unlicensed exchange of skills" would be financed and administered, how children would be motivated to learn the important but tediously acquired verbal and computational skills needed for survival in modern societies, and how individuals with valuable knowledge and skills would be motivated and rewarded for taking the trouble to impart them to others.

Illich also assumes that all or most human beings want to learn—the problem lies in the structure of obligatory formal education, not in individual attitudes and capacities. Carl Bereiter, whose arguments against compulsory education go beyond Illich's in certain respects, claims that this assumption is unwarranted. There is no evidence, he says, that very many people by nature desire knowledge. Since, moreover, formal education is innately authoritarian, nonequalitarian, irrational, and not very effective, people should have the right not to be educated. Bereiter does distinguish between training and education; it is the latter he feels should not be compulsory. Training, without all the trappings of education, should have a more honorable place in society, and the program Bereiter and Engelman developed for Head Start children (1966) is based upon these views. As Bereiter describes it:

> It simply gave intensive training to young children in reading, arithmetic, and expository language with no effort to shape personality or attitudes or to transform lower-class children into middle-class ones culturally. Nevertheless, unlike the typical Head Start program, this program did have an impact on children that was visible to the naked eye. For this we were accused of racism, fascism, playing God, of turning children into robots and destroying their childhood, their culture, their language, and so on.
>
> For a while I was puzzled by the violence of these reactions, but gradually it came to me that, although the changes we were producing in children were only changes in skills, they seemed like radical changes; and anyone who started producing radical changes in people could expect to provoke the same kinds of outrage and alarm. (Bereiter, 1974: 22–23)

While acknowledging the many weaknesses of formal educational systems, Hurn cautions against romanticizing the supposed benefits of breaking down the barriers between school and community and of "real" experience in the work place. Work placements for young people that provide anything beyond low-level, repetitive tasks are rare in a technologically developed society with an overcrowded labor market. And noting a tendency in recent years to make the local community or neighborhood the "focus of many of the hopes of those disillusioned with formal institutions," Hurn points out that not many communities are equipped to provide the kinds of personalized educational experiences that the reformers want.

> We can, and perhaps should, deplore the trends away from the solidary community in recent decades, trends, of course, that have led inexorably to the assumption of more and more responsibilities by specialized institutions previously the province of the community and the neighborhood. But we should not confuse a wish that the community should again become an organic and solidary institution with the assumption that it is already resurrected and ready to take on its traditional responsibilities of educating the young. (Hurn, 1978: 274)

In the view of most contemporary sociologists, educational change, like educational structure, reflects the time and place in which it occurs (or is proposed). Examination of historical and comparative materials also suggests a cyclical or back-and-forth quality about the major changes in educational systems—for example, the shifts between demands for centralization and decentralization of urban school systems documented by Ravitch; between demands for more attention to the "basics" and more attention to children's socioemotional development; between assignment of the major responsibility for learning to teachers or schools, with students as relatively passive beneficiaries or recipients of learning, and to students, with schools as mere providers of opportunities to learn.[6]

It is probably also true that any particular reform can deal with only a portion of the educational system or a subset of educational problems. Thus one of the most valuable services sociologists may contribute to the educational enterprise is to sensitize would-be reformers to the operation of educational systems as systems and to the ways in which reforms directed at one element of the system may have effects—sometimes undesired effects—on other elements. In the remaining pages of this book, we shall say more about the role of the sociologist as educational researcher and the kinds of research that seem to us most profitable for the immediate future.

The Sociologist's Contribution

Few students of the schooling process would disagree with the statement of the Swiss sociologist Kurt Lüscher that "as a rule the richly varied genetic potential is not exhausted to the full as a result of social environment" (Lüscher, 1971: 26), but there is a great deal of uncertainty over the appropriate role of the sociologist in the educational enterprise. There would seem to be at least three distinct role models, which I have termed for simplicity the *conceptualizer*, the *fact-finder*, and the *activist*.

In an article on the contributions of sociology to the field of education published twenty years ago, Gross summarized the conceptualist position as follows: "What the sociologist has to offer is basically a series of sensitizing and analytic concepts and ideas that will allow the practitioner to examine in a more realistic and more incisive way the multiple forces operating in his social environment" (Gross, 1959: 287). Many still feel that this is the appropriate position for the sociologist of education. In a recent review of the uses of social science in educational policy decisions, Levin (1976) concluded that research can best be used to frame the issues rather than "to obtain conclusive evidence on what is right and what is to be done" in a particular situation. And it does seem that the major payoffs in many substantive areas of sociology of education now depend more on theoretical development than on further instrumentation or data gathering, a point we shall return to later.

By contrast, others feel that the major function of the sociology of education is to provide reliable factual information on a wide range of specific educational problems and programs (see, for example, the quotation by Dyer at the beginning of Chapter 2). This approach is probably most valuable when it involves going beyond simple factfinding to search for the "unintended and unanticipated consequences of purposive social action" (Clark *et al.*, 1971: 2), though such an approach is not without hazard. As Coleman's career, in particular his research on the position of youth and on busing and white flight, makes abundantly clear, responsible research efforts do not always yield the results many people want to hear, and the researcher is often put in the unpleasant position of having to tell them what Max Weber termed "inconvenient facts" (Gerth and Mills, 1958: 147; see also Collins and Makowsky, 1978: 14–15).

Some favor a more active role for the sociologist of education, whether it involves designing and administering new schools and instructional materials or acting as advocate for a particular pedagogical model. Examples of the former are the simulation-games project at Johns Hopkins University, in which a group of sociologists constructed a series of instructional games simulating certain features of the socioeconomic environment, tested them in a variety of educational settings, and conducted evaluative research on their effects (Boocock and Schild, 1968), or the John Adams High School, an experimental school in Portland, Oregon, based on the model of the teaching hospital, which was designed and administered by a group of young social scientists who had been classmates at the Harvard Graduate School of Education (Fletcher, 1970).

Another variation of the activist role is advocacy sociology, which puts the sociologist in a role similar to a lawyer pleading a case for a client. Arguing that it is impossible for any piece of research to present a balanced picture of a complex educational issue, Rivlin proposes a "forensic social science" model, with the following procedures for assuring that all sides will be fairly represented:

> scholars or teams of scholars take on the task of writing briefs for or against particular policy positions. They state what the position is and bring together all the evidence that supports their side of the argument, leaving to the brief writers of the other side

the job of picking apart the case that has been presented and detailing the counter evidence. (Rivlin, 1973: 25. For a critical analysis of advocacy sociology, see Havighurst, 1975.)

A Research Agenda

The choice of research topic depends on many things, including the goodness-of-fit between the problems that educators find most pressing and the problems that researchers find intellectually interesting and suitable to the methodological tools at their disposal, as well as the research role model that fits the researcher most comfortably. The brief research agenda that follows undoubtedly reflects the interests and biases of the author as much as a rational set of implications drawn from the evidence presented in the preceding chapters. It should also be noted that not all scholars agree on the need for further research. Some of the reservations expressed appear to be grounded in a reluctance to gather yet more new data when so much already available has not been fully exploited (for example, Gordon, 1976), but at least a few scholars feel strongly that we already know enough to teach all children effectively, including the children of the poor, and that our failure to do so is far more a matter of politics than a matter of an inadequate research base (for example, Edmonds, n.d.).

While we basically agree with the many proponents of research conducted in the "natural setting" of the school—that is, of efforts to study more directly the actual workings of the "black box"—it does not seem that much more is to be gained by further descriptive case studies of a single class or school, at least until more highly developed theories enable us to place the findings from a particular situation in a more general context. Two kinds of research in natural settings that seem more useful at this point are: (1) multiple studies of natural experiments in education, especially where it is feasible for a researcher or team of researchers to observe an experiment from beginning to end; and (2) studies of learning environments in which experimental manipulation by the researcher is possible.

Natural experiments in education exemplify the kind of "intense but short-lived social phenomena" that Benjamin Zablocki finds a valuable source of evidence on social processes that are difficult for sociologists to isolate in the larger, slower-changing, formal organizations that comprise most of our social world. Zablocki is himself a student of intentional communities or communes, particularly the communitarian movement that flourished in this country during the 1960s and early 1970s. His interest in communes was generated by his belief that, because they experienced more radical and rapid change and had on the average shorter lives than more conventional communities, they offered one of the few natural sites for observing the entire life cycle of a social system large enough to contain all the major features of social structure but small enough to be studied as a whole by one or a small group of researchers—and moreover, that their existence was likely to occur within a time frame that allowed "study of processes whose natural time scales mesh with the time scale of research" (Zablocki, 1980: Chapter 1). Zablocki's study of over a hundred experimental communities is much more than an engrossing account of an exotic social variation; it provides rich comparative materials in sufficient quantity to reveal patterns in the emergence of normative order in such communities and the social factors that promote or destroy community stability.

Similarly, a report on a conference on alternative schools (Center for New Schools, 1972), attended by some thirty people who had designed, taught in, or studied such schools not only revealed an unexpected similarity of experience among a sizable sample of educational "inventions," each of whose creators had believed that it represented a unique learning community, but also provided valuable sociological evidence on the general processes of decision making in schools and the relationships between decision making and student attitudes, staff attitudes, and institutional context (for example, size, location, student-body composition, and relations with funding and accrediting agencies). The materials gathered on no-longer-existing experimental schools can of course be reanalyzed by sociologists, but it is regrettable that so few were extensively studied while they were "alive" by researchers not involved in their design and/or daily operation. Trained research teams prepared to identify promising educational experiments and to gather comparable data on their structure and dynamics throughout at least a major segment of their existence would seem to be a valuable research innovation.

As we saw in Chapter 2, the controlled experiment is generally held up as the ideal type of educational research. In fact it is a standard that is very difficult to approach in most real-life school situations. One of the most extensive and thoroughly evaluated experimental studies in recent years was the Planned Variation project, in which a large number of different pedagogical models were tested in a number of different Head Start and Follow Through programs throughout the country. The Planned Variation project was remarkable for its length and scope. Over thirty different models were tested in the Follow Through programs alone between 1968 and 1971, and over a thousand adults were involved in some phase of the project. However, the proceedings of a conference sponsored by the Brookings Institution in 1973, for the purpose of reviewing what had been learned from the project, documented the multiple difficulties of conducting large-scale field studies with experimental controls. The major problems seemed to be those of implementation, control, and length of any experimental treatment and evaluation. The editors of the conference report point out that the niceties of experimental design are only a small part of what must be taken into account in implementing successful experimental projects in school systems.

> If the technique of experimentation is to become a routine feature of educational program evaluation, detailed methodological knowledge of what constitutes a well-constructed experiment must be supplemented by equally detailed knowledge of the political and administrative intricacies of the existing educational system. The combination of the two is essential both because it gives foreknowledge of the administrative complexities of experimentation and because it contributes to the usefulness of experimental results. (Rivlin and Timpane, 1975: 34)

Random selection of subjects and assignment to experimental and control treatments, an important requirement of experimental design, is also difficult if not impossible to accomplish in large-scale educational research. In fact, the project staff in this case had to work with communities that volunteered to participate in the project, and even a compromise procedure of random assignment of pedagogical models to a large number of communities invited to "volunteer" was found to be too expensive, and not all communities were willing to test all models.

Yet another problem that plagued the project at every phase was shortage of time. The participants reported that more time should have gone into the development of the models before large-scale field testing was undertaken, the development of better outcome measures corresponding to the cognitive and noncognitive objectives of early education in general and alternative models in particular, and the development of methods for "monitoring what actually happened to the children in the programs, and measuring the extent to which sponsor models were implemented in local sites" (Rivlin and Timpane, 1975: 16). The authors estimated that the entire sequence of research and development activities for such a project, from initial experiments of models to dissemination of field test experiences, would require ten to twelve years.

Thus Zablocki's argument for studying short-lived, natural experiments becomes additionally convincing. In the natural experiment, though, the researcher is at the mercy of his or her subject, since he or she cannot control even the choice of innovation to be tested, let alone the selection of research site and subjects and the manner in which the innovation is introduced and administered. Comparable alternative treatments or nontreatments are often inadequate or absent altogether. The Nachlaot Integration project in Jerusalem, discussed in Chapter 13, illustrates a smaller-scale and thus more feasible kind of controlled experimental design. The experimental treatments involved only four different models (ethnic integration versus nonintegration, with or without an open-classroom environment), in a small number of schools in a single city. Not surprisingly, the results were considerably more clear-cut than those of the Planned Variation project. The Nachlaot project does not, of course, provide enough information on alternative modes of integration to indicate whether the one tested was the most effective one available—or even whether integration itself is the most effective way to raise the achievement levels of minority children under all circumstances.

Thus another valuable line of future research would be to extend the pioneering work of Campbell and Stanley (1963; mentioned in Chapter 2) on the special problems of experimental design in educational research, in particular conceptualizing strategies for balancing the requirements of the classical experimental model against those of the political and administrative structure and dynamics of school systems, and balancing the optimum length and scope of a given research project against the feasibility of obtaining adequate funding and the need to make short-term decisions about curriculum and teaching practices. Furthermore, if experimental research that is large-scale and long-term enough to produce adequate tests of new learning models is to begin in the foreseeable future, researchers will have to learn to work in larger research teams than they have been accustomed to in the past, and they will also have to learn how to communicate the need for such expensive projects to public and private funding agencies more convincingly than they have in the past.

As the above recommendations may already have suggested, we do not feel that there is much more to be learned from further large surveys in which attempts are made to "explain" individual learning differences by statistical analysis of a large number of "independent" variables, until theoretical developments provide a sounder framework for linking the variables causally. Indeed, the continuing debate over the *Equality of Educational Opportunity* survey indicates that further statistical analysis of already available data will produce little except essentially unresolvable arguments over the order in which variables are "fed into" the analysis. Methodological developments have extended the realm of feasible empirical data analysis dramatically during the past decade, but they cannot in themselves identify the important questions to be asked about the sociology of education and the variations in students' experiences and environments that most directly affect their learning.

The frustrating ambiguities in the results of both the large cross-sectional surveys and the longitudinal or experimental research reported in this book point clearly to the need for much more concentrated attention to the dependent variable(s). Sociologists who agree on almost nothing else are united by their discontent with the overemphasis of most schools and most research on a narrow set of cognitive skills. This limitation has been decried in numerous publications, some of which have gone as far as listing alternative schooling outcomes (particularly in the reports by McPartland, Epstein, and their colleagues at the Johns Hopkins Center for Social Organization of Schools). The next step is to conceptualize several of these alternative outcomes more fully and to develop instruments for measuring them. Similarly, instruments to measure the effects of different learning models and educational innovations are needed, since most innovations are not intended to teach the things measured by currently available standardized tests.[7]

In sum, the kinds of future research that seem most promising are of the sort that will flesh out the skeletal structure presented in Exhibit 2–1, clarifying the dimensions—perhaps adding to the ones now in the diagram or revising the ones already there—and filling the cells with specific theories or hypotheses explaining different patterns of learning (or lack of learning) in different areas of the system diagrammed in Exhibit 1–1.

Finally, an important recent development that we feel should be encouraged is greater attention to the role of the researcher, including recognition of the limitations of research dominated by white, male, middle-class academicians. Particularly with respect to such sensitive issues as educational equality and the achievement of minority children, we have seen that the characteristics of who is doing the research are more than coincidentally correlated with the outcomes obtained. For example, we saw that minority scholars have found that high achievement among minority students is not always positively correlated with assimilation into the majority culture, which majority scholars have tended to take for granted. There is no way to correct all the potential biases resulting from researchers' own social status, but a more balanced picture of the important issues of achievement and equity may be obtained by supporting the training of more researchers from societal subgroups that have been underrepresented in the academic world and by supporting more research projects by colleagues varying in race, gender, social class, and age.

Randall Collins has commented that a major task in building a truly scientific sociology is "to free ourselves from the dead weight of ideological commitments implicitly molding our vision" (Collins, 1975: 24), and Alvin Gouldner, in *The Coming Crisis of Western Sociology*, calls for a "reflexive" sociology, which involves a "deepening of the sociologist's own awareness, of who and what he is, in a specific society at any given time, and of how both his social role and his personal praxis affect his work as a sociologist," a development he considers as important as skill in producing "valid-reliable bits of information" (Gouldner, 1970: 494). Moving the sociology of education to the next developmental stage requires a combination of theoretical and methodological sophistication, self-awareness, and capacity to conceptualize learning problems from multiple points of view that can certainly not be achieved without major changes in the way sociological research is conducted. Finding ways to make these changes is a demanding but clearly worthwhile quest.

Notes

1. Edmond's arguments are supported by some of the findings on school management productivity discussed in Chapter 7, in particular the study by Wellisch *et al.*, 1978.

2. For a discussion of grounded theory and its application to educational research, see Richer, 1975.

3. For descriptions of a number of alternative schools and reflections on their strengths and weaknesses, see the special issue of the *Harvard Educational Review* on Alternative Schools (Volume 43, No. 3, August, 1972), and the various reports of the Center for New Schools, in Chicago. Silberman (1970) provides a good overview of this innovative era in education.

4. Named after the British school founded by A.S. Neill and popularized in his book by that name (Neill, 1961). Another book that influenced the free-school movement in this country was George Leonard's *Education and Ecstacy* (1968), which insisted that the two were synonymous.

5. Probably the closest real-life approximation to the school-as-research-institute model was the John Adams High School, an experimental school in Portland, Oregon, modeled on the teaching hospital. The original plans called for research activities ranging from systematic interviewing of a 10 percent random sample of school members to regular measurement of school climate to a computerized analysis of the costs and outcomes of alternative innovative teaching programs (Fletcher *et al.*, 1970). Unfortunately, the exigencies of daily school operation left little time for the research planned, and the group of young scholars who designed the school's programs and hired the original staff have since been replaced by more conventional personnel.

Another way of classifying Bredemeier's model is as an example of the pedagogical approach termed *individualized* instruction. While it shares certain of the practical difficulties of many individualized programs—in particular, it assumes almost unlimited amounts of interest, time, and energy on the part of the staff—it also has a clearer conceptual focus than most. For a presentation of major research and development efforts in individualized education, see Talmage, 1975.

6. Concerning the issue of responsibility, it is interesting to note that the demands for greater school and teacher "accountability" that have been aired in recent years echo earlier attempts to force the educational system to assume more responsibility for its successes and failures. For example, an 1817 Georgia state law forbade the state's commissioner of education to pay the salaries of teachers whose students had not made sufficient progress during the preceding quarter, and superintendents could be dismissed on similar grounds. (Lessinger, 1970).

7. Rivlin and Timpane point out that "standardized tests are explicity designed to give comparable measures of children's performance irrespective of what curriculum they have been exposed to, and hence are singularly ill suited for use as discriminators among curricula" (Rivlin and Timpane, 1975: 14).

Bibliography

Adams, R. S., and B. J. Biddle. 1970. *Realities of Teaching: Explorations with Videotape.* New York: Holt, Rinehart and Winston.

Adler, C. 1967. "Some Social Mechanisms Affecting High School Drop-Out in Israel." *Sociology of Education,* 40: 363–366.

———. 1973. "Inside Israel." In *World Politics and the Jewish Condition.* Ed. L. Henkin. New York: Quadrangle, pp. 147–177.

Alexander, C. N., and E. Q. Campbell. 1964. "Peer Influences on Adolescent Educational Aspirations and Attainments." *American Sociological Review,* 29: 568–575.

Alexander, K. L., M. Cook, and E. L. McDill. 1978. "Curricular Tracking and Educational Stratification: Some Further Evidence." *American Scoiological Review,* 43: 47–66.

Anderson, A. C. 1974. "Successes and Frustration in the Sociological Study of Education." *Social Science Quarterly,* 55: 282–296.

Anderson, G. T. 1970. "Effects of Classroom Social Climate on Individual Learning." *American Educational Research Journal,* 7: 135–152.

———, and H. J. Walberg. 1974. "Learning Environments." In *Evaluating Educational Performance.* Ed. H. J. Walberg. Berkeley: McCutchan.

Anderson, J. G., and F. B. Evans. 1976. "Family Socialization and Educational Achievement in Two Cultures: Mexican and Anglo-American." *Sociometry,* 39: 209–222.

Aries, Philippe. 1962. *Centuries of Childhood.* New York: Knopf.

Armor, David J. 1969. *The American School Counselor.* New York: Russell Sage Foundation.

Astin, A. W. 1972. *College Dropouts: A National Profile.* Washington, D.C.: American Council on Education.

Atkinson, John W. 1966. *An Introduction to Motivation.* Princeton, N.J.: Van Nostrand.

Averch, H. A. et al. 1974. *How Effective Is Schooling? A Critical Review of Research.* Englewood Cliffs, N. J.: Educational Technology Publications.

Bales, R. F. 1952. "Some Uniformities of Behavior in Small Social Systems." In *Readings in Social Psychology.* Rev. ed. Ed. G. E. Swanson et al. New York: Holt, pp. 146–159.

———, and E. F. Borgatta. 1955. "Size of Group as a Factor in the Interaction Profile." In *Small Groups.* Ed. P. Hare et al. New York: Knopf, pp. 396–413.

Bandura, A. 1969. *Principles of Behavior Modification.* New York: Holt, Rinehart and Winston.

Bane, Mary Jo. 1976. *Here to Stay: American Families in the Twentieth Century.* New York: Basic Books.

———, and J. Crouse. 1975. "Relating Human Abilities with Success Measures." Paper presented at annual meeting, American Association for the Advancement of Science.

Bargen, M., and H. J. Walberg. 1974. "School Performance." In *Evaluating Educational Performance.* Ed. H. J. Walberg. Berkeley: McCutchan, pp. 239–254.

Barker, R. G. et al. 1962. *Big School—Small School.* Report to U.S. Department of Health, Education and Welfare, Midwest Psychological Field Station, University of Kansas.

Bartel, H. W., N. R. Bartel, and J. J. Grill. 1973. "Sociometric View of Some Integrated Classrooms." *Journal of Social Issues,* 29: 159–173.

Barth, R. S. 1972. *Open Education and the American School.* New York: Agatha.

Bates, F. L., and V. K. Murray. 1975. "The School as a Behavior System." *Journal of Research and Development in Education,* 2: 23–33.

Bavelas, A. 1962. "Communication Patterns in Task-Oriented Groups." In *Group Dynamics.* Ed. D. Cartwright and A. Zander. Evanston, Ill.: Row, Peterson and Company.

Bayh, B. 1975. *Our Nation's Schools—A Report Card: "A" in School Violence and Vandalism.* Washington, D.C.: U.S. Government Printing Office.

Becker, H. 1968. "The Teacher in the Authority System of the Public Schools." In *The Sociology of Education.* Rev. ed. Ed. R. R. Bell and H. R. Stub. Homewood, Ill.: Dorsey.

Benedict, Ruth. 1946. *The Chrysanthemum and the Sword.* Boston: Houghton Mifflin.

Bennett, Neville. 1976. *Teaching Styles and Pupil Progress.* London: Open Books Publishing.

Bereiter, Carl. 1974. *Must We Educate?* Englewood Cliffs, N. J.: Prentice-Hall.

———, and Siegfried Engelmann. 1966. *Teaching Disadvantaged Children in the Preschool.* Englewood Cliffs, N.J.: Prentice-Hall.

Bernstein, Basil. 1961. "Social Class and Linguistic Development." In *Education, Economy and Society.* Ed. A. H. Halsey et al. New York: Free Press, pp. 288–314.

———, 1970. "Education Cannot Compensate for Society." *New Society,* 387: 344–347.

———, 1977. "Social Class, Language and Socialization." In *Power and Ideology in Education.* Ed. J. Karabel and A. H. Halsey. New York: Oxford, pp. 473–486.

Berry, J. W. 1966. "Temne and Eskimo Perceptual Skills." *International Journal of Psychology,* 1: 207–229.

Bettelheim, Bruno. 1969. *The Children of the Dream.* New York: Macmillan.

Bidwell, C. E. 1965. "The School as a Formal Organization." In *Handbook of Organizations.* Ed. J. G. March. Chicago: Rand McNally, pp. 972–1022.

———, 1969. "The Sociology of Education." In *Encyclopedia of Educational Research.* 4th ed. Ed. R. Ebel. New York: Macmillan, pp. 1241–1254.

Bidwell, C. E. 1973. "The Social Psychology of Teaching." In *Second Handbook of Research on Teaching*. Ed. R. Travers. Chicago: Rand McNally, pp. 413–449.

———, and J. D. Kasarda. 1975. "School District Organization and Student Achievement." *American Sociological Review*, 40: 35–70.

Blalock, Hubert M. Jr. 1961. *Causal Inferences in Non-experimental Research*. Chapel Hill: University of North Carolina Press.

———. 1972. *Social Statistics*. 2nd ed. New York: McGraw-Hill.

Blau, Peter M., and Otis Dudley Duncan. 1967. *The American Occupational Structure*. New York: Wiley.

Bloom, Benjamin S. 1968. "Learning for Mastery." *UCLA Evaluation Comment*, 1: 1–12.

———. 1976. *Human Characteristics and School Learning*. New York: McGraw-Hill.

Bloom, S. 1976. *Peer and Cross-Age Tutoring in the Schools*. Washington, D.C.: National Institute of Education.

Blyth, D. A., R. G. Simmons, and D. Bush. 1978. "The Transition into Early Adolescence: A Longitudinal Comparison of Youth in Two Educational Contexts." *Sociology of Education*, 51: 149–162.

Boocock, S. S. 1971. "A Funny Thing Happened on the Way to Maturity." *AAUW Journal*. 65: 13–16.

———. 1974. "Youth in Three Cultures." *School Review*, 82: 93–111.

———, and E. O. Schild. 1968. *Simulation Games in Learning*. Beverly Hills, Calif.: Sage.

Boulding, K. 1966. "Expecting the Unexpected: The Uncertain Future of Knowledge and Technology." Paper prepared for first area conference, Designing Education for the Future, Denver, Colorado.

Bowles, Samuel. 1968. "Toward Equality of Educational Opportunity." *Harvard Educational Review*, 38: 89–99.

———, and Herbert Gintis. 1976. *Schooling in Capitalist America: Educational Reform and the Contradictions of Economic Life*. New York: Basic Books.

———, and Herbert Gintis. 1977. "I.Q. in the U.S. Class Structure." In *Power and Ideology in Education*. Ed. J. Karabel and A. H. Halsey. New York: Oxford, pp. 215–232.

Boyle, R. P. 1966. "The Effect of the High School on Students' Aspirations." *American Journal of Sociology*, 71: 628–639.

Braun, C. 1976. "Teacher Expectation: Sociopsychological Dynamics." *Review of Educational Research*, 46: 185–213.

Bredemeier, H. C. 1968. "Schools and Student Growth." *Urban Review*, 3: 21–34.

———. 1978. "On the Concept of Equality and Its Attainment." Paper prepared for Rutgers Seminar on Sociological Contributions to Equity Theory, New Brunswick, N.J.

Brim, O. G. 1960. "Family Structure and Sex-Role Learning by Children." In *A Modern Introduction to the Family*. Ed. N. W. Bell and E. F. Vogel. Glencoe, Ill.: Free Press, pp. 482–496.

Brittain, C. V. 1963. "Adolescent Choices and Parent-Peer Cross-Pressures." *American Sociological Review*, 28: 385–390.

Brody, G. H., and B. J. Zimmerman. 1975. "The Effects of Modeling and Classroom Organization on the Personal Space of Third and Fourth Grade Children." *American Educational Research Journal,* 12: 157–168.

Bronfenbrenner, Urie. 1968. "Soviet Methods of Character Education." In *Comparative Perspectives on Education.* Ed. R. J. Havighurst. Boston: Little, Brown, pp. 57–65.

———. 1970. *Two Worlds of Childhood: U.S. and U.S.S.R.* New York: Basic Books–Russell Sage Foundation.

———. 1976. "The Experimental Ecology of Education." *Teachers College Record,* 78: 157–204.

Brookover, Wilbur B., and Edsel L. Erickson. 1975. *Sociology of Education.* Homewood, Ill.: Dorsey.

———, and Jeffrey M. Schneider. 1975. "Academic Environments and Elementary School Achievement." *Journal of Research and Development in Education,* 9: 82–91.

Brophy, J. E., and T. L. Good. 1970. "Teachers' Communication of Differential Expectations for Children's Classroom Performance: Some Behavioral Data." *Journal of Educational Psychology,* 61: 365–374.

———, and T. L. Good. 1974. *Teacher-Student Relationships: Causes and Consequences.* New York: Holt, Rinehart and Winston.

Brun-Gulbrandsen, S. 1971. "Sex Roles and the Socialization Process." In *The Changing Roles of Men and Women.* Ed. E. Dahlstrom. Boston: Beacon, pp. 59–78.

Burkhead, Jesse. 1967. *Input and Output in Large-city High Schools.* Syracuse, New York: Syracuse University Press.

Bushnell, J. H. 1962. "Student Culture at Vassar." In *The American College.* Ed. N. Sanford. New York: Wiley, pp. 489–514.

Cahman, W. J. 1949. "Attitudes of Minority Youth: A Methodological Introduction." *American Sociological Review,* 14: 543–548.

Campbell, D. T., and J. C. Stanley. 1963. "Experimental and Quasi-Experimental Designs for Research on Teaching." *Handbook of Research on Teaching.* Ed. N. L. Gage. Chicago: Rand McNally, pp. 171–246.

Campbell, E. Q. 1969. "Adolescent Socialization." In *Handbook of Socialization Theory and Research.* Ed. D. A. Goslin. Chicago: Rand McNally, pp. 821–859.

———, and C. N. Alexander. 1965. "Structural Effects and Interpersonal Relations." *American Journal of Sociology,* 71: 284–289.

Carnoy, M., and J. Werthein. 1977. "Socialist Ideology and the Transformation of Cuban Education." In *Power and Ideology in Education.* Ed. J. Karabel and A. H. Halsey. New York: Oxford, pp. 573–589.

Cartwright, Dorwin, and Alvin Zander. 1962. *Group Dynamics,* 2nd. ed. Evanston, Ill.: Row, Peterson.

Caudill, W., and G. De Vos. 1966. "Achievement, Culture, and Personality: The Case of the Japanese Americans." In *The Disadvantaged Learner.* Ed. S. W. Webster. San Francisco: Chandler, pp. 208–228.

Center for New Schools. 1970. *The Metro School: A Report on Chicago's Experimental School without Walls.* Chicago: Urban Research Corporation.

———. 1972. "Decision-Making in Alternative Secondary Schools." Report of a conference sponsored by UNESCO and Center for New Schools, Woodstock, Ill.

Chen, Theodore Hsi-en. 1974. *The Maoist Educational Revolution*. New York: Praeger.

Cicourel, A. V., and J. I. Kitsuse. 1963. *The Educational Decision-Makers*. Indianapolis: Bobbs-Merrill.

Clark, Burton. 1962. *Educating the Expert Society*. San Francisco: Chandler.

———. 1971. "Sociology and the Study of Education." Report of a planning conference for the National Institute of Education, Washington, D.C.

Clark, Kenneth. 1965. *Dark Ghetto*. New York: Harper and Row.

———. 1972. *A Possible Reality*. New York: Emerson Hall.

Clifford, M. M., and E. Walker. 1973. "The Effect of Physical Attractiveness on Teacher Expectations." *Sociology of Education*, 46: 248–258.

Cockerham, W. C., and A. L. Blevins. 1976. "Open School vs. Traditional School: Self-Identification Among Native American and White Adolescents." *Sociology of Education*, 49: 164–169.

Cohen, E. G. 1972. "Sociology and the Classroom: Setting the Conditions for Teacher-Student Interaction." *Review of Educational Research*, 42: 441–452.

———. 1973. "Open-Space Schools: The Opportunity to Become Ambitious." *Sociology of Education*, 46: 143–161.

———, and E. Bredo. 1975. "Elementary School Organization and Innovative Instructional Practices." In *Managing Change in Educational Organizations*. Ed. T. Deal and B. Baldridge. Berkeley: McCutchan, pp. 133–175.

Cohen, E. G., M. E. Lockheed, and M. Lohman. 1976. "The Center for Interracial Cooperation: A Field Experiment." *Sociology of Education*, 49: 47–58

Cohen, Rosalie. 1968. "Cognitive Styles, Culture Conflict and Non-Verbal Tests of Intelligence." Paper presented at annual meeting, Eastern Sociological Society.

Cole, Stephen. 1972. *The Sociological Method*. Chicago: Markham.

Coleman, James S. 1961. *The Adolescent Society*. New York: Free Press.

———. 1962. "Reward Structure and Allocation of Effort." In *Mathematical Methods in Small Group Processes*. Ed. J. H. Criswell *et al.* Stanford, Calif.: Stanford University Press, pp. 119–132.

———, Ernest Q. Campbell, *et al.* 1966. *Equality of Educational Opportunity*. U.S. Department of Health, Education and Welfare, Office of Education. Washington, D.C.: U.S. Government Printing Office.

———. 1968. "The Concept of Equality of Educational Opportunity." *Harvard Educational Review*, 68: 7–22.

———. 1969. "The Methods of Sociology." In *A Design for Sociology: Scope, Objective and Methods*. Ed. R. Bierstedt. Philadelphia: American Academy of Political and Social Science, pp. 86–114.

———. 1976. "Liberty and Equality in School Desegregation." *Social Policy*, 6: 9–13.

———, *et al.* 1975. *Trends in School Segregation 1968–73*. Washington, D.C.: Urban Institute.

Collins, Randall. 1975. *Conflict Sociology*. New York: Academic Press.

———, and Michael Makowsky. 1978. *The Discovery of Society*. 2nd ed. New York: Random House.

Committee of Concerned Asian Scholars. 1972. *China! Inside the People's Republic*. New York: Bantam.

Conant, James B. 1959. *The American High School Today*. New York: McGraw-Hill.

Connor, J. W. 1975. "Changing Trends in Japanese-American Academic Achievement." *Journal of Ethnic Studies*, 2: 95–98.

Cook, Thomas D., et al. 1975. *Sesame Street Revisited*. New York: Russell Sage Foundation.

Coons, John E., W. Clune III, and Stephen D. Sugarman. 1970. *Private Wealth and Public Education*. Cambridge: Harvard University Press.

———, and Stephen D. Sugarman. 1978. *Education by Choice: The Case for Family Control*. Berkeley: University of California Press.

Corwin, Ronald G., 1965. *A Sociology of Education*. New York: Appleton-Century-Crofts.

Crain, Robert L. 1968. *The Politics of School Desegregation*. Chicago: Aldine.

———. 1970. "School Integration and Occupational Achievement of Negroes." *American Journal of Sociology*, 75: 593–606.

———. 1971. "School Integration and the Academic Achievement of Negroes." *Sociology of Education*, 44: 1–26.

———. 1976. "Why Research Fails to Be Useful." In *School Desegregation: Shadow and Substance*. Ed. F. H. Levinsohn and B. D. Wright. Chicago: University of Chicago Press, pp. 31–45.

Crandall, Virginia, et al. 1960. "Maternal Reactions and the Development of Independence and Achievement Behavior in Young Children." *Child Development*, 31: 243–251.

———. 1964. "Achievement Behavior in Young Children." *Young Children*, 20: 77–90.

Cravioto, J. 1968. "Nutritional Deficiencies and Mental Performance in Childhood." In *Environmental Influences*. Ed. D. C. Glass. New York: Rockefeller University Press and Russell Sage Foundation, pp. 3–51.

Csikszentmihalyi, M., R. Larson, and S. Prescott. 1977. "The Ecology of Adolescent Activity and Experience." *Journal of Youth and Adolesence*, 6: 281–294.

Cusick, Philip A. 1973. *Inside High School: The Student's World*. New York: Holt, Rinehart, and Winston.

Dave, R. H. 1963. "The Identification and Measurement of Environmental Process Variables that Are Related to Educational Achievement." Unpublished doctoral dissertation, University of Chicago.

Davis, D. J., S. Kahan, and J. Bashi. 1976. "Birth Order and Intellectual Development: The Confluence Model in the Light of Cross-Cultural Evidence." *Science*, 196: 1470–1472.

Deci, E. 1975. *Intrinsic Motivation*. New York: Plenum.

Demos, John. 1970. *A Little Commonwealth: Family Life in Plymouth Colony*. London: Oxford.

Dentler, R. A. 1966. "Equality of Educational Opportunity: A Special Review." *Urban*, 1: 27–29.

de Shalit, N. 1970. "Children in War." In *Children and Families in Israel*. Ed. A. Jarus *et al*. New York: Gordon and Breach, pp. 151–182.

Deutsch, M. 1963. "The Disadvantaged Child and the Learning Process." In *Education in Depressed Areas*. Ed. A. H. Passow. New York: Columbia University-Teachers College Press, pp. 163–179.

Devin-Sheehan, L., R. S. Feldman, and V. L. Allen. 1976. "Research on Children Tutoring Children: A Critical Review." *Review of Educational Research*, 46: 355–385.

De Vries, D. L., and R. E. Slavin. 1976. "Teams-Games Tournament: A Final Report on the Research." Baltimore: Johns Hopkins University, Center for Social Organization of Schools, Report No. 217.

Dewey, John. 1928. *Democracy and Education*. New York: Macmillan.

Dodd, P. C. 1965. "Role Conflicts of School Principals." Final Report No. 4, Cooperative Research Project No. 853. Graduate School of Education, Harvard University.

Dornbusch, S. M. 1976. "A Theory of Evaluation Applied to Schools." Paper presented at annual meeting, Sociological Research Association, New York.

Doyle, D. P. 1977. "The Politics of Choice: A View from the Bridge." In *Parents, Teachers, and Children: Prospects for Choice in American Education*. J. S. Coleman *et al*. San Francisco: Institute for Contemporary Studies, pp. 227–255.

Dreeben, Robert. 1968. *On What Is Learned in School*. Reading, Mass.: Addison-Wesley.

———. 1973. "The School as a Workplace." In *Second Handbook of Research on Teaching*. Ed. R. Travers. Chicago: Rand McNally, pp. 450–473.

———, and Neal Gross. 1965. "The Role Behavior of School Principals." Final Report No. 3, Cooperative Research Project No. 853. Graduate School of Education, Harvard University.

Dubin, R., and T. C. Taveggia. 1968. *The Teaching-Learning Paradox: A Comparative Analysis of College Teaching Methods*. Eugene, Oregon: Center for the Advanced Study of Educational Administration.

Duncan, O. D. 1966. "Path Analysis: Sociological Examples." *American Journal of Sociology*, 72: 1–16.

Dunkin, M. J., and B. J. Biddle. 1974. *The Study of Teaching*. New York: Holt, Rinehart and Winston.

Durkheim, Emile. 1956, *Education and Sociology*. Glencoe, Ill.: Free Press.

———. 1961. *Moral Education*. Glencoe, Ill.: Free Press.

———. 1977. *The Evolution of Educational Thought*. London: Routledge and Kegan Paul.

Dyer, H. S. 1968. "School Factors and Equal Educational Opportunity." *Harvard Educational Review*, 38: 38–56.

Eckland, B. K. 1967. "Genetics and Sociology: A Reconsideration." *American Sociological Review*, 32: 173–194.

Edgar, D. E., and R. Warren. 1969. "Power and Autonomy in Teacher Socialization." *Sociology of Education*, 42: 386–399.

Edmonds, Ron. n.d. "A discussion of the literature and issues related to effective schooling." Harvard University, Graduate School of Education. Xeroxed paper.

Edwards, K. J., D. L. DeVries, and J. P. Snyder. 1972. "Games and Teams: A Winning Combination." *Simulation and Games,* 3: 247–269.

Eifermann, R. R. 1969. "Cooperativeness and Egalitarianism in Kibbutz Children's Games." Hebrew University, Department of Psychology. Unpublished paper.

Eisenstadt, S. N. 1956. *From Generation to Generation.* New York: Free Press.

Elam, Stanley, ed. 1973. *The Gallup Polls of Attitudes toward Education 1969–1973.* Bloomington, Ind.: Phi Delta Kappa.

Elder, G. H. 1965. "Family Structure and Educational Attainment." *American Sociological Review,* 30: 81–96.

Entwisle, D. R. 1966. "Development Sociolinguistics: A Comparative Study in Four Subcultural Settings." *Sociometry,* 29: 67–84.

———. 1970a. "Semantic Systems of Children: Some Assessments of Social Class and Ethnic Differences." In *Language and Poverty: Perspectives on a Theme.* Ed. F. Williams. Chicago: Markham.

———. 1970b. "To Dispel Fantasies about Fantasy-Based Measures." Baltimore: Johns Hopkins University. Mimeographed paper.

———, M. Webster, and L. Hayduk. 1974. "Expectation Theory in the Classroom." Report to U.S. Department of Health, Education and Welfare. Department of Social Relations, Johns Hopkins University.

Epperson, D. C. 1964. "A Re-assessment of Indices of Parental Influence in *The Adolescent Society.*" *American Sociological Review,* 29: 93–96.

Epstein, J. L., and J. M. McPartland. 1976. "Classroom Organization and the Quality of School Life." Baltimore: Johns Hopkins University, Center for Social Organization of Schools, Report No. 215.

———, and J. M. McPartland. 1977. "Family and School Interactions and Main Effects on Affective Outcomes." Baltimore: Johns Hopkins University, Center for Social Organization of Schools, Report No. 235.

Esposito, D. 1973. "Homogeneous and Heterogeneous Ability Grouping: Principal Findings and Implications for Evaluating and Designing More Effective Educational Environments." *Review of Educational Research,* 43: 163–179.

Faltermayer, E. K. 1968. "More Dollars and More Diplomas." *Fortune,* 77: 140–145.

Fan, K. H., and K. T. Fan. 1975. *From the Other Side of the River: A Self-portrait of China Today.* Garden City, New York: Anchor.

Farber, Jerry. 1969. *The Student as Nigger.* North Hollywood, Calif.: Contact Books.

Farley, R. 1976. "Is Coleman Right?" *Social Policy,* 6: 14–23.

Feldman, K. A., and T. M. Newcomb. 1969. *The Impact of College on Students.* Vol. 1. San Francisco: Jossey-Bass.

Field, W. F. 1951. "The Effects of Thematic Apperception on Certain Experimentally Aroused Needs." Unpublished doctoral dissertation, University of Maryland.

Finkelstein, B. 1975. "Pedagogy as Intrusion: Teaching Values in Popular Primary Schools in Nineteenth-Century America." *History of Childhood Quarterly,* 2: 349–378.

Finn, J. D. 1972. "Expectations and the Educational Environment." *Review of Educational Research,* 42: 387–410.

Fiske, E. B. 1978. "Small Classes Do Not Always Lead to Better Education." *New York Times* (July 30), A1, A16.

Flanagan, J. C. *et al.* 1962. "Studies of the American High School." Project Talent Office, University of Pittsburgh.

Flanders, Ned A. 1960. *Teacher Influence, Pupil Attitudes and Achievements.* U.S. Department of Health, Education and Welfare, Office of Education, Cooperative Research Monograph No. 12.

———. 1970. *Analyzing Teaching Behavior.* Reading, Mass.: Addison-Wesley.

Fletcher, Jerry, *et al.* 1970. "The School as a Center for Educational Change: A Prospectus." Portland, Oregon: John Adams High School. Mimeographed report.

Fraser, Stewart, ed. 1965. *Chinese Communist Education: Records of the First Decade.* Nashville: Vanderbilt University Press.

Friedenberg, E. Z. 1968. "The School as a Social Environment." In *The Sociology of Education.* Ed. R. R. Bell and H. R. Stub. Homewood, Ill.: Dorsey, pp. 186–198.

Fruchter, Benjamin. 1954. *Introduction to Factor Analysis.* New York: Van Nostrand.

Gans, H. J. 1976. "The Role of Education in the Escape from Poverty." In *Education, Inequality, and National Policy.* Ed. N. F. Ashline *et al.* Lexington, Mass.: Heath, pp. 61–72.

Garcia, H. 1975. "The Effects of a Redefined Assimilative Process upon Chicano Movement Participation." Yale University, Department of Sociology. Unpublished paper.

Gartner, A., M. Kohler, and F. Riessman. 1971. *Children Teach Children: Learning by Teaching.* New York: Harper and Row.

Gerard, H. B., and N. Miller. 1975. *School Desegregation: A Long-Term Study.* New York: Plenum.

Gerard, R. W. 1952. "The Biological Basis of Imagination." In *The Creative Process.* Ed. B. Ghiselin. Berkeley: University of California Press, pp. 226–251.

Gerth, H. H., and C. Wright Mills, eds. 1958. *From Max Weber: Essays in Sociology.* New York: Galaxy.

Getzels, Jacob W., and Philip W. Jackson. 1962. *Creativity and Intelligence.* New York: Wiley.

Gittell, Marilyn. 1974. *Participants and Participation: A Study of Local Policy in New York City.* New York: Center for Urban Education.

———, and T. Edward Hollander. 1968. *Six Urban School Districts: A Comparative Study of Institutional Response.* New York: Praeger.

Goffman, Erving. 1959. *The Presentation of Self in Everyday Life.* New York: Doubleday Anchor.

Goldberg, Marian L., *et al.* 1966. *The Effects of Ability Grouping.* New York: Columbia University—Teachers College Press.

Goodlad, John I. 1966. *School, Curriculum, and the Individual.* Waltham, Mass.: Blaisdell.

Goodman, Paul. 1960. *Growing Up Absurd.* New York: Random House.

Goor, A., and R. E. Sommerfeld. 1975. "A Comparison of Problem Solving Processes of Creative and Noncreative Students." *Journal of Educational Psychology,* 67: 495–505.

———, and T. Rapaport. 1977. "Enhancing Creativity in an Informal Educational Framework." *Journal of Educational Psychology,* 69: 636–643.

Gordon, Chad. 1969. "Self-Conceptions, Race and Family Factors as Determinants of Adolescent Achievement Orientations." Harvard University, Department of Social Relations. Unpublished manuscript.

Gordon, C. Wayne. 1957. *The Social System of the High School.* Glencoe, Ill.: Free Press.

———, and Leta M. Adler. 1963. "Dimensions of Teacher Leadership in Classroom Social Systems." Los Angeles: University of California, Department of Education. Mimeographed report.

Gordon, E. W. 1974. "Toward Defining Equality of Educational Opportunity." In *Equality of Educational Opportunity: A Handbook for Research.* Ed. L. P. Miller. New York: AMS Press, pp. 423–434.

———. 1976. "Education of the Disadvantaged: A Problem of Human Diversity." In *Education, Inequality, and National Policy.* Ed. N. F. Ashline et al. Lexington, Mass.: Heath, pp. 101–123.

Goslin, David A. 1966. *The Search for Ability: Standardized Testing in Social Perspective.* New York: Wiley.

———. 1969. *Guidelines for the Collection, Maintenance and Dissemination of Pupil Records.* New York: Russell Sage Foundation.

Gouldner, Alvin. 1970. *The Coming Crisis of Western Sociology.* New York: Avon.

Grant, W. V., and C. G. Lind. 1976. *Digest of Educational Statistics.* Washington, D.C.: U.S. Government Printing Office.

Gravenberg, O., and G. Collins. 1976. "Grades: Just a Measure of Conformity." *Humboldt Journal of Social Relations,* 3: 58–62.

Greeley, Andrew M., and Peter H. Rossi. 1966. *The Education of Catholic Americans.* Chicago: Aldine.

Green, A. W. 1946. "The Middle-Class Male Child and Neurosis." *American Sociological Review,* 11: 31–41.

Green, P. 1976. "Race and I.Q.: Fallacy of Heritability." *Dissent* (Spring), 181–196.

Green, R. L., and L. J. Hoffman. 1965. "A Case Study of the Effects of Educational Deprivation on Southern Rural Negro Children." *Journal of Negro Education,* 34: 327–341.

Green, T. F. 1969. "Schools and Communities: A Look Forward." *Harvard Educational Review,* 39: 221–252.

———. 1970. "Education and Schooling in Post-Industrial America: Some Directions for Policy." Paper presented to Committee on Science and Astronautics, U.S. House of Representatives, Ninety-first Congress.

Gronlund, Norman E. 1959. *Sociometry in the Classroom.* New York: Harper.

Gross, Neal, et al. 1958. *Explorations in Role Analysis.* New York: Wiley.

———. 1959. "Some Contributions of Sociology to the Field of Education." *Harvard Educational Review,* 29: 275–287.

———. 1965. *Who Runs Our Schools?* New York: Wiley.

———, and Robert E. Herriott. 1965. *Staff Leadership in Public Schools*. New York: Wiley.

Gross, Ronald, and Judith Murphey, eds. 1964. *The Revolution in the Schools*. New York: Harcourt, Brace and World.

Guilford, J. P. 1967. *The Nature of Human Intelligence*. New York: McGraw-Hill.

Guttentag, M. 1972. "Children in Harlem's Community Controlled Schools." *Journal of Social Issues*, 28: 1–20.

Hallinan, M. T. 1976. "Friendship Patterns in Open and Traditional Classrooms." *Sociology of Education*, 49: 254–265.

———, and N. B. Tuma. 1978. "Classroom Effects on Changes in Children's Friendships." *Sociology of Education*, 51: 270–282.

Hamblin, R. L., *et al.* 1969. "Changing the Game from 'Get the Teacher' to 'Learn.'" *Transaction*, 6: 20–31.

———, C. Hathaway, and J. S. Wodarski. 1971. "Group Contingencies, Peer Tutoring, and Accelerating Academic Achievement." In *A New Direction for Education: Behavior Analysis*. Ed. E. Ramp and W. Hopkins. Lawrence: University of Kansas Press, pp. 41–53.

Harman, H. H. 1967. *Modern Factor Analysis*. Chicago: University of Chicago Press.

Harvey, D. G., and G. T. Slatin. 1975. "The Relationship Between Child's SES and Teacher's Expectations: A Test of the Middle-Class Bias Hypothesis." *Social Forces*, 54: 140–159.

Hauser, R. M. 1971. *Socioeconomic Background and Educational Performance*. Washington, D.C.: American Sociological Association, Rose Monograph Series.

———. 1974. "Contextual Analysis Revisited." *Sociological Methods and Research*, 2: 365–375.

———, and W. H. Sewell. 1976. "On the Effects of Families and Family Structure." Madison: University of Wisconsin, Center for Demography and Ecology, Working Paper 32.

Havighurst, Robert J., ed. 1968. *Comparative Perspectives on Education*. Boston: Little, Brown.

———. 1975. "Sociology in the Contemporary Educational Crisis." *Journal of Research and Development in Education*, 9: 13–22.

Hawes, J. M. 1971. *Children in Urban Society: Juvenile Delinquency in Nineteenth Century America*. New York: Oxford.

Hawley, W. D. and B. Levin. 1978. "Wayward Coverage of School Desegregation." *The Washington Post* (Saturday, October 14), A17.

Hechinger, F. M. 1977. "No One Knows What Makes a Good School." *New York Times Fall Survey of Education* (November 13), 1, 14.

Henrysson, Sten. 1957. *Applicability of Factor Analysis in the Behavioral Sciences*. Stockholm: Almquist and Wiksell.

Herndon, James. 1968. *The Way It Spozed to Be*. New York: Bantam Books.

Hickrod, L. J., and G. A. Hickrod. 1965. "Communist China and the American Adolescent Subcultures." *China Quarterly*, 22: 170–178.

Holden, C. 1978. "California Court Is Forum for Latest Round in IQ Debate." *Science,* 201: 1106–1109.

Holt, John. 1964. *How Children Fail.* New York: Delta.

———. 1967. *How Children Learn.* New York: Pitman.

———. 1969. *The Underachieving School.* New York: Pitman.

Hopper, E. I. 1977. "A Typology for the Classification of Educational Systems." In *Power and Ideology in Education.* Ed. J. Karabel and A. H. Halsey. New York: Oxford, pp. 153–166.

Horner, M. S. 1970. "Femininity and Successful Achievement: Basic Inconsistency." In *Feminine Personality and Conflict.* Ed. J. M. Bardwick *et al.* Belmont, Calif.: Brooks Cole, pp. 45–74.

———. 1972. "Toward an Understanding of Achievement-Related Conflict in Women." *Journal of Social Issues,* 28: 157–175.

Hughes, E. C., *et al.* 1962. "Student Culture and Academic Effort." In *The American College.* Ed. N. Sanford. New York: Wiley, pp. 515–530.

Hunt, J. McV. 1961. *Intelligence and Experience.* New York: Ronald Press.

Hurn, Christopher. 1978. *The Limits and Possibilities of Schooling.* Boston: Allyn and Bacon.

Husen, Torsten, ed. 1967. *International Study of Achievement in Mathematics.* Vols. I and II. New York: Wiley.

Hyman, H. H., C. R. Wright, and J. S. Reid. 1975. *The Enduring Effects of Education.* Chicago: University of Chicago Press.

Illich, Ivan. 1970. "Why We Must Abolish Schooling." *The New York Review,* 15: 9–15.

———. 1971. *Deschooling Society.* New York: Harper and Row.

Inkeles, A. 1977. "The International Evaluation of Educational Achievement: A Review." *Proceedings of the National Academy of Education,* 4: 139–200.

Jackson, Philip. 1968. *Life in Classrooms.* New York: Holt, Rinehart and Winston.

———. 1971. "The Difference Teachers Make." In *How Teachers Make a Difference.* Washington, D.C.: U.S. Government Printing Office, pp. 21–31.

Jahoda, Marie, and Neil Warren. 1965. "The Myths of Youth." *Sociology of Education,* 38: 138–149.

Jencks, Christopher. 1969. "What Color Is IQ?" *New Republic,* 162: 25–29.

———, *et al.* 1972. *Inequality: A Reassessment of the Effects of Family and Schooling in America.* New York: Basic Books.

Jensen, A. R. 1969. "How Much Can We Boost IQ and Scholastic Achievement?" *Harvard Educational Review,* 39: 1–123.

Johnson, D. W., and R. T. Johnson. 1974. "Instructional Goal Structure: Cooperative, Competitive, or Individualistic." *Review of Educational Research,* 44: 213–240.

Johnson, M. E. 1976. "The Role of Perceived Parental Models, Expectations and Socializing Behaviors in the Self-Expectations of Adolescents from the U.S. and West Germany." Unpublished doctoral dissertation, Rutgers University.

Kaestle, C. F., and M. A. Vinovskis. 1978. "From Apron Strings to ABC's: Parents, Children and Schooling in Nineteenth-Century Massachusetts." In *Turning Points:*

Sociological and Historical Essays on the Family. Ed. J. Demos and S. S. Boocock. Chicago: University of Chicago Press, pp. S39–S80.

Kagan, J., et al. 1960. "Conceptual Style and the Use of Affect Labels." *Merrill-Palmer Quarterly,* 6: 261–278.

———, et al. 1963. "Psychological Significance of Styles of Conceptualization." In *Basic Cognitive Processes in Children.* Ed. J. C. Wright and J. Kagan, Monograph in Social Research on Child Development 28, No. 2, pp. 73–112.

———. 1964. "The Child's Sex Role Classification of School Objects." *Child Development,* 35: 1051–1056.

Kahl, J. A. 1953. "Educational and Occupational Aspirations of 'Common Man' Boys." *Harvard Educational Review,* 23: 186–203.

Kahn, R. L. 1956. "The Prediction of Productivity." *Journal of Social Issues,* 12: 41–49.

Kamin, Leon. 1974. *The Science and Politics of I.Q.* Potomac, Maryland: Erlbaum.

Kandel, D., and G. S. Lesser. 1969. "Parental and Peer Influences on Educational Plans of Adolescents." *American Sociological Review,* 34: 212–223.

Karweit, N. L. 1976a. "A Reanalysis of the Effect of Quantity of Schooling on Achievement." *Sociology of Education,* 49: 236–246.

———. 1976b. "School Influences on Student Interaction Patterns." Baltimore: Johns Hopkins University, Center for Social Organization of Schools, Report No. 220.

Katz, F. E. 1964. "The School as a Complex Social Organization." *Harvard Educational Review,* 34: 428–455.

Katz, M. 1972. "Attitudinal Modernity, Classroom Power and Status Characteristics." Paper presented at annual meeting, American Educational Research Association, Chicago.

Keniston, Kenneth, and the Carnegie Council on Children. 1977. *All Our Children: The American Family under Pressure.* New York: Harcourt Brace Jovanovich.

Keppel, Francis. 1966. *The Necessary Revolution in American Education.* New York: Harper and Row.

Kerr, N. D. 1964. "The School Board as an Agency of Legitimation." *Sociology of Education,* 38: 34–59.

Kessen, William, ed. 1975. *Childhood in China.* New Haven: Yale University Press.

Kett, J. 1974. "History of Age Grouping in America." In J. S. Coleman et al., *Youth: Transition to Adulthood.* Chicago: University of Chicago Press, pp. 9–29.

———. 1976. "The History of Age Grouping in America." In *Rethinking Childhood.* Ed. A. Skolnick. Boston: Little, Brown, pp. 214–234.

Kidd, T., and W. Woodman. 1975. "Sex and Orientation Toward Winning in Sport." *Research Quarterly,* 4: 475–483.

Kitano, Harry H. L. 1976. *Japanese Americans: The Evolution of a Subculture.* 2nd ed. Englewood Cliffs, N.J.: Prentice-Hall.

Klein, Z., and Y. Eshel. 1976. "A Further Investigation of the Effects of Integration and Special Educational Intervention in the Early Primary Grades." Jerusalem: Hebrew University, NCJW Research Institute for Innovation in Education.

Kleinberger, Aharon F. 1969. *Society, Schools and Progress in Israel*. Oxford, England: Pergamon.

Klitgaard, R. E., and G. R. Hall. 1973. *A Statistical Search for Unusually Effective Schools*. Santa Monica, Calif.: Rand Corporation.

Kohl, Herbert. 1967. *36 Children*. New York: Signet Books.

Kohn, M. L. 1959a. "Social Class and Parental Values." *American Journal of Sociology*, 64: 337–351.

———. 1959b. "Social Class and the Exercise of Parental Authority." *American Sociological Review*, 24: 352–366.

———. 1963. "Social Class and Parent-Child Relationships: An Interpretation." *American Journal of Sociology*, 68: 471–480.

———. 1976. "Social Class and Parental Values: Another Confirmation of the Relationship." *American Sociological Review*, 41: 538–545.

Komarovsky, Mirra. 1953. *Women in the Modern World: Their Education and Their Dilemmas*. Boston: Little, Brown.

Kounin, J. 1970. *Discipline and Group Management in Classrooms*. New York: Holt, Rinehart and Winston.

Kozol, J. 1970. *Death at an Early Age*. New York: Bantam.

Krasner, L., and L. P. Ullman, eds. 1965. *Case Studies in Behavior Modification*. New York: Holt, Rinehart and Winston.

———, and L. P. Ullman. 1966. *Research in Behavior Modification: New Developments and Implications*. New York: Holt, Rinehart and Winston.

Labov, William, et al. 1968. "A Study of the Non-standard English of Negro and Puerto Rican Speakers in New York City." Philadelphia: U.S. Regional Survey.

———. 1970. "The Logic of Nonstandard English." In *Language and Poverty*. Ed. F. Williams. Chicago: Markham.

Larkin, Ralph W. 1979. *Suburban Youth in Cultural Crisis*. New York: Oxford University Press.

Lau, L. J. 1978. "Educational Production Functions." Paper presented at National Invitational Conference on School Organization and Effects, San Diego.

Leacock, E. B. 1969. *Teaching and Learning in City Schools*. New York: Basic Books.

Lebra, Takie Sugiyama. 1976. *Japanese Patterns of Behavior*. Honolulu: University of Hawaii Press.

Lehne, Richard. 1978. *The Quest for Justice: The Politics of School Finance Reform*. New York: Longman.

Lein, Laura. 1973. "Speech and Setting: American Migrant Children in School and at Home." Unpublished doctoral dissertation, Harvard University.

———. 1974. *Families, Institutions and Child Development*. Cambridge, Mass.: Center for the Study of Public Policy.

Leiner, Marvin. 1974. *Children Are the Revolution*. New York: Viking.

Leonard, George B. 1968. *Education and Ecstacy*. New York: Dell.

Lessinger, Leon M. 1970. *Every Kid a Winner: Accountability in Education*. New York: Simon and Schuster.

Lever, J. 1978. "Sex Differences in the Complexity of Children's Play and Games." *American Sociological Review,* 43: 471–483.

Levin, H. M. 1976a. "A New Model of School Effectiveness." In *Schooling and Achievement in American Society.* Ed. W. H. Sewell, R. M. Hauser, and D. L. Featherman. New York: Academic Press, pp. 267–289.

———. 1976b. "Education, Life Chances, and the Courts: The Role of Social Science Evidence." In *Education, Inequality, and National Policy.* Ed. N. F. Ashline *et al.* Lexington, Mass.: Heath, pp. 73–100.

Levine, A., and J. Crumrine. 1975. "Women and the Fear of Success: A Problem in Replication." *American Journal of Sociology,* 80: 964–974.

Levitan, S. A., and K. C. Alderman. 1975. *Child Care and ABC's Too.* Baltimore: Johns Hopkins University Press.

Lewin, K., R. Lippitt, and R. K. White. 1939. "Patterns of Aggressive Behavior in Experimentally Created 'Social Climates.' " *Journal of Social Psychology,* 10: 271–299.

Liljestrom, R. 1966. "Sex Roles in the Mass Media and Books for the Young." In *Kynne eller Kon.* Stockholm: Raben o Sjogren, pp. 73–95.

Lindert, P. 1974. "Family Inputs and Inequality among Children." Madison: University of Wisconsin, Institute for Research on Poverty, Discussion Paper 218.

Litwak, E., and H. J. Meyer. 1973. "The School and the Family: Linking Organizations and External Primary Groups." In *The School in Society.* Ed. S. D. Sieber and D. E. Wilder. New York: Free Press, pp. 425–435.

Livingstone, D. W. 1968, "A General Model of the Internal Structure of National Educa-Systems." Baltimore: Johns Hopkins University, Department of Social Relations.

Lombard, Avima. 1973. "Home Instruction Program for Preschool Youngsters (HIPPY). Final Report." Jerusalem: Hebrew University, Center for Research on Education of the Disadvantaged.

Lortie, Dan C. 1971. "Structure and Teacher Performance: A Prologue to Systematic Research." In *How Teachers Make a Difference.* Washington, D.C.: U.S. Government Printing Office, pp. 51–65.

———. 1975. *Schoolteacher: A Sociological Study.* Chicago: University of Chicago Press.

Loy, J., S. Birrell, and D. Rose. 1976. "Attitudes Held Toward Agonistic Activities as a Function of Selected Social Identities." *Quest,* 26: 81–93.

Lucker, G. W., *et al.* 1976. "Performance in the Interdependent Classroom: A Field Study." *American Educational Research Journal,* 13: 115–123.

Lukes, Steven. 1973. *Emile Durkheim: His Life and Work.* New York: Harper and Row.

Lüscher, K. 1971. "Sociology and Educational Research—the Sociology of Educational Research." *Education,* 4: 22–30.

McAbee, H. V. 1958. "Time for the Job." *NASSP Bulletin,* 42: 41.

McArthur, R. 1967. "Sex Differences in Field Dependence for the Eskimo." *International Journal of Psychology,* 2: 139–140.

McClelland, David *et al.* 1953. *The Achievement Motive.* New York: Appleton-Century-Crofts.

———, *et al.* 1955. "Religious and Other Sources of Parental Attitudes Toward Independence Training." In *Studies in Motivation.* Ed. D. McClelland. New York: Appleton-Century-Crofts, pp. 389–397.

———. 1961. *The Achieving Society*. New York: Free Press.

Maccoby, Eleanor, ed. 1966. *The Development of Sex Differences*. Stanford: Stanford University Press.

———, and Carol N. Jacklin. 1974. *The Psychology of Sex Differences*. Stanford, Calif.: Stanford University Press.

McDill, Edward L., *et al*. 1967. "Institutional Effects on the Academic Behavior of High School Students." *Sociology of Education*, 40: 181–199.

———, *et al*. 1969. *Strategies for Success in Compensatory Education: An Appraisal of Evaluation Research*. Baltimore: Johns Hopkins Press.

———, and Leo C. Rigsby. 1973. *Structure and Process in Secondary Schools: The Academic Impact of Educational Climates*. Baltimore: Johns Hopkins University Press.

McGinley, P., and H. McGinley. 1970. "Reading Groups as Psychological Groups." *Journal of Experimental Education*, 39: 36–42.

McKay, H., *et al*. 1978. "Improving Cognitive Ability in Chronically Deprived Children." *Science*, 200: 270–278.

McKeachie, W. L. 1962. "Procedures and Techniques of Teaching: A Survey of Experimental Studies." In *The American College*. Ed. N. Sanford. New York: Wiley, pp. 312–364.

McNeely, A., and J. Buck. 1967. "A Study of Guidance Counselors at Three High Schools." Johns Hopkins University, Department of Social Relations. Unpublished paper.

McPartland, J. M. 1967. "The Relative Influence of School Desegregation and Classroom Desegregation on the Academic Achievement of Ninth Grade Negro Students." Baltimore: Johns Hopkins University, Center for Social Organization of Schools.

———, *et al*. 1976. "Productivity of Schools: Conceptual and Methodological Frameworks for Research." Baltimore: Johns Hopkins University, Center for Social Organization of Schools, Report No. 218.

———. 1977. "School Authority Systems and Student Motivation." Paper presented at annual meeting, American Educational Research Association, New York.

Maloney, T. and B. Petrie. 1974. "Professionalization of Attitudes Toward Play Among Canadian School Pupils as a Function of Sex, Grade, and Athletic Participation." *Journal of Leisure Research*, 4: 184–185.

Mao Tse-tung. 1967. *Quotations from Chairman Mao Tse-tung*. New York: Bantam.

Marjoribanks, K. 1972. "Environment, Social Class, and Mental Abilities." *Journal of Educational Psychology*, 63: 103–104.

Mauch, J. 1962. "A Systems Analysis Approach to Education." *Phi Delta Kappan*, 43: 158–161.

Mayeske, G. W. 1975. *Special Studies of Our Nation's Students*. Washington, D.C.: U.S. Government Printing Office.

Mayr, E. 1967. "Biological Man and the Year 2000." *Daedalus*, 96: 832–836.

Meddock, T. D., J. A. Parsons, and K. T. Hill. 1971. "Effects of an Adult's Presence and Praise on Young Children's Performance." *Journal of Experimental Child Psychology*, 12: 197–211.

Medley, D. M., and H. E. Mitzel. 1963. "Measuring Classroom Behavior by Systematic Observation." In *Handbook of Research on Teaching*. Ed. N. L. Gage. Chicago: Rand McNally, pp. 247–328.

Mendels, G. E., and J. P. Flanders. 1973. "Teachers' Expectations and Pupil Performance." *American Educational Research Journal*, 10: 203–212.

Merton, Robert K. 1957. *Social Theory and Social Structure*. Glencoe, Ill.: Free Press.

Meyer, J. W., et al. 1972. "The Impact of the Open-Space School upon Teacher Influence and Autonomy: The Effects of an Organizational Innovation." Stanford, Calif.: Stanford Center for Research and Development in Teaching, Report No. 21.

———, et al. 1977. "The World Educational Revolution, 1950–1970." *Sociology of Education*, 50: 242–258.

Michaels, J. W. 1977. "Classroom Reward Structure and Academic Performance." *Review of Educational Research*, 47: 87–98.

Milgram, R. M., and A. M. Milgram. 1976. "Creative Thinking and Creative Performance in Israeli Students." *Journal of Educational Psychology*, 68: 255–259.

Miller, Harry L. 1967. *Education for the Disadvantaged*. New York: Free Press.

Miller, L. M. 1963. "The Dropout: Schools Search for Clues to His Problems." *School Life* (May), 3.

Miller, S. M. 1976. "Types of Equality: Sorting, Rewarding, Performing." In *Education, Inequality, and National Policy*. ED. N. F. Ashline et al. Lexington, Mass.: Heath, pp. 15–43.

Minkovich, A., D. Davis, and J. Bashi. 1977. "An Evaluation Study of Israeli Elementary Schools." Jerusalem: Hebrew University, School of Education.

Minuchin, P. 1965. "Sex-Role Concepts and Sex Typing in Childhood as a Function of School and Home Environments." *Child Development*, 36: 1033–1048.

Moeller, G. 1968. "Bureaucracy and Teachers' Sense of Power." In *The Sociology of Education*. Ed. R. R. Bell and H. R. Stub. Homewood, Ill.: Dorsey, pp. 236–250.

Moise, E. 1964. "The New Mathematics Program." In *Revolution in Teaching*. Ed. A. de Grazia and D. A. Sohn. New York: Bantam, pp. 171–187.

Monahan, L., D. Kuhn, and P. Shaver. 1974. "Intrapsychic versus Cultural Explanations of the 'Fear of Success' Motive." *Journal of Personality and Social Psychology*, 29: 60–64.

Moore, G. A. 1967. *Realities of the Urban Classroom*. Garden City, N.Y.: Doubleday Anchor.

Moore, O. K., and A. R. Anderson. 1969. "Some Principles for the Design of Clarifying Educational Environments." In *Handbook of Socialization Theory and Research*. Ed. D. A. Goslin. Chicago: Rand McNally, pp. 571–613.

Morrison, A., and D. McIntyre. 1971. *Schools and Socialization*. Middlesex, England: Penguin.

Mullen, R. 1973. "Notes on Work-Education Aspects of Synanon's Interface program." San Francisco: Synanon Foundation. Mimeographed paper.

Munro, D. J. 1971a. "Egalitarian Ideal and Educational Fact in Communist China." In *China: Management of a Revolutionary Society*. Ed. J. M. Lindbeck. Seattle: University of Washington Press, pp. 256–301.

———. 1971b. "The Malleability of Man in Chinese Marxism." *China Quarterly*, 48: 609–640.

Murphey, M. J. 1973. "Educational Negotiation: Journal References." New York: Columbia Teachers College, Institute of Administrative Research.

Murray, H. A. 1938. *Explorations in Personality*. New York: Oxford.

Musgrove, F. 1964. *Youth and the Social Order*. Bloomington: Indiana University Press.

National Center for Education Statistics. 1976. *The Condition of Education*. Washington, D. C.: U.S. Government Printing Office.

———. 1978. *The Condition of Education*. Washington, D.C.: U.S. Government Printing Office.

Neill, A. S. 1961. *Summerhill*. New York: Hart.

Neubauer, P. B., ed. 1965. *Children in Collectives: Child-Rearing Aims and Practices in the Kibbutz*. Springfield, Ill.: Thomas.

Newcomb, Theodore M. 1952. "Attitude Development as a Function of Reference Groups: The Bennington Study." In *Readings in Social Psychology*. Ed. G. E. Swanson et al. New York: Holt, pp. 420–430.

———. 1962. "Student Peer-Group Influence." In *The American College*. Ed. N. Sanford. New York: Wiley, pp. 469–488.

Newman, F. M., and D. W. Oliver. 1967. "Education and Community." *Harvard Educational Review*, 37: 61–106.

Nielsen, H. D., and D. H. Kirk. 1974. "Classroom Climates." In *Evaluating Educational Performance*. Ed. H. J. Walberg. Berkeley: McCutchan, pp. 57–79.

Nisbet, John. 1961. "Family Environment and Intelligence." In *Education, Economy and Society*. Ed. A. H. Halsey et al. New York: Free Press, pp. 273–287.

Oettinger, A. G. 1968. "The Myths of Educational Technology." *Saturday Review* (May 18), 76–77, 91.

Okimoto, Daniel. 1970. *American in Disguise*. New York: Walker/Weatherhill.

O'Toole, J. 1975. "The Reserve Army of the Unemployed. 1. The World of Work." *Change* (May), 26–33, 63.

Panel on Youth of the President's Science Advisory Committee. 1974. *Youth: Transition to Adulthood*. Chicago: University of Chicago Press.

Paolitto, D. P. 1976. "The Effect of Cross-Age Tutoring on Adolescence: An Inquiry into Theoretical Assumptions." *Review of Educational Research*, 46: 215–237.

Parelius, Ann P. 1975. "Lifelong Education and Age Stratification: Some Unexplored Relationships." *American Behavioral Scientist*, 19: 206–223.

———, and Robert J. Parelius. 1978. *The Sociology of Education*. Englewood Cliffs, N.J.: Prentice-Hall.

Parsons, Talcott. 1951. *The Social System*. Glencoe, Ill.: Free Press.

———. 1959. "The School Class as a Social System: Some of Its Functions in American Society." *Harvard Educational Review*. 29: 297–318.

———. 1962. "Youth in the Context of American Society." *Daedalus*, 91: 97–123.

———, and Robert F. Bales. 1955. *Family Socialization and Interaction Process*. Glencoe, Ill.: Free Press.

———, and Gerald M. Platt. 1972. "Higher Education and Changing Socialization." In *Aging and Society*. Vol. 3. Ed. M. W. Riley *et al.* New York: Russell Sage Foundation, pp. 236–291.

Pearlin, L. I., and M. L. Kohn. 1966. "Social Class, Occupation, and Parental Values: A Cross-National Study." *American Sociological Review*, 31: 466–479.

Peleg, R., and C. Adler. 1977. "Compensatory Education in Israel: Conceptions, Attitudes, and Trends." *American Psychologist*, 32: 945–958.

Perlmutter, H. V., and G. DeMontmollin. 1952. "Group Learning of Nonsense Syllables." *Journal of Abnormal and Social Psychology*, 47: 762–769.

Persell, Caroline Hodges. 1977. *Education and Inequality: The Roots and Results of Stratification in American Schools*. New York: Free Press.

Peters, W. 1971. *A Class Divided*. New York: Doubleday.

Pettigrew, T. F. 1966. "Negro American Intelligence: A New Look at an Old Controversy." In *The Disadvantaged Child: Issues and Innovations*. Ed. J. L. Frost and G. R. Hawkes. Boston: Houghton Mifflin, pp. 96–116.

———, and R. L. Green. 1976. "School Desegregation in Large Cities: A Critique of the Coleman 'White Flight' Thesis." *Harvard Educational Review*, 46: 1–53.

Piaget, Jean. 1948. *The Moral Judgement of the Child*. New York: Free Press.

———. 1951. *The Child's Conception of the World*. New York: Humanities Press.

———. 1952. *The Origins of Intelligence in Children*. New York: International University Press.

Pine, F., and W. Olesker. 1973. "The School Failure as Tutor: An Exploratory Approach." *Journal of Youth and Adolescence*, 2: 183–200.

Pines, M. 1965. "What the Talking Typewriter Says." *New York Times Magazine* (May 9), 23, 74–80.

Price, R. F. 1970. *Education in Communist China*. New York: Praeger.

Ravitch, Diane. 1974. *The Great School Wars: New York City, 1805–1973*. New York: Basic Books.

———. 1977. "A Wasted Decade." *The New Republic* (November 5), 11–13.

Reynolds, D. 1977. "Schools Do Make a Difference!" Paper presented at conference on the Ecology of Childhood, Cornell University, Ithaca, New York.

Rhodes, A. L., and C. B. Nam. 1970. "The Religious Context of Educational Expectations." *American Sociological Review*, 35: 253–267.

Richer, S. 1974. "Middle-Class Bias of Schools—Fact or Fancy?" *Sociology of Education*, 47: 523–534.

———. 1975. "School Effects: The Case for Grounded Theory." *Sociology of Education*, 48: 383–399.

———. 1976. "Reference-Group Theory and Ability Grouping." *Sociology of Education*, 49: 65–71.

———. 1977. "The Kindergarten as a Setting For Sex-Role Socialization." Ottawa: Carleton University, Department of Sociology. Unpublished paper.

Ries, Jacob. 1968. *Jacob Ries Revisited: Poverty and the Slum in Another Era*. Edited with an introduction by F. Cordasco. New York: Anchor.

Riessman, Frank. 1962. *The Culturally Deprived Child*. New York: Harper.

Riley, M. W., *et al*. 1954. *Sociological Studies in Scale Analysis*. New Brunswick, N.J.: Rutgers University Press.

———., *et al*. 1955. "Adolescents Talk to Peers and Parents." Rutgers University, Department of Sociology, Mimeographed working paper.

———., *et al*. 1961. "Adolescent Values and the Riesman Typology: An Empirical Analysis." In *Culture and Social Character*. Ed. S. Lispet and L. Lowenthal. New York: Free Press, pp. 370–386.

———. 1963. *Sociological Research*. 2 vols. New York: Harcourt, Brace and World.

Rist, R. C. 1970. "Student Social Class and Teacher Expectations: The Self-Fulfilling Prophecy in Ghetto Education." *Harvard Educational Review*, 40: 411–451.

———. 1978. *The Invisible Children: School Integration in American Society*. Cambridge: Harvard University Press.

Ritterband, P., and R. Silberstein. 1973. "Group Disorders in the Public Schools." *American Sociological Review*, 38: 461–467.

Rivlin, Alice M. 1973. "Forensic Social Science." *Harvard Educational Review*, 43: 1–25.

———, and P. Michael Timpane, eds. 1975. *Planned Variation in Education: Should We Give Up or Try Harder?* Washington, D.C.: Brookings.

Robinson, H. B., N. Robinson, *et al*. 1974. Early Child Care in the United States of America: International Monographs on Early Child Care, No. 3. *Early Child Development and Care* 2, No. 4.

Rogoff, N. 1961. "Local Social Structure and Educational Selection." In *Education, Economy and Society:* Ed. A. H. Halsey *et al*. New York: Free Press, pp. 241–251.

Rosen, B. C. 1956. "The Achievement Syndrome: A Psychocultural Dimension of Social Stratification." *American Sociological Review*, 21: 203–211.

———. 1961. "Family Structure and Achievement Motivation." *American Sociological Review*, 26: 574–585.

Rosenbaum, J. E. 1975. "The Stratification of Socialization Processes." *American Sociological Review*, 40: 48–54.

———, and S. Presser. 1978. "Voluntary Racial Integration in a Magnet School." *School Review*, 86: 156–186.

Rosenberg, L. A., *et al*. 1966. "The Johns Hopkins Perceptual Test." Paper presented at annual meeting, Eastern Psychological Association.

Rosenthal, Robert. 1966. *Experimenter Effects in Behavioral Research*. New York: Appleton-Century-Crofts.

———, and Lenore Jacobson. 1966. "Teachers' Expectancies: Determinants of Pupils' IQ Gains." *Psychological Reports*, 19: 115–118.

———, and Lenore Jacobson. 1968. *Pygmalion in the Classroom*. New York: Holt, Rinehart and Winston.

Rossanda, R., M. Cini, and L. Berlinguer. 1977. "Theses on Education: A Marxist View." In *Power and Ideology in Education*. Ed. J. Karabel and A. H. Halsey. New York: Oxford, pp. 647–658.

Rossell, C. 1975. "School Desegregation and White Flight." *Political Science Quarterly,* 90: 675–695.

Rothbart, M. K., and E. E. Maccoby. 1966. "Parents' Differential Reactions to Sons and Daughters." *Journal of Personality and Social Psychology,* 4: 237–243.

Ryder, N. B. 1965. "The Cohort as a Concept in the Study of Social Change." *American Sociological Review,* 30: 843–861.

Sadler, M. E. 1900. *How Far Can We Learn Anything of Practical Value from the Study of Foreign Systems of Education?* London: Guilford.

St. John, Nancy. 1975. *School Desegregation.* New York: Wiley.

———, and Marshall Smith. 1969. "School Racial Composition, Achievement and Aspiration." Cambridge: Harvard Center for Educational Policy Research. Mimeographed paper.

———, and Ralph Lewis. 1970. "The Influence of School Racial Context on Academic Achievement." Cambridge: Harvard Graduate School of Education. Xeroxed paper.

Sanford, N., ed. 1962. *The American College.* New York: Wiley.

Sansan, as told to Bette Lord. 1964. *Eighth Moon: The True Story of a Young Girl's Life in Communist China.* New York: Harper and Row.

Sarason, Seymour B. 1971. *The Culture of the School and the Problem of Change.* Boston: Allyn and Bacon.

Scarr, S., and R. A. Weinberg. 1976. "IQ Test Performance of Black Children Adopted by White Families." *American Psychologist,* 31: 726–739.

Schooler, C. 1972. "Birth Order Effects: Not Here, Not Now." *Psychological Bulletin,* 78: 161–175.

Schwebel, A. 1969. "Physical and Social Distancing in Teacher-Pupil Relationships." Unpublished doctoral dissertation, Yale University.

Scrimshaw, N. S. 1968. "Infant Malnutrition and Adult Learning." *Saturday Review,* 51: 64–66.

Sears, R. R. 1965. "Development of Gender Role." In *Sex and Behavior.* Ed. F. A. Beach. New York: Wiley, pp. 133–163.

Seginer, R. 1978. "Familial Antecedents of Academic Achievement." University of Haifa, Department of Psychology and School of Education. Unpublished manuscript.

Selltiz, C., L. S. Wrightsman, and S. W. Cook. 1976. *Research Methods in Social Relations.* 3rd ed. New York: Holt, Rinehart and Winston.

Sewell, W. H. and V. P. Shah. 1968. "Social Class, Parental Encouragement and Educational Aspirations." *American Journal of Sociology,* 73: 559–572.

———, and R. M. Hauser. 1976. "Recent Developments in the Wisconsin Study of Social and Psychological Factors in Socioeconomic Achievements." Madison: University of Wisconsin, Center for Demography and Ecology, Working Paper 11.

Sexton, Patricia Cayo. 1967. *The American School: A Sociological Analysis.* Englewood Cliffs, N.J.: Prentice-Hall.

Shaw, M. E. 1932. "A Comparison of Individuals and Small Groups in the Rational Solution of Complex Problems." *American Journal of Psychology,* 44: 491–504.

Shaycoft, M. 1967. *The High School Years: Growth in Cognitive Skills.* Pittsburgh: American Institutes for Research and School of Education, University of Pittsburgh.

Shipman, M. D. 1968. *The Sociology of the School*. New York: Humanities Press.

Showell, B. 1976. "The Courts, the Legislature, the Presidency, and School Desegregation Policy." In *School Desegregation: Shadow and Substance*. Ed. F. H. Levinsohn and B. D. Wright. Chicago: University of Chicago Press, pp. 95–110.

Shur, Shimon. 1972. *Kibbutz Bibliography*. 2nd ed. Tel Aviv: Higher Education and Research Authority of the Federation of Kibbutz Movements.

Sidel, Ruth. 1972. *Women and Child Care in China*. New York: Hill and Wang.

Silberman, Bernard S., ed. 1962. *Japanese Character and Culture: A Book of Selected Readings*. Tucson: University of Arizona Press.

Silberman, C. E. 1970. *Crisis in the Classroom*. New York: Random House.

Simon, William, and John Gagnon. 1969. "Psychosexual Development." *Transaction*, 6: 9–17.

Simpson, R. L. 1962. "Parental Influence, Anticipatory Socialization and Social Mobility." *American Sociological Review*, 27: 517–522.

Slavin, R. E. 1977. "Building an Effective Classroom Reward Structure." Paper presented at annual meeting, American Educational Research Association, New York.

Smilansky, M. 1973. "Coping of the Educational System with the Needs of the Disadvantaged." In *Education in Israel*. Ed.C. Ormian. Jerusalem: Ministry of Education.

Sowell, T. 1977. "New Light on the Black I.Q. Controversy." *New York Times Magazine* (March 27), 56–63.

Spady, W. G. 1974. "Mastery Learning: Its Sociological Implications." In *Schools, Society, and Mastery Learning*. Ed. J. H. Block. New York: Holt, pp. 91–116.

———. 1976. "The Impact of School Resources on Students." In *Schooling and Achievement in American Society*. Ed. W. H. Sewell et al. New York: Academic Press, pp. 185–223.

Spilerman, S. 1971. "Raising Academic Motivation in Lower Class Adolescents: A Convergence of Two Research Traditions." *Sociology of Education*, 44: 103–118.

Spiro, Melford E. 1965. *Children of the Kibbutz*. New York: Schocken.

Statz, C. 1975. "The Chinese Dinner Method of Grading." Paper presented at annual meeting, American Sociological Association, San Francisco.

Stein, A. H., and M. M. Bailey. 1973. "The Socialization of Achievement Orientation in Females." *Psychological Bulletin*, 80: 345–366.

Stenholm, Britta. 1970. *Education in Sweden*. Stockholm: The Swedish Institute.

Stern, D., et al. 1975. "On the Continuing Evolution of Education Vouchers." Yale University, Institution for Social and Policy Studies. Mimeographed paper.

Stern, G. C. 1962. "Environments for Learning." In *The American College*. Ed. N. Sanford. New York: Wiley, pp. 690–730.

Sternglanz, S. H., and L. A. Serbin. 1974. "Sex Role Stereotyping in Children's Television Programs." *Developmental Psychology*, 10: 710–715.

Stinchcombe, Arthur L. 1964. *Rebellion in a High School*. Chicago: Quadrangle.

Stodolsky, S. S., and G. S. Lesser. 1967. "Learning Patterns in the Disadvantaged." *Harvard Educational Review*, 37: 546–593.

Strodtbeck, F. L. 1958. "Family Interaction, Values, and Achievement." In *Talent and Society*. Ed. D. C. McClelland et al. Princeton, N.J.: Van Nostrand, pp. 135–194.

Subcommittee on Elementary, Secondary, and Vocational Education of the Committee on Education and Labor, U.S. House of Representatives. 1977. *Hearings: Part I. General Issues in Elementary and Secondary Education.* Washington, D.C.: U.S. Government Printing Office.

Summers, A. A., and B. L. Wolfe. 1975. "Equality of Educational Opportunity Quantified: A Production Function Approach." Paper presented at winter meetings, Econometric Society, Philadelphia.

Talmage, Harriet, ed. 1975. *Systems of Individualized Education.* Berkeley: McCutchan.

Terman, L. M. 1923. *Intelligence Tests and School Reorganization.* New York: World Books.

———, and M. H. Oden. 1947. *The Gifted Child Grows Up.* Stanford, Calif.: Stanford University Press.

Thomas, G. E. 1977. "Race and Sex Effects on Access to College." Baltimore: Johns Hopkins University, Center for Social Organization of Schools, Report No. 229.

Toffler, Alvin. 1970. *Future Shock.* New York: Random House.

———, ed. 1974. *Learning for Tomorrow: The Role of the Future in Education.* New York: Vintage.

Turner, Ralph H. 1964. *The Social Context of Ambition.* San Francisco: Chandler.

———. 1968. "Sponsored and Contest Mobility and the School System." In *The Sociology of Education.* Ed. R. R. Bell and H. R. Stub. Homewood, Ill.: Dorsey, pp. 219–235.

U.S. Commission on Civil Rights. 1967. Racial Isolation in the Public Schools. Washington, D.C.: U.S. Government Printing Office.

VanGeel, T. 1978. "Parental Preferences and the Politics of Spending Public Educational Funds." *Teachers College Record,* 79: 339–363.

Veroff, J. *et al.* 1962. "Achievement Motivation and Religious Background." *American Sociological Review,* 27: 205–217.

Wagenaar, T. C. 1978. "School Structural Composition and Achievement: An Empirical Assessment." *Sociology and Social Research,* 62: 608–625.

Walberg, H. J. 1969. "Social Environment as a Mediator of Classroom Learning." *Journal of Educational Psychology,* 60: 443–448.

———, and S. C. Thomas. 1972. "Open Education: An Operational Definition and Validation in Great Britain and United States." *American Educational Research Journal,* 9: 197–207.

Wallace, Walter L. 1965. "Peer Influences and Undergraduates' Aspirations for Graduate Study." *Sociology of Education,* 38: 377–392.

———. 1969. *Sociological Theory.* Chicago: Aldine.

Wallach, M. A., and N. Kogan. 1965a. *Modes of Thinking in Young Children: A Study of the Creativity-Intelligence Distinction.* New York: Holt, Rinehart and Winston.

———, and N. Kogan. 1965b. "Cognitive Originality, Physiognomic Sensitivity and Defensiveness in Children." Final report to U.S. Office of Education on Cooperative Research Project No. 1316B. Duke University.

———, and N. Kogan. 1967. "Creativity and Intelligence in Children's Thinking." *Transaction,* 4: 38–43.

———, and C. W. Wing. 1969. *The Talented Student: A Validation of the Creativity/ Intelligence Distinction.* New York: Holt, Rinehart and Winston.

Waller, Willard. 1932. *The Sociology of Teaching.* New York: Wiley.

Waring, J. M. 1975."Social Replenishment and Social Change." *American Behavioral Scientist,* 19: 237–255.

Warren, R. L. 1973. "The Classroom as a Sanctuary: Discontinuities in Social Control." *American Anthropologist,* 75: 280–291.

———. 1975. "Context and Isolation: The Teaching Experience in an Elementary School." *Human Organization,* 34: 139–148.

Wegmann, R. G. 1976. "Classroom Discipline: An Exercise in the Maintenance of Social Reality." *Sociology of Education,* 49: 71–79.

Weick, K. E. 1969. *The Social Psychology of Organizing.* Reading, Mass.: Addison-Wesley.

Weinberg, C., and R. Skager. 1966. "Social Status and Guidance Involvement." *Personnel and Guidance Journal,* 44: 586–590.

Weisstein, N. 1969. "Woman as Nigger." *Psychology Today,* 3: 20–22, 58.

Weitzman, L. J., *et al.* 1972. "Sex-Role Socialization in Picture Books for Preschool Children." *American Journal of Sociology,* 77: 1125–1150.

Wellisch, J. B., *et al.* 1978. "School Management and Organization in Successful Schools (ESAA In-depth Study of Schools)." *Sociology of Education,* 51: 211–226.

Werts, Charles E. 1966. "Sex Differences in College Attendance." Evanston, Ill.: National Merit Scholarship Corporation Reports, Vol. 2, No. 6.

Weston, P. J., and M. T. Mednick. 1970. "Race, Social Class, and the Motive to Avoid Success in Women." *Journal of Cross-Cultural Psychology,* 1: 284–291.

White, Burton L., and Jean C. Watts. 1973. *Experience and Environment: Major Influences on the Development of the Young Child.* Englewood Cliffs, N.J.: Prentice-Hall.

White, R., and R. Lippitt. 1962. "Leader Behavior and Member Reaction in Three 'Social Climates.' " In *Group Dynamics.* Ed. D. Cartwright and A. Zander. Evanston, Ill.: Row, Peterson, pp. 527–553.

Whiting, B. B., ed. 1963. *Six Cultures: Studies of Child Rearing.* New York: Wiley.

———, and C. P. Edwards. 1973. "A Cross-Cultural Analysis of Sex Differences in the Behavior of Children Aged Three through 11." *Journal of Social Psychology,* 91: 171–188.

Wiley, D. E., and A. Harnischfeger. 1974. "Explosion of a Myth: Quantity of Schooling and Exposure to Instruction, Major Educational Vehicles." *Educational Researcher,* 3: 7–12.

———. 1976. "Another Hour, Another Day: Quantity of Schooling, a Potent Path for Policy." In *Schooling and Achievement in American Society.* Ed. W. H. Sewell *et al.* New York: Academic Press, pp. 225–265.

Williams, R. L. 1972. "Abuses and Misuses in Testing Black Children." In *Black Psychology.* Ed. R. Jones. New York: Harper and Row, pp. 71–91.

———. 1975. "The BITCH-100: A Culture-Specific Test." *Journal of Afro-American Issues,* 3: 103–116.

Wilson, Alan B. 1959. "Residential Segregation of Social Classes and Aspirations of High School Boys." *American Sociological Review,* 24: 836–845.

———. 1967. "Educational Consequences of Segregation in a California Community." In *U.S. Commission on Civil Rights, Racial Isolation in the Public Schools.* Washington, D.C.: U.S. Government Printing Office, pp. 165–206.

———. 1968. "Social Class and Equal Educational Opportunity." *Harvard Educational Review,* 38: 77–84.

Wilson, E. C. 1967. "A Model for Action." In *NEA, Rational Planning in Curriculum and Instruction.* Washington, D.C.: NEA Center for the Study of Instruction, pp. 155–193.

Wilson, W. J. 1977. "The Declining Significance of Race." Paper presented at annual meeting, Sociological Research Association, Chicago.

Winterbottom, M. R. 1953. "The Relation of Childhood Training in Independence to Achievement Motivation." Unpublished doctoral dissertation, University of Michigan.

Wirt, Frederich M., ed. 1975. *The Polity of the School.* Lexington, Mass.: Lexington Books.

———, and Michael W. Kirst. 1972. *The Political Web of American Schools.* Boston: Little, Brown.

Wright, B. J., and V. R. Isensten. 1977. *Psychological Tests and Minorities.* Washington, D.C.: U.S. Government Printing Office.

Wright, R. J. 1975. "The Affective and Cognitive Consequences of an Open Education Elementary School." *American Educational Research Journal,* 12: 449–468.

Zablocki, Benjamin. 1980. *Alienation and Charisma: American Communitarian Experiments.* New York: Free Press.

Zajonc, R. B. 1976. "Family Configuration and Intelligence." *Science,* 192: 227–236.

Zeigler, H., and W. Peck. 1970. "The Political Functions of the Educational System." *Sociology of Education,* 43: 115–142.

Zeigler, L. H., and M. K. Jennings. 1974. *Governing American Schools: Political Interaction in Local School Districts.* N. Scituate, Mass.: Duxbury.

Index

Ability, 102–123
 cognitive style and, 112–113
 creativity and, 113–119
 as distinct from achievement, 103
 measurement of intelligence, 104–108
 origin of intelligence, 108–112
 school performance and, 122
 sex differences in, 88–93
 testing of, 119–120
Ability grouping, 143–144, 171–173, 269
Academic success, *see* Achievement
Academic vs. productive work, 289–291
Accountability, 270–272
Achievement
 avoidance of, 92
 crosscultural differences in, 295–303
 as distinct from ability, 103
 and family position, 39–64
 and family structure, 65–83
 n Achievement Scale, 74–75
 peer group influence on, 212–241
 race and, 45–48
 religion and, 58–62
 sex differences in, 84–101
Achievement motivation, 74–75, 91
Activist function, 318–319
Adams, Henry, 135
Adler, Leta M., 148–149
Administration of schools, 132–136, 247–250
Adolescent peer group culture, 212–241
The Adolescent Society (Coleman), 212–220, 236
Age cohorts, 236–237
Age grouping, 142–143, 236
Age homogeneity, 170–171
Age structure of society, 236–238

Aggression
 motivation, 76
 sex differences in, 89
Alexander, C. N., 224–226
Alternative education, 285–295
 academic vs. productive work, 289–291
 egalitarianism, 293–295
 future research on, 320
 ideological instruction, 291–293
 individual vs. group orientation, 285–289
Alum Rock project, 272–274
American educational system, 8–10
American Federation of Teachers, 139
American Indians, 48
Amish children, 46–47
Analytic-cognitive style, 113
Analytic-descriptive style, 113
Anderson, Arnold, 312
Aries, Philippe, 8
Armor, David J., 141
Ascribed characteristics, 39–40
Aspirations, parental, 71–74
Attitude
 of public to schools, 256–258
 racial-ethnic differences in, 49–53
 variable in, 42, 193
Authoritarian leadership style, 148–149
Autotelic environment, 174
Autotelic rewards, 182
Averch, H. A., 201

Balance theory, 224–225, 240–241
Bales, R. F., 170
Bane, M. J., 67
Bargen, M., 201, 202
Barker, R. G., 193

351

Bartel, H. W., 163
Bashi, J., 69, 295
Bates, Frederick, 127, 129
Bavelas, A., 177
Becker, H., 227
Behavior modification, 180–182
Bennington College study, 220–221, 227
Bereiter, Carl, 316
Bereiter-Engelman program, 112
Bernstein, Basil, 44–45, 62
Bidwell, C. E., 130, 249–250
Birth order, 67–69
  and achievement, 39–64
Black Intelligence Test, 107
Blacks
  ability testing of, 106–107
  economic position of, 54
  and expectancy effects, 154–160
  language fluency of, 48
  mental-ability scores, 54–58
  school success of, 48–58
  segregation of, 264–274
  see also Race
Blau, Peter, 68
Bloom, S., 186
Blyth, D. A., 143
Boards of education, 250–251
Borgatta, E. F., 170
Boulding, Kenneth, 7
Bowles, Samuel, 119, 203, 204
Boyer, Ernest, 17
Boyle, R. P., 252–253, 255
Boys' achievement compared with girls', *see* Sex differences
Bredemeier, H. C., 314
Brody, G. H., 175
Bronfenbrenner, Urie, 25, 285–287
Brookover, Wilbur B., 200
Brophy, J. E., 161, 174
Brun-Gulbrandsen, S., 94–95
Bureaucracy of schools, 129–132, 247–250
Burkhead, Jesse, 253–255
Burt, Cyril, 111
Bush, D., 143
Busing, 266

Cahman, W. J., 47
California F scale, 149
Calvinist dogma, 60
Campbell, Ernest Q., 21, 28, 191, 224–226, 235, 321
Carnegie Council on Children, 67, 310
Catholic children, achievement and family position, 58–62
Caudill, W., 52–53, 59
Causal relationships, 29–35
Center for Interracial Cooperation, 159, 163
Central Midwestern Regional Educational Laboratory (CEMREL), 181
Central tendency, 64

Centuries of Childhood (Aries), 8
Change in education, *see* Reforms in education; Strategies for change
Childhood, changing view of, 7–12
Child spacing, 68
Children
  and family social position, 39–64
  and family structure, 65–83
  individual ability of, 102–123
  motivation of, 10–12
  parental influence on, 74–79
  school success of, 42–44
  sex differences in, 91–96
  in U.S. educational system, 8–9
  see also Students
Children of the Poor (Ries), 9
Chinese Americans, 54–58
Chinese educational system, 279, 288–292
Cicourel, A. V., 141
Civil Rights Act of 1964, 29
Clark, Kenneth, 63, 311
Classical experiment, 29–31
Classroom
  climate in, 182–188
  communication patterns in, 176–178
  evaluation in, 160–162
  expectancy effects in, 154–160
  grouping in, 169–173
  number of students in, 168–170
  open, 174–176
  reward structure in, 179–182
  role structure and relationships in, 146–166
  seating arrangements in, 173–174
  social context of, 170–173
  as a social system, 167–190
  student-peer relations in, 162–165
  teacher's role in, 147–151
  teacher-student relationship in, 151–162
  technology of, 173–178
Class size, 168–170, 299
Climate
  in classroom, 182–188
  of schools, 271
  social, 198–200
  of values, 218–222
Cognitive style, 112–113, 117
Cohen, Elizabeth, 146, 154, 164
Cohen, Rosalie, 113
Cohorts, 237
Coleman, James S., 21, 27, 28, 33, 48–49, 59, 180, 191, 212–220, 222–223, 228–229, 234–238, 264–265, 303, 309
College attendance
  and family aspirations, 71–74
  and peer status, 224–226
  and religious background, 60–61
  and sex roles, 99
Collins, Randall, 323
The Coming Crisis of Western Society (Gouldner), 323

Communes, research on, 319
Communication in classroom, 176-178
Community
 relationship with schools, 251-260
 size, 252-253
Community-controlled schools, 270-272
Comparative education, *see* Crosscultural comparisons
Compensatory education, 112
Competence motivation, 10-11
Compulsory education, 316
Conant, James B., 193
Conceptualist function, 318
Connor, J. W., 53-54
Contextual effects, 194-198, 220-222
Control
 of environment, 51-52
 of self, 43-44
 by teachers, 138-139
Coons, John, 245, 249, 263-264
Counselors, 140-142
Crain, Robert, 248-249, 251, 267
Crandall, Virginia, 75
Creativity, 112-119
 concepts of, 113
 defined, 112-113
 "playful" component of, 115-116
 sex differences in, 117-118
 tests of, 114-115
Crosscultural comparisons, 277-305
 academic vs. productive work, 289-291
 achievement differences (IEA project), 295-303
 alternative schools, 285-295
 comparative research, 277-279
 egalitarianism, 293-295
 ideological instruction, 291-293
 individual vs. group orientation, 285-289
 national educational systems, 284-295
 society-school relations, 279-284
 system structures, 283-285
Cross-sectional studies, 28-29
Culture-free tests, 106-107
"Culture of poverty," deprived children, 62-63
Culture-specific tests, 107
Cusick, Philip A., 206, 235-236

Data
 comparability, 278
 gathering, 26-27
Daughters, sex role of, 94-96
Dave, R. H., 77
Davis, D., 295
Davis, D. J., 69
Death at an Early Age (Kozol), 12
Decision making, in family, 78-79, 81
Degrees, advanced, 87-88
Democratic leadership, 148-149
Demography
 theories, 20
 variables, 193
Dependent variable, 4
Deprived children, *see* Disadvantaged children
Deschooling, 316
Desegregation, 251, 264-274
Design of research, *see* Research design
Deutsch, Martin, 62, 102
Developed vs. developing countries, 280, 302
Developmental stages, 10-12
De Vos, G., 52-53, 59
Dewey, John, 4, 127, 128
Disadvantaged children
 ability testing of, 104-108
 and "culture of poverty," 62-63
 linguistic advantage of, 46-47
 and school failure, 41
Discipline, parental, 42-43
Dispersion of scores, 64
Dornbusch, Sanford, 127, 161-162
Dreeben, Robert, 5, 20, 65, 146, 151, 171, 176, 259
Duncan, O. D., 68
Durkheim, Emile, 3-4, 6, 146, 151, 176, 277, 279, 309, 310
Dyer, H. S., 17, 191

Economic class position, 54. *See also* Socioeconomic status
Edgar, D. E., 138, 139
Edmonds, Ron, 311
Education
 alternative, 285-295
 American, 8-10
 change (reforms) in, 260-274, 313-317
 Chinese, 279, 288-292
 compensatory, 112
 compulsory, 316
 crosscultural comparisons of, 277-303
 government's role in, 260-261
 inequality in, 262-274, 293-295, 321
 Israeli, 280, 287, 295
 Russian, 285-286
 and sociology of learning, 4-16
 worldwide expansion of, 281-283
Educational attainment
 of parents, 224-226
 by sex, 86-87
Educational Opportunity, see Equality of Educational Opportunity
Educational research
 agenda for future, 319-323
 current state of, 309-317
 design of, 17-37
 methodology of, 21-36
 sociology's contribution to, 317-323
 see also Research design
Educational Research Service, 168
Educational sociology, 16. *See also* Sociology of learning

Educational systems, *see* National educational systems
Effectiveness of school, 191–211
  methodology for measuring, 206–209
  nonhuman resources, 203–206
  school climate, 198–200
  school size, 103–104
  social climate, 198–200
  social context, 194–198
  strategies for evaluating, 192–193
  student characteristics, 193–200
  teacher characteristics, 200–203
Eifermann, R. R., 288
Eisenstadt, S. N., 213–214
Empirical measurement, 22–24
Employment of parents, 69–70
Entwisle, Doris, 45–47, 74, 91, 159
Enumeration district, 196
Environmental press, 186–187
Environment outside school, *see* External Environment
EPL (Executive Professional Leadership), 133–134
Epperson, D. C., 230–231
Equality in education, 262–274, 293–295, 321
Equality of Educational Opportunity (EEO) survey, 21–29, 33, 48–52, 69, 74, 147, 191, 197, 200–205, 209–210, 278
Ethnicity, and mental-ability scores, 54–58
Evaluation
  of classroom performance, 160–162
  of schools, 192–193, 206–208
Examiner bias, 54
Expectancy effects, 154–160
Expectation training, 159
Experimental controls, 29–32, 320–321
Experimental schools, 320. See also Alternative education
Experimenter effect, 31
Expressive-feminine role, 93–94
External environment of schools, 245–276
  government, 260–261
  professional administration, 247–250
  public, 251–260
  school board, 250–251
  strategies for change in, 262–274

Factfinding function, 318
Factor analysis, 32–33
Family
  aspirations of, 71–74
  birth order in, 67–69
  interrelationships in, 65–83
  parent-child interaction in, 74–81
  and race, 45–88
  recent social trends in, 67
  relationship with school, 65–66
  and religion, 58–62
  size of, 67–68
  social position and school success, 39–64
  socioeconomic status of, 40–48, 219
  structure and school success, 65–83
  values of, 71–74
  see also Parents
Farber, Jerry, 167
Farley, R., 265–266
Fathers
  and child's sex role, 95–96
  employment of, 69–70
  presence of, 69–70
  see also Parents
"Fear of success," 92
Federal Reserve Bank of Philadelphia study, 202, 205
Female-male differences, *see* Sex differences
"Feminine mystique," 93
FIAC (Flander's Interaction Analysis Categories), 182–186
Field, W. F., 91
Field setting, 25
Flanders, Ned A., 21–28, 184–186
Follow Through program, 320
Frankenstein, Carl, 294
Friedenberg, Edgar Z., 277
Friedman, Milton, 272
Future research, 319–323

Gans, Herbert, 72, 74
Garcia, H., 81
Gender
  role, 84
  stereotyping, 88, 97
  see also Sex differences
From Generation to Generation (Eisenstadt), 213
Genetics, and intelligence, 108–112
Gerard, R. W., 102, 266
Getzels, Jacob W., 114–116
Gifted children, and ability grouping, 171–173
Gintis, Herbert, 119
Girls' achievement compared with boys',
  see Sex differences
Gittell, Marilyn, 248, 258
Goldberg, Marian L., 147, 171–172
Good, T. L., 161, 174
Goodman, Paul, 105
Goor, A., 118
Gordon, Chad, 69, 72
Gordon, C. Wayne, 148–149, 222–223
Gordon, Edmund, 39, 277
Goslin, David A., 105, 106, 119, 120
Gouldner, Alvin, 323
Government, role of in education, 260–261
Grades
  and classroom performance, 160–162
  and classroom reward structure, 179–183
  as measures of learning, 22–23
Graduation rates, by sex, 86–88
Green, Arnold, 77
Green, P., 111
Green, T. F., 280–281
Grill, J. J., 163

Gross, Neal, 133, 139, 249, 259, 318
"Grounded theory, " 312
Group orientation, 285–289
Group size, classroom, 169–170
Guidance counselors, 140–142
Guttentag, M., 271–272

Hallinan, M. T., 228
Halo effect, 224
Hamblin, R. L., 182
Harvey, D. G., 158
Hauser, R. M., 197
Hawthorne effect, 36n. *See also* Novelty effect
Head Start, 316, 320
Hechinger, F. M., 201, 204
Heredity and IQ, 108–112
Herndon, James, 12
Herriott, Robert E., 139
Hierarchical order in schools, 131–132
High School Characteristics Index (HSCI), 186
High schools
 adolescent peer culture in, 212–241
 size of, 193–194
Hollander, T. Edward, 248, 258
Holland's educational system, 280
Holt, John, 12, 128, 153, 303
Home environment, 80–81. *See also* Family
Home-intervention programs, 83, 315
Hopper, E. I., 282–283
Horner, M. S., 92
How Children Fail (Holt), 153
How Children Learn (Holt), 153
How the Other Half Lives (Ries), 9
Hughes, E. C., 227
Human development, 10–12
Hunt, J. M., 108–110
Hurn, Christopher, 6, 17, 56, 291, 317
Husen, Torsten, 86, 296–301

Ideological instruction, 291–293
IEA, *see* International Project for the Evaluation of Educational Achievement
Illich, Ivan, 316
Income level, and achievement, 254
Independence
 of child, 75–76
 training, 81
Individual ability, *see* Ability
Individual vs. group orientation, 285–289
Inequality in education, 262–274, 293–295, 321
Instrumental-masculine role, 93–94
Integration, racial, 268–270. *See also* Desegregation; Segregation
Intelligence
 and creativity, 113–119
 environment-heredity arguments on, 108–112
 and family structure, 68–69
 measurement of, 104–108
 origin of, 108–112
 six differences in, 78

Intelligence and Experience (Hunt), 108
Intelligence quotient (IQ) tests
 as ability measure, 104–108
 consequences of, 119–120
 and expectancy effects, 155–157
 and family SES, 71–74
Interaction Analysis Categories (FIAC), 182–186
International Project for the Evaluation of Educational Achievement, 205, 296–303
Interpersonal relationships
 in classroom, 151–165, 175
 in family, 65–83
 and high school achievement, 224–226
 of teachers, 151–162, 182–188
Intrinsic motivation, 10–11
IS-201 schools, 270–272
Israel, educational system in, 280, 287–295

Jacklin, Carol, 84, 88–91
Jackson, Philip, 114–116, 146, 150, 151, 167, 176
Jacobson, Lenore, 154–158, 186, 269–270
Japanese Americans, 52–53
Jencks, Christopher, 40–41, 102, 119, 191, 205, 245, 263, 267, 272–273, 309, 310
Jennings, M. K., 248, 250
Jensen, A. R., 102, 104, 108–112
Jews, achievement of children, 58–62
John Adams High School, 318, 325n
Johns Hopkins University studies, 159, 180, 318

Kagan, Jerome, 113, 117
Kahan, S., 69
Kahl, J. A., 71, 256
Kahn, R. L., 163
Kamin, Leon, 111
Kandel, D., 231
Karweit, N. L., 205
Kasarda, J. D., 249–250
Katz, F. E., 128
Kenniston, Kenneth, 67
Kett, Joseph, 142, 212, 236
Kibbutz, 287–295
Kitsuse, J. I., 141
Kogan, N., 114–118
Kohn, Melvin, 42–44, 98
Komarovsky, Mirra, 92
Kounin, J., 153
Kozol, Jonathan, 12

Laboratory setting, 25–26
Labov, William, 48
Laissez-faire leadership style, 148–149
Larkin, Ralph W., 235
Lau, L. J., 201
Leadership styles, 148–149
Learning
 change and, 5
 components of, 5–6
 definition of, 4

Index

Learning (cont'd.)
 measurement of, 22–24
 in schools, 4–7
 sociology of, 3–16, 317–323
 system, 12–15
 theories of, 18–21, 312–313
 time spent in, 205–206
Learning Environment Inventory (LEI), 187–188
Leavitt, H. J., 177–178
Legislation on educational reform, 260–261
Lein, Laura, 67
Less-developed societies, 302
Lesser, G. S., 54–58, 231
Lever, J., 96
Levin, H. M., 208–209, 261, 318
Lewin, K., 148–149
Life in Classrooms (Jackson), 146
Lifelong education, 9
Linguistic development, 44–48
 rural-urban differences in, 46–47
Lippitt, R., 148
Livingstone, D. W., 283–285
Lombard, Avima, 294, 315
Longitudinal studies, 28–29
Lortie, Dan C., 162
Lüscher, Kurt, 317

McClelland, David, 60, 61, 74, 91, 287
Maccoby, Eleanor, 84, 88–91
McDill, Edward, 32–33, 198–200, 220, 258–259
McKeachie, W. L., 169
McPartland, J. M., 78–79, 98, 147, 176, 179, 206–207, 226
Magnet schools, 268–270
Mao Tse-tung, 292
Marjoribanks, K., 80
Masculine-instrumental role, 93–94
Matching, 31
Mathematics achievement
 crosscultural differences in, 296–303
 sex differences in, 85–86
Measurement
 of central tendency, 64
 of dispersion, 64
 of intelligence, 104–108
 of learning, 22–24
Median score, 64
Medical students study, 227–228
Medley, D. M., 148
Mellon Foundation study, 226
Mental-ability scores, 54–58. *See also* Intelligence quotient (IQ)
Merton, Robert, 313
Methodology
 agenda for future, 319–323
 current state of, 309–317
 experimental controls, 29–32
 measurement of learning, 22–24
 production function analysis, 208–209

 and research design, 21–35
 sample, 24
 setting, 25
 statistical controls, 32–35
 systems analysis, 207–208
 and theory in educational research, 35–36
 time factor, 27–29, 206–207
 see also Research design
Metro school program, 315
Mexican-Americans, 81
Meyer, John, 281–282, 313
Meyers (McDill, Meyers, and Rigsby), 32, 198–200
Michaels, J. W., 179
Migrant laborers, families of, 47–48
Miller, H. L., 30
Miller, N., 266
Minkovich, A., 295
Minorities
 and expectancy effects, 154–160
 mental ability scores, 54–58
 school success, 45–58
 see also Blacks; Race
Minuchin, P., 98
Mitzel, H. E., 148
Mobility, upward, 72, 74, 282
Model building, *see* Research design
Moeller, G., 131, 137–138, 139
Moore, O. K., 174, 182
Moore, Omar, 30
Moral instruction, 291–293
Moreno, 162
Mothers
 and childrens' sex roles, 94–96
 employment of, 69–70
 good parenting by, 79–81
 influence compared with influence of child's peer group, 231–233
 presence of, 69–70
 textbook gender stereotyping of, 97
 see also Parents
Motivation
 of child by parent, 74–79
 of children, 10–12
 sex differences in, 91–93
Multicollinearity, 206
Multiple regression analysis, 33
Multivariate analysis, 32
Murray, Virginia, 127, 129, 196
Musgrove, F., 212, 232

n Achievement scale, 74–75, 91–92
Nachlaot Integration Project, 294, 321
Nam, C. B., 61
National educational systems, 281–303
 alternative models, 285–295
 American, 8–10
 differences in achievement among, 295–303
 expansion of, 281–282
 structure of, 284–295
National Education Association, 139

National Institute of Education, 23
National Longitudinal Study of the High School Senior Class of 1972, 99
National Principalship Study, 133, 259
Natural-setting research, 319–321
Need-Press Model, 186–187
"Neighborhood" community concept, 255
Newcomb, Theodore M., 220, 224
Nonhuman school resources, 203–206
Norms, social, 5
Novelty effect, 30–31
Null hypothesis, 35
"Nurturance" schooling, 314

Office of Economic Opportunity, 272–273
On What Is Learned in School (Dreeben), 5, 146
Open classroom, 174–176
Oriental Americans, 48–58
Our Country (Educational Research Council of America), 97
Outside-school environment, *see* External environment of schools

Panel on Youth, 236–238
Paradigmatic response, 45–46
Parelius, Ann P., 52
Parelius, Robert J., 52
Parents
  aspirations of, 71–74
  behavior of, 74–79
  and childrens' sex roles, 94–96
  and child's school success, 42–44
  and community-controlled schools, 270–272
  educational level and child's college aspirations, 224–226
  employment of, 69–70
  "good," 79–81
  influence compared with influence of youth's peers, 229–236
  interaction with child, 74–79
  involvement in schools, 258–260
  presence of, 69–70
  and socialization of sex roles, 94–96
  values of, 71–74
  voucher plans for, 272–274
  see also Family
Parkway Program, 315
Parsons, Talcott, 4, 213, 283
Path analysis, 33–34
Peer culture of adolescents, 212–241
  Coleman's findings on, 214–220
  components of, 215
  and peer status, 222–224
  and role in society, 236–239
  strength of, 229–236
  value climate studies, 220–222
Peer effect, 92
Peer status, 162–164, 217–224
Peer tutoring, 164–165
Penn State Pyramid Plan, 164–165

People's Republic of China, 279, 288–292
Performance evaluation, 160–162
Permeability, 259
Pestalozzi, Johann, 9
Peters, W., 160
Pettigrew, T. F., 111
Philadelphia schools study, 202, 205
Physical resources of schools, 203–206
Piaget, Jean, 10–11
Planned Variation project, 320, 321
Play patterns of boys and girls, 96–97
Poverty
  "culture" of, 62–63
  and school failure, 41
Preschool programs, 10
Press scales, 186–187
Presser, S., 268–270
Principals, 132–136
  relationship with teachers, 136
  role in school hierarchy, 132–135
  and student productivity, 133–135
Probability sample, 24–25
Production function analysis, 208–209
Productive work for students, 289–291
Professional administration, 247–250
Project Talent, 103, 194, 197, 254
Protestantism, and achievement, 60–62
Psychology of learning, 4
Public
  attitudes of, 256–258
  parents as, 258–260
  relationship with schools, 251–260
Puerto Rican children, 48–58
Punishment, parental, 42–43
Pygmalion in the Classroom (Rosenthal and Jacobson), 158

Questionnaires, 23

Race
  and achievement, 45–48
  inequities based on, 311
  and parental aspirations, 72–73
  permanence of, 40
  and school effectiveness, 195–198
  segregation by, 264–274
  visibility of, 40
Radical critics, 147, 303
Random sample, 24–25
Rapaport, T., 118
Ravitch, Diane, 317
Rebellion in a High School (Gordon), 228
Reference groups, 162, 173, 194
Reforms, in education, 260–274
  government's role in, 260–261
  strategies for, 262–274
  summary of recent, 313–317
Regression analyses, 202–203
Relational cognitive style, 113

Religion
    instruction in, 291–293
    and school success, 58–62
Research
    agenda for future, 319–323
    crosscultural, 278–279
    multicollinearity in, 206
    production function analysis, 208–209
    on school effectiveness, 206–209
    and systems analysis, 207–208
Research design, 17–37
    causal relationships, 29–35
    elements of, 18
    experimental controls, 29–32
    measurement, 22–24
    methodology, 21–36
    sample, 24
    setting, 25
    statistical controls, 32–35
    theory, 18–21, 35–36
    time factor, 27–29
Responsive environment, 174
Retarded, labeling of, 249–250
Retentivity, 299–301
Revolution in the Schools
    (Gross and Murphy), 12
Reward structure, 179–182
Rhodes, A. L., 60–61
Richer, S., 96–97, 173
Ries, Jacob, 9
Riessman, Frank, 62
Rigsby (McDill, Meyers, and Rigsby), 32, 198–200
Riley, John, 232–234
Riley, Matilda, 232–234
Rist, R. C., 158, 174, 268
Rivlin, Alice M., 318
Rogoff, N., 251–252, 255
Role
    hierarchy, 131–132
    structure in classroom, 146–166
Rosen, B. C., 42, 75
Rosenbaum, J. E., 143–144, 268–270
Rosenthal, Robert, 21, 24, 25, 28, 31, 154–158, 186, 269–270
Rossell, C., 265
Rural-urban differences in linguistic development, 46–47
Russian educational system, 285–286
Rutgers University study, 233–234

Sadler, M. E., 245
St. John, Nancy, 266–267
Sample size, 25
Sampling unit, 25
Sanford, Nevitt, 226–227
Sarason, Seymour, 132, 136, 140, 142, 173
Schooler, C., 69
Schooling, purpose of, 6–7

Schools
    administration of, 247–250
    alternative, 285–295, 320
    as behavior sets, 129
    boards of education for, 250–251
    as bureaucracies, 129–132
    change in, 262–274
    classroom role structure, 146–166
    classroom as social system, 167–190
    community-controlled, 270–272
    crosscultural studies of, 281–303
    desegregated, 264–268
    differential treatment of sexes in, 96–98
    effectiveness of, 191–211
    environment of, 245–305
    evaluation of, 192–193, 206–208
    external environment of, 245–276
    functions of, 6–7
    government's effect on, 260–261
    hierarchical order of, 131–132
    as institutions, 128–129
    learning in, 4–7
    magnet, 268–270
    "nurturance," 314
    open, 174–176
    physical resources of, 203–206
    principals of, 132–135
    reform of, 313–317
    relationship with public, 251–260
    relationship with society, 279–284
    secondary, 212–241
    size of, 103–104, 297–298
    social climate of, 198–200
    social context of, 194–198
    as social systems, 127–145, 167–190
    sociologist's view of, 128–132
    special services personnel in, 140–142
    teacher characteristics in, 200–203
    time spent in learning in, 205–206
    vertical organization of, 143–144
School success, *see* Achievement
"School without walls," 315–316
Schwebel, A., 174
Sears, Robert, 95–96
Seating assignments, 173–174
Seginer, R., 77
Segregation, racial, 251, 264–274
Selection, educational, 282–283
Self-concept, 51
Self-control, parental attitude toward, 43–44
SES, *see* Socioeconomic status
Setting, in research design, 25
Sewell, William, 28, 41
Sex differences
    in abilities, 88–93
    and achievement, 84–101
    and advanced degrees, 78–88
    in creativity, 117–118
    crosscultural comparisons on, 301–302
    and intellectual development, 78
    in motivation, 91–93

parental behavior and, 94–95
in performance, 85–88
in personality traits, 88–93
in school achievement, 84–101
in school treatment, 96–98
and sex-role socialization, 93–98
Shaw, M. E., 169
Shevsky index, 252
Shipman, M. D., 127
Siblings
IQ scores of, 109
position in family, 67–69
Significance tests, 33, 35
Simmons, R. G., 143
Simpson, R. L., 229–230
Single-parent families, 68
Size
of class, 168–170
of family, 67–68
of schools, 103–104
Skager, R., 141
Slatin, G. T., 158
Small groups, 169–170
Smilansky, M., 293
Smith, Adam, 272
Social-class differences, 98–99
Social climate of schools, 198–200
Social context of schools, 194–198
Social environment outside of school (external environment), 245–276
Socialization, and sex roles, 84–101
Social norms, 5
Social system, class as, 167–190
Social System of the High School (Gordon), 222
Society
relationship to learning, 278
relationship with schools, 279–284
youth linkage with, 236–238
Socioeconomic status (SES)
and achievement, 40–48
and community relationship with schools, 252–256
crosscultural differences in, 301
and effectiveness of school, 194–198
and high school rebellion, 228–229
and IQ, 71–74
in Israeli schools, 295
and linguistic development, 44–48
and sex differences, 98–99
in Wisconsin study, 33–34
Sociograms, 162
Sociology of learning, 3–16, 317–323
activist role in, 318–319
and changing views on children, 7–12
compared with educational sociology, 16
conceptualist role in, 318
and education, 4
factfinding in, 318
findings summarized, 309–313
functions of, 317–319
future research agenda for, 319–323

and learning system, 12–15
in schools, 4–7
theories on, 18–21
Sociology of Teaching (Waller), 152
Sociometric analysis, 162–163
Sons, sex role of, 94–96
Sowell, T., 56, 60
Spady, William, 6–7, 191,197–198, 201,203
Spatial ability, 89
Specialization, crosscultural differences in, 301
Special services personnel, 140–142
Stanford University Center for Interracial Cooperation, 159, 163
Stanley, J. C., 321
Statistical, controls, 32–35
Status
in adolescent peer group, 217–220
of students among peers, 162–164
see also Socioeconomic status
Stein, A. H., 186
Stern, D., 186
Stern's Organizational Climate Scales, 271
Stinchcombe, Arthur L., 228–229, 281
Stodolsky, S. S., 54–56, 58
Strategies for change, 262–274
community-controlled schools, 270–272
desegregation, 264–268
magnet schools, 268–270
vouchers, 272–274
Strodtbeck, F. L., 22, 26, 58–60, 77, 79
Student-exposure effects, 205–206
Students
adolescent culture of, 217–241
age grouping of, 142–143
characteristics of, 193–200
counseling services for, 140–142
family social position, 39–64
family structure and interrelationships, 65–83
individual ability of, 102–123
position in school structure, 142–144
relationship with peers, 162–165
relationship with teachers, 151–162
and school effectiveness, 193–200
and school size, 103–104
sex differences among, 84–100
and social climate in school, 198–200
and social context of school, 194–198
and teacher expectations, 154–160
Success in school, *see* Achievement
Sugarman, Stephen, 249, 263–264
Summerhill model, 314
Summers, A. A., 204, 208
Superintendents, 248–249, 251
Synanon, 291
Syntagmatic response, 45–46
Systems analysis, 207–208

Talented students, 268–270
Talk in classroom, FIAC analysis of, 182–186
"Talking typewriter," 30–31, 174

Teachers
  classroom role of, 147–151
  and effectiveness of school, 200–203
  evaluation by, 160–162
  expectations of student performance, 154–160
  experienced, 201–203
  leadership styles of, 148–149
  measurement of interaction with students, 182–188
  measures of effectiveness of, 148–149
  professional organizations, 139–140
  relationship with students, 151–162, 182–188
  role in hierarchy, 135–140
  salaries of, 202
  sense of control, 138–139
Teaching
  compared with other professions, 150
  definition of, 147
  as professional role, 150–151
Tele relations, 162
Television, and linguistic development, 46
Terman, L. M., 58
Tests and testing
  biases of, 23, 106–107
  consequences of, 119–120
  of significance, 33, 35
  standard, 23
Theory
  compared with methodology, 35–36
  of learning, 312–314
  sociological, 18–21
Thomas, Gail, 99
Thomas, S. C., 175
Thomas, W. I., 154
Time
  as research factor, 27–29, 206–207
  spent in learning, 205–206
Toffler, Alvin, 7
Tracking, 143–144
Turner, Ralph H., 223–224, 252, 256, 282
Tutoring by students, 164–165
Two Worlds of Childhood (Bronfenbrenner), 286
"Typewriter, talking," 30–31, 174

Unit efficiency, 170
Upward mobility, 72, 74, 282
Urban-rural differences in linguistic development, 46–47

Value climate
  contextual effects, 194–198
  in high schools, 218–220
Value system
  of Jewish vs. Catholic families, 59–60
  parental, 71–74
  of U.S. and Japan, 52–53
Vassar College study, 226–227
Verbal ability
  sexual differences in, 89
  and socioeconomic status, 44–48
Veroff, J., 61–62

Vertical organization of schools, 143–144
Vouchers, educational, 272–274

Wagenaar, T. C., 259–260
Walberg, H. J., 175, 187–188, 201, 202
Wallace, Walter L., 221–222
Wallach, M. A., 114–118
Waller, Willard, 39, 152, 179
Warren, R. L., 138, 139
The Way It's Spozed to Be (Herndon), 12
Weber, Max, 60, 130, 248, 310, 318
Wegmann, R. G., 153
Weinberg, C., 141
Weisstein, Naomi, 84
Werts, Charles E., 99
White, Burton L., 65, 79–80
White flight, 264–266
Whiting, Beatrice, 96
Whiting, John, 96
Who Runs Our Schools? (Gross), 249
Wiley, D. E., 205–207, 294
Williams, Robert, 107
Wilson, Alan, 195, 199
Wilson, E. C., 255, 256, 266
Wisconsin Study of Social and Psychological Factors . . . , 33–34, 41, 83
Wolfe, B. L., 204, 208
"Woman-as-nigger," 93
Women in the Modern World (Komarovsky), 92
Word associations, 45–46
Work programs, 289–291
Wright, R. J., 175–176

Youth
  changing views on, 7–12
  linkage with larger society, 236–238
  peer group culture of, 212–241

Zablocki, Benjamin, 319, 321
Zajonc, R. B., 68–69
Zeigler, L. H. 248, 250
Zimmerman, B. J., 175